UNSTOPPABLE BRILLIANCE

First published in 2006 by Liberties Press
51 Stephens Road | Inchicore | Dublin 8 | Ireland
www.libertiespress.com | info@libertiespress.com
Editorial: +353 (1) 402 0805 | sean@libertiespress.com
Sales and marketing: +353 (1) 453 4363 | peter@libertiespress.com
Liberties Press is a member company of Clé, the Irish Book Publishers' Association

Trade enquiries to CMD Distribution
55A Spruce Avenue | Stillorgan Industrial Park | Blackrock | County Dublin
Tel: +353 (1) 294 2560
Fax: +353 (1) 294 2564

Copyright © Antoinette Walker and Michael Fitzgerald, 2006
Foreword copyright © Kathy Sinnott

ISBN 0–905483–03–1

2 4 6 8 10 9 7 5 3 1

A CIP record for this title is available from the British Library

Cover design by Liam Furlong at space.ie
Set in 11.5-point Garamond

Printed in Ireland by Colour Books
Unit 105 | Baldoyle Industrial Estate | Dublin 13

UNSTOPPABLE BRILLIANCE

IRISH GENIUSES AND ASPERGER'S SYNDROME

ANTOINETTE WALKER AND MICHAEL FITZGERALD

Contents

ACKNOWLEDGEMENTS

From genesis to birth, the journey of any book is filled with many a twist and turn along the way. Scrutinising the lives of Irish geniuses has ensured countless exciting moments on this book's passage, and for this we greatly appreciate the contributions of a number of people. First and foremost we would like to thank Seán O'Keeffe and Peter O'Connell of Liberties Press, without whose vision, professionalism and diligence this book would not have seen the light of day. For discussions, insights and support of diverse kinds we are grateful to Pat Matthews (President of the World Autism Association), Viktoria Lyons, Michael Gill, Brendan O'Brien, Maria Lawlor, Jerry Harper, Ioan James, John Richmond, Bill Tormey, Emmet and Elisabeth Arrigan, Theresa Scott, Anna Coonan, Patricia Maloney, Ellen Cranley and Aoife O'Connor. For sharing her ideas and aspirations in the foreword of this book we are also grateful to Kathy Sinnott MEP. A special word of thanks and appreciation is extended to the many parents of children with autism, as well as persons with autism/Asperger's syndrome, who continue to educate us over the years. For their unfailing help we thank the librarians at Trinity College Dublin, in particular Virginia McLoughlin, Joe O'Brien, Philomena Nicholson and Joseph McCarthy; at the Royal College of Surgeons, in particular Joan Moore; and at Dublin City Library and Archive Collections. Finally, Antoinette would like to thank her parents, Michael and Anne, and family and friends, while Michael would like to thank his wife Frances and sons Owen, Mark and Robert, for their support and forbearance in the writing of this book.

FOREWORD

We were reminded in a recent 'disABILITY' campaign to focus on a person's ability, not his or her disability. This reminds us of the obvious fact that, for example, even though a man cannot walk, he may be able to read, write and talk. It also attempts to make us aware that a woman who has a visual impairment can not just hear but may hear better than a sighted person.

But there is a deeper meaning. Ability is not necessarily just what the person can do, apart from what he or she cannot do and apart from any compensating skills. For some people, the ability is the disability itself.

In *Unstoppable Brilliance: Irish Geniuses and Asperger's Syndrome* by Antoinette Walker and Michael Fitzgerald, we have the stories of gifted men and women whose ability *and* disability was Asperger's syndrome. They were gifted with the aspergic ability to, on the one hand, give themselves completely to the pursuit of their interests, and on the other to bypass the distractions and obstacles of life, not as hurdles to be jumped, but as irrelevancies to be ignored or not even noticed. They were men and a woman who were able to trail-blaze to the frontiers and to penetrate the centre, laying bare the heart of maths and science, Aboriginal and modern man, language and politics.

This is the uniqueness of their 'abled' achievement. Many bright people travel the same paths but get sidetracked along the way. Consequently, when these geniuses with Asperger's syndrome arrived at their destination, they found it a solitary place. But here too the aspergic ability equipped these geniuses for survival in isolation and more productivity.

We who have benefited from their ability should be grateful because Asperger's syndrome, though an ability, is also a disability with a burden of pain. Their legacy, which we now enjoy, was achieved at a price of loneliness and social, emotional and physical struggle both for the person and those that loved them.

Many people in Ireland today have Asperger's syndrome. Not all are 'geniuse' but, in my experience, all are gifted and have special areas of talent. It is my hope that the stories in this book will force us to ask ourselves some important questions. Why are children with Asperger's often diagnosed so late in Ireland? And why, when that diagnosis finally comes, does it seem to close instead of open doors. Why, given the very individual needs of people with Asperger's, are there so few specialised services to meet those needs? Where are the information and training services for teachers, parents and employers? What does our high-pressure exam-based education system do to the student with Asperger's? Why is there little outreach to young adults with Asperger's to help them establish themselves in work and in the community. Where is a policy of understanding support for a family of a child or a parent with Asperger's? Why are so many people with Asperger's misdiagnosed as having a mental illness? And why are so many of these misdiagnosed people medicated to the point of developing a mental illness?

Finally, why are Asperger's and other autistic spectrum disorders still seen as psychiatric or psychological conditions, with no recognition of the medical problems that cause them? It is no coincidence that most of the people in this book suffered poor health, especially gastrointestinal disease, poor immune protection and eye problems. Why, despite years of campaigning, is there still no medical treatment for autistic spectrum disorders in Ireland? And are we cherishing people with Asperger's syndrome, and their gifts?

It is my fervent hope that celebrating great Irish people who had Asperger's will somehow give all of us a greater awareness of the people in our midst who share this ability/disability. I hope too that *Unstoppable Brilliance* will inspire the political descendants of de Valera, Emmet and Pearse to take seriously both the potential and the plight of all people with Asperger's in Ireland today.

Kathy Sinnott MEP, *March 2006*

INTRODUCTION

There is something about genius that intrigues. Being in the presence of someone with exceptional talents and abilities is no ordinary event and the memory of it can stay with us long afterwards. Because nature throws up geniuses only very rarely, we are aware of just how exotic a species they are. We do not expect them to be normal and take for granted their enigmatic, odd and bizarre ways. They can also sometimes inspire ridicule and fear and may not always be likeable figures. Richard Ellmann, the celebrated biographer of James Joyce, believed that the Irish are gifted with more eccentricities than Americans and Englishman. To be average in Ireland, he felt, is to be eccentric. Perhaps Ellmann was a little biased; nonetheless, the nine characters in this book – all of them Irish – showed remarkable abilities and were strange and complex individuals indeed.

Is there a biological basis to genius? It is the contention of this book that there is. The Latin origins and derivations of the word would suggest so: *genus,* meaning 'family', *ingenium,* 'a natural disposition or innate capacity', and '*gignere',* to beget. Recognising that eccentricity is part and parcel of genius, many, such as theatre and opera director Jonathan Miller, would argue that geniuses have 'normal' psychological disabilities rather than some mere disorder. This book attempts to put a name on those 'normal psychological disabilities' with a diagnosis of Asperger's syndrome, an autistic spectrum disorder. In essence, it is a forensic look at the trappings of genius.

All geniuses possess a unique kind of intelligence. The paediatrician Hans Asperger observed that highly original thought and experience was found in some autistic children and believed that this could lead to exceptional achievements later in life. He wrote about 'autistic intelligence' – a kind of intelligence untouched by tradition and culture. According to the neurologist Oliver Sacks in his book *An Anthropologist on Mars,* this form of intelligence is unconventional, unorthodox, strangely pure and original and related to the intelligence of pure creativity. Certainly, the characters discussed in this book, regardless of their chosen field, possessed this kind of intelligence: primitive and pure, intuitive and instinctive, and marked by a moral intensity. All of these characters were willing to take intellectual risks by combining what may have looked like unrelated ideas to produce something radically new.

*

All of the figures discussed in this book showed significant Asperger traits and recognisable genius. Only a clinical assessment would ultimately confirm a diagnosis of Asperger's syndrome, and this is clearly not possible. Even so, it is possible to make substantial claims about the subjects. Why is it necessary to make a retrospective diagnosis, one might ask, and label these people? Why diagnose the departed? There is no doubt that focusing on deficits and disorders serves to reinforce negative connotations of the condition. But Asperger's syndrome is also associated with magnificent, at times almost superhuman, abilities, and these need to be accentuated too. The nature of the syndrome, in which some areas of the brain are hyperdeveloped and others are underdeveloped, means that it brings both blessings and burdens. By extension, the path of genius never easy.

In making a retrospective diagnosis of Asperger's syndrome, it is vital to gain as much detail as possible about the minutiae of the lives of the individuals concerned. Descriptions, impressions, opinions and the perceptions of those who observed these people at close quarters have as much value as their legacies and historical record. Indeed the seemingly trivial or the throwaway comment can offer a wealth of information. Biographies – authorised, standard or well known – and memoirs of family and friends have been used to glean as many facts as possible. Those with Asperger's syndrome in general have reduced capacities for autobiography but, where such works were attempted, we have included them. To all intents and purposes, this book is a snapshot of these Asperger geniuses; it is not intended to be exhaustive.

Three spheres of interest have been selected: politics, science and the arts. Traditionally, Asperger's syndrome was associated with those in science and engineering fields, but there is growing awareness that it is also seen in those in positions of political leadership and among creative artists. The nine figures that inhabit these spheres were all extreme figures, and most are household names in Ireland – in many cases, around the world. All of them were born in Ireland, but some – like so many of their contemporaries – left the country due to famine, war, disillusionment or upheaval of one kind or another. Three iconic figures from Irish politics have been selected: Robert Emmet, Éamon de Valera, and Pádraig Pearse. From the sphere of mathematics and science, we have included Robert Boyle, the Father of Chemistry, the brilliant Trinity College mathematician William Rowan Hamilton, and Daisy Bates, ethnographer of the Aborigines. There are many 'Asperger geniuses' from Ireland's celebrated literary heritage; W. B. Yeats, James Joyce and Samuel Beckett are the ones who are discussed in this book.

The predominance of male figures reflects the fact that autistic spectrum disorders affect men four times as much as they do women. The decision to select Daisy Bates was based on the fact that she exhibited considerable Asperger's traits, often to extremes. Others who could have been discussed in this context include Margaret Anna Cusack, the Nun of Kenmare, Dame Kathleen Lonsdale and the eccentric Speranza (Lady Jane Wilde).

*

Autism as a condition has been with us through the ages but it was ascribed no name until the early 1940s, when psychiatry became an increasingly specialised discipline. Two physicians working independently, Leo Kanner in Baltimore and Hans Asperger in Vienna, coined the words 'autistic' and 'autism' from the Greek word *autos,* meaning 'self'. It was a condition marked by considerable impairment in relation to language and communication. No two individuals with autism are the same, and there can be huge variations in the degree of the condition, reflecting the heterogeneity of the condition. Nowadays we know that a spectrum of autistic disorders exists. Roughly speaking, at the low-functioning end of the scale is 'classical autism', where children are often mute, with severe disabilities and retardation, whereas those with higher abilities, or 'high-functioning' individuals, are at the other end. Asperger's syndrome is located at the high-functioning end of the autistic spectrum. High-functioning autism and Asperger's syndrome – terms which are often used interchangeably – can be differentiated on the basis of the desire and ability to form relationships. There is a tendency for those with Asperger's syndrome who perhaps have more language skills to want to make relationships with people but to lack social know-how, whereas those with high-functioning autism tend to be less interested in making relationships. Nonetheless, they are all on the autistic spectrum.

In western culture, many euphemisms for autism abound, not least in Ireland. Those described as 'the village fool', 'not the full shilling', 'touched' or a 'queer hawk' may today be termed autistic. The nonsensical talk or *ráiméis* of the Irish fool (*amadán*) might in fact have been the idiosyncratic language of autism. Indeed, Shakespeare's wise fool, with his primitive, intuitive intelligence, may have been on the autistic spectrum too.

So what exactly does it mean to have Asperger's syndrome? In 1944, the Austrian paediatrician Hans Asperger described the condition which we now call Asperger's syndrome. The condition was fundamentally based on a problem with social interactions, as he saw it. In practice, people with this condition have problems with the to and fro of conversation and social interaction. In speech, they often use a high-pitched tone of voice or a monotonous one. They have problems reading non-verbal behaviour, or body language. They frequently engage in monologues which do not require the listener to interact with them, or else do not give listeners sufficient context on what they are speaking about – much to the confusion and consternation of listeners. Much of this is related to difficulties in seeing things from other people's perspectives and in understanding social and emotional relationships.

People with Asperger's syndrome are often described as enigmatic, odd or eccentric. In reality, they are severely puzzled about the social world and social interactions. At times they can feel like an alien, living on a different planet from other people. As a consequence, they spend their lifetime trying to work out the pattern in the chaos around them. The interests of people with Asperger's syndrome are frequently very narrow and specialised. Because of their enormous capacities for work, their phenomenal energy, their persistence, and their tendency to have a very narrow focus, they are usually successful in life. Essentially, they are driven more by their internal worlds and their internal ideas than by the social environment. As a result, they tend to be apolitical or take little interest in world affairs unless these things directly impinge on their consciousness.

By and large, people with Asperger's syndrome are very rigid, controlling and dominating. Characteristically, they develop rigid routines and rituals. They dislike change and strive for what is called 'preservation of sameness'. In terms of sensory perception, they can be oversensitive or hypersensitive to touch, noise, smell and other stimuli, and they are often fussy eaters. Their motor co-ordination can be poor, and they are frequently clumsy. At times, they have difficulty separating fact from fiction – something which often earns them a reputation for lying and deceit. Contrary to popular belief, they can have massively creative imaginations, though as children they tend not to engage in pretend play and take all meanings literally. It is not uncommon for people to perceive them as being narrow, eccentric, narcissistic and grandiose.

Because of their social difficulties, they can suffer from depression and indeed often exhibit a great deal of anxiety. In the past it was not uncommon, given their difficulties with separating fact from fiction, for them to be misdiagnosed as having schizophrenia and being inappropriately placed in services for persons with schizophrenia or similar institutions. Indeed, adults with Asperger's syndrome are still commonly misdiagnosed as schizophrenic. Depending on the severity of depression and the difficulties they experience in terms of social interaction, they can develop suicidal ideas, and indeed suicide is not rare among members of this group. Some people with Asperger's syndrome can also be plagued by poor health in general.

In school, their poor social interaction can give rise to difficulties, and they are often misdiagnosed by teachers as having 'conduct disorder' due to behaviour problems. They may show little interest in formal education and be daydreamers in class. In the past, many people with autistic spectrum disorders were only diagnosed as having learning disability – the 'slow learners' – or were misdiagnosed as having learning disability and confined to the learning-disability services. We now know that a dual diagnosis of autism and learning disability is not uncommon. These people therefore require special interventions for both autism and learning disability. Furthermore, they require special speech and language programmes, special communication skills programmes and special help with reading non-verbal behaviour.

At secondary school, people with Asperger's syndrome often drop out due to bullying or depression, or because of their difficulties in managing social interaction. As they are seen as odd, different or peculiar, they are often a target for bullying. Indeed Yeats, Joyce and Beckett were all bullied at various stages of their schooling. At university – if they get there – they have an extremely high drop-out rate in their first year because of problems with social interaction, organisation and social awareness. Feeling lonely and isolated, they can experience the world as being against them, and they often show paranoid traits in early adulthood and later.

Often a harsh superego or an autistic superego is seen in those with Asperger syndrome: in other words, they suffer excessively from a sense of duty or propriety. In psychoanalytical theory, the superego is the part of the personality that represents the conscience. Here, ethical and moral values reign supreme, and there is a constant striving for perfection. Feelings of guilt and failure may arise if they believe that certain codes and standards have been breached or impugned, especially those involving unacceptable desires. This can frequently lead to conflict because of the failure to appreciate or understand the viewpoint of others, and the standards they expect from other people can be unacceptably high.

The issue of control is of major significance too. With autistic spectrum disorders, there may be some impairment of the neurons in the amygdala of the brain, which is associated with emotion and aggression. For this reason, 'troublesome' behaviour can be associated with the condition. Many autistic individuals can be aggressive towards themselves or others: this is referred to as 'autistic aggression'. Conversely, they can also be extremely passive.

Those with Asperger's syndrome also have a poor sense of identity or self. As a result, they are often engaged in a constant search for identity and may adopt multiple roles or reinvent themselves in some way – something known as identity diffusion. As children, they may refer to themselves in the third person. In their lifetime, they may have numerous quite different roles or occupations. Normally, a person builds up an identify by imitation and identification with parents and others during childhood, and by seeing how they affect others around them. Due to problems with eye contact, reading non-verbal behaviour (i.e. noticing faces and emotions expressed on faces) and empathy issues, the development of a sense of self is affected in people with Asperger's syndrome, who instead have a highly unusual personal identity. Despite having a prodigious memory for facts, they often cannot personalise memory and have a poor sense of identity in its classic form. In fact, it could be said that they find it hard to recognise or know what it means to be themselves. Not surprisingly, many writers, Yeats, Joyce and Beckett included, were consumed with the search for an identity, and this indeed became a primary focus of their work. The failure to develop an identity is also linked to the way in which those with Asperger's syndrome see themselves in relation to sequential time. They have considerable difficulties experiencing time in sequence or chronologically and tend to live in the 'here and now'. As a consequence, they seldom learn from past mistakes and are often doomed to repeat them.

Sexual identity is often not fixed in a person with Asperger's syndrome. Over their lifetime, this identity may become even more fluid or undefined than that of an average, or neurotypical, person. Sexual states ranging from celibacy to promiscuity and every orientation in between are possible. For example, Robert Boyle remained celibate all his life, while Beckett was promiscuous for all of his. A distinction must be drawn here between sexual desire and sexual acts. Often, because of their social impairment and autistic superego, forming sexual unions may be problematic for people with Asperger's syndrome, despite the existence of intense desire. What is clear is that those with Asperger's syndrome tend to remain immature personalities.

*

Autistic intelligence tends to be concentrated in the areas of language, music and logic. All of those discussed in this book were gifted to varying degrees in one or more of these areas – in some cases, as in that of Joyce, in all three areas. By nature, they are extremely logical and analytical, and their thinking is concrete, which makes them good mathematicians though lesser poets, as in the case of Hamilton and de Valera. If they do not play a musical instrument, they can still appreciate music and musical form architectonically – i.e. in terms of its artistically pleasing structure. Language is especially important to those with Asperger's syndrome – not least the writers – and they often have their own idiosyncratic forms of it. They are frequently great linguists and polyglots. Daisy Bates, for example, could speak 188 Aboriginal dialects, in addition to several modern and classical languages. How languages are taught to those with Asperger's syndrome has a substantial bearing on the ease with which they are acquired, however. The traditional emphasis on teaching rules of language or grammar, for example in Latin and Greek, makes their acquisition easier for someone with Asperger's syndrome. This also applies to modern languages. A unique situation occurs with the teaching of the Irish language in Ireland: the teaching of Irish poses great difficulties for those with Asperger's syndrome, often necessitating exemptions from State exams. Certainly some of the individuals in this book, including Boyle and Joyce, had difficulties learning Irish and abandoned it, although in general they were excellent linguists. The modern emphasis on getting a 'sense' of the language at the expense of grammar, and on empty rote learning, does not work for those with Asperger's syndrome. For example, among other things the unusual syntax, aspiration (pronouncing sounds with the exhalation of breath) and dependent forms of the Irish language are bewildering to them and the logic of the language is extremely hard to grasp. Crucially, those with Asperger's syndrome need to know the rules of a language first in order to form a mental image of it. Once the rules are known, however, the language can be acquired, as evidenced by the experiences of Pearse and de Valera.

Language, often peculiar, is vital for expression in those with Asperger's syndrome. Talking about her autism in *An Anthropologist on Mars,* animal scientist Temple Grandin explained that she does not have an unconscious and does not repress memories and thoughts like normal people. Indeed, you could say that autistic speech or narrative is uncensored and free-flowing – truly free association. The unconscious and psychoanalysis certainly preoccupied many of the characters discussed in this book. Both Beckett and Joyce, though they were interested in these ideas at first, in the end rejected psychoanalysis. 'Mystery of the unconscious?' Joyce declared. 'What about the mystery of consciousness?' In fact, you could say that autistic narrative is the mystery of consciousness. It is no wonder that Joyce's writing has been described as 'psychotic' and *Finnegans Wake* as the product of a 'clever schizophrenic', by psychiatrist Nancy Andreason.

In terms of autistic intelligence, in routine clinical practice there is a tendency to use the diagnosis autism when the IQ is below 70 and Asperger's syndrome when the IQ is above 70. The term 'autistic savant' refers to people with autism but who have limited intelligence. About 10 percent of those with autism are autistic savants; these people have exceptional skills in certain areas, for example in music or as calculating prodigies. The 1988 Hollywood film *Rain Man* was one of the first movies that depicted the life of an autistic savant, in the form of the character played by Dustin Hoffman. Psychologist Beta Hermelin believes that about 1 or 2 out of 200 people with autistic spectrum disorders have genuine talent. The term 'Asperger savant' is used for people with Asperger's syndrome and huge creativity – the kind of creativity that many of the people in this book exhibited.

*

The National Autistic Society in the United Kingdom puts the prevalence of all autistic spectrum disorders, including Asperger's syndrome, at slightly under 1 percent of the population. In Ireland, with a population of nearly 4 million, this would give a figure of just under 40,000 people. Specifically, NAS puts the prevalence of Asperger's syndrome at 36 per 10,000. autistic spectrum disorders tend to be about four times more common in boys than in girls. We have no idea what the prevalence of Asperger savants in society is, though it is likely to be quite rare. Problems with prevalence data in Europe led the EU Commission in 2006 to fund a project called the European Autism Information System to measure the incidence of the disorder. Estimating the prevalence of the condition is often difficult and controversial due to differences in the ways that cases of autism are identified and defined, and with differences in study methods and changes in diagnostic criteria.

Diagnosis is directed towards children on the autistic spectrum because of the need for early diagnosis and intervention. Children do not grow out of autism, but with early intervention they can learn to cope with the condition and interact with others better. Many adults living with Asperger's syndrome or high-functioning autism have never been diagnosed and are oblivious to their condition, even though they may be aware that they do not quite fit into society.

Given these statistics, the condition is present among a significant portion of the population. This has major implications for education, health services and indeed employment services. In the work environment, those with autism often need sheltered or supported employment, unless they find their niche in a particular field.

*

Autism and Asperger's syndrome are neurobiological disorders associated with abnormalities in numerous areas of the brain. These abnormalities essentially cause a lack of integration in the brain. There appear to be problems with nerve cell migration in the womb and also with the pruning of brain cells after birth, which may explain why autistic individuals retain many childhood traits. This leads to major difficulties in social interaction – but also results in the flowering of their special talents. In essence, persons with Asperger's savantism tend to have even less integrated brains, with modules that are hyperdeveloped and developed out of balance with other areas of the brain. Because this kind of talent has a large genetic component, it is not surprising that it shows itself early in life. Environmental factors are probably necessary for the development of the condition too but these are of minor importance: for example, Asperger musicians being exposed to music at an early age.

The cause of autism is largely genetic, with heritability accounting for approximately 90 percent of the condition. Because the condition has a polygenic basis, several genes are involved in the condition. Most importantly, autism is not caused by parental rearing or behaviour, as was believed in the past. Indeed, at one point autism was said to be due to 'refrigerated mothers', something which caused enormous distress and guilt for parents.

At present, there are a number of theories that try to explain the lack of integration in the brain, but none of them explains the condition conclusively. A number of physical theories focus on the left and right hemispheres of the brain. Some medical experts believe that autism is associated with left-hemisphere impairment, while Asperger's syndrome is associated with right-hemisphere deficits. (The right hemisphere processes information involved in spatial imaging, social interaction and emotions, and, it could be said, 'thinks visually'; the left hemisphere is concerned with logic, order, language, arithmetic and sequential time, and thinks in words and numbers.) Within the hemispheres, the major areas affected in autism are believed to be the frontal lobes (which help to plan, coordinate, control and execute behaviour), the limbic system (the centre of emotions, including the amydala) and the cerebellum, which coordinates movement and is responsible for social interaction. All of these areas are high in white matter – the support cells involved in sending messages to various parts of the brain, like telephone wires. In autisic children, the cerebellum and frontal lobes can be bigger than normal, giving a larger head circumference. In recent times, autism has also been seen in terms of an extreme male brain or extreme maleness. Research into the effects of testosterone in the individual, from conception through the various stages of human development, is ongoing.

There are also a number of competing psychological theories in relation to autism. None explains autism in its entirety, though all explain it in part. The 'theory of mind' hypothesis focuses on social and communicative deficits, where people have difficulty attributing mental states to themselves or others, i.e. they are not able to see things from another person's perspective. The 'executive function' theory is concerned with primary cognitive impairment in a variety of mental processes. These processes can include organisational skills, planning, future-oriented behaviour, selective attention, maintenance of attention or vigilance, inhibition and creativity. This theory can explain the repetition seen in those with autism and why mistakes are likely to be repeated. Finally, the 'weak central coherence' theory looks at cognitive abnormalities in the way information is processed. This theory explains why those with autism have exceptional skills at processing detail but fail to see the 'big picture' and see the world in a fragmentary way. Given that autism is a neurobiological disorder, research on the subject today stretches into many other fields of biomedicine, including neurobiology, neuroimaging, genetics, immunology, language and communication, nutrition and proteomics – the study of proteins.

*

That something pure and primitive emanates from those with Asperger's syndrome, and especially Asperger geniuses, becomes more evident when their lives are examined. Their intelligence is unconditioned by tradition and society. In fact, their development is somewhat arrested, and they retain a juvenile or childlike disposition all their lives. This immaturity stretches across all aspects of development: physical, emotional, social and, not least, in relation to intelligence and imagination. Physically, for example, those with autism can manifest clumsy gaits, unusual voice patterns, delicate constitutions, and boyish or girlish complexions well into adulthood. Emotionally stunted, they show reduced emotion or affection or else react aggressively, throwing tantrums. Having little ability to empathise with others or understand the motives of others, they can be childishly unforgiving and vengeful.

Traits of risk-taking and fearlessness often never leave the Asperger genius. In fact, risk-taking is a defining trait of gifted and creative geniuses. The Asperger imagination retains much from childhood too: its vividness and potency, which induces all manner of fears and paranoia, and also its sense of awe and wonder. A kind of arrested development seems to go hand in hand with genius. For instance, in explaining why his young tenor voice had stayed unchanged all his life, James Joyce declared: 'It's because I've not developed. If I had matured, I wouldn't be so committed to this *folie* of writing 'Work in Progress' [*Finnegans Wake*].'

It is now well known that those with autism think visually or in pictures. As a result, they tend to think in concrete images and have only a fragmented picture of reality. In general, they have unusual responses to sensory stimuli – visual, auditory, gustatory, tactile and olfactory – which fire their imaginations even more. In effect, they have extraordinary imaginations and prodigious memory for retaining images as facts. This ability to think in pictures is enormously helpful when speaking in public, for instance. This may explain why they make good public speakers, or can talk literally for hours. Nowadays, thinking in pictures when speaking in public is a basic skill taught in communications courses.

The instinct for simplicity and asceticism can be seen at the heart of the Asperger genius too. Certainly the Asperger mind gravitates towards the abstract and the absolute. Regardless of the chosen field, there is a focus on simplicity, beauty, immortality and truth. Pearse, for example, certainly expressed a pure notion of Irish nationality or patriotism, given his obsession with absolutes and ideals. The potency of the imagination is also linked to religion, and a certain religious disposition can be seen in those with Asperger's syndrome. Although established religion is by and large (though not always) rejected because of their non-conformity, religiosity in the Asperger person remains with them all their life. In their make-up, there can also exist a curious attraction to metaphysics, the supernatural and esoteric subjects – usually in the search for knowledge or absolute truth. In recent years, geneticists have discovered a genetic predisposition to be interested in spiritual or religious matters. This genetic profile may also explain why these people seem to have an inherent need for ceremony, repetition and ritual in their lives.

*

In the development of human society, society needs its Asperger geniuses to push the boundaries of knowledge and bring benefits to everyone. The fact that geniuses see further and deeper into the nature of things than ordinary minds makes such advances possible. Living in a somewhat autistic world means that they are less connected to social distractions and can experience time as a continuum and not chronologically – and thus can see life from the viewpoint of eternity, as it were.

Society becomes more efficient at ensuring its survival and ennobling its spirit not only through advances in science and technology but also in relation to art, music, literature, architecture and politics – indeed every facet of human endeavour. People listen to the Asperger genius because of their dominating presence, their powerful rhetoric, and their way of using their abilities to ensure that their visions are realised. For the genius, however, the yoke is not always easy nor the burden light. Conflict is at the heart of creativity. The search for identity and the social impairment that Asperger's syndrome brings, paradoxically propels the genius onwards. Genius is not a mantle that someone with Asperger's syndrome readily adopts, it is innate. Once unleashed in the right conditions, its brilliance is unstoppable.

FEATURES OF ASPERGER'S SYNDROME

ESPECIALLY INVOLVING EXCEPTIONAL TALENTS AND ABILITIES

Because of the heterogeneity in autistic spectrum disorders, there can be considerable variety or difference in the features observed.

SPEECH & LANGUAGE

Idiosyncratic or peculiar language:
– Fascination with words
– Word repetition or echolalia
– Pronoun reversal/poor syntax/literal meanings (difficulty with figurative language)
Inventive use of language: neologisms/liking for word games/puns/
    rhymes/capacity for poetry
Higher verbal IQ
Linguists/polyglots
Monologues
Pedantic/verbose/malapropisms
Unusual voice qualities: high-pitched tone or monotone/unusual stress patterns
Simple, slapstick humour/talent for mimicry and impersonation

SOCIAL IMPAIRMENT

Liking for solitude
Solitary pursuits
Difficulty showing emotions, especially affection
Variable desire for company: selective company/preference for family members, close friends
Difficulty reading other people's minds and behaviour
Failure to recognise faces
Lack of empathy
Gullibility/naivety
Excessive formality/robotic
No turn-taking/adapting content of speech to listeners
Inappropriate behaviour/rudeness
Childlike capacity/immaturity (in adulthood)

NARROW INTERESTS

Limited/eccentric interests
Intense focus on one or two subjects
Preoccupied with own agenda/self-motivated/autodidactic/insatiable curiosity/avid reader
Non-compliant/non-conformist
Originality of thought/innovative/inventive
Intense concentration/hyperfocus/phenomenal energy
Excellent rote memory for facts and details
Preoccupation with details
Computer-style thinking
Preoccupation with parts of objects, especially mechanical
Difficulties prioritising, except own interests
Poor organising abilities, except own interests
Collecting instinct

NON-VERBAL BEHAVIOUR

Repetitive routines or rituals (compulsive)
Desire for sameness
Repetitive motor mannerisms: hand/toe/finger flapping, rocking
Impaired sequential time: being 'in their own world'/living in the 'here and now'
Few facial expressions (apart from anger or misery)
Lack of eye contact
Innocent, charming faces, flashing eyes
Autistic charisma/poise

MISCELLANEOUS

Identity diffusion
Poor autobiographical memory
Cannot construct narratives of self
Restlessness
Potent imagination/fears, paranoid traits
No pretend play (as children)
Difficulty differentiating fact from fiction
Musical ability/understanding of musical form
Controlling and aggressive (autistic aggression)
Hypersensitive to criticism
Vengeful
Autistic superego/harsh conscience/moral intensity or, rarely, the opposite
Religiosity/interest in metaphysics/supernatural/immortality
Co-morbidity/impaired or poor health, especially depression/poor hygiene

SENSORY PERCEPTION/MOTOR CO-ORDINATION

Good visuo-spatial skills
Unusual reactions to sensory stimuli:
– hypersensitive, especially hearing, touch, smell, sight (colour)
– hyposensitive, especially touch, hearing
Synaesthesia (mixing up of senses)
Absolute pitch
Food fads
Insensitivity to pain
Attention deficits
Delayed sensory processing
Peripheral perception – peering, squinting
Anxiety due to sensory overload
Huge capacity for observation
Fragmented perception – e.g. seeing only the door handle in a room
Motor clumsiness/awkward motor movements
Poor handwriting
Clumsy, awkward gait
Poor balance (proprioreception)
Poor muscle tone/lax joints
Rapid movements
Unusual postures
Poor aptitude for sports

1

ROBERT EMMET

Emmet had indeed mastered everything but human nature.

W. B. YEATS, *Emmet, the Apostle of Irish Liberty*

Every nation has its iconic figures, its blemish-free martyrs whose names are invoked in times of political upheaval. Ireland has Robert Emmet. His death in 1803 at the age of twenty-five leading a failed uprising against the British forces in Ireland spawned a republican legacy which the passage of time has done little to diminish. That said, contemporary views on him tend to be polarised. Emmet as one of the founding fathers of the Irish Republic and one of its favourite sons now competes with Emmet the inept romantic on a fool's errand. Whichever way you look at his legacy, the fact remains that Emmet was extraordinarily gifted and talented. He was a genius: a creative genius in inspirational oratory and military design and strategy. Even so, his genius was unmistakably flawed in that he lacked pragmatism and insight into human nature – both qualities that are crucial in the conduct of war and are often deficient in those with Asperger's syndrome.

As an individual, Emmet was highly enigmatic and complex and had all the hallmarks of an Asperger genius. Indeed, the memoirs and accounts of him that exist follow a certain pattern for remembering and commemorating geniuses. His fine qualities and achievements are automatically emboldened for posterity. Emmet is thus presented as the ulti-mate revolutionary hero, the Che Guevara of his time, and his name is commemorated in song and verse down through the ages. And like many a martyr, his execution elevated him to the status of a saint, and he has been thus venerated ever since.

*

Dr Robert Emmet's position as the State Physician and Governor of St Patrick's Hospital, Dublin ensured that his youngest son Robert was born into privileged society on 4 March 1778. The family, of Protestant persua-sion, was considerably wealthy and lived at a well-appointed residence on St Stephen's Green, now housing the Royal College of Surgeons. His wife gave birth to seventeen children in all, of whom only four survived infan-cy, reflecting the huge infant-mortality rates of the time. Robert, the youngest, had two much older brothers, Christopher Temple and Thomas Addis, and an older sister, Mary Anne, all exceptional minds in their own right. Several descriptions of Emmet emphasise his average height, slight and delicate frame, angular face, expressive eyes, and hyperactivity.

An account of Emmet by Comtesse d'Haussonville in *Robert Emmet* is quite perceptive. This woman was the granddaughter of Madame de Staël, a leading French intellectual of her time who had known Emmet in Paris:

> He was above the middle stature, rather slight and delicate, although endowed with nervous strength which enabled him easily to support great fatigue. He walked with a quick step, and all his movements were rapid. The portraits remaining of him have been made from memory after his death, and the painter, it is said, preoccupied with his tragic fate, has given him a sad sombre expression which he had not in the happy days of life. His countenance was pleasing and *distingué*. His hair was brown, and his complexion quite pale; the eyebrow was arched, and the eyes black and large with dark eyelashes, which gave to his looks a remarkable expression of pride, penetration and mildness. His nose was aquiline and his mouth slightly disdainful.

Indeed, one of the most striking physical aspects of Emmet – like so many people with Asperger's syndrome – was his eyes and visage. Described by historian Dr R. R. Madden in *The United Irishmen, Their Lives and Times* as thin and alert and having a 'sharp visage and expressive countenance', Emmet's eyes were 'small, bright and full of expression: his nose sharp, remarkably thin and straight'. Madden also confirmed that Emmet was of moderate height and had a quick step. Emmet's former mathematics tutor at Trinity, the Rev Thomas Elrington, described his complexion as 'dirty-brownish' and said that he looked somewhat pockmarked from a distance. He walked briskly but did not swing his arms. This reference to Emmet not swinging his arms when walking is interesting, as it is frequently seen in those with autism. The quick step and brisk walking would certainly suggest that he was hyperkinetic and full of nervous energy – he also had a nail-biting habit – but he possibly had motor co-ordination problems too. (Emmet's elder brother Tomas walked with a stooped gait, as did his niece Jane Erin.) Although Elrington refers to him as not being near-sighted, Emmet had less than perfect vision and certainly, as he grew older, needed to wear spectacles like his brothers, possibly for short-sightedness. It is interesting to note d'Haussonville's description of his large, penetrating eyes, which occurs with autism, but there is no mention of any poor eye contact. Retaining a youthful quality, he sported a boyish air into adulthood.

There was something unassuming about Emmet, and his features were infused with a calm self-possession, a trait commonly seen in those with autism. This was something of which his grand-nephew Thomas Addis Emmet was also aware: in *Memoir of Thomas Addis and Robert Emmet,* he wrote about Emmet's 'wistful, elusive expression of a dreamer of dreams'. Indeed, a certain charm was evident even when he was not in the throes of public debate. For her part, Madame de Staël revealed that his charisma only became apparent when he was 'animated by an important issue'. Certainly the sharp distinction between the taciturn Emmet and the ignited Emmet is made too by his friend Thomas Moore of *Irish Melodies* fame:

> With a repose of look and manner indicating but little movement within, it was only when the spring was touched that set his feelings, and through them his intellect, in motion, that he at all rose above the level of ordinary men. On no occasion was this more particularly striking than in those displays of oratory with which, both in the Debating, and the Historical, Society, he so often enchained the attention and sympathy of his young audience. No two individuals, indeed, could be more unlike to each other, than was the same youth to himself, before rising

to speak, and after – the brow that had appeared inanimate, and almost drooping, at once elevating itself to all the consciousness of power, and the whole countenance and figure of the speaker assuming a change as of one suddenly inspired.

*

Wherever he went, Emmet made a strong impression. Curiously, the comments of others often succinctly capture what it means to be an Asperger genius. D'Haussonville's view of Emmet could be a character sketch of many individuals discussed in this book:

> [He] exhibited at an early age rare and brilliant faculties, a singular blending of enthusiasm and sagacity, a great power of concentration, an ardent and poetical fancy, combined with an exact and penetrating intellect – which made him equally fit for literary and scientific pursuits. He distinguished himself, also, by an indomitable energy of will, united to great gentleness of disposition – a combination always typical of the truly heroic character. It is not uninteresting to observe how the first trials of superior minds are marked even from childhood.

According to his grand-nephew's account, Emmet was a precocious child who entered school at an age earlier than was customary for young boys: 'from the beginning, this child was noted for his readiness in acquiring know-ledge; he was always in advance of his class, and he maintained this position until he left school'. By the age of fourteen, philosophical tracts were well within his intellectual grasp; these included Thomas Locke's *On the Human Understanding*, which he read at his own volition. His personal copy is still extant, and the section on government is heavily underscored or boxed off, while the margins are crammed with his detailed notes. Contemporaries, biographers and historians all agree that he displayed extraordinary intelligence and clearly had a high IQ. A brilliant student with an enquiring mind and passion for knowledge, he excelled in mathematics and science, in particular at Trinity College Dublin, which he entered at the age of fifteen, and went on to win several academic awards in his time there. Indeed, a high proportion of those with Asperger's syndrome have a natural aptitude for mathematics and science, being especially good at engineering subjects. Remarkably, Emmet built a laboratory at home to further his scientific investigations

30

and conducted various experiments. The interest in gadgets, invention and novelty-seeking – nowadays seen in gadgetry such as mobile phones and iPods – was particularly marked in Emmet's case and later came to the fore with the various artillery and pyrotechnics he invented for the 1803 rebellion.

Emmet reserved his energy for his narrow all-embracing interests – mathematics, chemistry and patriotism – and combined them in the single cause of Irish freedom. It is worth noting that Asperger geniuses have in the past shown both political interests as well as mathematical interests, notably Éamon de Valera. Emmet's singleness of purpose was apparent to everyone with whom he came in contact. Historian Marianne Elliot in *Robert Emmet: The Making of a Legend* describes him as 'zealous and single-minded', while historian Patrick Geoghegan in *Robert Emmet: A Life* refers to his 'infectious enthusiasm'. Not surprisingly, he was frequently described as possessing 'nervous energy' and having absolute concentration in the pursuit of his interests. He also showed a dogged insistence in staying with a problem until it was solved – regardless of dangers and threats to his personal health. These features are perfectly illustrated by Madden in a well-quoted incident from his youth where he accidentally poisoned himself:

> [Emmet] was in the habit of making chemical experiments in his father's house, and on one occasion nearly fell a victim to his ardour in his favourite pursuit. Mr Patten, a brother-in-law of T. A. Emmet, had been staying at his father's, and on the occasion referred to, had assisted Robert in his experiments. After Mr Patten had retired, the former applied himself to the solution of a very difficult problem in *Friend's Algebra*. A habit which he never relinquished, when deeply engaged in thought – that of biting his nails – was the cause of an accident which proved nearly fatal to him. He was seized with the most violent inward pains; these pains were the effects of the poison he had been manipulating, corrosive sublimate. [He] had, unconsciously, on putting his fingers to his mouth, taken, internally, some portion of the poison. Though fully aware of the cause of his sufferings and of the danger he was in, he abstained from disturbing his father, but proceeded to his library, and took down a volume of an encyclopaedia which was in the room. Having referred to the article 'poison', he found that chalk was recommended as prophylactic in cases of poisoning from corrosive sublimate. He then called to mind that Mr Patten had been using chalk with a

turning lathe in the coach-house; he went out, broke open the coach-house door, and succeeded in finding the chalk, which he made use of, and then set to work again at the puzzling question, which had before baffled his endeavours to solve. In the morning, when he presented himself at the breakfast table, his countenance, to the language of my informant (who was present) 'looked as small and as yellow as an orange'. He acknowledged to this gentleman that he had suffered all night excruciating tortures, and yet he employed his mind in the solution of that question, which the author of the work acknowledged was one of extraordinary difficulty, and he succeeded in his efforts.

From an early age, Emmet's enthusiasm for military history and strategic planning was obvious in his choice of reading matter, from which he frequently learnt tactics and pictured various troop manoeuvres, much like Winston Churchill did more than a century later. It comes as no surprise that Emmet was steeped in national politics, as his father filled the minds of his children with strong moral and patriotic principles. Something of a radical patriot himself, Dr Emmet was forceful in his views on Catholic emancipation and nationalist issues and dreamt of Ireland becoming independent. Leading political thinkers of the day and United Irishmen such as Dr William Drennan regularly dined at the Emmet home, and their ideas inevitably rubbed off on the youngest Emmet. Frequently, Dr Emmet discussed politics in considerable detail with Irish patriot and parliamentarian Henry Grattan, who later remarked that it was 'an extravagant sort of patriotism' that was foisted on the Emmet children.

Across the Atlantic, the American War of Independence had a profound effect on the Emmet family and provided a model for Irish freedom. Emmet was inclined to daydream, like Yeats and Pearse, and his mind was filled with visions of freeing Ireland, as George Washington had done for America. One such incident, recalled by Moore, occurred when Emmet sat beside him at the piano while he played a traditional air, inspiring Emmet to break free from his reverie and exclaim: 'Oh, that I were at the head of twenty thousand men marching to that air!'

Committed to action, it was natural that Emmet would follow in the footsteps of his brother Thomas and become active in the United Irishmen. He joined the United Irishmen club at Trinity College – though he reputedly never took the oath – and was secretly involved in recruiting students and preparing for rebellion. This was a highly dangerous move, as he faced both expulsion from the college and criminal prosecution if discovered. Yet he continued nonetheless, showing his trademark fearlessness – evident in some people with autism. Prior to the 1798 rebellion, however, there was a routing of subversive elements within the university, and Emmet and twenty-two others were effectively expelled following an inquisition, otherwise known as a 'visitation'. Initially, Emmet had boycotted the proceedings and had sought to resign from the college in advance, but a ruling from the Irish Lord Chancellor, the Earl of Clare, prevented any student from taking his name off the college books.

It was at Trinity College that Emmet used his powers of oratory to get across his nationalist messages and influence fellow students. He was frequently described as a brilliant orator with astonishing debating powers. Naturally, he had been looked upon with suspicion by the college authorities. The subsequent failure of the 1798 rebellion and the death of Theobald Wolfe Tone, founder of the United Irishmen, was a bitter blow for Emmet. The arrest and imprisonment of his brother Thomas, first in Dublin and then in Scotland, for his involvement as one of the leaders only served to further Emmet's commitment to the nationalist cause.

A deeper immersion in patriotism on the part of Emmet came in 1800, when he became secretary of a secret United Irishmen delegation to France – to which many of the rebels had fled following the failure of the rebellion. There he moved among the higher echelons of Napoleon Bonaparte's military in an effort to secure their help in overthrowing British rule in Ireland. In particular, Emmet sought a treaty signed between the United Irishmen and France in advance of a rebellion, along the lines of that obtained by Benjamin Franklin on behalf of America. Such a treaty never materialised. According to Elliot, Emmet was a 'single-minded negotiator with talents as a military tactician, at least on paper, and a young man who commanded the respect of a number of hardened senior figures in the French government and military command.'

Emmet's skills as a military tactician were certainly honed in France. There he studied manuals on military tactics – although he had no real practical experience of warfare. What little knowledge he acquired on this subject largely came from books; previously, in Ireland, he and an associate, Malachy Delany, had amended a military handbook written by Surgeon Thomas Wright, who had smuggled guns for the rebels in 1798.

New ideas on insurgency and revolution in particular were to be found in *Extracts from Colonel Tempelhoff's History of the Seven Years War*. A famous mathematician, Georg Friedrich von Tempelhoff was also a colonel in the Prussian army and a distinguished artillerist. Madden notes Emmet's obsession with the details of this military treatise:

> [His copy is] throughout annotated in pencil, in Emmet's hand, with all the care and application of a man who had given to every line of the work the minutest attention. The marginal notes and underlined passages have reference particularly to military operations in mountainous countries, and to the advantages which an observer of a quick and experienced eye may draw from attack and defence. 'One may plainly see,' says Madden, 'that the reader has passed days and nights in the study of these works, and one may thereby judge of the nature of the preoccupations by which, from his youth, Robert Emmet was absorbed.'

In particular, Emmet was impressed with Tempelhoff's detailed flanking manoeuvres to surprise the enemy. He became increasingly enamoured with the view that using the element of surprise was the only way for a small army to defeat a much greater one. Surprise was to be a principal strategy in the 1803 rebellion.

It was also in Paris that Emmet's penchant for novelties and invention brought his creative genius to the fore. Indeed, he presents a classic picture of a person with Asperger's syndrome: a preoccupation with mechanical objects and gadgets, a talent for drawing, and excellent visuospatial skills. An artistic flair was evident too from his many designs, such as the attractive seal of the United Irishman. In all likelihood, he had good fine motor skills, as he was adept at sketching, drawing and design.

Geoghegan notes that it was in Paris that Emmet developed his interest in unorthodox military weapons, explained partly by the influence of the inventor Robert Fulton, but also because the use of gadgetry appealed to his scientific nature. This surely must have been an immensely fertile period in Emmet's life, stimulated by his contact with advanced artillerists and skilled political and military leaders, and culminating in his decision to return to Ireland in 1802 to join fellow rebels Thomas Russell, William Dowdall, Michael Quigley and William Hamilton in order to stage a new rebellion, reputedly instigated by Colonel Despard.

Upon his return, the planning and organisation of the rebellion occupied all his time. Though not the instigator of the rebellion, he was a considerable organiser of it and went to enormous lengths to prevent the mistakes of the 1798 rebellion occurring again. He relied on the rebels of '98 rising again, this time with the aim of taking the capital first, with the provinces to follow suit. Naturally, he was preoccupied with secrecy, given that the large network of government spies and informers had been the downfall of the '98 rebel leaders. As a consequence, with great flair and originality he devised ways to communicate and establish the bona fides of messengers with special signals. One method was the use of 'ivory counters', according to Miles Byrne, a veteran of the 1798 rebellion who had joined forces with Emmet. These counters were branded with one, two or three marks of varying importance and were given to messengers when they were delivering orders. The number of marks on a counter corresponded to the significance of a message: the fewer the marks, the higher the priority.

Insufficient arms had been another issue in 1798. This time round, Emmet established a number of arms depots in Dublin and commissioned the manufacture of blunderbusses and pistols and a range of other weapons. In fact, Emmet came up with numerous designs and inventions for ingenious gadgetry, motivated as much by enthusiasm as necessity: he comes across as an early-nineteenth-century version of Q, the quartermaster extraordinaire in the James Bond movies. Among other things, Emmet designed exploding beams to impede cavalry or infantry, hollow beams for carrying pikes in secret, and hinged pikes that could be worn under greatcoats. He even had plans for landmines filled with glass and nails, though these plans were not realised in his lifetime.

A house in Patrick Street, Dublin was acquired as an operational headquarters, and Emmet putting his visual-spatial skills to good use constructed secret closets large enough to accommodate pikes, firearms and ammunition for ten thousand men. After the failed 1798 rebellion, he had developed some skill in devising trapdoors and tunnels. Fearing that he would be arrested like his brother, he had hidden in his home in Milltown for six weeks, constructing various trap doors, hiding places and tunnels.

The range of his firearm inventions was also impressive. Perhaps the most remarkable was a prototype for the modern rocket; Emmet made it longer and used metal casing instead of a shorter and paper-cased version. Undoubtedly, his interest in rockets and explosive devices began in earnest while he was in France, where he met the American inventor Robert Fulton, then designing torpedoes, underwater mines and submarines for the French. Many believe that the fire rocket which William Congreve was credited with inventing in 1807 may have been influenced by Emmet and Fulton, although it is possible that Emmet improved on a type that was already being used in India against the British. All of this new technology was aimed at using the element of surprise to overcome the enemy.

Mounting a rebellion with Emmet at the helm became possible because he had the charisma, the mettle, the planning ability and the financial legacy from his father, according to biographer Seán McMahon in *Robert Emmet*. In the matter of getting sufficient men, Emmet relied heavily on his ability to persuade the masses of the success of the mission. Many people fell under his spell, including his fellow rebel Miles Byrne, who was conscious of his genius in persuading people to believe in the struggle. Not alone could Emmet hold sway over the minds of Trinity men but also those from lower social classes who were recruited for the rebellion in 1803. Typical of many orators with specific aims, his emotional appeal was often more important than the facts on the ground. This propaganda element was obvious both in France and Ireland, with Emmet reporting that the French would invade and support a rebellion, and is confirmed by Elliot, who says that 'a good deal of embroidery in what Robert Emmet was telling potential supporters for the United Irishmen in Paris had not yet received assurances'.

Despite the fact that he was only in his early twenties, Emmet showed leadership qualities as he matured into the role. As an authoritative figure, he inspired many men under his command, including the recruited former soldier Sergeant Matthew Doyle. According to Byrne, Doyle was inspired by Emmet's 'powerful and eloquent language' and 'felt highly honoured and flattered' in his company. Where Emmet showed leadership, however, it was of an inspirational nature rather than being based on skilled command. Like many Asperger geniuses, he possessed charisma in abundance and exuded a calm confidence which inspired men, even when all seemed lost. Geoghegan notes that, on the night of the rebellion, 'the 23rd of July, with his plans in tatters, Robert Emmet displayed eye-cool nerve. He never lost control of his emotions and at all times maintained an outward air of confidence and determination'. Indeed, this was not far removed from the unnerving calm of legendary SAS hero Paddy Mayne or Montgomery of Alamein.

On paper, nothing seemed to be overlooked in respect of Emmet's planning. Taking his cue from the American Declaration of Independence, he drafted the proclamation of the provisional government, which encapsulated the ideological aims of the people of Ireland – not least freedom of religion. The proclamation set down how to administer the country during and after the rebellion, mindful of the will of the people, and a code of conduct for Irish soldiers:

> This solemn declaration we now make. We war not against property. We war against no religious belief . . . we war against English dominion . . . if we are to fall, we will fall where we fight for our country.

Indeed, his words still resonate centuries later. In fact, elements of the declaration were also used by Pádraig Pearse when he came to draw up the 1916 Proclamation. Like Pearse, Emmet's planning even extended to the elaborate military dress of the leaders: he was neither the first nor the last political leader to be taken by French fashion! Making the Irish leaders appear like French generals with plumes and gold epaulettes was another tactic to inspire confidence that French aid was at hand. Emmet the poet was ever conscious of the power of symbolism! There is also the sense that there were no half-measures with him: everything should be done properly or not at all. This obsession with detail and precision is unquestionably a feature of Asperger's syndrome.

While he clearly showed talent when it came to military planning, the execution of the plans was another matter. Geoghegan sums up Emmet's plan for the rebellion as ingeniously flawed. It is true to say that he was skilled at the mechanical details of the rebellion but was not the best of strategists. The rebellion failed for a number of reasons, but chiefly because there were insufficient arms and men. Into the mix were also thrown poor communication, bad luck, incompetence and lack of discipline. Geoghegan notes that Emmet's optimism and enthusiasm provided the rebellion with its driving force and dynamic but that these traits were also its undoing. In truth, Emmet was probably too optimistic and too little aware of his shortcomings. As he put it himself: 'I thank God for having gifted me with a sanguine disposition.'

On the question of arms, although veterans such as Miles Byrne attested to how 'brilliant' Emmet's plan was, Byrne had misgivings about some of his priorities, for example his focus on novel rather than ortho-dox weaponry. At heart here is the question of common sense and the ability to establish priorities – somthing that is usually in short supply in Asperger's syndrome. When the time came for fighting, there were not enough blunderbusses or pistols. Emmet's gunsmith was late in the prom-ised delivery of arms; promises of money for guns never materialised, and corrupt patriots made off with Emmet's money at the eleventh hour. The lack of arms had a detrimental impact on the morale of the soldiers and consequently affected the number of men who were prepared to fight. For instance, when a contingent of Kildaremen arrived in the capi-tal and saw how few arms there were, they promptly returned home.

Undeniably, Emmet's optimism was misplaced, yet those around him were taken in by the power of his rhetoric nevertheless. In relation to the events of 1803, Byrne in his memoirs stated that 'Mr Emmet's powerful, persuasive language and sound reason, all coming from the heart, left it impossible for any Irishman, impressed with a desire for his country's independence, to make objection to his plans.' At a meeting between Byrne, Michael Dwyer and other 1798 rebel leaders in May 1803, Emmet claimed he had sixty thousand men committed to the rebellion – an aston-ishing claim. Byrne was later to say that, had he known that Emmet depended on the 'lower orders', he would have put him right. The naive and trusting Emmet took the assurances of men at face value, and expect-ed at least nineteen counties to join the rebellion.

A mixture of incompetence and bad luck, including an explosion at the Patrick Street arms depot, resulted in the date of the rebellion being brought forward, according to Byrne. The sheer incompetence too was astonishing: numerous operations were bungled and fuses for the various munitions were mixed up. But once the fighting started, perhaps the lack of discipline was the most shocking. Wild drunkenness and wanton vio-lence, such as the killing of Lord Kilwarden, the Chief Justice, meant that Emmet's supposedly massive fighting force descended into a rabble of ninety men.

Poor communication marred the success of the rebellion even fur-ther. On the night of July 23, the supply of men was further hampered when false reports of the rebellion being postponed resulted in many recruits staying away. An order for Dwyer's men to march on Dublin never reached him. No one was quite sure what to do. In fact, too great a preoccupation with secrecy helped lead to the collapse of the rebellion. The way in which Emmet handled the demands of communication and secrecy speaks volumes about his character. The charge of being impractical or lacking in pragmatism is often levelled at him – sometimes, perhaps, unfairly. Where secrecy was concerned, he was a realist. He had learnt the lessons of the 1798 rebellion, which had failed largely because many of the leaders were arrested on the word of informers. Even as a student at Trinity College, the need for secrecy was uppermost in his mind. There he had rebuked his friend Tom Moore over an unsigned article that drew attention to the possibility of sedition within the college. Where Emmet parted company with the pragmatists was in his inflexible approach to secrecy, which perhaps bordered on paranoia. When communication was vital, Emmet was not capable of being judicious and lacked common sense. This feature is seen over and over again in those with Asperger's syndrome. The memoirs of Henry Grattan confirmed the view that Emmet had little pragmatism, despite his intellect:

> He was a clever man, but devoid of prudence and of judgement. His objects were quite visionary; yet he was an honourable enthusiast.

Emmet's decision to abandon the rebellion came only with the realisation that he could not mount a serious assault on Dublin Castle. His subsequent trial for treason and execution was not something that Emmet had reckoned on, despite his vision of a liberated Ireland. The rebellion resulted in Emmet and twenty-one others being executed and several thousand being imprisoned. History has certainly recorded Emmet's audacious attempt to free Ireland. On 27 September 1803, *The Times* of London wrote:

> He possessed that enthusiasm which forms its projects without deliberation, pursues them under a heated imagination, and consequently fails in the execution of them. The plan he conceived was wild, imaginary, and impracticable.

His trial continues to fascinate. In 2005, Mr Justice Adrian Hardiman in *History Ireland* described it as nothing more than a 'show trial': there was insufficient evidence to convict him but the Crown was intent on executing him for treason nonetheless.

*

There are no accounts of Emmet having any speech and language difficulties as such. If he had, they most likely had been corrected or modi-
fied by the extensive elocution lessons he received from Samuel Whyte,
whose grammar school on Grafton Street he attended as a boy. Many
accounts attest to the loud and powerful nature of Emmet's voice. It was
described as 'loud, strong and clear' on the day of his trial. Geoghegan
records that, in an account of Emmet's speech from the dock by the government informer Henry Brereton Code, Emmet's voice could be heard
at the outer doors of the courthouse. This was attributed to Emmet's
power of voice projection from his long experience of public speaking.
That said, his voice was measured, as Geoghegan notes:

> There was nothing boisterous in his delivery, or forced or affected in his
> manner; his accents and cadence of voice, on the contrary, were exquis-
> itely modulated.

In addition, Emmet never appeared nervous or showed any fear in
public speaking, whether in his maiden speech at the Historical Society or
his speech from the dock. On one occasion at the Historical Society, however, when a contentious motion – 'Ought a soldier to consider the
motives of a war, before he engages in it?' – was hotly debated, he was
subjected to such intense and sustained heckling and jeering by a large
crowd that he lost concentration, 'broke down' and returned to his seat,
and was unable to respond to the opposing speaker's arguments. While
this seems out of character for the normally composed and collected
Emmet, it is possible that he was hypersensitive to noise and that the bar-
racking – to which he was unaccustomed – might have upset his equilibrium.

Great powers of oratory ran in the Emmet family. By all accounts, his
elder brothers Temple and Thomas Addis were powerful orators too.
Temple, who was endowed with possibly a greater intellect than Emmet,
distinguished himself in debating at TCD's Historical Society and went on
to have a brilliant law career, although his life was cut short at the age of
twenty-eight by an illness from which he never recovered. Temple was
renowned for his ability to speak in images rather than facts, leading
Henry Grattan Junior to declare that his only fault was that he could not

speak prose: 'Everything was poetry.' Judging from this capacity to think in pictures, it is quite possible that Temple too had Asperger traits.

This rhetorical flair was evident too in Emmet, who also distinguished himself in debating at the Historical Society. Henry Grattan was impressed by Emmet's speaking abilities: 'he possessed the powers of eloquence in a surprising degree', as he put it. Clearly Emmet had an ear for music and rhythm, as his speech was frequently punctuated by eloquence and euphony. The ability to think in pictures, by having an acute visual aesthetic, sustained Emmet for hours when he was speaking in public. Perhaps the speech that is inextricably linked to Emmet and his legacy is his speech from the dock. After being found guilty of treason, he delivered a brilliant speech in court which, Geoghegan notes, both inspired future generations and ensured his own immortality. It ended with the famous words:

> Let no man write my epitaph; for as no man who knows my motives dares now vindicate them, let not prejudice or ignorance asperse them. Let them rest in obscurity and peace: my memory be left in oblivion and my tomb remain uninscribed, until other times and other men can do justice to my character. When my country takes her place among the nations of the earth, then, and not till then, let my epitaph be written. I have done.

Like many an Asperger genius, Emmet also had a flair for languages and from childhood could speak and write Latin and French well. Certainly he also had some familiarity with Irish, as it was spoken to the servants and during family holidays to County Kerry, where his mother's people lived. It is unknown whether he was in any way proficient in the language or not. His phenomenal memory is perhaps also evident in that he was a good speller. Certainly Geoghegan refers to the fact that Dr Emmet believed that good spelling was a sign of a good education and encouraged high standards in his children.

*

There is little information about Emmet's sense of humour, but he clearly possessed one. Geoghegan calls it 'a quirky sense of humour' – which certainly could be a byword for autistic humour. Certainly an inventive way with words was evident in him, leading several historians to remark that he delighted in word games and neologisms. When writing poetry, he used the pen name 'Trebor' ('Robert' spelt backwards). In devising the various aliases, such as 'Ellis' and 'Hewitt', that he used to conceal his identity in Ireland, there was an element of playfulness as well. The name 'Ellis' was chosen, according to Geoghegan, because it was similar to his own surname in that it contained five letters, a capital 'E', a double consonant, a vowel and a final consonant. The choice of 'Hewitt' and its chiming with 'Emmet' also points to a love of rhyme in this poet.

One incident relayed by Geoghegan also shows his peculiar humour. When first arrested, Emmet was taken to Kilmainham Jail, where his cousin St John Mason was also being held. Mason bribed the prison guard, George Dunn, into helping Emmet escape. A farcical plan was devised by Emmet that, if the governor had left the prison for dinner but sentries were present in the hall, Dunn would hide Emmet's escape clothes in a washroom, where Emmet would go to change. Dunn was to whistle 'God Save the King' as a signal for Emmet to proceed to the washroom. Emmet found the incongruity hilarious. Indeed, this kind of simple slapstick is a particular favourite among those with Asperger's syndrome. Alas for Emmet, the escape plan did not succeed: Dunn was a government spy, and Dublin Castle was duly informed.

It is quite likely that Emmet and the woman he loved, Sarah Curran, shared the same sense of humour – a rather simple kind. His letters to her are filled with humorous anecdotes that made her laugh. Geoghegan notes that there was a playful side to Sarah and that she had a great capacity for laughter – which possibly sustained her in times of crisis. In one of her final letters to Emmet, she writes: 'You know I can laugh at the worst of times.' Another was signed off: 'I long to know how your wife and ten small children are.' We know that Emmet's brother Thomas had a great sense of humour too. According to Geoghegan, he took delight in entertaining his family and would attempt to sing 'with a most discordant sound – to create a laugh – which he always heartily enjoyed'. A penchant for novelties was certainly found in Emmet, and this contained an element of playfulness too. He wrote poems in invisible ink, which turned purple when the parchment was treated with certain chemicals.

*

In his short life, there are many episodes where Emmet showed extraordinary visual memory skills, common to those with Asperger's syndrome. During his many debates, he displayed an incredible memory, enabling him to speak for hours. His trial lasted more than thirteen hours: he must have been exhausted, forced to fast and stand in the dock all day, but his energy was undiminished, as were his tremendous powers of concentration. Such was his intense focus that he frequently spoke without a script or notes or any kind of aide-mémoire. Just before he was led away for execution, he quickly penned a letter to the Chief Secretary, William Wickham, who was responsible for military intelligence in Ireland. The letter is remarkable in that Emmet knew precisely what to say and did so calmly and precisely, despite the strain that he was under. In the approximately two-hundred-word letter – eloquent to the end – Elliot notes that he wrote 'in a strong, firm hand, without blot, correction or erasure'.

*

So much has been written about Emmet, with no sparing of superlatives, that it can be difficult to get a realistic impression of the man – one not filtered through the eyes of uncritical followers. This is especially true in terms of how he related to people. Despite the scarcity of original sources, a picture emerges of Emmet as socially awkward. Signs of him being ill at ease in society are revealed by his brother Thomas's brother-in-law, John Patten, who speaks of 'the extreme diffidence of Robert'. Patten notes that Emmet 'was so modest, reserved and retiring' that he seemed unaware of his abilities. An awareness that he did not fit into society was noticeable early on, and his 'apparent unfitness for society' or 'unwillingness to engage in active intercourse with men of the world', as Madden puts it, gave rise to some uneasiness in his father where his career was concerned. Even so, Dr Emmet was absolutely convinced that strength of character and leadership lay beneath his son's taciturn exterior and that, when the time came, Emmet would more than prove his worth.

Emmet is described as something of a recluse by Marianne Elliot; this is a feature sometimes encountered in those with Asperger's syndrome. Elliot also notes that, as a young child, Emmet appeared to have few companions of his own age. During his student days, he came across as a 'rather serious and quiet young man' and certainly did not go in for the usual student predilections. Instead he lived at home and refrained from any pranks or riotous behaviour. Despite the effusive praise that his friend Tom Moore normally heaped on him, it is likely that Moore's belief that Emmet was 'wholly free from the follies and frailties of youth' is accurate. It suggests that Emmet had an autistic superego, whereby he lived by a severe moral code – much like Robert Boyle. All in all, the impression is that Emmet's lifestyle was above reproach and that he was rather prim and proper. There are no records of Emmet creating any social faux pas as such, although he was a poor time-keeper and often arrived late for debates. Records from the Historical Society at Trinity College show that he was regularly fined for late attendances. This unpunctuality likely suggests that his mind was engrossed elsewhere and that he had a tendency to live in the 'here and now' – as do many people with autistic spectrum disorders.

Nonetheless, Emmet was not entirely socially isolated or reclusive. His charm, kindness and generosity meant that he naturally drew people to him and was well loved. Indeed, the barrister Charles Phillips stated firmly that 'everyone loved, everyone respected him'. Equally, Emmet could be controlling, dominating and black-and-white in his ideas, which made him a good leader of men. At a personal level, he had many acquaintances, but possibly few that he could call close friends or confidants. Although he was able to form attachments, these were generally among those who shared his interests or were childhood friends: men like Thomas Moore, Richard Curran, Archibald Douglas and Dacre Hamilton, a student who shared his passion for mathematics at Trinity College.

In France, Emmet developed a reputation for being enigmatic and elusive: British government intelligence reports of the time revealed that 'he lived very privately at Paris'. There is also the suggestion that he may have been depressed for a period in France, or at least to have been 'moody and withdrawn'. Adding to the view that Emmet was uncomfortable in general society, during his time in Paris he went to great efforts to avoid attending dinners, soirées and suchlike. It seems unlikely that this was due entirely to his concern for security and secrecy. He had few friends in the city and mainly associated with William Lawless, a former surgeon; Gabrielle, the Marquise de Fontenay and a family friend; and a mysterious 'Englishman' visiting Paris. Geoghegan says that Emmet refused to dine in public and stubbornly insisted on meeting guests in the residence of this Englishman. Again, the people he did meet in France were those that had common interests, such as Tadeusz Kosciusko, the Polish patriot and veteran of the American War of Independence, who had led an unsuccessful uprising in Poland in 1794 against Russia; the American ambassador Robert Livingston; the scientist Louis-Nicholas Vauquelin, who discovered chromium; and the American political writer and diplomat Joel Barlow. Though Emmet spoke perfect French, according to Elliot, he did not mix in French society, apart from attending the anti-Bonapartist salon of Madame de Staël – then a hive of intellectuals and radicals. There is no information on how frequently he attended her salon, however. As for French society in general, with his sharp moral code, it is possible that he was shocked by the aristocratic excesses and scandalous fashions of the French and chose to avoid them. Given his acute sense of decorum, this supports the view that Emmet was rather conservative and prudish in his tastes.

There are also indications of an emotional, immature personality with some hypersensitivity. Clearly the impression of a highly sensitive young man is found in the 1802 diary of Irishwoman Catherine Wilmot, travelling on the Continent, quoted in Eliot's *Robert Emmet: The Making of a Legend*:

> His colour comes and goes so rapidly, accompanied by such a nervousness of agitated sensibility, that in his society I feel in a perpetual apprehension lest any passing idle word should wound the delicacy of his feelings. For tho' his reserve prevents one's hearing many of his opinions, yet one would swear to their style of exaltation, from their flitting shadows blushing across his countenance in everlasting succession. His understanding they tell me is very bright.

Clearly, on these occasions the powerful and persuasive Emmet was well hidden under a rather juvenile, even feminine, façade. His tendency to blush in company would seem to indicate so. Even when reproaching his friend Moore, this was done with an 'almost feminine gentleness of manner', according to Moore. The Peter Pan quality of Emmet's character also comes across in descriptions of him as a naive and impulsive dreamer: Patten speaks of his 'boyishness of air'; James Tandy, son of Napper Tandy, one of the founders of the United Irishmen, described the rebellion as 'puerile' and called Emmet 'that highly gifted but infatuated boy'.

Extremely close family ties and loyalties are often seen in those with Asperger's syndrome. Emmet enjoyed a particularly close relationship with his family which exile did little to diminish. The bond between mother and son was particularly strong: he was her seventeenth child (she had buried thirteen infants), and she was hugely protective of him. In fact, he was her firm favourite. In some ways Emmet conforms to the notion that exceptional men are the sons of their mothers: Mrs Emmet too had a 'delicate and proud nature, a lively sensibility and a penetrating intellect', according to the Comtesse d'Haussonville. The Comtesse notes too that Robert above all other sons resembled his mother most and that the love she bore him inspired her with 'especial solitude', to which he responded beyond all her expectations. This would certainly fit with Freud's view of the favourite child doing particularly well in life. Emmet possibly enjoyed the company of children too. He certainly had time for his nephews and nieces, and bequeathed his prize possession of a watch, which he had inherited from his grandfather, to his nephew Robert.

As regards relationships with women, Emmet's name is indelibly linked to that of Sarah Curran. Indeed, in his romantic liaison with Sarah he became an unlikely romantic icon. This is not so surprising given his idealist, romantic imagination and lack of emotional maturity. Sarah, the daughter of wealthy barrister John Philpot Curran, who had defended several United Irishmen, lived in Rathfarnham and came to know Emmet through his friendship with her brother Richard. The ability to form and sustain intimate relationships regularly proves difficult for those with Asperger's syndrome, yet it is clear that Emmet and Sarah's was no ordinary relationship. From adolescence, Emmet had developed a sort of reverential deference for women, according to Patten, believing that they 'preserved more traces of their original purity and excellence' than could be found in men.

Those with autistic spectrum disorders certainly have a great capacity for feelings, which can make them sensitive in the extreme. Luckily for Emmet, his profound love for Sarah was reciprocated. In a love letter to Emmet, Sarah expressed the nature of their close bond: 'and such is the perfect confidence that I feel subsists between us that I have no fear of misconstruction on your part of any uneasiness I feel.' For Emmet's part, the night before his execution he wrote to Richard Curran to inform him of his feelings and concern for his sister Sarah, conveying the nature of their romance:

> I intended as much happiness for Sarah as the most ardent love could have given her. I never did tell you how much I idolised her. It was not a wild or unfounded passion, but it was an attachment increasing every hour, from an admiration of the purity of her mind and respect for her talents. I did dwell in secret upon the prospect of our union. I did hope that success, while it afforded an opportunity of our union, might be a means of confirming an attachment which misfortune had called forth.

Undoubtedly, Sarah had certain qualities that appealed to Emmet's chivalrous nature, especially her 'pure mind' and 'talents'. These 'talents' we can take to be her musical abilities. Geoghegan notes that she was a talented musician: she was an able pianist and harpist, and had a fine singing voice. She was also one of the first people in Ireland to have recognised the supreme genius of Mozart only a few years after his death. Like all his family, Emmet had a deep appreciation for music too – as do many people with Asperger's syndrome, though they are not always capable of singing or playing an instrument themselves. From her time as a loyal servant of his in Butterfield Lane, Rathfarnham, Anne Devlin remembered that Emmet sometimes hummed a tune, but 'he was no great singer'.

Other aspects of Sarah's nature appealed to the romantic Emmet. Clearly she was charming, and her frail beauty was particularly attractive to him. Insightfully, Geoghegan says that there was something 'fey and ethereal' about her. Indeed, this otherworldliness only added to her pure quality in Emmet's eyes. In addition, she cut a slightly tragic figure, having endured a deeply unhappy childhood, with the loss of her mother, the death of a sister, banishment from the family home, and a cold and indifferent father. Nonetheless, behind the frail beauty was a reserve of strength and a deep religious faith which surely must have impressed Emmet too.

It could be argued that Emmet's romantic liaison with Sarah was not 'normal' but was rooted in courtly and chivalrous notions – reflecting, to a degree, the social class he inhabited. In this respect, it was an idealised love: he idolised Sarah. Indeed, this capacity to idolise women is certainly found in those with Asperger's syndrome. Emmet's sense of courtly honour is even more pronounced in that he hoped that a successful rebellion would establish his credentials with Sarah's family and make him worthy to win her hand. His idolising of Sarah was also his undoing, however. As a fugitive, he imprudently failed to destroy her love letters, which contained details of the uprising; these letters ultimately incriminated them both. As regards other women, the Marquise de Fonteney in Paris and Anne Devlin in Dublin were largely maternal figures to Emmet, either being his confidante or offering him support of various kinds, or both.

That Emmet lacked a good understanding of human nature is quite clear and there is more to this than just the immaturity of youth. The charge of being a poor judge of men is often made against him, and for the most part this is true – and singularly points to Asperger's syndrome. Given to extremes, he was either far too trusting or far too distrusting. As Geoghegan puts it:

> While Robert Emmet might have been a good leader, he was a terrible judge of men. Always too trusting, it was one of the main reasons why the rebellion failed: he had taken at face value the declarations of support and believed every promise that he received. In prison he allowed himself to be completely deceived by George Dunn, whose treachery implicated the very person he wanted to protect the most. But the great betrayal was still to come. Leonard McNally, the trusted defender of the United Irishmen, reported everything he said back to Dublin Castle.

The fact that his defence barrister, Leonard McNally, was a government spy was an act of colossal treachery on McNally's part, yet Emmet went to his grave with no inkling of it, believing him to be a man of honour. Unquestionably, the innate naivety associated with autism was present in abundance in him, and left him open to betrayal.

*

History is full of leaders, from Alexander the Great to Lawrence of Arabia, who take huge moral responsibility for correcting ills and oppression – typically with a sharp sense of duty. Emmet was another such leader. The qualities of duty, honour, loyalty, chivalry and trust were all extremely pronounced in Emmet's case. In fact, it points to Emmet having a harsh superego or autistic superego. His moral code was forged at an early age through the influence of his parents, who instilled in him their version of radical patriotism but also charity towards the sick and destitute of Dublin. Elliot notes that the Emmet family was known for its charitable work and that Mrs Emmet was often accompanied by her youngest son on her visits among the poor. The close bond between mother and son continued throughout Emmet's life and partly prompted his return to Ireland in 1802, though it was ultimately his sense of duty towards Ireland that precipitated his homecoming.

His honesty of purpose and feelings of guilt over Ireland's oppression and his parents' sacrifices made the need to assuage that guilt more urgent. Clearly, he was conscious that his parents had made great sacrifices by not impeding his brothers and himself in their pursuit of Ireland's freedom, despite the obvious risks involved. Too often, Emmet is criticised for naivety, yet paradoxically he was fully aware of the risks involved in him returning home. In a letter to the Marquise de Fontenay, he writes: 'I believe I am myself on the point of making a sacrifice by returning to Ireland', which could be 'a very painful one to me'. At the time of his father's death in December 1802, he played the role of dutiful son, making the arrangements for the funeral and giving much-needed emotional support to his mother.

On the question of chivalry, Emmet seems more at home as a medieval knight than a wayward rebel. His chivalry was particularly expressed in his loyalty to his fellow rebels after the failed rising. As a fugitive, he refused to flee to France after so many of his men had been arrested and imprisoned. In the matter of his liaison with Sarah Curran, however, Emmet's sense of chivalry was absolute. In prison, the fear that he had incriminated Sarah Curran by keeping her love letters and had thus endangered her life wounded him deeply. He was overcome with guilt: 'There have been moments in my imprisonment when my mind was so sunk by grief on her account that death would have been a refuge.' The burden of guilt left him in the invidious position of pleading guilty at his trial and accepting certain death, provided that her letters were not used as evidence against either him or her. His fate was sealed but he was immortalised as the utter romantic hero – dying for love of lady and land.

Nonetheless, his innate nobility was also signified by sincerity, dignity, gratitude and pride. In the face of adversity, during his trial and subsequent execution, he showed remarkable stoicism and dignity – something that has drawn comments from several historians, not least Marianne Elliot, who writes that 'Robert Emmet greeted the news of his guilt with a callous indifference', while Geoghegan notes that 'Emmet's self-confidence and defiant countenance unnerved some'. His unfailing good manners and politeness during this time were puzzling, and the enigmatic Emmet really comes to the fore. His final act before he left Kilmainham Jail was to write a letter to William Wickham, as the representative of the British administration. In many ways, it was a strange letter – neither strictly necessary nor to be expected at this time. His gratitude extended to the administration for treating him well and with kindness as a prisoner, and for the mildness of the administration: had they wished, they could have stamped out Emmet and his followers' subversive actions with greater ferocity. And he would never claim that the British were 'remiss' in not detecting the conspiracy sooner. Far from being obsequious, the writing of this letter was the genuine and sincere act of an honourable man who had nothing left but his pride and dignity. Similarly, he shook hands with his jailers; at the gallows, he gave money to his executioner and even went so far as to help him place the noose around his neck. From the time his trial began until he mounted the gallows to meet his death, he showed no fear: he put propriety before fears or nerves.

The superego takes many forms, not least pride and vanity. Emmet was a proud young man who refused offers of financial help while in Paris, including that offered by the Marquise de Fontenay. At the time, many of the United Irishmen and refugees – including Wolfe Tone's family – were petitioning for relief, having fallen on hard times in France. It appears that Emmet was not avaricious or self-aggrandising and that his needs were modest and simple. The entire legacy Emmet received from his father upon his death was spent on artillery and sundries for the 1803 rebellion, as well as the costs involved in housing several of the leaders of the rising in his unfurnished home in Rathfarnham in the preceding months.

From Lord Macaulay to Madden, accusations of vanity and egotism have often been thrown at Emmet. Commenting on Emmet's rebellion, Macaulay declared: 'I fear the vanity of a young man, with no principles, was his ruling motive in the murderous affair of 1803.' There is no evidence of personal vanity in Emmet as such, however. John Patten, who had occasion to observe Emmet at close quarters, begged to differ:

Robert had not a particle of vanity in his composition. He was the most free from self-conceit of any man I ever knew. You might live with him for five years – aye, for ten years – in the same house – in the same room, even, and never discover that he thought about himself at all. He was neither vain of his person nor his mind.

This also shows how enigmatic, private and secretive Emmet was and, moreover, how controlling he was in maintaining a distance from other people.

What is clear is that Emmet had an innate sense of justice – as do many with Asperger's syndrome – which made him intolerant of any abuses of power. For this reason, he disliked Napoleon for his treatment of small nations such as the Netherlands and was loath to enter into any agreement with him, once declaring: 'I consider Bonaparte as the most savage tyrant.' His sharp moral code was reflected too in the proclamation of the provisional government which he drew up, in particular the code of conduct for soldiers. For those who violated the common laws of morality during warfare and were guilty of torture, free-quarter, rape and murder, there would be no harbouring or toleration of them by the new state – or indeed protection for them from the rough justice of the people.

There is little in the various accounts of Emmet to indicate that he showed excessive autistic aggression as such. Even so, in his brother's account, he could be outspoken against the corruption and abuses that existed throughout the country. The extent to which he was controlling or critical of others was expressed in his need for secrecy, which possibly at times bordered on paranoia. Clearly he could be stubborn, but he appears to have borne criticisms well – something which is not common for people with Asperger's syndrome – but perhaps reflected his huge need for self-control. On rare occasions, the mask slipped, however, and he apportioned blame or disapproval. On his return to Rathfarnham following the failed rebellion, he parried his loyal servant Anne Devlin's disapproval by saying: 'Don't blame me, the fault is not mine.' Similarly, at his trial, prosecuting counsel William Plunket's listing of the shortcomings of the failed rebellion provoked extreme dissatisfaction on Emmet's part. On hearing Plunket's 'I expose to the public eye the utter meanness and insufficiency of its resources', Emmet's demeanour changed from one of 'manly firmness' to one of total contempt. According to a yeoman who was present, Emmet assumed 'an air of haughty and offended dignity'.

*

The unique repetitive mannerisms of those with Asperger's syndrome are often expressed in a variety of ways, such as rocking, swaying, head-bouncing, foot-tapping or rhythmic arm-, leg- or hand-jiggling. Emmet showed signs of such repetitive and stereotypical movements. In his case, these stereotypies were probably in response to the sensory overload of an attentive or hostile environment, or ways of sustaining his train of thought. These were most noticeable when he was speaking in public or out walking. Geoghegan writes that Emmet had a peculiar habit of sway-ing his body: from his earliest days at Trinity College, '[Emmet] had devel-oped a habit of swaying his body when he spoke in public, and he seemed to use this as a metronome to modulate his style.' On another occasion when he delivered a speech with his back to a fireplace, his hand moved rhythmically backwards and forwards along the chimney piece to empha-sise certain arguments. Another mannerism that was obvious in court was the continued gentle rhythmical tapping of his fingers on the palm of his hand 'for added emphasis' during a speech. This was most evident during his speech from the dock.

Another repetitive mannerism occurred when he was out walking, which he did religiously. He carried a little cane that he would tap rhyth-mically on the ground when he was deep in thought. Miles Byrne, in his *Memoirs,* recalls a meeting with Emmet and United Irishman Thomas Cloney in Harold's Cross. Byrne observed the rebel leader approaching 'walking along and musing, and tapping the ground with his little cane, in his accustomed way'.

*

The many facets to Emmet's character serve only to deepen the enigma of the man. There is some evidence of identity diffusion too, with his constant need to reinvent himself in the shape of orator, poet, inventor, revolutionary, martyr, and so on. Geoghegan writes that part of the par-adoxical nature of Robert Emmet was the 'curious combination of poet and warrior'. Although Emmet had some talent for poetry, his verses were not highly original or remarkable. Influenced by the Romantic poets of the time – Coleridge, Southey, Shelley and others – Emmet's poetry is distinctively dramatic, containing impassioned pleas for action or laments for dead heroes. Moreover, the rhyming couplets are often strained and contrived.

Many Asperger geniuses at some point pursue occupations that seem bizarre and out of character. Emmet's other occupation in his short life was in tanning. Upon his return to Ireland in 1802, he had no means of earning a living and decided to learn a trade by going into partnership with John Patten and a tanner called Norris.

A martyr or messianic identity is sometimes found in the Asperger genius too. For rebel leaders, the figure of Christ the redeemer is inevitably bound up with notions of personal sacrifice, suffering and, ultimately, death. It is not insignificant that, at the time of Emmet's arrest, a handwritten commentary on the passion of Christ was found in his possession. Certain words were heavily underscored: 'the innocent victim . . . oppress'd – afflicted – bleeding – dying'. Over a century later, the same thinking was present in Pádraig Pearse, but to a far greater extent. Not surprisingly, given their failures, many consider these national heroes to have been delusional or, as Yeats put it, to have suffered the 'delirium of the brave'. There was clearly a religiosity or sense of religion in Emmet's imagination. Though he was not a regular churchgoer and was not particularly committed to Anglican services, Emmet was avowedly Christian. In his final hours, he was conscious of his sins and asked to receive the sacrament.

A desire for public recognition for one's achievements is at the heart of the Asperger genius. In Emmet's speech from the dock, we get a concern for immortality and how he would be perceived in time to come. He admits that he was a 'man to whom fame is dearer than life'. With an eye to posterity, Emmet wrote – for his brother – a detailed account of the plans and preparations for the rebellion. In effect, this was the culmination of his life's work, written as a progress report on Ireland's fight for freedom, where all the disasters are catalogued, along with his thoughts on how they could have been rectified had things been different.

*

That Emmet was both a genius and a prodigy is beyond question. A friend of his at Trinity College, Archibald Douglas, wrote that 'so gifted a creature does not appear in a thousand years'. Time and again, we find the word 'pure' used to describe exceptional minds. Emmet's grandnephew Thomas Addis refers to Emmet's 'purity of mind' and 'purity of intention', while the political philosopher William Godwin concluded that Emmet was 'a man of a very pure mind' – though he lucidly added that he was also a 'meteor and ephemeral', no doubt shorthand for 'the good die young'. Thomas Moore too wrote about Emmet's purity:

> Were I to number, indeed, the men among all I have ever known, who appeared to me to combine in the greatest degree pure moral worth with intellectual power, I should, among the highest of the few, place Robert Emmet . . . how capable he was of the most devoted passion events afterwards proved. The pursuit of science, in which he eminently distinguished himself, seemed at this time the only object that at all divided his thoughts with the enthusiasm for Irish freedom, which in him was an hereditary as well as national feeling.

His pureness of mind took many forms, whether in the pursuit of love of woman or country. And typically, his romantic imagination was bursting with heroes legendary and real. In his formative years, he received a classical education, where his mind was exposed to heroes from antiquity. Later, he was influenced by George Washington and heroes of the American War of Independence such as the Polish general and patriot Tadeusz Kosciusko. All these heroes, alive or dead, were more real to him than the people around him. Charles Philips, a friend of the Curran family, confirms this view:

> His mind was naturally melancholy and romantic – he had fed it from the pure foundation of classic literature, and might be said to have lived not so much in the scene around him as in the society of the illustrious and sainted dead. The poets of antiquity were his companions, its patriots were his models, and its republics his admiration.

Moreover, Emmet's romantic imagination meant that he was stoical to the end: he whispered the words *'Utrumque paratus'* from Virgil's *Aeneid* to his cousin St John Mason as he passed into Green Street Courthouse for his trial. He was 'prepared for either' fate: death or life.

The impact of Emmet's letters and orations, in particular his speech from the dock, was phenomenal – it was reported in *The Times,* the *London*

Chronicle and the *Dublin Evening Post* – and affected the minds of both oppressed and oppressors, to say nothing for the legions of intellectuals and patriots on both sides of the Atlantic. Lord Norbury who tried Emmet, was actually reduced to tears, as were many who left Green Street Courthouse the day of his trial. Indeed, Emmet's letter to Wickham had such a profound effect on Wickham that he resigned his position as Chief Secretary soon after. Romantic poets such as Southey, Coleridge and Shelley succumbed to the dazzling eloquence of the speech too, as did Abraham Lincoln, who reputedly learnt it by firelight in his Kentucky cabin.

2

PÁDRAIG PEARSE

Two influences go into the making of every artist, apart from his own personality – if indeed, personality is not only the sum of these two influences – the influence of his ancestors and that of his contemporaries.

PÁDRAIG PEARSE

Over the entrance to St Enda's School, founded by poet and teacher Pádraig Pearse, a wooden panel depicted the boy Cúchulainn taking up arms before the druids in the Hall of Heroes. The motto of this much-loved Celtic hero served as Pearse's creed too: 'I care not though I were to live but one day and one night provided my fame and my deeds lived after me.' After Pearse proclaimed the Irish Republic from the steps of the General Post Office in Dublin on Easter Monday, 24 April 1916, and set in train a revolution that would culminate in Ireland achieving independence from Britain in 1922, he became an iconic figure and martyr in Irish history. His legacy is mixed, however: one man's revolutionary hero is another man's murderer. Indeed, the far-seeing Pearse predicted that people would 'say hard things for us now, but later on, they will praise us.' In fact, Pearse's reputation continues to swing back and forth.

Many historians note that Pearse remains an elusive and enigmatic figure. Certainly he was a man of contradictions: he abhorred violence, destruction and cruelty yet saw these things as a necessary means to a desired end. Undeniably, Pearse was a unique individual who achieved remarkable things in his short life. An oratorical and educational genius, his ability to see further than others meant that he was no armchair idealist or dilettante but, ultimately, a man of action. He overcame seemingly insurmountable odds to achieve – or at least put into practice – his ideas on nationalism, language and education. Given his enormous talents and his enigmatic, eccentric, immature and contradictory nature, Pearse can be understood in terms of Asperger's syndrome.

*

In demeanour, Pearse had definite poise and charm. This was present from an early age: indeed his stepsister Emily noted the 'wonderfully calm self-possession' on the face of the young page boy on her wedding day. In appearance, Pearse retained his boyish looks throughout his life and was somewhat fresh-faced; he was also tall and had a high, smooth forehead and a rather stately bearing. In public, he generally wore a solemn, earnest expression on his face. By all accounts, Pearse suffered from short-sightedness and had a distinct cast or squint, or some unspecified eye disfigurement, in his left eye. This may also indicate some problems with maintaining eye contact. He was self-conscious about this and as a result posed for photographs showing his right profile. In his youth he wore spectacles but he changed them for pince-nez in adulthood. His sister Mary Brigid remembered his most beautiful strong, even teeth, and his tendency to dress in black gave him a clergyman-like appearance. Allied with his powers of rhetoric and determination, Pearse's demeanour and appearance made him a forceful personality. His charisma mesmerised his audiences: his pupil and later comrade Desmond Ryan admitted that 'to live with him was to fall under his persuasive spell'.

*

In Pearse, the remarkable strength of will and huge reserves of energy common in the Asperger genius are present. The absolute dedication to his interests – the Irish language, literature, education and nationalism – is there in abundant measure. Though the focus of his interests was narrow, it was all-consuming, and marked by an unusual intelligence similar to his father's. Pádraig Pearse, who was born on 10 November 1879, was described as 'bright, serious and, like his father, self-motivated' by historian Seán Farrell Moran in *Patrick Pearse and the Politics of Redemption*. Despite his humble origins, Pearse's British-born father, James Pearse, became a highly respected stone carver, and examples of his work can be found in many Dublin churches today, including the Church of Saints Augustine and John on Thomas Street. His father's success was fuelled in part by a desire to make something of himself in the world and by his thirst for education and learning. This, coupled with a liberal and broad-minded outlook, led to him amassing a large library in the family home on Great Brunswick Street (now Pearse Street) in Dublin. An avid reader from his earliest days, Pearse would spend hours on end reading. His sister Mary Brigid recounts how 'one seldom saw him without a book open before him, or tucked away under his arm'. Books concerning Ireland were favourites, along with children's stories and nature studies – indicating a curiosity about the natural world often seen in those with Asperger's syndrome. This pattern of reading followed him into adulthood: indeed, such was his deep concentration when reading that he developed a reputation for unpunctuality, whether for dinner or when giving public lectures.

Attending the nearby Christian Brothers School on Westland Row, Pearse was intelligent and industrious and adapted to the school's renowned system of rote-learning and cramming to pass exams. Unlike many others with Asperger's syndrome, he did well at school, despite the rigorous, exam-oriented system. His creative instincts also found expression at Westland Row: according to his school friend Eamonn O'Neill, Pearse was especially good at English composition and won a special prize for an essay at the Intermediate examination. In addition, he also had a particular liking for mathematics.

An absolute dedication to the Irish language and literature was fostered from an early age too. Hailing from north County Meath, his mother's people spoke Irish, and various accounts are documented by Pearse in his incomplete autobiography *The Home Life of Pádraig Pearse,* edited posthumously by his sister Mary Brigid. In 1893, he began to learn Irish at CBS, and he soon excelled at the subject, although he continued to do well in English, French and Latin – showing the good linguistic skills that many with Asperger's syndrome possess. He finished his schooldays with what historian Ruth Dudley Edwards describes in *Patrick Pearse: The Triumph of Failure* as a regard for the English classics and a passionate love of the Irish language and literature. In December 1896, at the age of sixteen, his enchantment with literature led him to establish the New Ireland Literary Society, where his dramatic abilities and debating skills were put to good use in various venues around Dublin. His energy and enthusiasm were boundless: various kinds of scholarly papers were read by the prolific Pearse, along with readings and recitations from Irish literature provided by others.

Influenced by the Irish-language scholar Thomas Flannery, Pearse had joined the Gaelic League at the age of fifteen. He soon became passionately interested in promoting a scholarly interest in the language and helping to save it from extinction. He was committed to the ideals of the League and moved quickly through its ranks, being elected onto the Executive Committee in 1898. With absolute commitment, he also attended central branch meetings and organised various events, giving scholarly lectures and teaching Irish. In fact, he was a veritable whirlwind of ideas and action. Dudley Edwards notes that, during his first two years on the committee, he had the most regular attendance of any member: he missed just six out of 109 meetings – and these only because of other League business!

It was in his role as editor of the Gaelic League's newspaper, *An Claidheamh Soluis,* from 1903, however, that he became a force to be reckoned with. His six years as editor of the paper was one of single-minded devotion to it, and the publication became a platform for his views. Like some with Asperger's syndrome, he was naturally opinionated and had a steady stream of ideas on a host of topics. His talent for writing also found expression in the many short stories and poems he contributed to the newspaper. Overall, *An Claidheamh Soluis* was extremely successful: by the time Pearse finally gave up the editorship in 1909, it had increased its circulation substantially. Summing up his friend's contribution to the Gaelic League, Eamonn O'Neill says that, in the dozen or so years Pearse spent there, Pearse's life was one of 'the most arduous toil for the language-teaching, editing, speaking, and attending a wearying round of committee meetings'.

It was perhaps in the area of education that Pearse commanded the greatest respect. By and large, he was a courageous pioneer in Irish education. His educational articles in *An Claidheamh Soluis* were thought-provoking and aimed at the formulation of possible future government policy on the language; they also introduced ideas on bilingualism, courtesy of a trip to Belgium in 1905 to see at first hand how the teaching of Flemish and French were co-ordinated. Famously, he railed against the Irish education system: his ideas in this area culminated in an essay entitled 'The Murder Machine', published in pamphlet form in 1916. In this essay he argued convincingly that the Irish educational system, based on an English model, was deliberately designed to destroy the spirit of Irish children. The purpose of this system, according to Pearse, was effectively to create 'willing or at least manageable slaves'. This was achieved by an exam-orientated curriculum with an emphasis on rote-learning, the recitation of long passages, and strict discipline – all of which did little to develop the minds of pupils, in his experience.

It was his belief that education should have nothing to do with the 'manufacture of things, but with fostering the growth of things' instead. According to educationalist Séamus Ó Buachalla in *A Significant Irish Educationalist,* mere reform of the educational system was not adequate for Pearse but 'an act of creation was necessary'. Like many Asperger geniuses, he wanted something radically new to replace the old system. While many of these arguments may seem commonplace today, in the early twentieth century they were novel and ground-breaking in Ireland.

Having established himself as a theoretical educationalist, Pearse – the doer – tried to modernise the educational system and remove the tight state bureaucratic control of it. His view of education involved a fosterage system, rooted in Celtic mythology, which recognised children as individuals in their own right. There was a considerable practical aspect to his theory: he recognised that children are not all equally academically gifted but appreciated that it was most important to bring out the best in each child. In essence, Pearse was promoting a *mens sana in corpora sano* philosophy – where true education consisted in a healthy balance of learning, self-expression and sport. Armed with such ideas, which had little chance of being implemented by government, Pearse decided to found his own school. This also came at a time when he was anxious to make something of his life, as his father had.

The setting up of an all-Irish school was to prove extremely challenging for Pearse. Yet what he lacked in prudence and maturity, he made up for in determination and energy. Though beset with financial difficulties – the school was entirely privately funded – the experiment was highly successful. For the most part, the success of St Enda's was due to Pearse's remarkable will and talent as an educator. According to a master at St Enda's, F. O'Nolan, who had also been a clerk in the secretariat of the Gaelic League, Pearse had boundless energy: 'To say that he was working-working-working all the time conveys but a faint idea of his concentrated energy.'

At St Enda's, Pearse was innovative, putting into practice his philosophy of education, according to Elaine Sisson writing in *Pearse's Patriots: St Enda's and the Cult of Boyhood*. This philosophy was based on providing written educational materials in Irish, teaching Irish as a vernacular language, improving teaching methods – especially in the teaching of languages, with the use of bilingualism and the Direct Method, a way of teaching language principally through conversation – and using modern visual teaching aids. Years later, when the Irish state came into existence, Pearse's own literary works – in simple Irish – proved to be perfect material for the Irish-language curriculum set out by the Department of Education. In terms of managing the pupils, Pearse achieved his ends mainly through encouragement and good discipline: corporal punishment was rarely used at St Enda's. Instinctively, Pearse believed – rather naively, it must be said – that boys were essentially truthful beings. In the financial management of the school, however, Pearse was grossly naive and highly impractical, especially with regard to the ill-judged move of the school from Ranelagh to the outer-Dublin suburb of Rathfarnham. Moreover, even when on the verge of bankruptcy, he overstretched himself further with other projects that needed funding.

Throughout his life, Pearse continued to produce plays and poetry – with mixed success. The plays he staged at St Enda's were highly successful: these included *Fionn, Mac-Ghníomharta Chuculain, Íosagán,* and *The Destruction of the Hostel* – the last also performed at the Abbey Theatre. Pearse was not as successful as a novelist, however. Like some writers with Asperger's, his works were largely plotless and lacked credible characterisation. Dealing with mythic heroes like Cúchulainn – essentially one-dimensional figures due their epic nature – suited Pearse better. These characters did not require an underlying complexity or subtlety of mind from Pearse's perspective. The lack of central coherence in autism, or the ability to see the big picture, clearly found expression in his inability to write a novel, where plot does require a sustained development of ideas. Certainly his short pieces are best: his stories, poems, plays and polemics. Indeed, Moran argues that, in Pearse's immature writings, he was still in many ways that 'young, dreamy, and lonely boy'.

At some point, Pearse's many interests crystallised into an all-consuming love for Ireland. Many historians agree that he was the most unlikely of revolutionaries, given his reserved, shy and socially awkward disposition. Nonetheless, the progression to nationalism was a natural one for Pearse, given his loyalties to Irish literature and the Irish language.

Pearse had inherited certain political leanings from his father: support for the Irish Parliamentary Party and an admiration of Parnell. The downfall of Parnell, however, left him disillusioned with politics, as it had so many others. In practice, Pearse at first took a passive interest in politics and set little store by party politics. Nonetheless, with his innate sense of right and wrong, he would give credit, where he felt it was due, to some British-government policies – mainly those that related to education. Not surprisingly, this did little to endear him to nationalists and only reinforced the image of him as a loose cannon.

Pearse's disenchantment with Irish parliamentary politics and his move towards militarism came in 1912, with the third Home Rule Bill, whose slow progress through parliament demoralised even its most ardent supporters. Given his exceptionally vivid and romantic imagination, at this time Pearse became more and more immersed in the legacies of Irish rebel heroes such as Robert Emmet, Wolfe Tone and John Mitchel. By giving policing measures to the Irish, the Home Rule Bill also prompted the rise of military forces – first the Ulster Volunteers in the North and subsequently the Irish Volunteers in the South. In what was clearly a defining moment, Pearse co-founded the Irish Volunteers in 1912 with Eoin MacNeill and several others and, typically, threw himself wholeheartedly into its activities.

The historian Joe Lee notes that Pearse was a natural leader. In his role as headmaster at St Enda's, Pearse was used to wielding authority and knew how to manipulate men and circumstances for his own ends. It could also be said, however, that he was not above allowing himself to be manipulated too. As a result, Pearse assumed the leadership during the Rising as if it were his natural right.

Added to this arrogance were his abilities as a speaker. Certainly many of those with Asperger's syndrome speak with absolute conviction and sincerity, and this was overwhelmingly the case with Pearse. As his commitment to violence and sacrifice grew more intense, given his desire for radical change, he met with an ever-increasing enthusiasm from those he admired most. He certainly never grew tired of repeating the same message over and over again: for him, his ideas remained continually fresh. Again, this kind of repetition and commitment to the same message is frequently found in those with Asperger's syndrome.

In 1914, Pearse was allowed to join the Irish Republican Brotherhood (IRB), the secret paramilitary organisation revitalised in 1908 under Thomas Clarke. Pearse's membership of the IRB had been resisted for some time, as many considered him 'excessively vain' and 'possibly emotionally disturbed', according to Moran. Nonetheless, once he became a member, he was committed to infiltrating the non-political Irish Volunteers and helping move them towards a military solution. When this approach failed – and indeed split the organisation in 1914 – the resultant National Volunteers became more firmly wedded to armed struggle, which inevitably led to the Easter Rising.

Despite being a member of the IRB Military Council, Pearse had very little to do with the planning of the Rising: this speaks volumes about his lack of tactical abilities. It appears, however, that Pearse and many others believed that the Rising would be successful once the large shipment of arms had been delivered and the nationalist forces mobilised. When the arms did not materialise and Eoin MacNeill cancelled the manoeuvres for Easter Sunday, Pearse still believed the action was possible, and he countermanded MacNeill's orders and postponed the rising by a day. The ensuing confusion meant that, on Easter Monday, fewer Volunteers turned out than had been anticipated. Nonetheless, the unpragmatic Pearse, consumed with idealism, believed right to the end that the Rising would succeed.

There is no record that Pearse ever fired a shot during the Rising – or indeed that he could handle a rifle. It fell to James Connelly, with his military experience in the British army, to effectively take control of the uprising. In the days he spent in the besieged GPO, Pearse occupied himself writing propaganda and discussing Irish literature with Joseph Plunkett, who was dying with tuberculosis. The Rising lasted one week and was a military failure, despite the bravery of the men and women who had fought in it. As a symbolic act, however, it was an unmitigated success.

*

By nature, Pearse was shy, silent, introspective and socially inept. To judge from various accounts, he had a number of social impairments that made mixing and socialising with people quite difficult. He has been variously described as 'quiet', 'shy', 'reserved' and 'socially awkward'; he certainly had little capacity for social chit-chat. Eamonn O'Neill, a friend of his from CBS Westland Row, remembered him as 'a grave, sweet, silent boy' who was extremely reserved at school and kept very much to himself. Yet in spite of his shyness, Pearse was popular, and was liked and respected by his fellow pupils, whom, O'Neill believes, sensed that great strength and intellect lay behind the reserve. Although there is no suggestion that he was bullied, his time at school was marked by an increasing introspection and he certainly did not mix much with his peers, preferring books to school sports.

The extent to which Pearse got on well with people usually depended on whether they shared his goals and ideas or not: a typical scenario for people with Asperger's syndrome. According to his friend Mary Hayden, on the whole Pearse was a 'silent man', except when in the company of a few people whom he knew well, but he rarely revealed his deeper feelings even to them. When preaching to the converted, he was guaranteed to have friends for life. Consequently, he could relax in their company, and joke and be kind and generous. If not, he tended to be insensitive, though he was by nature kind and unselfish, as Dudley Edwards notes.

Both Pearse and his brother Willie tended to avoid the company of others. In this respect, Mary Brigid Pearse recalls that 'neither of my brothers was quite like other boys. Neither joined in the usual rough sport beloved of schoolboys, and they were rarely mischievous. They both loved home and were content to stay there.' Desmond Ryan, a veteran of the GPO, refers to Pearse's reclusive nature:

He had no petty vices nor meannesses, and to live with him was to fall under his persuasive spell. He was a recluse and mystic. . . . The testimony of his friends is unanimous: they all loved him even when his faults stood out before their eyes.

In fact, Pearse struck Hayden as an unusual character because he was so absolutely free from affectation of any kind: he was 'so perfectly simple'.

Pearse probably inherited some of his father's detachment. The first Pearse marriage was not a harmonious one, and James Pearse's wife Emily died from spinal inflammation, leaving behind two young children, Emily and James. One cannot rule out Asperger's traits in his case either: James Pearse too was a quiet, taciturn man who kept to himself. In autobiographical notes, Pearse remarks that his father did not have many 'intimate friends' and rarely had visitors to the house. His characteristic reserve seemed to dominate his second marriage to Pearse's mother, Margaret Brady, too:

> He was very silent, and spoke once or twice during the course of a meal; breaking some reverie to say something kind to my mother or something funny to one of us. . . . Occasionally at night . . . the deep reserve of his nature would break down . . . he would lift one of us, and press our face against his face, and put his arm around us, and draw us close against his stone-dusty blouse.

On many occasions, Pearse's behaviour was quite inappropriate. To an outsider, he seemed to have a reckless disregard for paying bills incurred by St Enda's. He genuinely failed to understand why tradesmen and creditors would get angry over unpaid bills, since he was not profiting himself, and his school was a noble enterprise. He expected all and sundry to wait indefinitely until the money turned up. Although this was no way to run a business, Pearse tended to appeal to the noble side of his creditors – if such existed! At the height of his financial difficulties at St Enda's, with the school about to go into liquidation, Pearse set up a newspaper, *An Barr Buadh,* yet never questioned the viability of such an enterprise. As far as he was concerned, his causes were beyond question.

Undoubtedly, Pearse sometimes had problems reading or understanding the attentions or motives of others. Also, he often talked at cross purposes. For example, his debating society, the New Ireland Literary Society, frequently put on plays and recitals. On one occasion, *Hamlet* was to be performed followed by a recital. Though he had a great love for music, he was rather vague about it. When his sister, who was to accompany the singers on the piano, asked what key they singers wished to sing in, as they had supplied no sheet music, he replied: 'Oh, the common-or-garden key!' When he was told that no such thing existed, because of the different pitches in which the various singers sang, he responded: 'Oh, these fellows all sing in the *medium* voice. The common-or-garden key, you know!' When his by-now-rather-agitated sister replied that even those who had 'medium' voices sang in different keys, Pearse still did not get the message. 'Quite so,' he agreed, 'the common-or-garden key.' Finally, his sister gave up, exasperated.

A fairly famous episode of Pearse's inappropriate behaviour is recounted by Eamonn O'Neill. In his capacity as an officer of the executive committee of the Gaelic League, Pearse decided to wear evening dress to an early ard-fheis of the League. This was entirely out of keeping with what the rank-and-file Gaelic Leaguers considered appropriate dress: Pearse looked more like a British-establishment figure than what was considered to be a true Irishman. Essentially, Pearse failed to interpret or read what others expected of him. It is hardly surprising, however, that with his sharp sense of duty and decorum Pearse would chose to wear something formal for the occasion.

For a good portion of his life, empathy was found wanting in Pearse. Coming from a comfortable middle-class home, he was quite far removed from the social ills of the day. He could relate very little to the rising tide of socialism sweeping Dublin under the stewardship of James Larkin and James Connolly. His view of the Irish peasantry was heavily romanticised too. When he wrote about the peasant's way of life, his work did not always reflect the great hardships they endured. For example, he wrote of their folk songs: 'Pure they are and spotless as the driven snow, like the souls and lives of those who sing them; sweet they are as the scent of the wild mountain flowers which grow in their native homes.' Perhaps most controversially, he accused Irish emigrants of being traitors to the Irish state. As a consequence of his poor insight, he remained detached and naive. Nonetheless, in later years he became more socially conscious, especially regarding the poverty, misery and human isolation that existed in Irish society.

Despite Pearse's social handicaps, he was not entirely immune to the reactions of society. He certainly had a sense that he was different. On one occasion, he declared that the effect of being a product of two traditions – English on his father's side and Irish on his mother's – 'made me the strange thing I am'. It is Asperger's syndrome rather than his mixed heritage that accounts in the main for his character, however. Always conscious of his social shortcomings, he knew that he was incapable of making small talk and generally did not put people at ease, preferring to flee their company instead. In typical self-publicising style, he wrote in his self-established paper *An Barr Buadh* a most revealing and frank insight of himself:

> Pearse, you are too dark in yourself. You don't make friends with the Gaels. You avoid their company. When you come among them you bring a dark cloud with you which lies heavily on them. The fellow who was talkative before you came falls silent. The fellow who was merry and laughing before falls into a melancholy fit. Is it your English blood that is the cause of that, I wonder? . . . However, you have the gift of speech. You can make your audience laugh or cry as you please. . . . The gay and sunny Pearse is seen too seldom, and generally at public meetings and in Sgoil Eanna. . . . I don't like that gloomy Pearse. He gives me the shivers. And the most curious part of the story is that no one knows which is the true Pearse.

This account also expresses the many personas of Pearse: the multiple personalities and identity diffusion that figures so highly in Asperger's syndrome.

The nature of Pearse's friendships, where they existed, is also worth close scrutiny. All their lives, Pearse and his brother Willie were inseparable. In fact, it is likely that Pearse had no intimate friend other than Willie. Certainly, Pearse recognised Willie as his true companion. As he put it: 'as a boy he was my only playmate: as a man he has been my only intimate friend'. Indeed, Ruth Dudley Edwards describes Willie as Pearse's 'comrade, confidant, intimate, support, mirror, doppelgänger'. In general, Pearse's male friends included those with whom he shared interests, such as Eamonn O'Neill, Thomas MacDonagh and Joseph Plunkett, among others.

Like many with Asperger's syndrome, Pearse was most comfortable among family members and often remained socially awkward outside that domain, a fact noted by Moran:

> Around most people he was still the shy, quiet, priggish figure he had always been. Though animated with family and his few close friends, he was almost never so forceful or assertive in personal relationships as he could be when on the stage. His political role was limited; it did not force him to be anything more than a propagandist, and it avoided his very real social limitations. We know that when he spoke to crowds, he moved them deeply – a possible result of his own tendency to be transformed by patriotic rhetoric. Those causes that he felt deeply made the clumsy Pearse into the inspired teacher or charismatic political leader, succeeding in ways he never experienced in his personal life.

As for Pearse's liaisons with women, they seem to be non-existent, other than his close friendships with Mary Hayden, who shared many of his Gaelic League activities, and his sisters. In the company of women, he could be 'chronically shy', as Desmond Ryan's two sisters observed when they helped out in the GPO during the Easter Rising. Indeed, there is no credible evidence that Pearse ever courted a woman or had sexual relations with one. In a letter to his friend Mary Hayden, he seemed to suggest that he would never marry and was wedded to his causes – again a phenomenon of Asperger's syndrome. Given his emotional immaturity, Pearse's attitude to women was ambivalent: he viewed women in either an idealised form or else as a maternal helpmate. Yet even though Pearse idealised women, particularly young girls, he had scant knowledge of them. Hayden says that he understood the lower or even the lighter side of women very little: 'He looked on the purity, the power of the self-sacrifice, which is to be found more commonly in women than in men, as something divine.' In this sense, Pearse felt that he could understand them because these qualities were strong in his own nature too.

On this point, the question of Pearse's sexual orientation inevitably arises. Given his lack of interest in women, many have automatically assumed that he was homosexual. However, there is no evidence to suggest that this was the case either. That said, Pearse clearly prized male friendships that featured a certain homoeroticism. In many aspects of his life, however, Pearse bore all the hallmarks of an ascetic monk. With his autistic superego, he could exert huge self-control – celibacy, in this case. Had he been aware of any homosexual tendencies, he probably would have been more guarded, given the social mores of the time, and possibly, in light of his rigid moral code, repressed them.

By and large, people with Asperger's syndrome, given their emotional immaturity, are more comfortable in the company of younger people. Pearse generally got on far better with children than with adults. His great love of children and the enjoyment he took from their company was observed by many. From his days spent in Connemara at a Mrs Connolly's house, she observed how he 'entered into all their fun; understood intimately the child mind, and became one of themselves'. At St Enda's, F. O'Nolan too observed Pearse's 'fatherly tenderness' and deep insight into boys' hearts and characters. Because the fantasy element was strong in the immature Pearse, he relished the world of young children, in which he did not have to interpret social codes.

Moreover, Pearse tended to idolise children, much as he did women, especially what he considered their divine nature. Undeniably, he took great delight in the male form, in particular the physical beauty and prowess of Gaelic warriors and young boys – the *macaomh*. So spontaneous and rapturous were his descriptions or elegies of male acquaintances that his innocence seems rather obvious. There is no evidence that his perhaps excessive love of boys, especially his young charges, was unwholesome or harmful: there is nothing to suggest that he was a pederast or paedophile. For all his moral authority, he never inspired fear in boys but rather awe, respect and adoration. Even so, his gross naivety often leaves some of his poems and short stories open to misinterpretation. His innocence was shattered somewhat when his friends Thomas MacDonagh and Joseph Mary Plunkett, alarmed at his English translation of his poem *'A Mhic Bhig na gCleas'* ('Little Lad of the Tricks'), brought their concerns to his attention.

> Little lad of the tricks,
> Full well I know
> That you have been in mischief
> Confess your fault truly.

I forgive you, child
Of the soft red mouth:
I will not condemn anyone
For a sin not understood.

Raise your comely head
Till I kiss your mouth:
If either of us is the better of that
I am the better of it.

There is a fragrance in your kiss
That I have not found yet
In the kisses of women
Or in the honey of their bodies . . .

Typical of the naivety seen in those with Asperger's syndrome, Pearse reputedly was hurt and bewildered that such unsavoury inferences could be drawn from his poetry. Another example of a rather risqué piece of writing is *'Lá Fa'n Tuaith'* ('A Day in the Country'), a fantasy that concludes with Pearse getting into bed with a young boy. It must be remembered, however, that Pearse was a product of late Victorian and Edwardian culture, which romanticised childhood and in which fantasy and adventure were the prevailing genres, such as in *Peter Pan, Alice in Wonderland, The Swiss Family Robinson* and *The Railway Children* – books adored by the young Pearse.

Those with Asperger's syndrome also have an affinity for animals: they response purely on instinct to them. Pearse had a special regard for animals, which were frequently depicted in his books and plays. In particular, he loved watching the arrival and departure of swallows each year. His gentleness towards animals was also seen at St Enda's, where he installed a menagerie of sorts in the agricultural part of the school. The unjust treatment of animals was not tolerated by him: the only expulsion from his school occurred after a pupil was cruel to a cat.

*

There are no accounts that Pearse had any speech and language difficulties as a child. From his own recollections, he quickly learned the alphabet and how to spell. He did have a stammer, which became quite noticeable when he was delivering a lecture. Moran writes that Pearse had to overcome a pronounced stammer in order to speak in public, and that this perhaps accounts for the 'peculiar pistol-like and jerky delivery' he had when talking. F. O'Nolan remembers that, in his interview for a job at St Enda's, Pearse spoke in 'abrupt, nervous phrases'. Many others, including Roger Casement and Stephen McKenna, recall that he spoke in a 'peculiar' manner. Clearly, Pearse had unusual voice qualities which affected his fluency, which can often occur in those with Asperger's syndrome. In the delivery of his speeches, Pearse lacked spontaneity and relied heavily on careful writing and rewriting of his scripts. This lack of spontaneity again features strongly in those with Asperger's syndrome. Certainly his controlling nature would not have left anything to chance: no doubt he practised his speeches until he felt confident.

At times, Pearse lapsed into his own idiosyncratic form of language. According to Moran, there are reports that, when Pearse and Willie spoke to each other, they did so in a kind of baby talk. It is possible that this was prompted by the easy intimacy they shared, but it discommoded others in their company, who were more accustomed to the serious-minded Pearse. The use of malapropisms can also be found in those with Asperger's syndrome, and Pearse was no stranger to them. The architect and critic Joseph Holloway attended one of Pearse's lectures at the Catholic Commercial Club in 1899, where Pearse gave what could be described as a wildly effusive account of Irish saga literature. In the highly excited delivery, several malapropisms caught Holloway's attention: 'I noticed that Mr Pearse used many words à la Mrs Malaprop in most inappropriate places and made use of such remarks as "handed down by word of mouth" etc. which struck me as quite funny.'

Like many with Asperger's syndrome, Pearse was a good linguist and mastered a number of languages easily: French, Latin and Irish. He was also a powerful orator and an important rhetorician for Irish republicanism. In fact, like Emmet and de Valera he had a genius for oratory. Many people with Asperger's syndrome are good at speechifying to large or even small groups: they can often capture a crowd and hold them spellbound. Pearse's powers of oration were evident from an early age. As a prominent member of the school debating society, he earned a reputation as a fine speaker. His style was clearly one of flamboyance and exaggeration. His fellow student Eamonn O'Neill recounts that Pearse had a good deal of the 'grand manner' in speaking. From an early age, his family too were aware of the force and sincerity of his 'histrionic powers'. His sister Mary Brigid notes how, all his life, he was a devoted disciple of the dramatic art:

> When he was a mere child he began to write plays and teach us how to act them. The fine art of elocution always made a strong appeal to him; and his manner of reciting was peculiarly impressive and arresting. Even in the quiet parts of his pieces there was ever a hidden fire – and ardent sincerity – held in check, but burning fervidly all the while.

History records that Pearse's most memorable speeches were the Robert Emmet commemoration in 1911 and the graveside oration for the Fenian O'Donovan Rossa in 1915. The Emmet commemoration speech was highly emotive, appealing for guilt to be assuaged and calling for a great act of atonement for the shame of the Irishmen who failed to come to Emmet's aid. It was the graveside oration for O'Donovan Rossa that proved to be the pinnacle of Pearse's oratory, however. There was no mistaking its intent – he preached revolution:

> . . . the seeds sown by the young men of '65 and '67 are coming to their miraculous ripening today. Rulers and Defenders of Realms had need to be wary if they would guard against such processes. Life springs from death: and from graves of patriot men and women spring living nations. The Defenders of this Realm have worked well in secret and in the open . . . but the fools, the fools, the fools! – they have left us our Fenian dead, and while Ireland holds these graves, Ireland unfree shall never be at peace.

Pearse tended to reserve the 'grand manner' for speeches or dramatic situations only. Away from the crowd, when immersed in his work, he was rather taciturn – so much so that F. O'Nolan says that he never spoke a single word that was not necessary. People with Asperger's syndrome can exhibit either an economy of speech or its opposite, loquaciousness, depending on the occasion. Pearse also had an instinct for publicity and would do anything to get his message across – something that is not uncommon in those with Asperger's syndrome.

*

Pearse's grave, serious-minded demeanour often gave the impression that he was devoid of all humour: his boyhood confessor, Father George O'Neill, stated that Pearse was a religious enthusiast 'of the sombre, humourless kind'. Nonetheless, Pearse did have a sense of humour. Commenting on Pearse's sense of humour found in *An Claidheamh Soluis,* Dudley Edwards calls it a kind of 'heavy whimsy' which was 'always limited' and very late in developing. In recollections from family and friends, it is clear that Pearse had a quirky sense of humour, something that is not uncommon in those with Asperger's syndrome. He had a great liking for practical jokes, slapstick humour, simple jokes, puns, wordplay and neologisms. According to his sister Mary Brigid, Pearse possessed an 'acute sense of humour', and he appreciated a joke told against himself more than anyone she ever knew.

Frequently, various domestic incidents gave rise to his 'unbounded hilarity'. What is funny for someone with Asperger's syndrome is not necessarily funny to others, however. Humour involves reciprocity: the sharing of laughter with others. Often, Asperger-type humour is not shared, and this was certainly the case with Pearse. His sense of humour was not always appreciated by his brother and sister, and it sometimes gave rise to friction. Mary Brigid gives an account of a staging of *Macbeth* at their home, where Pearse was in the title role and she was Lady Macbeth:

> Pat's risibility always completely overcame him the instant he addressed me by any endearing term, and he used to break into uncontrollable laughter! This made the whole business absolutely farcical. . . . I used to become seriously annoyed.

Invariably, on every occasion when Pearse had to be 'endearing' towards Lady Macbeth, he collapsed into great mirth – even when performing for the local priest! Often the humour was rather slapstick and bore all the hallmarks of an Oscar Wilde farce. On one occasion at the family home, Pearse mistook the arrival of a new maid for a distinguished female visitor and greeted her with great ceremony and pomp – much to the maid's astonishment. On learning the truth, Pearse became 'uproarious', and it took him some time to regain his composure.

Those with Asperger's syndrome also find wordplay and puns highly amusing. As an adult, Pearse took particular delight in a house guest's description of a fluid for killing slugs called 'Slugeen'. Needless to say, this gave rise to rather inappropriate behaviour for a grown man: he was seized with such an uncontrollable urge to laugh that he had to bury his head in a sofa cushion and stifle his laughs behind the gentleman's back – much to the latter's bewilderment.

Pearse also enjoyed mimicking and impersonation. The many dramas and practical jokes he performed at home and at St Enda's gave him endless opportunities for indulging in this kind of humour. In addition, his lifelong predilection for dressing up as a woman or a beggar – and tricking people into believing that he was someone he was not – was a favourite with him.

*

The desire for sameness and repetition was strong in Pearse. For instance, he seemed to have no desire to leave the family home permanently. In his home life, the familiarity of things and people no doubt brought him enormous comfort and security. In an autobiographical account, he acknowledges the impact of his home life from an early age:

> And continually my thoughts have gone back to the places that were first familiar to me, and my ear has heard the voice that it first heard. I will set it down to my credit, I have never loved any place better than those old places; or any voice better than those old voices. . . . Two things have constantly pulled at cross-purposes in me: a deep homing instinct, a desire beyond words to be at home always, with the same beloved faces, the same familiar shapes and sounds about me; the other, an impulse to seek hard things to do, to go on far quests and fight for lost causes.

In his work, Pearse never tired of stating the same arguments over and over again: about the Irish language, education and nationalism. Dudley Edwards notes that Pearse 'showed no signs of growing out of this habit of endlessly repeating a message that remained fresh only to himself'. He also had a desire for routine and repetition. For example, like many with autistic spectrum disorders, he loved model railways and anything with a mechanical action. Living in such close proximity to Westland Row Station and later at Sandymount must surely have fostered his great love of trains. His sister Mary Brigid recalls how, in his youth, he would spend hours travelling on the Liffey viaduct – known as the Loop Line – that connected Westland Row Station with Amiens Street Station (now

Pearse Station and Connolly Station, respectively), going backwards and forwards between one terminus and the other!

*

On many issues, Pearse spoke with great moral authority, as though vested with powers from a higher order. Such was his conviction in the absolute correctness of his actions and beliefs that he would reject all advice and criticisms. At times, he would be quite vocal in his opposition to any criticism, or else would simply push on with his plans regardless. Typically, he believed in doing things his way or not at all.

The superior air Pearse sported gave people cause to regard him as snobbish, priggish and pompous, and he could certainly be vain and self-righteous. By his own admission, his major flaw was pride. Even in childhood, there is the suggestion that he was aggressive, mostly verbally, if things did not go his way. Dudley Edwards makes reference to his bad temper in childhood, though he conquered it somewhat in later years. He would stand up to anyone, teachers included, if they attacked his brother Willie. Needless to say, frequent references to Pearse's dominant personality are made, especially by his family. His father too was described as a formidable and somewhat pompous individual.

His commitment to circumscribed interests inevitably leaves Pearse open to the charge of narrow-mindedness and arrogance. Pearse's hugely controlling nature was most evident in his role as editor of *An Claidheamh Soluis*. As a rule, Pearse liked to control the agenda of the paper and set himself up as the nation's sage and nanny. All his life he was extremely didactic: most of what he wrote or said was in order to educate and inform his readers and audience – again, something that is classically seen in those with Asperger's syndrome. According to Moran, 'he set out to tell the readership, all of whom were already devoted disciples of the Irish language, where the truth lay and what their own allegiances should be'.

Frequently, he censored texts if he felt they were 'improper'. Despite his great celebration of Irish literature, he had an aversion to crude or bawdy elements in native Irish humour and bowdlerised stories or poems when they appeared in the *Claidheamh* or other publications in which he was involved. Neither was he consensus-driven. On one occasion, he turned the *Claidheamh* into a broadsheet without consulting anyone about it. The fact that serious losses were incurred as a result was of little consequence to him. Certainly this type of autocratic behaviour is commonly seen in those with Asperger's syndrome.

Frequently, Pearse failed to see others' points of view. His stances were often controversial and antagonistic, and were based on naivety and insensitivity. Before 1912, Moran argues, he was basically 'politically illiterate'. In general, politics requires a good knowledge of the situation on the ground and insight into human nature – which in turn calls for being a sharp judge of men, mood, nuance and intent – qualities not necessarily found in those with Asperger's syndrome. There was a common perception that Pearse's political thinking was immature or simplistic, as Moran points out:

> The various political intrigues of the Gaelic League, while fascinating to Pearse, confused and disturbed him. He had little understanding of the various political subtleties, a problem that was compounded by his natural acquaintance to a constitutional process he understood little. While fellow nationalists expected him to be consistent, his political insensitivity caused him to stumble. It is understandable that the overly sensitive and unprepared Pearse felt the pressure of this criticism more than many others might have. Teaching boys furnished a kind of independence and isolation that allowed his unsystematic mind freely to spin his own brand of nationalism, away from the prospect of critical opinion.

He ran into considerable trouble when he welcomed the Irish Council Bill of 1907, which would give the Irish control over taxation but would not deliver Home Rule. The Bill was rejected wholeheartedly by Irish parliamentarians; Pearse, however, supported it, as it would give the Irish full control over schools and education. Frequently, he was verbally aggressive in condemning various actions, regardless of class, creed or status. On one occasion, he took a stand against the Irish bishops on the issue of whether Irish should be an essential subject in University College Dublin and was unsparing in his criticism of the bishops' reluctance to promote Irish. On another occasion, he chastised the bishops' lack of commitment to Ireland's cause after they failed to make reference to the Irish language in their Lenten Pastorals of 1903. Furthermore, Pearse opposed the paying of fees to teachers for teaching Irish during school hours: he contended that Irish should be integral to the system. On many occasions he rebuked leading literary figures, including W. B. Yeats and J. M. Synge, if their standards fell short of his – which was not hard! Pearse was forthright in his condemnation of Synge's *The Playboy of the Western World*, for what he saw as its caricaturing of Irish life and its moral repugnance, when it was first produced in the Abbey Theatre in 1907.

Pearse certainly elevated the Irish language at the expense of English. This fact irked the young James Joyce, who attended some of Pearse's classes at the Gaelic League – and subsequently left in disgust, labelling Pearse a bore. It must be said, though, that Pearse matured in some respects in relation to this issue: much later, he came to respect Anglo-Irish literature.

Pearse's response to criticism was often hostile. Once, in 1910, in response to being attacked once again for his lack of political acumen, he bragged angrily to Desmond Ryan: 'Let them talk! I am the most dangerous revolutionary of the whole lot of them!' Another defence of Pearse's was to meet criticism with victimhood: he saw himself as the League's willing slave, who was battered and abused by those who did not agree with him. By 'exposing' those around him as being less committed than him, Pearse could claim moral justification for his inflexibility, according to Moran:

> Pearse was exposed as obviously immature in his espousal of narrow-minded and naive opinions that allowed little room for disagreement. He quietly yet firmly rejected those who did not support him as being less committed than himself. This inflexibility got him into trouble more than once.

Certainly the moral justification for Pearse's actions had its roots in his rather messianic or spiritual mission: he felt that right was on his side. The historian F. S. L. Lyons argues that, in order to understand the Rising, we must first understand Pearse. Pearse's conception of Ireland, Lyons argues, was essentially spiritual: a lifetime's exposure to Irish myth, legend and rebel heroes led him to identify them with the sacred. In his pamphlet *Ghosts,* Pearse chastised the preceding generation of nationalists for their fundamental error when it came to their view of Ireland:

> They have conceived of nationality as a material thing, whereas it is a spiritual thing. . . . They have not recognised in their people the image and likeness of God. Hence the nation is not to them all holy, a thing

77

inviolate and inviolable, a thing that a man dare not sell or dishonour on pain of eternal perdition.

The incitement to blood sacrifice and violence grew stronger and stronger in Pearse's writings and speeches. He appealed to the nobler side of the Gael and the cruel effects of the years of oppression: 'Bloodshed is a cleansing and a sanctifying thing, and the nation which regards it as the final horror has lost its manhood. There are many things more horrible than bloodshed; and slavery is one of them.'

Such constant aggressive and naive criticism repelled many, and made Pearse an unpopular figure. Time and again he alienated many leading members of the Gaelic League, when his views conflicted with official League views and policies. Indeed, the League during Pearse's tenure was riven with factional disputes, prompting its founder, Douglas Hyde, to claim that Pearse had damaged the very ideals of the movement.

*

There is evidence to suggest that Pearse had a harsh superego or conscience. All his life, he had a strict sense of duty, especially towards his mother. A dutiful son, he lavished affection and attention on her, yet his devotion to her was markedly juvenile, even into adulthood. In effect, his immaturity had all the hallmarks of arrested development: he never left home permanently to become a fully-fledged individual in society. Such was Pearse's strict sense of propriety, full of moral restriction, that he earned a reputation for being a prude. Dudley Edwards notes that, at seventeen, Pearse's reserve, his near-obsessive devotion to work and his disapproval of smoking, drinking and swearing combined to produce a priggish and intolerant young man – an outlook which took several years to mellow. According to Mary Hayden, anything coarse disgusted him: 'From a doubtful story or jest he shrank as from a blow. Never, in all the years I knew him, did I ever hear from his lips even the mildest "swearword".' It comes as no surprise that people sometimes shrank from meeting him.

Many, including F. O'Nolan, have attested to Pearse being 'a mighty moral force'. Certainly, as we have seen, people from politicians to bishops and literary figures at times felt the weight of his censure. Perhaps surprisingly, Pearse could sometimes be less stringent in his reading of certain rights. In fact, he was not always a faithful follower of the conventions of the day, and he knew the limitations of 'respectable society'. Propriety was dispensed with if it interfered with his sense of natural justice. His high regard for women also saw him support what he saw as their rights: he argued for equal pay and opportunities for women, and for them to have the right to vote. Indeed, he strongly supported the suffragettes – although he abhorred their destruction of property. He also called for more women to be appointed to the Senate of the National University. In this respect, by the standards of the time he was rather enlightened.

Pearse's sense of failure and guilt were equally acute. He was frequently plagued with feelings of guilt: for not being an honourable Irishman, for letting the nation down, for experiencing financial difficulties in the running of his school, and for not becoming a better-known poet and playwright. For those with Asperger's syndrome, what they do is invariably never enough – it never quite satisfies them. Their life's work might be dismissed as rubbish by themselves or indeed others, or they might have a certain amnesia about what they have achieved thus far. Part of this can be explained by their failure to see their life in its broader context. The ever-present need to assuage their guilt inevitably involves the need for concrete action: in Pearse's case, the aim of carrying out a blood sacrifice rather than waiting, apparently indefinitely, for Home Rule. Pearse was filled with such compulsion at times that it inevitably gave rise to disturbing elements in his make-up. Desmond Ryan, always at close quarters to observe his former teacher, recounts:

> There was a disconcerting side to Pearse, especially in his earlier years. No honest portrait can hide certain shadows; a Napoleonic complex which expressed itself in a fanatical glorification of war for its own sake, an excess of sentiment which almost intoxicated him both on the platform and in private ventures, a recklessness in action and the outlook of a very respectable Dubliner who has never left his city or family circle for very long. . . .

*

From the many occupations and activities that Pearse engaged in throughout his relatively short life, it is clear that issues of self-identity existed.

The identity diffusion commonly seen in those with Asperger's syndrome appears to have been a feature of his life too. He certainly had a love for titles and at various times could boast – albeit tenuously in some cases – of being a sculptor, barrister, poet, dramatist, writer, linguist, educator, headmaster, journalist, soldier, orator, revolutionary and, of course, patriot. This conflict of identity often fosters creativity and action – the ultimate aim of which is to gain public recognition and thus put a stamp of approval on a particular identity. With Pearse, issues relating to his sexual identity were also added to the mix.

Pearse's instinct for publicity and didacticism spread across several occupations – he was journalist, essayist, poet, dramatist and propagandist, as the occasion demanded. He frequently came a cropper with regard to balancing idealism and realism, however. In the financial management of his school, he was hopelessly inept, yet he was an exceptional teacher. As a soldier, he lacked a common language with the soldiers under his command, he could not fire a rifle or give orders, and he was a poor tactician; yet his air of calm confidence and self-possession was a huge morale-booster to the soldiers in the GPO during the Rising.

While it is true to say that, at some level, Pearse felt inferior and socially inadequate, as he was not emotionally equipped to deal with adults, fundamentally he did not have a coherent sense of himself or a self-identity. At the heart of his immature personality, this lack of self-awareness meant he could only contemplate himself at a distance. As he put it himself in the autobiographical *Home Life of Pádraig Pearse*:

> There has been so much tempest in my life that the quiet places in which my childhood were spent, and the quiet voices that sounded there, seem to me sometimes not to have belonged to my life at all, but to have been part of the life of another of whom I have heard or read, or whom I have imagined: one whom I can observe with considerable detachment as the story of his days pieces itself together in my mind again, and his dreams come back to me.

His words also reveal his inability to personalise memory – something that is often deficient in a person with Asperger's syndrome.

Throughout his life, a love of impersonation prompted his elder stepsister Emily to remark that he was self-repressed. There are numerous accounts of Pearse dressing up as a woman or a beggar, often aided and abetted by Willie or his cousin Mary Kate or nephew Alfred. This repetition would seem to suggest that the dressing up was not just idle play but instances of more compulsive behaviour. At the age of ten, Pearse frequently liked to dress up as a priest in vestments and carry out various rituals, such as 'May Devotions', which involved carrying lighted candles and reciting the rosary and litany in a procession of siblings. His fondness for impersonation was not confined to his childhood years, however: it continued into his teens, and he was certainly still masquerading as women and beggars by his late twenties, before he founded St Enda's school. As we have seen, Pearse had an extraordinary capacity for fantasy, and saw himself as a hero saving others from distress. As a result, he took to his newfound role as saviour of the nation with aplomb, according to his sister Mary Brigid:

> He liked to dress up and masquerade as different, strange, rather eccentric people – principally females. He would frequently dress himself in any old clothes he could rummage out, and present himself at the hall door, disguised as a woman in motley garb. . . . [Pearse] was really very clever at 'making up', and was able to disguise even his boyish treble, making it appear old and cracked. He and Mary Kate, our cousin, were incessantly playing pranks of this sort.

According to his nephew Alfred, who joined him in begging around Donnybrook, Pearse's aim was 'to find out, by experience, how it felt to beg'. Pearse was evidently so absorbed in the task that he became quite a successful beggar, regularly receiving alms. This practice did not stop in Dublin, however: in Connemara, he also dressed up in shabby clothes, went unshaven for days, and set off with a stick along the country lanes as 'a man of the road'. This experimentation was clearly an attempt of sorts to resolve his identity diffusion. There is nothing to suggest that it was conscious transvestism; here again, there is an instinctive innocence about Pearse. It would appear that, as with James Joyce, the feminine and masculine sat side by side in Pearse. As he put it: 'The woman in us loves to sit by our own fireside; the man in us urges us forth on divine adventures.'

*

Given his vivid and powerful imagination, it is not surprising that Pearse had some sensory impairment or sensitivities. From early childhood, he had an acute visual awareness and suffered from fears and phobias. Like Beckett, he was afraid of the dark as a small boy – with the result that his mother or great-aunt Margaret sometimes had to sit with him at night. The fear of strange beings and spectres lurking on the darkened staircase at night terrified him so much that he was often afraid to venture downstairs.

Pearse's short-sightedness did not lessen the impact of his acute visual aesthetic, however. He rejoiced in nature, especially trees, and delighted in beautiful scenery. The type of landscape he favoured in particular was the desolate beauty of the Aran Islands and the Twelve Pins in Connemara. Those with Asperger's syndrome also have a particular liking for 'nice' faces and can keep them in their memory for a long time. Pearse clearly recalled his mother's 'kind true eyes', 'the softness of her cheek' and 'the music of her voice'. He also had a keen sense of hearing but tended to be hyposensitive to particular types of sound too. Loud music certainly did not disturb him. Although he loved music, he had no ear for it. When it came to his poetry, too, the sounds of nature were evocative for him: in 'On the Strand of Howth', he refers to the 'minstrelsy of birds, the 'lone sea-gull screams' and the 'chanting music' of the blackbird and thrush. In his recollections, sounds are inextricably linked to memories from childhood, much like they were for Proust. Pearse notes:

> Much more clearly defined in my memory are the characteristic sounds of the room [living room]: the carolling of the black fire-fairy, the ticking of a clock, and the rhythmic tap-tapping which came all day from the workshop. In this tap-tapping there were two distinct notes: one sharp and metallic, which I knew afterwards to be the sound of a chisel against hard marble; the other soft and dull, subsequently to be recognised as the sound of a chisel against Caen stone. In the one case the chisel was struck by an iron; in the other by a wooden mallet.

An acute sense of balance too was evident in his sister's recollections. Pearse himself remarks that he had a 'faculty of remaining still for a long time': as a young child, he liked to be drawn and painted by artists and sculptors who were acquainted with his father. In later years, he developed a fondness for boating, though he was a poor sailor: whenever the family's small craft left the shelter of Dún Laoghaire harbour, Pearse became seasick, although he experienced no such problems when rowing on the calm waters of the River Liffey near Chapelizod. His sense of balance was also affected when walking. By all accounts, he walked with a noticeable gait, which Sinéad de Valera described as 'lumbering' and 'heavy'. According to Roger Casement, Pearse seemed 'physically awkward and had a curious heavy gait'.

Pearse probably had some motor clumsiness, which is sometimes seen in people with Asperger's syndrome, although his handwriting was quite neat. During childhood, he appears to have been quite unathletic and to have exhibited poor physical abilities, and in general preferred more cerebral pursuits like draughts. His school friend Eamonn O'Neill recounts, however, that in later years Pearse joined the school boxing and football clubs. Though his team was often beaten, Pearse himself would invariably put up a good fight. He also learnt to swim at the age of thirty and was by all accounts an excellent rower – both activities where fine motor co-ordination is not required.

As a child, Pearse seems to have been hypersensitive to touch. Whenever his aunt came to visit, she was not supposed to touch him: it was considered taboo by Pearse. Many children with autism are hypersensitive to the pressure of clothes on their body or may not like various textures. This may have been the case with Pearse: he remarks that he liked 'to stand – or, better still, to lie – without my clothes in the warmth of the fire, and to think out my thoughts.' As an adult, he had a liking for the same type of clothes, mostly black, and also kilts: it is possible that certain textures, colours and fabrics appealed to him. The lack of intimacy that the sexually immature Pearse seems to have shown may have been associated with touch too. He also seems to have been hyposensitive to extremes of temperature. According to Mary Brigid: 'to such discomforts as excessive heat, or cold, or wet, he appeared indifferent.'

Hypersensitivities in taste were quite evident in Pearse's life too. This commonly occurs in those with autism: they often have a taste for sweet things or junk food. All his life, he enjoyed a stick of sugar barley or Turkish Delight. As Mary Brigid notes: 'My brother was extremely fond of sweet things – jam, sugar, honey and the like.' His sweet tooth often got him into trouble: once, over a period of days, he robbed flat gelatine sweets that his father had used to patch up a cracked window-pane!

According to Mary Brigid, he had a particular weakness for currants, raisins and candied peel. Each year, the task of stoning the fat raisins for the Christmas cakes and puddings fell to Pearse – who managed to eat more than he supplied! He was also fond of nuts, especially coconuts and almonds, which he devoured whenever he could, even if it meant pilfering from his mother's kitchen.

Pearse was also no stranger to food fads. As a young man, he became a vegetarian, as did his brother Willie, and they took their main meals in a vegetarian restaurant on College Street. They soon tired of this diet, however, and returned to their regular one. Pearse's tastes in general were often simple or ascetic, Mary Brigid reports: 'Of intoxicants he did not even know the taste; he did not smoke; he took little interest in what he ate.'

Although there is no suggestion that Pearse had poor health, he could be gloomy, and there are mentions of him suffering bouts of depression. Some commentators believe that the insurgents' suicidal mission during the Easter Rising was directly related to Pearse's depression. However, there is no evidence whatsoever that he was suffering from depression or suicidal thoughts when he pushed on with plans for the Rising. Clearly, the intensity and eccentricities of Pearse's character often led people to think that he was mad. It is hardly surprising that Ryan, who later fought alongside him in the GPO, commented that 'Pearse in his dashing moods struck you as quite insane.'

*

Questions inevitably arise about what kind of mind Pearse had, and whether his mental make-up was predetermined by his Asperger's syndrome. Sinéad de Valera, the wife of Éamon de Valera, described Pearse as having a 'beautiful mind', while his friend Mary Hayden thought that it was of 'a strange and unusual type'. Without doubt, it was exceptional, and typical of the Asperger genius. Pearse was blessed with a vivid imagination from an early age. During childhood, in his mind he would transform his home into all manner of exotic places and creatures: ships on the high seas, Roman chariots, jungle-roaming elephants, knights in quest of the Holy Grail, sandy deserts or steep mountainsides, and in all of these scenarios he was cast in the role of explorer, adventurer and, especially, hero. These adventures generally had a half-real quality for Pearse which he could never quite shake off: he suffered the sorrows and enjoyed the triumphs of the adventures too much.

Like Lord Jim in Joseph Conrad's novel of the same name, he was forever seeking some action that would indisputably crown him as a hero. From the age of seven, his great-aunt Margaret sang him songs about heroes like Napoleon. Her stories of the deeds of Irish heroes such as Wolfe Tone, Robert Emmet, John Mitchel and O'Donovan Rossa were burnt into his imagination, as were the supposed glorifying and sanctifying effects of war. Like Yeats, Pearse was a daydreamer who also had visions at night. His visions were no idle dreams, however. From the age of sixteen, he dreamt of founding a school where children could be cherished and fostered and the Irish language could be spoken freely and fluently. He also dreamt of giving his life in the cause of Irish freedom.

A certain religiosity or spiritual dimension was also to be found in Pearse, which is not uncommon in the Asperger genius. Pearse's sister Mary Brigid declares that he was a man of deep religious feeling, a dedicated churchgoer and a daily communicant, whenever possible. Stories abound as to how he was so anxious to get to church once that he jumped from a tram while it was still moving, fell, and severely cut his face, and was distressed that he had missed the Holy Day of obligation. Pearse's father also took an interest in religion. A liberal free thinker, he built up a considerable library containing books on comparative religions, literature, history and politics. There is a feeling too that the repetition of ritual and the ceremony of Catholic rites appealed to Pearse's dramatic side. Indeed, this could be explained by his strict adherence to duty and desire for sameness. Certainly, like Joyce, his favourite ceremonies were the ones performed during Holy Week: the enacting of the crucifixion and resurrection.

Pearse did not blindly accept Roman Catholic orthodoxies, however. Indeed, the Jesuit Francis Shaw was critical of Pearse's heretical and unorthodox views of the Catholic faith. Dudley Edwards comments that Pearse was not an orthodox Catholic, although he was 'assiduous in its practices'. He certainly reinterpreted the basic tenets of Catholicism over the years and refashioned them. His membership of the IRB, for example, would have brought automatic excommunication from the Catholic Church, but he chose to ignore this fact. One could say that Pearse's Celtic paganism and Roman Catholicism co-existed quite happily. According to

Mary Hayden, 'all his life he was a devout Catholic, but of religion he seldom spoke. The unseen world appeared very close to him; and the belief which he often (by way of jest) professed in ghosts, fairies and old legends was, I think, only half-assumed.' Indeed, the mystical element in his thinking is closely linked to the figure of Jesus Christ, who held particular appeal for him and with whom he identified. Indeed, the heroism, death and redemption of Christ have been archetypal for many writers and poets, from Joyce to Yeats, regardless of their religious persuasion. Beyond doubt, Pearse had something of a mystical temperament, which coloured his imagination. Moran notes how he had 'esoteric interests', including an obsession with metaphysical, esoteric subjects such as folk tales and fantasy – an obsession that was not confined to his writings but also coloured his political views. As we have seen, this mystical or esoteric temperament is commonly found in the Asperger imagination. A fairly accurate description of Pearse in this regard is given by Desmond Ryan's father, W. P. Ryan, who wrote in 1911 that Pearse was 'a scholar with a child-spirit, a mystical temperament and a Celtic nature, in the heroic and constructive sense'.

From the many accounts and memoirs of Pearse, he would seem to fit the criteria for an Asperger genius. Many of his aspirations, foresight and experiments came to fruition in the decades after his death, when the Irish Republic was established and his ideas on education and child welfare gained ground. Because of his special regard for children, which encompassed all citizens of the island, Protestant and Catholic, he enshrined his desire for their protection into the Proclamation of the Irish Republic: 'all the children of the nation should be cherished equally'. When it came to writing the Irish Constitution later, this aspiration would influence de Valera too.

Pearse's setting up of St Enda's school paved the way for the development of similar schools across the country decades later. The recent growth of the Irish-medium schools or *gaelscoileanna* has been extraordinary: there were fewer than twenty in 1972, and there are currently 194 in the thirty-two counties (excluding the Gaeltacht) – a shift for which the visionary Pearse is in large measure responsible.

3

ÉAMON DE VALERA

All propaganda, no human life . . . He will fail through not having enough human life to judge the human life in others.

W. B. YEATS on Éamon de Valera

As a founding father of the Irish Republic, Éamon de Valera scarcely needs an introduction. With a political career that spanned seventy years, he has given rise to as much acrimony as admiration. Yet even his political opponents would agree that he was a political genius. As a political leader with an international reputation, he gained an authority which many, including Conor Cruise O'Brien, believed had not been seen since the fall of Charles Stewart Parnell in 1890.

As with all Asperger geniuses, however, de Valera was unmistakably flawed. He could be both innovative and archly conservative, sincere and devious, sensitive yet lacking in empathy, erratic and consistent, pontifical and provincial, pragmatic and absolutist. His innate dignity was matched with toughness; asceticism with materialism; charisma with coldness. The sum of these contradictions led many to conclude that de Valera was either mad or a genius. Indeed, the Irish peer Lord Granard declared that de Valera was 'on the borderline between genius and insanity': a typical assessment of an Asperger genius.

*

In appearance, de Valera was tall and thin. There is no reference to him avoiding eye contact, but his brown, bespectacled eyes were often described as 'flashing' and 'burning'. With increasing age, his face became more deeply etched. A lurching gait was noticeable: this was described by American academic Mary C. Bromage in her biography *De Valera* as 'forward bending' – giving the impression of a slight stoop. In demeanour, he possessed great charm, and had the warm smile and self-possession so often seen in the Asperger genius. Indeed, his whole persona could be mesmeric. A former teacher at Blackrock College, County Dublin, remarked that he had 'a certain dignity of manner, a gentleness of disposition'.

*

Éamon de Valera was born in New York on 14 October 1882 to an Irish mother, Kate Coll, and a Spanish father, Juan Vivion de Valera. At the age of two, Éamon was sent to live with his mother's people in Bruree, County Limerick, while his now-widowed mother remained in New York. Having distinguished himself at school in Bruree and Charleville, County Cork, he won a scholarship to Blackrock College in Dublin and completed his education at the then Royal University, where he flourished as a mathematics teacher while developing an ever-deepening interest in the politics of the day. His immersion in Irish politics for more than seventy years would see de Valera progress from teacher to soldier, military leader, revolutionary, first minister, founder and leader of the Fianna Fáil Party, Taoiseach for three spells and statesman, climaxing with him serving as President of Ireland for two terms. Aside from his intense focus on national politics, he had obsessive interests in mathematics and the Irish language.

Typically of the man, his interests sometimes collided – to bizarre effect. As Taoiseach, he once told the economist Patrick Lynch to prepare a paper on how the theory of relativity could be applied to politics. Hardly a job for an economist, you might think! Nonetheless, Lynch duly went off to the National Library, as de Valera had suggested, and produced a piece of calculated nonsense which delighted his boss no end. In 1940, under an act of government, de Valera established the Dublin Institute for Advanced Studies for his pet subjects: Celtic studies and theoretical physics. A lifelong admirer of William Rowan Hamilton's general theory of dynamics and its impact on quantum mechanics in the work of the Austrian physicist Erwin Schrödinger, de Valera invited Schrödinger to Ireland to become director of the School for Theoretical Physics at the Dublin Institute, where he stayed until his retirement in 1955. The parliamentarian and journalist William O'Brien declared that, when it came to defending his political views, de Valera would defend a thesis as though it were a point in pure mathematics with more than the 'French bigotry for logic'. During his public life, mathematics was a source of relaxation to de Valera, and he subscribed to many journals, often jotting notes in the margins and corresponding with eminent mathematicians and physicists of the day.

His interest in mathematics was apparent from an early age: according to one biographer, M. J. MacManus in *Eamon de Valera: A Biography,* at the local school in Bruree de Valera enjoyed lessons and 'books using sums'. That said, like many a genius he could become bored easily and often played truant, for which his uncle, Patrick Coll, severely disciplined him. De Valera's keen intelligence was apparent to all, though, and like Hamilton, he had a natural aptitude for the theoretical side of elementary mathematics. His subsequent education, at the Christian Brothers School in Charleville, County Cork, and at Blackrock College, County Dublin, also attests to his prowess in mathematics. Studying for his Bachelor of Arts at the Royal University of Ireland, later University College Dublin, he experienced an epiphany of sorts on discovering the writings of the French mathematician Camille Jordan. At the time, the Irish education system viewed mathematics as a tool to solve problems, whereas the French regarded it as the science of numbers. Innovatively, the analytical de Valera compiled a textbook on elementary arithmetic when teaching students at Carysfort Training College in Blackrock.

The shift from a practical to a pure view of science appealed to de Valera. Having been seduced by Hamilton's quarternions – an algebraic formula that expresses rotations in four dimensions – these became a focus of his studies. His interest in astrophysics, electro-optics, spectroscopy, quarternions and metaphysics waned somewhat on his marriage and later impending fatherhood, however. One could say that, in his twenties, the 'abstract' de Valera gave way to de Valera the pragmatist. He abandoned his thesis on quarternions and, having decided on a career in teaching instead, took a diploma in education. If he had pursued his interest in mathematics, he may well have become a mathematician of note. Certainly, the tale was often told of how he was one of only nine people in the world who could fully understand the implications of Einstein's law of relativity at the time.

From boyhood, de Valera was self-motivated, hard-working and persistent in relation to both his studies and his interest in nationalism. Certainly, he grew into the role of revolutionary. The Easter Rising of 1916 brought him to national prominence as Commandant of the Third Battalion of Irish Volunteers. He had joined the Irish Volunteers in 1913 not out of a desire for revolt but with the aim of defending Ireland, as he saw it. He later joined the secret oath-bound Irish Republican Brotherhood, on the condition that he would only take and not give orders, as he did not want to take a leadership role. At the end of the Rising, he was spared the fate of many of the other leaders of the rebellion – death by firing squad – because of his American citizenship.

De Valera had absolute conviction in his ideals and abilities which sustained him through his long career in politics. He frequently exhibited the kind of concrete thinking found in those with autism. The fanciful or imaginary did not interest him, and he was not given to reading novels – with the exception of detective novels, often the reading material of choice for those with Asperger's syndrome. On one occasion, when asked to write a school essay on 'Making Hay While the Sun Shines', he was at a loss and could think of nothing to say except: 'What other time would you make hay?' Such misinterpretations of literal and implied meanings would become a theme of de Valera's life: this trait certainly seriously affected his ability to communicate with others. Indeed, all the hallmarks of an Asperger genius were found in de Valera: the penetrating intellect, the intense focus and passion, the deep concentration, the prodigious memory, the absolute conviction, the rigid discipline and repetition, the industry, the precision and exactitude. Given these qualities, de Valera, like Emmet, showed considerable talent as a military planner. His capacity for great concentration was evident prior to the Rising, when he immersed himself in completing a detailed reconnaissance of the south-eastern approaches to the city, studying troop movements, and undertaking meticulous tactical and logistical planning, so as to leave little to chance when it came to military action. A particular memory of one soldier who remembers de Valera on the eve of the Rising is found in Tim Pat Coogan's *De Valera: Long Fellow, Long Shadow*:

> He was able to tell each Company Captain what he would find to his advantage or disadvantage when he got there. . . . He was able to discuss every detail, even the places where it would be possible to procure an alternative water supply, where we could definitely find tools for such things as loopholing walls and making communications. . . . I cannot remember a query put to him that he was not able to answer.

De Valera applied this capacity for concentration to whatever situation he faced, whether it was a mathematical problem or an important matter of state. His son Terry de Valera in *A Memoir* remembers 'how often I observed, at times of great stress or crisis, how he sat or stood in silence, joining his hands together, holding his extended index fingers pressed to his lips, deep in thought and displaying an enviable concentration.'

De Valera's sense of discipline and repetition too were remarkable. He worked long hours – often well into the night. Mary Bromage notes that as Taoiseach he worked twelve hours or more every day; others claim that the figure was closer to eighteen hours. As Chancellor of the National University of Ireland, a position he held from 1921 until his death in 1975, by all accounts he hardly ever missed a meeting. Clearly, he had huge reserves of energy for political activities too, including meeting crowds the length and breadth of the country, and in America attending numerous rallies and meetings.

In fact, de Valera was constantly 'on duty' and rarely took holidays. Any small periods of free time he did have were taken up with walking, playing chess, reading and religious practices. Even when imprisoned, notably in Lincoln Jail in 1918, de Valera would encourage his fellow Irish inmates to plan their regime of reading, religious devotion and physical exercise. Beneath this discipline lay a hierarchical view of the world, influenced in part by the power structures of Roman Catholicism and by his own concrete thinking. The chain of command or pecking order was carefully observed by de Valera and required due respect and deference. According to Coogan, de Valera insisted on 'strict procedural behaviour and observance of spheres of influences'.

Allied to de Valera's nationalism was his great love of the Irish language; indeed, his involvement with the Gaelic League became a springboard for later political action. It was through Irish lessons that he met his future wife, Sinéad Flanagan, who became his teacher. She describes him as 'an exacting pupil, fond of giving posers'. This trait was also noticed by his son Terry, who speaks about his father's 'passion for accuracy in the use of words'. In public office, his careful scrutiny of documents often led to distress on his part over a misplaced comma.

Beyond doubt, de Valera was endowed with extremely strong leadership qualities. He commanded the respect of his men, and their confidence was not misplaced. In the fighting throughout Easter week 1916, he showed great concern for his men's safety and, more importantly was an effective commander, unlike Emmet and Pearse. He demonstrated enormous courage and bravery in his defence of Boland's Mills. Indeed, a lack of fear, or absence of awareness of danger, is typical of those with autism, and can account for the considerable bravery and heroism sometimes exhibited by these people. When de Valera received the order to surrender from Pearse, he disbelieved it at first, as his battalion was holding its own against the British forces and had indeed inflicted heavy causalities on them. That said, rumours also existed that he had some class of 'breakdown' during the Rising, in that his behaviour was highly emotional and erratic.

De Valera is frequently described as having possessed political genius. Certainly he knew about the prerequisites of power: information and possessing the means to acquire, manipulate and control it, and the need to have the support of the people. In his desire to be a dominant political force, de Valera had an iron determination to bring about change. In this respect, he was a pragmatist. Through his political leadership he achieved the people's support, using all the means at his disposal: charisma, sincerity, fear, patriotism and deviousness. A former teacher at Blackrock College recognised de Valera's talents in terms of 'a capability of adapting himself to circumstances, or perhaps I should say of utilising those circumstances that served his purpose'. Compromise was not something de Valera recognised – again, a common trait among many with Asperger's syndrome – neither was it in his nature to be politically accommodating or consensus-driven. In all likelihood, he would not have felt at home with today's more consensual politics. Bromage notes that 'never had he felt cut out for the give and take, the partisan manoeuvre, the legislative compromise'.

De Valera's absolute conviction and inflexibility were evident in many of the political actions he took. As President of the Second Dáil he rejected the Anglo-Irish Treaty that had been negotiated by his delegates with the British prime minister David Lloyd George in London in 1921, although he had failed to attend the negotiations himself. The principle of external association – the establishment of Ireland as a republic within the Commonwealth – an idea advanced by de Valera, was rejected by the British in favour of a compromise, partition. In many respects, 'external association' was an original and innovative concept but was before its time. Indeed, another British colony, India, would achieve such status in 1947. De Valera, unlike delegates such as Michael Collins and Arthur Griffith, did not view partition as a stepping stone to a united Ireland. His and others' rejection of the Treaty set in train the horrific Civil War, which convulsed the nation and saw de Valera cast into the political wilderness to all intents and purposes for a decade.

De Valera's inflexibility and moral leadership was evident too when, as head of the government during the Second World War, he adopted a position of neutrality: he did not want Ireland to be dragged into another war and was wary of the possibility of Britain re-invading Ireland, given the chance. He stood firm against the dominant powers of Britain, the United States and Germany – for good and for ill – when those countries looked for support from Ireland during the war. In fact, his inflexible view on neutrality meant that, on two occasions during the war, he turned down the offer of a united Ireland by Neville Chamberlain and later Churchill in exchange for Ireland's entry into the war – arguably a disastrous decision, given the subsequent Troubles in Northern Ireland.

Under de Valera's stewardship, Ireland became a republic, although the question of partition and a united Ireland would remain unsolved. During the 1930s, he made a great impact as an international statesman when he addressed the League of Nations, especially in his capacity as President of the Council of the League in 1932 and President of the Assembly of the League in 1938. He later removed many of the provisions of the Treaty: he abolished the oath of allegiance, the post of Governor General and the right of appeal to the Privy Council; he also got back the Irish ports from the British, drafted the Irish Constitution (which was enacted in 1937), and in 1949 took Ireland out of the Commonwealth. By 1938, he had fixed the land annuities issue – relating to money that the British government had loaned to Irish landlords before the Government of Ireland Act of 1921 and which the landlords had agreed to repay – and thus ended the economic war with Britain. It should be noted, however, that he was also responsible for the economic war: ie he solved a problem that he himself had created! In assessing de Valera's career in this period, historian John A. Murphy, in an article published in the *Sunday Independent* on 6 March 2005, is fulsome in his praise:

> What is remarkable about de Valera's skilful Anglo-Irish policy in the 1930s is that he managed to achieve quite revolutionary aims without outrageously twisting the lion's tail. A classic case of *suaviter in modo fortiter in re* ('gentle in manner, resolute in execution').

Even as *persona non grata* after the Civil War – many held him personally responsible, due to his refusal to accept the Treaty, for the bloodshed of the conflict – de Valera retained his instinct for politics and his opportunism when it came to seeking and maintaining power. He founded the Fianna Fáil Party in 1926 and spent decades building up the apparatus of what was to become the most successful political party in the country. To this day, de Valera's mark remains indelibly on the party: it was moulded on his fervently loyal grassroots base and formidable personality, as well as his attention to detail – everything of local value that might affect the outcome of an election was passed up the ranks of the party – his opportunism and pragmatism, and desire to control and manipulate information though propaganda – or what might now more commonly be referred to as spin-doctoring. In this respect, his establishment of the *Irish Press* newspaper in 1931 was a crucial measure to bolster the popularity of Fianna Fáil.

The Irish Constitution enshrined de Valera's unique vision of Ireland. It has been hailed worldwide as a remarkable document for its clarity and structure and for its concern with the preservation of basic human rights. Indeed, other nations, such as India and South Africa, that subsequently gained independence from imperial powers were influenced by it when drawing up their own constitutions. Clearly, the document was drafted with near-mathematical precision and logic. De Valera was guided by the principle of the common good, whereby personal freedom and liberties were balanced by social regulation. He consulted with the Holy Ghost Fathers, whom he knew and respected from his time at Blackrock College, notably John Charles McQuaid, later Archbishop of Dublin. Significantly, however, de Valera resisted attempts by the hierarchy to make Roman Catholicism the established religion of the country, and have an even greater alignment of Church and State. De Valera, who had fought so hard for Irish sovereignty, was not about to hand it back to the Catholic Church, notwithstanding his own deeply held Catholic faith.

The Constitution is not without its limitations, however. In this area, de Valera's narrow-mindedness and stringent personal moral code are cast in sharp relief. Most notably, by enshrining marriage and the family as the inviolable bedrock of Irish society, he diminished the rights of working women and same-sex couples. Naturally, the conservative tone of the Constitution attracted criticism from women's rights groups and feminists. In many ways, de Valera can be said to have rowed back on the spirit of the more liberal 1916 Easter Proclamation, with its avowal of the rights of all men, women and children.

*

Despite the plethora of biographies on de Valera, accounts of his early life are extremely sketchy. We have no knowledge as to how quickly he learned to speak. We do know, however, that he learned to read quickly and that he was an avid reader of stories featuring Irish heroes, both legendary and modern. At school in Bruree, he was a star reader – typical of many with Asperger's syndrome – and competitive about it too, forcing himself to go to school on one occasion when he had measles so that others would not favourably impress the inspector in his absence! As was customary at the time, he read books on the lives of the Irish partiot Patrick Sarsfield and Napoleon, and *The Scottish Chiefs* by Jane Porter – a boys' book on Scottish chieftains that was popular in Ireland at the time. According to M. J. MacManus, one of the Christian Brothers in Charleville, read tales about Wellington's victories to his class. On one occasion, de Valera forlornly exclaimed: 'But Brother, have we no generals of our own?' Clearly the imagination of the young de Valera was ignited when the Brother recounted tales of Owen Roe and Hugh O'Neill: 'Éamon sat there gripping the desk, all on fire.' Later, at Blackrock College, he developed a love for the Classics that continued throughout his life. Indeed, the romantic aspects of heroes and heroism fired his imagination.

De Valera had an extraordinary memory for detail and retained this faculty into old age. He seems to have inherited this skill from his mother. Kate de Valera reputedly won a Spelling Bee competition in the United States, and could always correctly identify the many flowers, plants and shrubs in her garden whenever she was asked.

Not surprisingly, given his prodigious memory and logical mind, he was a good linguist and mastered Latin, Greek, French and later Irish. Unlike many with Asperger's syndrome, however, de Valera appears to have had no great difficulty in learning Irish. We know, however, that he worked hard at learning the language. The fact that he was highly motivated to do so, given his almost obsessive interest in Irish culture and his future wife being his teacher may account for his having overcome any obstacles in this area. Indeed his father, Juan Vivion de Valera, was something of a linguist himself and was proficient in Spanish, English, French and German. All his life, de Valera retained a love for languages, studying and using them whenever he could, including writing messages in Latin from Lincoln Jail during 1918–19.

As is so often the case with those with Asperger's syndrome, de Valera's brilliance was not always reflected in the exam results he attained. Indeed, it was a matter of some soreness on his part that he only obtained a pass degree in mathematics for his Bachelor of Arts degree. The cause of this was not want of ability but want of application. Sport and drinking took up much of his time during this period of his life.

The language that de Valera employed was often stereotyped and repetitive, and even idiosyncratic at times. The British civil servant Tom Jones observed how, in negotiations with Lloyd George, de Valera used a limited vocabulary and talked mainly of ideals, constantly returning to the 'same few dominating notions'. This approach is certainly classically autistic. Although de Valera had adequate speech, he showed a marked impairment in his ability to sustain a conversation or dialogue with others. According to fellow patriot Piaras Beaslai, de Valera made a very bad chairman: 'He was intensely verbose, wasting a great deal of time on elaborate explanations of the simplest points, with many repetitions, speaking in the tone of a schoolmaster to children.'

At Blackrock College, de Valera received elocution lessons as part of the curriculum. He evidently showed a natural ability for public speaking: his first recitation impressed the teacher, who dubbed him another Daniel

O'Connell. An extremely apt comparison, as events would prove! Like Emmet, de Valera could speak in public for hours without notes. De Valera possessed little of the eloquence of Emmet or Pearse, however, and his delivery was often poor. Sometimes his speeches were rather dull, lacking in wit or humour, and delivered in the halting, didactic tone of a schoolmaster. Changes in vocal quality are common in Asperger's syndrome, and de Valera's was either characteristically high-pitched or low and monotonous. That said, some of his pieces of rhetoric were masterful, such as his St Patrick's Day radio broadcast in 1943, or his radio reply to Churchill in 1945. In the St Patrick's Day broadcast, he presented his vision of a Hibernian utopia:

> That Ireland which we dreamed of would be the home of a people who valued material wealth only as a basis of right living; of a people who were satisfied with frugal comfort and devoted their leisure to the things of the spirit – a land whose countryside would be bright with cosy homesteads, whose fields and villages would be joyous with the sounds of industry, with the romping of sturdy children, the contests of athletic youths and the laughter of comely maidens, whose firesides would be forums for the wisdom of serene old age. It would, in a word, be the home of a people living the life that God desires that man should live.

On such occasions, his message came across as direct, simple and burningly sincere. Like many Irish people, he could not pronounce 'th' sounds in English; for his supporters, this only added authenticity to his rural origins. Rhetoric rather than reality is something for which those with Asperger's syndrome have an abundant talent; rhetoric became a hallmark of his speeches and indeed the modus operandi of the political party he founded.

Language held its own appeal for de Valera, in the form of wordplay and the use of slang. Perhaps the most infamous example of this is the term 'totty twigging' (girl-watching), which he took great delight in using in his younger days. As explained by Father Seán Farragher in *Dev and His Alma Mater,* de Valera picked up this local slang on social outings to Cashel during his time teaching at Rockwell College in Tipperary.

Like many with Asperger's syndrome, de Valera found it easier to communicate by letter than through speech. Indeed, people with Asperger's syndrome can make excellent diarists and they are often prolific letter writers, preferring to avoid face-to-face contact. De Valera was an inveterate correspondent – and, incidentally, a collector of pens. Coogan notes that he had the ability to sound 'warm and moderate' in print while at the same time acting in a 'hard and unyielding manner'. Certainly his letters to his wife Sinéad would support this view. These letters, full of concern, advice, longing and affection, were written during times away from his family – absences that were, it must be admitted, sometimes not entirely essential and often unnecessarily prolonged. Completely absorbed in his work, de Valera often took only a passive interest in his family.

*

The impression of a dour, humourless, rather prim and proper de Valera has gained particular currency in Ireland. It is far from true that he had no sense of humour at all, however. Rather he had a quirky or peculiar sense of humour, such as is commonly seen in those with Asperger's syndrome. His sense of humour was unsubtle and often involved wordplay. In *Unique Dictator: A Study of Eamon de Valera,* Desmond Ryan, while noting how many of de Valera's critics considered him to be a 'dull, pedantic, piqued professor . . . who lacked humour', cites the civil servant and economist T. K. Whitaker, who worked closely with de Valera and had the following to say about his sense of humour:

> [De Valera] had a very strange sense of humour. I remember once I was over in the Dáil . . . advising the Minister for Finance during a Budget debate. Suddenly Paddy Lynch appeared at my shoulder. He said that [de Valera] had sent him over to ask me did I know what an Epicycloid Circle was. Paddy said he did not know for the life of him what he meant. So I said I was no expert but I thought it was a circle enclosing a smaller circle which it touched tangentially. Paddy came back later . . . to say that Dev was delighted. He was to tell me two things. Firstly that the Taoiseach said that it was reassuring to know there was someone in Finance who understood mathematics. Secondly that the tangential nature of the two circles touching contained about the same contact with truth as did the Opposition's attack on the Budget!

At home, de Valera's children saw their father's simple, playful, punning humour first-hand. Terry recounts an incident when he and his brother Ruairi were playing with lead soldiers in the corner of the play-room, where they also took their meals, when de Valera came in for his tea of boiled eggs and brown bread. After correcting Ruairi for saying that they were attacking the 'English' rather than the more generic 'enemy' – not wishing to foster a hatred of Ireland's nearest neighbour in his sons – de Valera left the table and, with a broad grin, threw the empty eggshell, which landed on the 'enemy'. As he left the room, he announced: 'And there's a shell on them.'

The game of charades is universally loved by those with autism, and de Valera was no exception. Terry recounts another incident when cha-rades were played by the family and some guests at the family home in, Bellevue, Blackrock. After disappearing for some time, his father's team, comprising Frank Aiken, Dr Jim Ryan and Gerry Boland, re-entered the drawing room on their hands and knees with a large pair of antlers strapped to de Valera's head; all of the men were wailing like wild animals. Mimicking was another area where de Valera, like Joyce, showed talent. Terry mentions that his father enjoyed recounting his great escape from Lincoln Jail, when he had to run the gauntlet of courting soldiers in a nearby village. He relished playing the part of a tipsy Australian soldier arm in arm with his girl, and had all the gestures and the accent off to a 'T'. De Valera also liked cartoons – all the more so if they featured the politics of the day. His loft bedroom in Bruree was covered with political cartoons from the weekly *Freeman's Journal.*

De Valera enjoyed jokes, though, like Pearse, not bawdy or profane ones. Like Pearse too, there are instances of him finding it hard to con-tain his laughter in various situations. One concerned an occasional visi-tor to the house, Canon Breen, who had a habit of prefacing every sen-tence with: 'I have noticed . . . ' This phrase was employed to great effect in the de Valera household, with the result that on one occasion when the Canon began to speak, de Valera could barely contain himself. He quick-ly bent down, on the pretext of tying his shoelace, in order to conceal his spluttering. Clearly, de Valera and his wife Sinéad shared the same kind of humour: Terry mentions the good-humoured banter they engaged in, often drawing on her urban and his rural origins: she came from Dublin, he from Bruree. De Valera also had a penchant for rhymes. He composed one for Sinéad after she had been enthusing about how much she loved the Dublin Mountains:

I've seen the Rockies and the Alps
The Appalachians and the Urals.
That they are singular, all agree
But the Dublin hills are plural!

In the Dáil, de Valera could be extremely quick-witted, and there are accounts that he liked to hoodwink the Opposition using Latin words. When this was drawn to his attention, however, he responded: 'No, those words are Greek!' His humour often drew on a kind of concrete thinking. In response to Lloyd George's exasperation with de Valera – 'Dealing with de Valera is like trying to pick up a piece of mercury with a fork' – he responded humorously with: 'Why doesn't he try a spoon?'

Coogan too refers to de Valera's 'grisly sense of humour'. This relates to a story told by de Valera's biographers Lord Longford and T. P. O'Neill that, when lunching at Blackrock College, de Valera – charged with reading Bible lessons at mealtimes – found a passage from Saint Alphonsus on death, which included a lengthy description of a corpse devoured by worms: 'As the boys choked over their food, he dwelt lovingly on every detail.' As well as finding the passage amusing, he was oblivious to the disgust and discomfort it engendered in those around him and was perhaps deliberately winding up his audience!

*

De Valera showed considerable impairment and inappropriate behaviour when it came to social interaction. Like many an Asperger genius, he liked solitude but, given his absorption in affairs of state, was not always able to indulge it. Whenever he was imprisoned and forced into solitary confinement – which he was on a number of occasions – the solitude never disturbed him, and he would use the time to do things he particularly enjoyed, such as reading and studying. Records of de Valera's early life in Bruree are vague, so it is impossible to know whether he mixed easily with his peers or kept to himself. We know that his time was fairly well occupied with farmwork, which included many solitary tasks. He also included in his pastimes solitary activities such as reading, 'digging for springs' and fowl-shooting.

The general impression of de Valera's childhood years is that he was unhappy and isolated. Due to the economic hardship experienced by his family in America, he was effectively abandoned by his mother at the age of two and brought back to Ireland to be reared by a rather stern uncle in Bruree. His Aunt Hannie, who was a maternal figure to him, emigrated a year after he arrived in Ireland, and his grandmother died when he was six. Longford and O'Neill record that, when his closest friend left the neighbourhood, de Valera wrote to his Aunt Hannie to plead with his mother to allow him to return to America. His pleas fell on deaf ears, however, as his mother now had a new life with a new husband and son. So from the age of six until his marriage at twenty-seven, his home life was exclusively male. Moreover, to all intents and purposes he was an orphan. His mother may have possessed certain autistic traits; Coogan remarks that there was a 'certain coldness in her psychological make-up'. Indeed, he asserted that, had Kate really wanted her son with her, she would have been able, given her determination and forcefulness, to persuade her new husband to accept him.

Throughout de Valera's life, close friendships, where they existed, tended to be with males and with those he shared common interests, such as politics, religion or the Irish language. He had a wide circle of acquaintances and maintained a number of close friendships over the years. De Valera did not entertain very much, except for this close-knit circle of friends, according to his son Terry. While many friendships were forged in politics, such as that with Frank Aiken, others were non-political, like that with Dr Robert Farnan, who sheltered and supported him financially whenever he was a fugitive during the War of Independence and Civil War and acted as something of a confidant for him. Other friends were from his schooldays, such as Frank Hughes, who was best man at his wedding. Over time, the community of Holy Ghost Fathers, particularly at Blackrock College, become an extended family to him, and he was never more at home than when attending events and social activities at the college, such as the annual sports day – apart from a ten-year period following his rejection of the Treaty when he was *persona non grata,* which affected him profoundly. Beyond that, however, de Valera had few close friends – although he was generally surrounded by acolytes who were only too willing to do his bidding. Indeed, he commanded enormous respect and loyalty from several quarters, notably from his secretary, Kathleen O'Connell – something that is invariably seen in charismatic leaders.

In his dealings with women, de Valera showed a certain degree of ambivalence: he saw them either in supportive roles or in an idealised way. This sprang from a certain emotional immaturity, which is often evident in those with Asperger's syndrome. By today's standards, his view of women is repressive at worst and old-fashioned at best. He tended to see women in supportive roles rather than as colleagues, and appreciated their talents, efficiencies and loyalties only in that capacity. In his mind, they were the backbone of society, the glue that held and sustained faith, family and society – whether as mothers, nurses, teachers, nuns, secretaries and so on – but not pioneers in any way.

The only instance when they were allowed to step out of that role was when they became symbolic of a higher order. The women who were involved in the Easter Rising or were related or connected in any way to its martyrs, such as Countess Markiewicz and Margaret Pearse, mother of Pádraig and Willie Pearse, were somehow seen as sacrosanct. Women certainly did not figure much in de Valera's Cabinets. Instead, his idealisation of motherhood was enshrined in the Irish Constitution, while safeguarding the rights of women meant no more than not forcing them from the home to work – to the detriment of the family – as had been the case with his own mother.

Like many young men, de Valera reputedly had 'an eye for the women'. After a short romance at the age of twenty-seven, he married Sinéad Flanagan, who was four years older than him. Despite her talents, intellect and independent spirit, Sinéad's marriage to de Valera became a traditional one: he the breadwinner, she the homemaker. She had a deep love of literature and poetry in particular, as well as acting, and had many interests in common with her husband, including a devotion to teaching, the Irish language, the Gaelic League, the Catholic faith and patriotism. On her marriage to de Valera, she gave up all of her literary and cultural activities, despite the fact that she had previously been extremely active in the Gaelic League. Notoriously shy, she avoided public life, with the exception of de Valera's time as President, when protocol was observed. Indeed, people with Asperger's syndrome often marry shy people.

In *Long Fellow, Long Shadow*, Coogan describes Sinéad's marriage to de Valera as far from serene. Marriage could not have been easy for her; one gets the sense that she raised her seven children single-handedly while de Valera was absent for long periods, either engaged in military activities or affairs of state, on the run, in jail, or fund-raising and lobbying in

America. Nonetheless, he clearly depended on her and drew strength from her deep religious faith and common sense – something that is often deficient in people with Asperger's syndrome. (When the newlyweds first set up home together, Sinéad sent de Valera out to buy some basic items; he later arrived back from an auction much pleased with his purchases of a huge brass chandelier, a worthless cello and two copper plates adorned with rural scenes!) To his credit, he appreciated women's common sense and grasp of practicalities, and once advised his son Vivion to 'listen to the women' carefully.

There was a tendency in de Valera to compartmentalise people, even his wife. In many respects, he was rather patronising, keeping Sinéad in the dark about various events, and his long periods away, especially in America, brought little comfort. Unbeknownst to him, she was smuggled into America in 1920 on a false passport arranged by Michael Collins for a surprise visit. Rather than responding to her sudden arrival with affection, however, he was positively annoyed at her dramatic appearance, no doubt feeling ambushed and experiencing a loss of control. She spent a miserable six weeks, mainly holed up in a hotel, while he continued lobbying for support for the republican cause. He reputedly told her that her place was 'at home with the children'. In her recollections, relayed by her son Terry, she admitted: 'It was a huge blunder for me to go to America. I derived neither profit nor pleasure from my visit. I am not one who is easily bored, but I had nothing really profitable to do and spent a good deal of time in the hotel.' Essentially, her marriage was a typical 'Asperger marriage' in that she looked after her husband completely, but there was little reciprocity from him.

Like many people with Asperger's syndrome, de Valera had a natural affinity for children. He spent long periods away from home, however, particularly during the War of Independence and Civil War, and not surprisingly was a remote figure to his children, Vivion, Mairín, Éamonn, Brian, Ruairí, Emer and Terry. According to Terry, 'the family seldom saw my father during this time. Mother told me that he hardly saw me for the first two years of my life [1922–24]. He was frequently away from home, including his many tours in the United States.' Six weeks after his arrival back in Ireland in 1921, de Valera still had not seen his children – although the most wanted man in Ireland, Michael Collins, had unfailingly seen them every week in his absence. Terry also remembers his father being

103

heavily involved in affairs of state and the launch of the *Irish Press,* which prevented him from joining them on holidays in Wicklow or elsewhere. Like an amiable uncle, he frequently brought back presents for his young children from his trips, such as balloons with ships' names on them. He clearly shared with them a liking for storytelling, regaling them with various accounts of his voyages on ocean-going liners such as the *Leviathan* and the *Majestic.* As a result of his absences, his children learned to live without him, but when these drew to a close following the end of Civil War hostilities, another era dawned – that of the disciplinarian who expected high standards from his children. In the biography by Longford and O'Neill, de Valera's son Éamonn remembers:

> As a child I feared my father, and resented his intrusion into our lives. He had been in prison and in America, and on his return I found it hard to accept the stricter discipline he enforced. . . . Although my father loves children, he has not been able to communicate well with them. Looking back, I realise that he has never really appreciated the difficulties and shortcomings of minds less gifted than his own.

This is something that the children of those with Asperger's syndrome constantly encounter, which can often bring tension and conflict. In essence, de Valera could not understand the motivations or perspectives of others, something which made meaningful communication difficult.

*

In negotiations or Dáil debates, de Valera was described as aloof and often cold, but never shy and retiring. In the right company – often sycophantic, as deference was always welcome – he could be convivial, and he was capable of great charm and courtesy. By no means did everyone experience this charm, however. Despite those with Asperger's syndrome having difficulty communicating effectively with others, they are filled nevertheless with the need for companionship and at times can be quite verbose, if not 'chatterful', as the politician Tim Healy describes him in *De Valera: Long Fellow, Long Shadow.*

De Valera's ability to communicate in negotiations and meetings was impaired: there was no turn-taking or sharing of attention, appreciating the context of a meeting, reading body language, and so on. In fact, he was unable to tell if people grew bored or their attention waned. Conversations or dialogue with him tended to be exhaustive history lessons, in which he reverted to 'teacher mode' and monopolised the conversation. Indeed, he exasperated Lloyd George and the unionist leader Sir James Craig by not discussing practical issues and failing to 'do business', as it were. It is little wonder that Craig found him 'impossible'.

At a political level, de Valera's communication deficits meant that he had little empathy and was narrow-minded. His decision to go to America in 1919 clearly had no regard for what the Irish people would have wished – i.e. not to be deserted by their leader at an extremely difficult juncture. Unlike Emmet and Pearse, de Valera is hardly ever described as being naive: with him, it was more a case of wilful ignorance. His lack of empathy with Irish-American republicans and Protestant unionists alike often meant that he did not take the time to educate himself about these people's concerns and modi operandi. Even with people he supposedly understood – the native Irish – he showed remarkable lack of empathy in his handling of the twin ills of unemployment and emigration, despite his mother's people, the Coll family, having experienced it first-hand. Moreover, the economic war waged with the British, and the power struggles in which he engaged with his Industry and Commerce Minister, Seán Lemass, did little to improve the lot of the Irish people while de Valera was Taoiseach. Many historians argue that, if anything, he made matters far worse. Longford and O'Neill state that one of de Valera's most remarkable characteristics was his quality of detached judgement when it came to affairs of state. Indeed, his judgements tended to be devoid of personal prejudice and the outcome rather of cold, logical reasoning. This was a strength in some senses: he was a very difficult man to 'buy' or win over.

As an adolescent spending his first night boarding at Blackrock College, his lack of empathy was apparent. He failed to see how another pupil of his own age was so upset from homesickness, while de Valera felt that he was in heaven. His son Vivion reveals that, as a teacher, de Valera was unable to appreciate the difficulties experienced by students who were less gifted than himself. According to Father Farragher, in his early years de Valera did not rate himself highly as a teacher. Examination results showed that his students had done either extremely well or very badly – which suggests that students who did not have natural ability yet were in obvious need of extra tuition were not well served. In addition, de Valera tended to be impatient with students who failed to grasp the rigours of mathematical theorems. Indeed, his son Terry was hounded by his father with maths lessons. He frequently got cross with the boy, who came to dread the lessons intensely. De Valera also decided to give Latin lessons to Terry: these consisted of Latin prayers for the most part. Presumably Terry did not enjoy these much either!

In many ways, de Valera had a deeply sensitive nature, though. During his time in Lincoln Jail, he developed a rapport with the Anglican prison chaplain who visited him regularly in his cell. Following the armistice on 11 November 1918, the clergyman came to visit de Valera as usual, and they discussed the outcome of the war. The chaplain was suddenly overcome by grief. Upon telling de Valera that he had lost his son in the war, de Valera was filled with compassion and placed his arms around the sobbing clergyman. In the authorised biography, his son Éamonn reveals a hypersensitive father:

> Tears and laughter are very close to the surface of his character. The commonly held view that he is aloof and austere is untrue. His natural reserve and self-discipline have so been misinterpreted.

According to Terry, he was very 'compassionate and highly sensitive, greatly concerned for the welfare of others, especially when there was a sickness in the family'. At other times, however, he exhibited an indifference to the feelings or difficulties experienced by others. He once advised his school friend Frank Hughes to 'let what the world and your neighbours think be damned' and pulled him up for paying too much attention to the opinions of others when seeking to achieve his goals. De Valera's manner towards the soldiers under his command was especially austere and formidable. In the Irish Volunteers, he was responsible for drilling the soldiers: he would give orders in Irish, despite the fact that none of the men understood the language!

*

De Valera showed considerable self-control and willpower throughout his life – which often left friends and opponents alike guessing at what his intentions might be. Indeed, so enigmatic were many of his discourses that they appear like an autistic narrative, almost impossible to decipher.

Controlling behaviour is commonplace in people with Asperger's syndrome and frequently takes the form of secrecy, power struggles, manipulation, hostility to criticism and autistic aggression. In de Valera's case, his controlling behaviour could be both subtle and overt. Sometimes his self-discipline kept his emotions in check, while at other times, hot-blooded, he vented his fury. Not surprisingly, he became a figure not to be trifled with. There were possibly some Asperger traits in the de Valera or Coll family make-up that he inherited. His mother Kate Coll was known to be bossy and something of a formidable figure herself. Like Samuel Beckett's mother May, there was no frivolity about her and she was intensely private. Bromage notes that Kate pursued a strict pattern of life, keeping to her own home and venturing out for Mass only.

Fundamentally, de Valera was obsessed with maintaining power and control, whether this concerned dealing with the British or the Irish-American patriots, the running of his government, the suppression of subversives, censorship laws, economic policy, the *Irish Press* or, ultimately, his legacy. His desire for control was so pronounced that it sometimes bordered on the paranoid and dictatorial. (It was not for nothing that Desmond Ryan entitled his biography *Unique Dictator: A Study of Éamon de Valera.*) There are untold instances throughout de Valera's life where he would not yield to the opinions or authority of others, unless for strategic reasons. You could say, as Coogan does in his biography, that his creed was one of *non serviam* ('I will not serve') with all its connotations of pride. In his time in Lincoln Jail during the War of Independence, he freely exerted his will, refusing to conform to prison regulations. He was described by his fellow prisoner Seán Etchingham as 'unbending and unbreakable'.

In his dealings with Michael Collins, de Valera earned a reputation for deviousness and manipulation. At the heart of the jockeying for control was de Valera's desire to be seen as the figurehead of the republican movement in Ireland, although he was lobbying and fundraising in America for eighteen months. His return to Ireland in early 1921 was precipitated by the news that the British wished to enter into peace negotiations with Collins, the de facto military leader in Ireland at the time. De Valera set about exerting control once more; he did not always believe in the efficacy of the guerrilla warfare masterminded by Collins and insisted on battles being fought along more conventional lines. It remains a matter of controversy that de Valera sent Collins to London in his stead to negotiate a treaty which, many believe, he knew was impossible to deliver. A number of ploys were used by de Valera to cow people into submission too. Coogan writes about an incident during a meeting with Collins when de Valera had tried to outmanoeuvre Collins and the IRB but failed, whereupon he lost his temper and pushed the desk to one side, half-screaming and half-shouting: 'Ye may mutiny if you like, but Ireland will give me another army.' The methods of intimidation he used are analysed by Coogan:

> These calculated shows of temper often worked for him in a one-to-one situation, when he would use an array of psychological tricks: calculated hissing-type breathing through the nostrils, like a pressure cooker coming to a boil, that could only be averted by doing whatever it was he wanted; the deliberate silences; the piercing, accusatory glances; the long walk to a huge desk with a chair placed in front for the penitent or supplicant; the demoralising mood change from kindliness to anger; the unexpected hardness that always underlay his deceptively rambling circumlocutory manner in negotiations.

Once returned to power in 1932, he removed any threats to his position: in 1939, he proscribed the fascist Blueshirts and the IRA and arrested all leaders, holding them in custody for the duration of the Second World War. When fund-raising in American during the late 1920s for the establishment of the Fianna Fáil newspaper the *Irish Press,* de Valera toured numerous newspaper offices in various states to see equipment and operations, always posing the same question: 'How do you control it?' As a board member, he appointed himself controlling director of the *Irish Press* with omnipotent executive functions, a position he retained until he became President, at which point control of the paper passed to his son, Vivion. In 1959, he attempted to get rid of proportional representation from the Irish electoral system – the system under which he had been become Taoiseach and which protected minority groups by enabling them to secure representation in the Dáil. When the matter was put to the people in a referendum, however, it was duly rejected.

Another instance of de Valera's controlling nature in action was the draconian censorship laws enacted at the behest of Archbishop McQuaid.

Books and material that were deemed indecent or which contained foul language were banned by the Censorship Board, and the censorship laws were strictly enforced in the 1950s. Works of literature were the first casualties, and frequently writers of international renown, including Ernest Hemingway, James Joyce and Samuel Beckett, fell foul of the law.

The ability to deal with criticism is often severely lacking in people with Asperger's syndrome. De Valera's approach to criticism was either to ignore it or react aggressively to it, depending on the situation. Certainly he had a notorious temper and exhibited a degree of autistic aggression in this respect. Perhaps the best example of this involved his handling of the Treaty. He sent delegates to negotiate with Lloyd George while he deliberately stayed behind in Dublin. Moreover, the delegates had no clear, concise document of the terms and settlement to work towards, other than the briefest and vaguest of notes from de Valera – not an insignificant detail, given de Valera's passion for precision and detail. His inordinate pride, and the prospect of losing face as a result of not delivering external association, prompted him to take defensive action and denounce the delegates. Consequently, he was extremely hostile towards both the Treaty supporters and the critics of external association, and did not spare the vitriol when the matter was debated in the Dáil. Even the pressing advice of his close friend and confidant Dr Robert Farnan not to reject the Treaty was categorically ignored. It could be said that his autistic aggression in no small measure contributed to the Civil War.

De Valera later took great umbrage at the decision of the Irish bishops to express their disapproval of the Civil War by withholding the sacraments from republicans. As a devout Catholic and daily communicant, de Valera was affected by this action. Not one for social graces or to let injustices pass, especially when on the receiving end, he complained volubly to Pope Pius XII years later when he met him face to face. The Pope was harangued about the 'misguided' actions of the Irish bishops who had operated beyond their sphere of influence, as de Valera deemed it. Needless to say, the Pope was speechless.

Although, as already mentioned, people with Asperger's syndrome rarely compromise, de Valera was forced to do so in order to avoid the end to his political career. Possibly his biggest compromise was made in 1927. He, along with his fellow Fianna Fáil TDs, entered Dáil Éireann to take their seats, but first had to swear the oath of allegiance to the Crown, which they had previously resisted doing. Although they were prepared to take the oath, as it transpired they were admitted to the Dáil without doing so. Similarly, de Valera's departure from Dáil Éireann, in 1959, was swift and decisive: he knew when he was beaten. After Dr Noel Browne TD probed into the business dealings of the *Irish Press* and exposed de Valera's obvious conflict of interest in relation to the newspaper, he handed over the reins of power to Seán Lemass, ostensibly so that he would be free to become President.

De Valera was obsessed with secrecy and generally kept things close to his chest. The need for secrecy in many instances was strategic, but it was also closely bound up with suppressing anything that would affect his legacy and place in history. At the end of the Easter Rising, he kept the decision to surrender from his men and surrendered separately before being led back to inform his Volunteers of the surrender, ostensibly to avoid being humiliated in front of his men. In office, he rarely delegated responsibility and reputedly told his Cabinet very little. When pressed for an answer, he invariably would not commit himself – much to the exasperation of colleagues – leaving many to conclude that he was indecisive. According to the historian John Bowman in *De Valera and the Ulster Question, 1917–1973,* de Valera preferred to 'minimise written records', and the policy of his wartime government was to do their work 'orally as far as possible':

> As a leader, de Valera did not easily delegate responsibility. He always remained – to his supporters – 'The Chief', and in power tended to take initiatives which, in any 'open' system of government, would have been the result of collective cabinet decisions. Reinforcing a natural instinct for privacy and secrecy was a personal sense of self-justification which dated from the Treaty and Civil War period.

As de Valera grew in international stature, he came to handle criticism more adroitly. He skilfully saw off Churchill's rebuke of Ireland's neutrality policy after the Second World War. De Valera's radio reply was calculatedly tardy but restrained, perhaps showing the degree to which he had matured into a statesman, and he turned in a powerful piece of rhetoric which won widespread approval:

> I know the reply I would have given a quarter of a century ago. But I have deliberately decided that that is not the reply I shall make tonight.

110

I shall strive not to be guilty of adding any fuel to the flames of hatred and passion which, if continued to be fed, promise to burn up whatever is left by the war of decent human feeling in Europe. . . .

Mr Churchill is proud of Britain's stand alone, after France had fallen and before America entered the war. Could he not find in his heart the generosity to acknowledge that there is a small nation that stood alone not for one year or two, but for several hundred years against aggression; that endured spoliations, famines, massacres in endless succession; that was clubbed many times into insensibility, but that each time on returning consciousness took up the fight anew; a small nation that could never be got to accept defeat and has never surrendered her soul?

Towards the end of his time as Taoiseach, his mettle declined somewhat. One-time senator and chairman of the Commissioners of Public Works, Joseph Connolly, reflected on the waning of lively debate at the time:

In my latter talks with de Valera, I formed the opinion that he no longer welcomed discussion, much less criticism, and that what he wanted beside him was a group of 'yes men' who agreed with everything and anything that the party (with himself as leader) approved.

*

Just like his controlling urges, the superego was harsh in de Valera's case too. You could say that he had an acute sense of right and wrong – as is often the case with people with Asperger's syndrome – though this should not be taken to mean that he led a life of complete moral rectitude. His innate sense of morality was shaped by his Catholic upbringing and formative years in the community of the Holy Ghost Fathers, where he was a boarder and then a teacher at Blackrock College. Despite some minor youthful intemperance, de Valera was abstemious where cigarettes and alcohol were concerned, though he did take a drink on occasion.

An innate sense of natural justice made de Valera rail against the perceived ills of society and against oppression, and he naturally identified with the underdog. He did not care for the legal profession, as he believed that the administration of justice was not always weighted in favour of righting wrongs – and, not least, because his political opponents were often lawyers. An obligation to the poor was instilled in him from his time in Blackrock College, which had close associations with the St Vincent de Paul Society. An earnest de Valera often visited impoverished families in the Blackrock area and later became President of the Society established in Blackrock College. According to his son Terry, he subscribed generously to charities, frequently giving more than he could afford.

Even so, deep ambiguities existed where his sense of justice was concerned. When in power, social justice was not a burning issue for him: the national interest often superseded the rights of the poor and disadvantaged, and he preferred to concentrate on waging the economic war with Britain. On the international stage, de Valera's sense of justice was more spirited: he believed that minority rights and the rights of small nations should be upheld, and protected against oppressors. It was his tenure as President of the Assembly of the League of Nations in 1938 that brought him into contact with fascism, then sweeping Europe, and he championed the rights of smaller nations. He disliked and distrusted the dictator Mussolini, whom he considered to be an 'arrogant, bumptious little man', according to Terry.

De Valera's superego was also expressed somewhat in his austere and frugal tastes. He told Mary Bromage that 'I believe that I live as simply as most people. . . . A number of expenses that the average person has, I have not got. I do not smoke or drink; I do not entertain to any extent.' His main indulgence was his love of books: despite his failing eyesight, he continued to collect them into old age. Clearly, the collecting instinct so frequently seen in those with Asperger's syndrome was present in de Valera too.

In practice, though, his frugality was far from severe: he also cared a great deal about symbolism, as he knew that it touched the hearts and minds of people and was the thing that converted thoughts and emotions into votes. To hold public office meant upholding prestige and the trappings of power. Hence he ran up costly hotel bills during his time in America, when he stayed at the Waldorf Astoria and lavishly entertained Irish Americans with an eye to winning favour among them. He also had well-appointed residences in Blackrock (admittedly rented) and expensive motor cars. More controversially, the establishment of the *Irish Press* gave rise to allegations of profiteering and fraud on the part of de Valera, who, with considerable business acumen, converted the company into a lucrative family concern over time. The argument that money was a motivating factor in de Valera's life is not entirely persuasive, however. His view that he held a 'moral trusteeship' of the *Irish Press* is credible – albeit an arrogant view of the situation. The fiduciary interest in the *Irish Press* was one that was not ultimately shared by the de Valera family, as argued by many.

Given de Valera's strong moral code, he expected everyone else to live by his standards. According to T. Ryle Dwyer in *De Valera: The Man and the Myths,* one of his first acts upon coming to power in 1932 was to reduce his own salary by 40 percent and that of his ministers by 33 percent. In addition, the shameful pay and conditions of the staff at the *Irish Press* featured regularly in disputes and would make an employer blush today. In essence, the messianic and empathy-deficient de Valera, looking into his own heart to see what the people of Ireland wanted, expected those under his command, whether soldiers or staff, to put up with tough conditions – be it food rations or slave labour – for the common good.

This same sense of duty and propriety governed how de Valera felt he should conduct himself in both public and private life. He was a stickler on the subject that the privilege of office should not benefit his private life. According to Terry, his father believed that he should not accept a car provided by the State, as his cars were his own to use as he saw fit for family purposes. According to Father Farragher, de Valera was noted for his attendance at the funerals of those to whom he owed a debt of gratitude or with whom he was closely associated, particularly among the Blackrock community. Nonetheless, his sense of duty in attending funeral sat well with his political instincts too: a personal show of solidarity and support would reap electorate benefits. In fact, he set in train a practice of politicians scrambling to attend funerals which became de rigueur in every parish the length and breadth of the country.

Frequently, de Valera's autistic superego gave rise to controversy, perhaps most famously on the occasion of his visit to the home of the German ambassador, Dr Eduard Hempel, in 1945 to offer his condolences on the death of Hitler. While this action may have flown in the face of de Valera's aversion to imperial aggressors, the keen sense of protocol that motivated it cannot be underestimated. Throughout his life, de Valera was a stickler for duty and discipline, and even when all was falling apart around him, he would insist on observing procedural matters in order to keep order amidst the chaos. Although the offer of condolence showed a gross insensitivity and lack of empathy for the fate of the Jewish people, what weighed more heavily on de Valera's mind was the exemplary conduct of Dr Hempel during the war, as a model of courtesy and rectitude. The Irish leader had no wish to humiliate him at the moment of Germany's defeat, as the leaders of the 1916 Rising had been. Indeed, all his life de Valera adhered rigidly to rules of warfare and protocols on how states should behave towards one another.

Needless to say, de Valera, like many with Asperger's syndrome, could be exasperating or downright odd with regard to issues of protocol. At the end of the Rising, having surrendered to Captain Hitzen and then signalled for his men to leave their HQ at Boland's Bakery, de Valera 'deliberately and meticulously' locked the entrance to the premises, according to Bromage. This certainly echoes Robert Emmet's own dignity and honour in the face of defeat.

The tension between right and wrong inevitably gives rise to guilt in some instances. There is little or no evidence that de Valera experienced guilt, and this raises the possibility of a psychopathic element to his personality: that he was incapable of feeling guilt or empathy. It could be speculated that his guilt manifested itself in anxiety – in the form of panic attacks or nervous fits – or in his need to make atonement. Eyewitnesses during the 1916 Rising claimed that he had a 'nervous breakdown', and Coogan relates how these eyewitnesses recalled seeing 'a tall, gangling figure in green Volunteer uniform and red socks running around day and night, without sleep, getting trenches dug, giving contradictory orders and forgetting the password so that he nearly got himself shot.' Possibly de Valera's condition in this case was induced by exhaustion, the stress of the military situation, and his first real experience of bloodshed: it was certainly the only time he took part in combat. In addition, in 1922, he may have had some kind of breakdown on learning of the death of Collins. When news of the assassination reached him, he was travelling on foot over high ground from Cork to Callan, County Kilkenny. Reputedly, he was too distressed to talk and walked separately from the eight-man escort, talking and muttering aloud to himself, and was possibly reduced to tears, according to Coogan in *Michael Collins: A Biography*. That said, many would argue that, in presiding over the erection of memorials to Collins, de Valera exhibited complete emotional detachment. It is possible too in de Valera's case that the absolute conviction associated with Asperger genius may have rationalised any guilt he experienced.

*

The need for routine and repetition was highly expressed in de Valera's life. One feature of autism, preservation of sameness, was certainly evident in him. Preservation of sameness can ensure the illusion of safety, order and stability in an otherwise chaotic world. For the majority of his life, he lived in Blackrock, County Dublin – in either Blackrock College or its immediate environs, notably Cross Avenue. The rigid discipline of the college – which was monastic even for boarders, with early rising, study, Mass, and measured repetition thereafter of classwork, meals, recreation and further study – meant that de Valera felt comfortable with routine and carefully built it into his life. For instance, as President, he would visit the oratory in the Áras five times a day.

Preservation of sameness can also be seen in the way in which he tried to maintain a Hibernian utopia of old. According to Coogan, he 'idolised the ethos of the peasant patriarchy' from whence he had come. As a consequence, he tried to sustain this vision of the past with all the conviction of an Old Testament prophet. Like Joyce with his desire to preserve forever Edwardian Dublin, de Valera wanted to perpetuate the simple, honest, God-fearing life of the native Irish.

Another feature of the preservation of sameness present in de Valera was his manner of dress. For dramatic effect, he frequently dressed in clerical, black attire when he roved the country to address the people – something that can be seen also in Pearse and Yeats. He wore a long black overcoat, a black suit (occasionally with a black tie) and a large black hat. In his younger days, he wore homespun trousers, giving a country-boy look and lending an eccentric air to his appearance. Coogan cites a description by one of de Valera's contemporaries:

> His appearance is extremely remarkable . . . his clothes, of rough homespun, also make him conspicuous; and he often wore a most unusual cap, with a prominent peak and a cap folded across the top, rather like an airman's helmet.

*

It is impossible to paint a single picture of de Valera because his personality was multifaceted and he was different things to different people. In essence, he exhibited the kind of identity diffusion found in those with Asperger's syndrome. There is strong evidence to suggest that he lacked a coherent sense of self and was obsessed with matters of self, race and place throughout his life – much like Joyce. Inevitably, this was underpinned by a combination of insecurity and egotism. Over the years, his family origins came under serious scrutiny. The lack of reliable records of his parents' marriage in New York and the circumstances of his birth meant that his origins were shrouded in mystery and inevitably gave rise to speculation that he was illegitimate. This seems unlikely, however, given the evidence.

It could be said that de Valera's identity was in a constant state of evolution. As his life progressed, even his name was not a fixed entity. It underwent one change after another: George was the name registered on his birth certificate; Edward was on his baptismal certificate; he was called Eddie, or even Eddie Coll, as a boy because of difficulties both pupils and teachers had in pronouncing 'de Valera' at school; he was nicknamed the 'Dane Coll' by his schoolmates – a name which his uncle Patrick was called too (possibly a corruption of 'Dean' because his uncle served at Mass, according to Coogan); later, 'Eddie' was changed to the Irish version, 'Éamon'; 'Dev' became a nickname that stuck and which he used himself; finally, he was happy for all and sundry to call him 'Chief' in later years. In many respects, de Valera was the quintessential tribal chieftain who commanded great respect and loyalty, if not fealty, from his compatriots and followers: Ernie O'Malley, Harry Boland and Cathal Brugha, amongst others. The Easter Rising was certainly the watershed in his life: his leadership qualities had been forged and recognised there, and he had became a hero – and was worshipped ever after as one.

His identity was also bound up with messianic notions found in many Asperger geniuses. Like Emmet and Pearse, he identified with the Christ-like figure of the Redeemer and believed in the virtue of suffering. He once declared that the generation that does not suffer for its country leaves no mark on history. No one came to represent the close alliance of Church and State more than de Valera, and he earned a reputation as a lay pontiff. Certainly, he was happy to promote this view of himself as a Catholic statesman. Papal recognition of his work followed: in 1933 he received the Grand Cross of the Order of Pius IX, in 1959 he became a Knight Commander of the Order of St Gregory the Great, and in 1960 he was made an Associate Member of the Holy Ghost Congregation.

Clearly his identity diffusion spawned an obsession with titles, always with a view to status and the power associated with it. Many of these titles were august, such as Chancellor of the NUI or President of Ireland. Some were harmless, like Professor of Mathematics – although technically he was not qualified as such. Others were highly controversial: while lobbying in America, he promoted himself from the Príomh Aire (First Minister) of the 1919 Executive Council or First Dáil to President of the Irish Republic without a mandate to do so.

One thing for sure is that he wanted people to consider him as being Irish and not a blow-in from America. His immersion in the Irish language could also be seen as part of this need for self-identity – it being the language his grandmother spoke – although he was also keenly aware of how learning Irish could improve his prospects as a teacher. In later years, when others attacked him in government, calling him a Spanish Jew, based on his father's origins, he went to great lengths to assert his credentials, deeming it a topic worthy of a Dáil address. Obviously the matter was important enough for de Valera to take the trouble in 1936 of engaging the services of the Spanish ambassador, Leopold Kerney, to look into his Spanish origins. According to Terry de Valera, the ambassador established his father's Spanish connection, tracing the family to its origins in Galicia and later Andalucia. From there, the family could be traced back to Spanish and Roman nobility, in particular crusading knights in the service of King Alfonso XI. This no doubt pleased the Chief!

The Asperger genius often has an obsession with immortality and their place in history and the scheme of the cosmos. Clearly, de Valera was obsessed with his legacy. From an early age, he had inklings of his own importance or, as Coogan says, 'intimations of the brilliant career' that lay ahead of him. One of his trademarks was collecting and storing documents, mindful that one day they would be valuable records. Mementoes of his time at Blackrock were kept – anything from sports-day programmes to photographs and entrance-exam cards. Moreover, where his legacy was concerned, de Valera showed that objective reality was a work in progress. Over time, he would give varying accounts of the same event, such as how he joined the IRB, his reasons for going to America in 1919, or the circumstances surrounding his rejection of the Treaty. Frequently, these stories are marked by contradictions and distortions, if not outright lies. This blending of fact and fiction also reflects the Asperger-like inability to personalise memory, resulting in a tendency to live in the here and now and reinterpret the past accordingly. In fact, Asperger geniuses are good revisionists of the details and chronology of their lives.

Clearly, de Valera was wary not to put anything in writing that might compromise him or put him in a poor light. His recollections were carefully cultivated at the expense of Michael Collins. Collins's role in his life, especially the great care he had taken of Sinéad and the de Valera family while de Valera was in America, was downplayed. Furthermore, he went to great lengths to deny all posthumous honours to Michael Collins. Indeed, Coogan, in an article published in *The Irish Times* on 31 January 2005, described him as rather 'mean-spirited' in his failure to acknowledge Collins's legacy. Curiously, there is no de Valera memoir of the 1916 Rising. Perhaps he felt that drawing attention to a nervous fit or breakdown would tarnish his legacy.

Habitually, de Valera sought to influence historians and biographers. The authorised biographers Lord Longford and T. P. O'Neill were constrained by editorial conditions laid down by him. In 1964, a group of historians were invited to Áras an Uachtaráin to discuss questions, which they had to submit in advance, about de Valera's career. These attempts to control his legacy stifled serious academic research, according to John Bowman:

> [De Valera's] instinct not to commit the most sensitive material to paper, the rumoured destruction of some files, the occasional removal of papers by some ministers, the failure to employ professional archivists within government departments, and the generally tardy policy concerning access – all of these factors result in serious problems for the historian of Irish politics since independence.

Less seriously, his identity diffusion was reflected in his penchant for disguise and impersonation. Although de Valera's disguises were mainly borne out of necessity during wartime, others were adopted from whimsy or mischief, and he certainly had a flair for the dramatic. Like Pearse, he cut a credible figure in his travels. A bearded or moustachioed de Valera is frequently seen in pictures of the time. On one occasion, when he was on the run during the Civil War, he grew a beard, removed his glasses, and dressed like an American tourist, along with Frank Aiken and Austin Stack, on their way to an IRA meeting. He evidently dressed as a priest on more than one occasion – once, as a joke, complete with the Prefect's biretta and soutane in Blackrock College. In 1922, when travelling to the Irish Race Congress in Paris, he dressed up and pretended to be Father Patrick Walsh – a priest friend – complete with his passport. This was perhaps done for the sheer fun of it: Coogan argues that there was no real need for him to be incognito, as the British no longer wished to arrest him.

*

Like many people with Asperger's syndrome, de Valera had some sensory impairments or perceptual differences. Though visually impaired, he was acutely observant. As far as can be ascertained, he maintained eye contact with people. Like Joyce, his eyesight was particularly bad; from his early twenties, he wore glasses, possibly for short-sightedness at first, and he underwent a series of eye operations during his lifetime. In the 1930s, he attended the same ophthalmologist as Joyce, Dr Alfred Vogt, in Zurich for a detached retina. Certainly by the end of his life he was effectively blind.

There is also evidence of unusual hearing responses in de Valera. His hearing was exceptionally acute, if not supersensitive – much to chagrin of those who tried to whisper behind his back! Furthermore, he does not appear to have been hypersensitive to loud noises, as often happens among people with Asperger's syndrome. In fact, as an adolescent he enjoyed shooting fowl, and he is reputed to have said that he had 'a love of guns', according to MacManus. In terms of balance and proprioception (which relates to the senses that monitor body and limb position), it appears that de Valera experienced problems like severe seasickness and vertigo. He dreaded having to make transatlantic voyages – which he did many times – according to Terry. He memorably encountered vertigo during the Easter Rising, when in charge of the battalion headquartered at Boland's Mills. Terry writes that his father, along with several of his men, climbed the nearby distillery tower and hoisted a green flag, with a harp at its centre, on top of the tower to fool the British into thinking that it was held by rebel forces. Despite the threat from sniper fire, de Valera was more afraid of the vertigo he had to endure.

De Valera might possibly have displayed a rocking motion, similar to the kind observed in Emmet when he spoke in public. Bromage notes that de Valera was seen to sway backwards and forwards during one Dáil debate when he was vigorously questioning ministers over issues relating to poverty:

> As emotion bore through his statistics and his statements, his voice rose, his long dark hair fell over his forehead and, pressing the tips of his long fingers on the desk in front of him like a pivot, he swayed backwards and forwards.

Like many people with Asperger's syndrome, he had a deep appreciation of music: classical music, ballads and popular airs, and even birdsong. Violin virtuoso Fritz Kreisler and tenor Count John McCormack were counted among his favourites. Though de Valera liked to sing, he had no singing voice as such, according to Terry, even though Terry's grandfather, Juan Vivion de Valera, was an accomplished musician.

Much has been made of de Valera's simple tastes, and these tastes may have extended to his dietary requirements too. He preferred plain fare, partly due to his upbringing but also as a result of his personal preferences. In general, de Valera seemed to have enjoyed reasonably good health; he lived to the age of ninety-two. Sleep disturbances are a common feature of those with Asperger's syndrome, and de Valera, while he generally had uninterrupted sleep at night, was plagued with sleepiness during the day. At school in Blackrock, he would frequently fall asleep during study periods or in his room. Coogan mentions that this condition persisted throughout his life, to the point where, in public office, he considered getting a 'standing desk' to counteract the sleepiness.

There appears to be little evidence of motor clumsiness on de Valera's part. According to his son Terry, his father played an 'excellent game of rugby', although others would say that he dominated the ball and was not a team player at all. Once, at Blackrock, he insisted that he take all the penalties – with a most unsuccessful outcome! Clearly he could handle firearms safely, so there appears to be no indication that he had poor fine motor co-ordination. From his many letters and accounts of his spells in prison, he kept physically fit, playing many games, including handball and tennis. Like many other hypersensitive individuals, de Valera had a great love of nature and animals. He displayed an obvious affection, bordering on the sentimental, towards domestic animals, which was shared by his wife. Over the years, a succession of cats and dogs – and hens, in one case – became part of the extended de Valera household. Indeed, he once wept over the death of the family canary, which had escaped from its cage, according to Terry.

*

The religiosity or spiritualism that marks many Asperger geniuses was present in abundance in de Valera. In his case, spirituality was filtered through Christian principles, and a thorough grounding in religious dogma that he had received from the Christian Brothers and Holy Ghost Fathers. As a young man in Blackrock College, he contemplated joining the priesthood, but his vocation was never encouraged by the religious superiors. Nonetheless, throughout his life he had a certain monastic disposition. At the age of eighty, when his wife's health was declining, he considered resigning the presidency and joining the Blackrock Community as a lay brother, in the event of his wife predeceasing him. Yet like Pearse, de Valera was not an orthodox Catholic, and his independent streak often made him a formidable opponent of churchmen. Longford and O'Neill make reference to a profound admirer of de Valera's who once remarked that 'he would have made such a good Protestant'! This comment reflects de Valera's emphasis on private prayer and righteousness, whereby, as Longford and O'Neill remark, he 'always remained a man of ineradicable private judgement; a man not only with a most sensitive conscience, but with the self-confidence to live and die by what it told him.'

A mind that is open to the spiritual world is often linked to a romantic or poetic imagination. The heroic romanticism present in de Valera was forged in his childhood and formative years. His grandmother died when he was six, but not before she had filled her grandson's imagination with stories and sagas from Ireland's culture, using expressions from the disappearing Irish language. A love of Irish heroes was fostered in the young de Valera, and his nationalist impulses were sharpened by his uncle, Pat Coll, and parish priest Father Eugene Sheedy. After the 1916 Rising, de Valera held Pearse as one of his greatest heroes. Another hero was Machiavelli's Prince. The importance of this work for de Valera, with its ideal state as a republic and the necessity for citizen armies, should not be underestimated. He carried this book around with him and recommended it to young people, such as Richard Mulcahy, who were entering politics. Perhaps the most important message he took from *The Prince* was that achieving real political ends was not possible through a middle way of moderation, temporizing, consensus and caution – all of which are anathema to the Asperger genius. Indeed, his wife Sinéad summed up the essential difference in her husband: 'In small things, Dev is very much given to weighing up things: he sees all the difficulties and takes all the precautions. On the other hand, when a big matter is at stake, he will go boldly forward.'

Like Emmet and Pearse, de Valera had a liking for poetry. He was particularly encouraged by the works of the nationalist poet James Clarence Mangan and by the English Catholic mystic poet Francis Thompson. In fact, his passion for mathematics and metaphysics often found expression in poetry, of which he wrote a great deal while in prison:

When I behold thee filled am I with hope
Quarternia
And realms new yield my soul extended scope
Quarternia.

De Valera, as an Asperger genius, could boldly stride forward and become a strong moral leader. Yet his lack of empathy left him open to the charge of insensitivity and failure to see the human needs and desires of his people. As a political leader, he tried to reconcile two visions: Ireland as an island nation, independent, united and self-contained, and Ireland that had an international outlook and was part of the community of nations, enjoying good relations with leading powers such as America and Britain. It could be said that this clash of isolationism and integration reflected de Valera's own autistic struggle to be both part of something and yet separate from it.

4

ROBERT BOYLE

He that said it was not good for man to be alone placed the celibate
amongst the inferior states of perfection.

ROBERT BOYLE, Letter to John Evelyn, *Works,* vol. vi

For many Irish people, Robert Boyle evokes classroom memories of
Boyle's Law of Gases and little else. Nowadays, so rapidly has science
advanced that the work of the trailblazer Boyle is taken largely for granted. The seventeenth-century Father of Chemistry, though born in
Ireland, spent the greater part of his life in England. There he embarked
on a brilliant scientific career that coincided with the establishment of the
foremost British scientific academy, the Royal Society. His single most
important contribution to science was to establish the experimental
method; in so doing, he laid the cornerstone of modern science. After
Boyle and his contemporaries, science was no longer something that was
discussed philosophically but something grounded on observable fact.
Meticulously, he recorded every detail of his experiments, no matter how
trivial or bizarre they might appear, and published the results for the benefit of all. This novel approach in time became the norm, and today we
have thousands of journals publishing research results. Indeed, so seriously is empiricism taken today that to 'publish or perish' shapes the rep-
utations of scientists and scientific institutions everywhere.

Impressions of Boyle through the ages paint a picture of a science-loving saint. However, Boyle was far from being the tranquil figure depicted but was a highly complex individual. A close scrutiny of his life reveals certain Asperger traits.

While there is no definitive biography of Boyle, numerous accounts and commentaries are found in collected volumes of his work or collections of correspondence, among them R. E. W. Maddison's *The Life of the Honourable Robert Boyle* (1969) and Michael Hunter's *Robert Boyle by Himself and His Friends* (1994). Other biographical details can be gleaned from Roger Pilkington's *Robert Boyle: Father of Chemistry* (1959). Fortunately, in *An Account of Philaretus During His Minority,* Boyle himself gave an account of his early life in the guise of a third person.

From these accounts emerge a genius for devising experiments and a man with an insatiable curiosity. He showed a dogged determination to understand the natural world and was hyperkinetic in the pursuit of this goal. Yet Boyle was no impartial scientist: he fundamentally believed that God was at the centre of a mechanical universe and that it was the scientist's duty to make sense of His handiwork where possible. Like Einstein, he felt that pure or unbridled reason was not enough to understand nature and the universe.

*

Born on 20 January 1627 in Lismore Castle, County Waterford, Robert Boyle was the fourteenth child of the Great Earl of Cork and his wife Catherine Fenton. In appearance, Boyle was tall and thin. He had a delicate pallor and was somewhat frail, due to the ill health that plagued him all his life. In one account, Maddison describes him as 'tall, thin and effeminate'. Indeed, feminine features or androgyny can sometimes be seen in those with Asperger's syndrome. Various paintings and etchings from the time show his delicate features: large, dark, expressive eyes under arched eyebrows, a rather long face with a straight, sharp nose, and large, generous lips. There are no accounts of whether he avoided eye contact or not.

No mention of Robert Boyle is possible without reference first being made to his father, Richard Boyle. The story of Richard Boyle's rise to fame and fortune is perhaps one of the most incredible tales of its kind. Born in England in 1566, the law clerk landed in Ireland at the age of twenty-two with £27 in cash, a diamond ring, a gold bracelet, some clothes, a rapier and a dagger, according to Pilkington. With these his only worldly goods, and not short of ambition, the adventurer set about acquiring property and position in Elizabethan Ireland with ruthless determination. Such was his cunning and enterprise that he has been styled the first great capitalist entrepreneur and the Bill Gates of his day. By the time his fourteenth child, Robert, was born, the sixty-year-old Richard owned vast swathes of land in Munster, including Sir Walter Raleigh's estates, and had acquired the title 'Great Earl of Cork'. In subsequent years, he became Lord Justice of Ireland, the Lord High Treasurer and a member of the English Privy Council. His means of accruing property was based on a thoroughgoing knowledge of land deeds and conveyancing and, crucially, strategic marital alliances. His first marriage, to heiress Joan Apsley, enabled him to build up his holdings and improve his position in society. Following her death in childbirth, his next marriage, to Catherine Fenton, daughter of Irish Secretary Sir Geoffrey Fenton, paved the way for him to amass lands and titles at a phenomenal rate. His income from rents alone was far greater than that of any other subject under King Charles I. Being in favour at Charles's court also meant that he could exploit protocols and obtain new patents when the titles of any of his estates were in doubt. Once his own position was secure, he set about arranging marriages for his children to members of leading British and Irish noble families.

Asperger traits found in the father were almost certainly replicated in the son, despite their diverging interests. The trait that enabled Richard Boyle to accumulate such wealth and position was an all-encompassing focus on his interests that lasted his entire lifetime. A sharp intelligence and shrewd business acumen, with a great attention to detail and observable fact, saw the Earl plough back most of the profits into his huge estates. In outlook, he was certainly progressive and innovative. Frequently labelled ruthless, corrupt, vain and boastful, the Great Earl justified his land grab under the then prevailing view that it was God's providence to bring civilising ways to the Irish natives, according to Nicholas Canny in *The Upstart Earl*.

In keeping with what his father considered a gentlemanly upbringing, Robert Boyle's education consisted of private tutoring and schooling at Eton College, followed by the grand tour of continental Europe. At Eton, Boyle was a keen student, and his exceptional intelligence soon became evident. He was particularly fortunate that all his tutors, whether at Eton or privately, encouraged and stimulated him intellectually. Recognising that he was dealing with a prodigy, John Harrison at Eton in particular handled Boyle adroitly, relaxing or reinforcing discipline where necessary in order to fuel the youth's curiosity and passion for knowledge. The unorthodox tutor also brought the Classics to life for the young Boyle, in particular the conquests of Alexander the Great. Typically of Asperger geniuses, Boyle was an avid reader. Books became his constant companions, not least medieval romances such as *Amadis of Gaul* and other chivalrous tales. His immersion in these tales, not surprisingly, fired his romantic imagination. After four years at Eton, Boyle and his brother Francis went on a tour of European cities under the care of a French tutor called Isaac Marcombes. In Geneva, he received an extremely rounded education from Marcombes and excelled at such subjects as rhetoric, logic, Latin, Roman history, Old and New Testament criticism, arithmetic and geometry – though he later admitted that he had no talent for mathematics.

Through Marcombes, Boyle learned about the radically new ideas of the age originating from Descartes, Galileo and Francis Bacon. His first real interest in science emerged during a trip to Italy at the age of fifteen. His exposure to Galileo's work and tomb prompted a fresh wave of daydreaming on the structure of the universe. Once again, his books accompanied him wherever he went. Francis Boyle remarked that his brother's pockets were constantly stuffed with books, and even when he was walking downhill or roaming across the Italian countryside, his head was stuck in a book. From his account of his travels in *Philaretus,* it is clear that Boyle was highly observant and that he absorbed all manner of information about his surroundings and the interaction of the local people. Clearly he had good visuo-spatial skills and an eye for design: he freely gave judgements on the architecture of the various European cities he visited. In 1641, the tour was cut short by the onset of rebellion in Ireland, and by the time the rebellion had ended, in 1643, the Earl of Cork had incurred extensive property losses, which took their toll on both his fortune and his health. Before long, he was dead; his favourite son Robert was barely sixteen years old.

*

The decision to devote his life to the pursuit of knowledge was something akin to a religious conversion for Boyle. In adolescence, he experienced a crisis of faith that took some years to resolve. Bearing all the hallmarks of a Romantic engagement with nature such that the poet Shelley might have had, Boyle had a dramatic epiphany during a thunderstorm in Geneva. The outcome was that Boyle would believe that the world was mechanical, orderly and consistent, and worked according to God's laws of motion. This view ran counter to the traditional view of science at the time. In leading universities such as Oxford, science, or 'natural philosophy' as it was then called, was based on Scholasticism, which incorporated the ideas of Aristotle and medieval Christian theology. It did not advocate a mechanical universe. More crucially for Boyle, the ideas of natural philosophy were debated rather than observed and recorded as facts. Theory dominated experimentation. Fearing that a Scholastic education at Oxford would lead him away from the true pursuit of science, he decided against it. More and more, his thinking was influenced by the Renaissance philosopher Francis Bacon, who sought to put scientific inquiry on a better footing. Such enquiry, Bacon believed, should involve the recording of observed facts, more use of experiment, and accurate observation. But while Bacon philosophised about this radical departure from the traditional method, it was Boyle who put it into practice.

Displaying an independent and original mind – essential to the Asperger genius – Boyle went his own way. Still in his late teens and eager to conduct experiments, he set up a laboratory on a property in Stalbridge, Kent, which he had inherited from his father. Fortunately for science, Boyle led a privileged life that allowed him to devote entire days to the study of nature without the pressing need to be gainfully employed. Having the means to engross himself in chemistry clearly gave him great pleasure. He wrote to his sister Katherine that 'the delights I taste in it make me fancy my laboratory a kind of Elysium'. Like Newton, experiments in alchemy occupied a good deal of his time, and his interest in the subject never waned. This interest was not based on the avarice associated with the attempt to convert base metal to gold but was borne from pure curiosity. In essence, alchemists were the first chemists: they genuinely believed in the medicinal and religious connotations of gold.

Despite not having a grounding in science from Oxford, Boyle was never short of influential figures or mentors to guide his thinking or act as a springboard for his ideas. Around this time, he started to correspond with Samuel Hartlib, the most prominent communicator of scientific ideas at the time. Boyle discussed with Hartlib the problems he encountered, such as the compression of air. Pilkington writes that, by the age of twenty, Boyle was accepted and even looked up to by the 'leading virtuosi of the day' – John Wilkins, John Wallis, John Evelyn, Robert Moray, Christopher Wren and William Petty – natural scientists who gravitated towards each other from the mid-1640s onwards to discuss new experiments and the ideas of Francis Bacon in what they styled the 'Invisible College'. Eventually, this led to the formation of the Royal Society in 1660. Among them, Boyle, with his 'unusual brilliance', was completely at home. His move to Oxford in 1654 was to become one of the most fertile scientific periods in his life. Having been schooled in the technical and practical aspects of chemistry by a Mr Staehl from Strasbourg, Boyle went on to build a substantial laboratory over the next fourteen years and employ numerous assistants, notably Robert Hooke, who later gained scientific recognition in his own right. Scientists in Boyle's time were no longer forced to work in isolation or secrecy, as they had before.

Showing the hallmark of the Asperger genius, Boyle was curious about every aspect of whatever he was studying and observed the results with tremendous precision. He displayed great ingenuity in devising trials or experiments for whatever phenomena he was concerned with. Indeed, the Scottish chemist Dr George Wilson noted the skill with which Boyle interpreted the phenomena he witnessed. In fact, both Boyle and his father had a sharp ear and keen eye for what was going on around them – in the father's case, analysing a political situation. Yet there was something of the scientist in the Earl too. He had been an avid horticulturist, according to Canny, in particular tending to his orchards, and he had wanted to graft apple trees with those first planted by Sir Walter Raleigh. The Earl too was practical and logical and insisted on the 'superiority of knowledge derived from experience', according to Canny.

In fact, there was hardly a branch of knowledge that did not claim Robert Boyle's attention. Pilkington sums it up by saying that to Boyle we owe the secrets of fire, air, water, animals, vegetables, fossils, and phosphorescence. Ably assisted by Robert Hooke and his vacuum or air pump, Boyle conducted pioneering experiments on gases. He demonstrated the physical properties of air and found that it could be weighed and was necessary for combustion, respiration and the transmission of sound. Using the air pump, Boyle's was able to describe the relationship between the pressure and volume of a gas. He found that the more the space or volume of a gas is reduced, the higher its pressure, and thus Boyle's Law entered the scientific lexicon. Indeed, the pressure cooker as we know it today works on the principle of Boyle's Law. In addition, he found that the weight of an object varies with changes in atmospheric pressure. In 1660, the results of a range of experiments using the air pump were contained in *New Experiments Physico-Mechanical, Touching the Spring of Air and its Effects*. The pressure of a gas was then rather charmingly called the 'spring'. *The Spring of the Air,* as it became known, was hailed as a breakthrough at the time and established Boyle as the foremost scientist of the period.

Boyle's method was based on careful observation, accurate experiments and inductive reasoning. In 1661, in *The Sceptical Chymist,* he disagreed with the Aristotelian view that nature consisted of four elements – fire, water, air and earth – and that they could be converted from one into another. Also, he disagreed that all matter contained the alchemists' three principles of mercury, sulphur and salt, inherited from Paracelsus. These were mythical substances and should be abandoned, Boyle argued. Aristotle's belief that nature abhorred a vacuum was also disputed. These theories, Boyle found, did not accord with the observable facts, especially in light of the knowledge gleaned from the use of the air pump. Furthermore, he believed that all substances are composed of minute particles or corpuscles which differ in their arrangement or motion – a belief that would pave the way for atomic theory. Pilkington sums up Boyle's contribution to science:

> There was hardly a department of science in which he was not thoroughly proficient, and his influence upon the development of scientific thought was unequalled. No other man of science of Boyle's day and generation played so large a part in shaping the intellectual climate of the future, and not until Darwin did another scientist bring about such a change in the attitude of philosophers and public alike to the phenomena of the world in which they lived. This is all the more remarkable when it is remembered that Boyle had such notable contemporaries as Isaac Newton. In terms of precise formulation of theory Newton's

achievements were infinitely greater, but it was Boyle whose works were eagerly bought and read the moment they came from the press.

Boyle can claim credit for many discoveries in the development of modern chemistry which are taken for granted today: litmus paper and the distinction between acids, bases and neutral solutions; the distinction between mixtures and compounds; the definition of an element as anything that cannot be broken down into simpler substances, and the use of the hydrometer. Having isolated phosphorous, he was the first to create the match – albeit admittedly not in a useable form. Showing considerable prescience, he experimented with a form of refrigeration, with electricity and with preserving food by vacuum-packing.

His fascination with human anatomy and healing led to many contributions to medical science and medicines: experiments on the composition of blood and possible transfusions; physical properties of semi-permeable membranes; and remedies for various ailments. One of Boyle's first forays into science was in pharmacology, prompted by his own delicate constitution and his various ailments. In an age when purgatives were a universal remedy, laxatives and enemas were often administered to him at Eton; this engendered in Boyle a lifelong distrust of doctors and dispensers. This distrust prompted him to study, compile and classify his own cures for various ailments. Later, Dr William Petty had given him instruction in anatomy and physiology, and a thorough grounding in experimental procedures. In his lifetime, his 'cures' ran to several hundred prescriptions, many of which have survived to this day. Ailments ranging from agues to breast cancer, jaundice and scurvy received the benefit of his wisdom – though many of the cures would be considered dubious today. A valuable lesson from Petty was that the cures Boyle used in medicating himself had not been proven sound: 'medicaments not sufficiently tried by those that administer or advise them'.

Because theism informed his view of science, Boyle was overcautious, or slow to draw conclusions. Even so, his experiments did not allow him to make sizeable or universal claims. This led many commentators to suggest that he was ambivalent, if not flexible, in his views. Indeed, the philosopher Leibniz was astonished that Boyle had not arrived at a theory of chemistry after meditating on it for so long. By Boyle's own admission, the mechanical laws of nature did not always explain certain things, such as the incorporeality of the soul, miracles or the supernatural. But in areas where ambiguities existed, Boyle explained them away as mysteries of the divine God, and too difficult for humans to comprehend. Pilkington writes that Boyle spent his life in the pursuit of nature 'through a great variety of forms and changes, and in the most rational as well as devout adoration of its divine author.' It could be argued that Boyle was so absorbed in the microdetails of nature and was so reluctant to draw conclusions because he failed to see the big picture. This inability is often associated with a lack of central coherence found in those with Asperger's syndrome.

*

There is no record of any speech and language delay on Boyle's part. The first five years of his life were spent in fosterage, where he learned to speak. Mixing with native Irish children, he also picked up some Irish words. His earliest education was overseen by a private French tutor and the family chaplain, who taught him to read and write at the age of five. According to Canny, Boyle had been taught to write in a 'fair hand' and to speak French and Latin by the age of eight. The fact that he had mastered these skills so well endeared him greatly to his father.

In speech, Boyle had a soft voice and spoke with studied caution. However, in various letters of the time there are references to his habit of stammering and repetition of words. This habit developed before the age of five and persisted all his life, being most pronounced in times of stress or excitement. This was in an age when stammering was looked upon as an infirmity and referred to as 'defective speech'. The severity of the condition was described in a letter by the Italian scientist Lorenzo Magalotti, who says that Boyle had 'some impediment in his speech, which is often interrupted by a kind of stammering, which seems as if he were constrained by an internal force to swallow his words again and with the words also his breath, so that he seems so near to bursting that it excites compassion in the hearer.' Given his puritan cast of mind, Boyle attributed this 'defect' to God's retribution. When he was being fostered, he had mocked the local children who stammered, later convincing himself that the habit had stayed with him because he had imitated them.

With a flair for logic and a highly retentive memory, Boyle had a great aptitude for languages. When living abroad, he took to writing in French because, like Beckett, it was the language in which he could express himself best. Some Irish was acquired from his country nurse during fosterage and, later, formal lessons were given by a tutor hired by his father to teach both brothers while they were at Eton. However, they never mastered the language to any extent. There are no accounts of what methods the tutor used to teach Irish to the young Boyle. In his forties, Boyle's obsession with religion prompted the study of biblical languages. Contemporary translations and commentaries on the Bible had done little to satisfy his desire for greater detail and accuracy. Over the period of a year, he embarked on a study of not only Hebrew and Greek but also the Chaldaic, Syriac and Arabic languages, like William Rowan Hamilton. Ever the autodidact, he learned Syriac on his own because he failed to find a teacher!

In terms of language, Boyle revolutionised the way experiments were described. Previously, this was done either in Latin or using symbols, which meant that experiments could not always be replicated. In one fell swoop, Boyle transformed the style of presenting experimental data into direct and plain English. The science historian Dr John Young, in the online Literary Encyclopaedia, remarks that Boyle as a scientific writer was exceptional for his lucidity and precision. In contrast, he notes that Boyle's assistant George Starkey was wilfully obscure, using 'symbolic allegories, often in doggerel verse, or interspersing them with violent personal invective against rival chemists'. In time, the lucid style of expression developed by Boyle became the policy of the Royal Society.

In terms of his style of writing, a distinction must be made between Boyle's scientific and his religious and literary writings. With the latter, his style was fairly stilted, wordy and florid, in the literary fashion of the time. This could be read as a certain hyperactivity in his writing. In later life, Boyle was rather embarrassed by this style. Maddison draws attention to the fact that, in his earlier writings, Boyle was conscious of his 'own occasional verbosity, and the use of over-long complex periods'. The essayist Eustace Budgell stated that 'his style is far from being correct; that it is too wordy and prolix; and that though it is for the most part plain and easy, yet, that he has sometimes made use of harsh and antiquated expressions'. Certainly a verbose and digressional style is commonly seen in those with Asperger's syndrome: William Hamilton is another case in point.

It is evident that Boyle took great delight in language, creating neologisms and engaging in wordplay – a typical Asperger trait. 'Meleteticks' was the name he coined for his frequent musings and mediations, which he later fleshed out in his writings. In his trademark desire for precision, nouns or verbs were invented (and their derivative terms) to more accurately reflect the work in hand. The most memorable are 'indigation' and 'indagate', which led to 'indagator' and 'indigative', to describe a search or investigation of nature. He was also the first person to use the term 'analysis' to explain the results of his experiments in chemistry. In written speech, he regularly made up exalted titles or pseudonyms for various people: his own persona was referred to as 'Philaretus' ('the lover of virtue'), while his sister Katherine was addressed as 'Sophronia' ('of sound mind').

Frequently, the playful side of Boyle and his quirky sense of humour are perhaps lost in his ever-pious public perception. There was a sardonic tone to his humour, and his early letters are interspersed with witty asides. Though Bishop Burnet, in his funeral oration, remarked that there was little levity or frolicking in Boyle's nature, this was not entirely true. Certainly when entertaining young ladies, his penchant for practical jokes emerged – something fairly frequently found in those with Asperger's syndrome. Like a magician, he would mock, frighten and amaze them with tricks such as burning paper impregnated with weak spirit of wine, or staining items with silver nitrate.

*

The ability to immerse oneself wholeheartedly in work or thought is something that is seen time and time again in the Asperger genius. Often the seeds of this practice are sown in daydreaming in youth. Daydreaming is not so idle and functionless as might be imagined but can be the start of a fermentation of ideas which can gain expression years later. Like W. B. Yeats and Isaac Newton, from his teenage years Boyle was a notorious daydreamer, and the practice persisted all his life. Furthermore, whether engaged in scientific work, religious or literary writings, or learning scriptures, he showed an astonishing ability to immerse himself in his work and concentrate deeply. The incredible energy which he invested in his work is reminiscent of his father too. The outcome of such rigid discipline was that Boyle worked at a phenomenal rate and became a prolific writer, completing more than forty books in his lifetime.

Repetition and routine was found too in his extensive note-taking and journal-keeping. Like his father, who had kept records and detailed journals for decades, Boyle was a voluminous writer. According to Pilkington, Boyle, having spent the day observing in great detail, would write notes on whatever ideas or musings he had had that day: 'in the evenings he would sit alone by the fireside in the quiet of the manor house to write notes of the thoughts which had occurred to him during the day, and the incidents or observations which had prompted them'. After his death, he left seven volumes of correspondence, forty-six volumes of miscellaneous papers, and eighteen volumes of notebooks, many of which were never published. His published experiments on nature alone contained forty-two volumes, and clearly were hugely popular in their day. It is obvious too that Boyle enjoyed more fame in his lifetime than posthumously. Indeed, his latest publication was so eagerly awaited that various methods to speed up production were employed, according to Pilkington:

> Robert Boyle's books were certainly widely read. His forty-two volumes ran through a total of more than two hundred editions – an average of nearly five per book – and his complete works were twice reprinted within the century after his birth. He had to employ professional editors and proof-readers to keep pace with the flow of his output, and the latest work from his pen was so urgently solicited by printers that some of his papers were communicated piecemeal and set up in type before they were even completed.

The desire for repetition and sameness was certainly present in Boyle. He had a rigid pattern of behaviour, whether it concerned his dress, medication, society or working practices. For the last twenty-three years of his life, which he shared with his sister Katherine, they would start the day with meditation and private prayer. An ordered, monastic routine was one he dearly loved – not unlike de Valera. After prayers, Boyle would retire to his laboratory for the morning. In the afternoon, the great and the good flocked to their house in Pall Mall in London, yet as Boyle grew more infirm, the number of visitors had to be curtailed. He would often work late into the night. Over the years, his bedroom became an extended laboratory, and increasingly cramped. Maddison quotes one letter that describes it: 'Glasses, pots, chemical and mathematical instruments, books and bundles of papers did so fill and crowd his bed-chamber that there was but just room for a few chairs; so as his whole equipage was very philosophical without formality.' His library contained more than three thousand books, but they were not always in an ordered fashion. Again, as with so many Asperger geniuses, the task of organising books and papers fell into abeyance.

*

Boyle has been variously described as diffident, shy, retiring, introspective, serious and reserved, and there are many instances where he does indeed cut a solitary figure. Precocious as a child, he preferred the company of books to that of his peers, as frequently occurs with those with Asperger's syndrome. As an adolescent, he would spend four or five hours alone in the fields, acting out imaginary roles of great heroes. Later, he enjoyed solitary pursuits such as reading, fishing, hawking and walking, especially in the company of his pet spaniel. Regardless of where he lived, he was given to roaming about the countryside on his own, lost in thought – as indeed did W. B. Yeats, Joyce, Beckett, Hamilton, Pearse, de Valera and Daisy Bates – and would turn his mind to arithmetic problems to rein in his thoughts when they went 'a-gadding', as he put it. He often worked alone in his laboratory, though he did employ some assistants, becoming more dependent on them as his eyesight failed. Particularly at Stalbridge, he lived the life of a recluse, sometimes breaking his solitude to come to London to visit his sister Katherine and meet members of the Invisible College.

Beyond doubt, Boyle was a highly sensitive and anxious individual, particularly in his childhood and formative years. By the time he was sixteen, he had lost his mother and father, his siblings Margaret and Lewis, and his much-admired brother-in-law, Lord Barrymore. Indeed, his hyper-sensitivity was later apparent when, according to his close friend Bishop Burnet, 'the tenderness of his nature' was such that he was unable to watch or carry out anatomical dissections, especially of animals, though he knew that the knowledge that he could gain from such experiments would be instructive.

During his schooldays at Eton, Boyle appears to have been popular with the other boys, but he was extremely studious and hated being called away from his books. Like many with Asperger's syndrome, he gravitated

towards the company of adults more than his peers. In fact, the precocious Boyle, still not a teenager, was a frequent guest at the Provost's table
and was able to converse effortlessly with visiting scholars and men of the
world.

Like many with Asperger's syndrome, Boyle had close family bonds.
He and his brother Francis, who had been educated together, were particularly close, and Francis often emulated him. Boyle's older brother Roger,
Lord Broghill, was also a regular correspondent. In later life, Boyle tended to mix only with those who shared his interests in science and religion.
He had hundreds of acquaintances, thanks to the fame and acclaim he
received in his lifetime, but few close friendships. His male friendships,
which were based on common intellectual interests, included those with
Robert Hooke, John Evelyn, Dr William Petty and many others who
became founding members of the Royal Society. His profound preoccupation with religion led to a friendship with Bishop Burnet which lasted
thirty years: it is believed that Bishop Burnet was Boyle's confidant.

With his increasing fame, many demands were made on Boyle's company. Like Spinoza, who may also have had Asperger's syndrome, he
found social visits tedious and wasteful of his time. At the height of his
fame, when he was living in London with his sister, the visits became so
out of hand that the family were forced to publish a notice restricting
their receptions 'unless upon occasions very extraordinary' to 'Tuesday
and Friday forenoon, and Wednesday and Saturday afternoon', so that
Boyle could conserve time and energy for his work. He would often work
elsewhere to avoid wasteful interruptions, escaping to private lodgings
somewhere else in London or resting with relatives not far from the city.
Though he was interested in the world from the viewpoint of science, he
held himself aloof and independent from major contemporary events –
the Civil Wars, religious persecution and the Restoration. His autistic
detachment from the affairs of the world and personal piety surely gave
him an otherworldly and eccentric air. The fact that he was so apolitical
also indicates how his inner sense of time was very much in the 'here and
now', much like Joyce and Beckett.

No matter how absorbed he was in his researches, letters reveal that
Boyle was unfailingly generous, gentle, courteous and kind. These qualities meant that he became a trustworthy figure and also helped his ideas
to become accepted. Moreover, Boyle had considerable charm in terms of

both his social manners and his powers of conversation. History does not record whether he made any social faux pas or lacked empathy. Whenever he was in an awkward position, silence was his usual response, but it is clear that he put himself under severe pressure to be civil, as Bishop Burnet notes:

> He was exactly civil, rather to Ceremony; and though he felt his easiness of access, and the desires of many, all Strangers in particular, to be much with him, made great wastes on his Time; yet as he was severe in that, not to be denied when he was at home, so he said he knew the Heart of a Stranger, and how much eased his own had been, while travelling, if admitted to the Conversation of those he desired to see; therefore he thought his Obligation to Strangers was more than bare Civility, it was a piece of Religious Charity in him.

The loss of his mother at a tender age clearly had a huge impact on the young Boyle and his social impairment. A complex man, the Earl of Cork was not always consistent and logical in the matter of rearing his children, and indeed showed many Asperger traits, not least emotional detachment and controlling behaviour. For much of Robert's upbringing, the Earl was absent from his life, and it fell to tutors to make up any shortcomings and provide all sorts of guidance and education.

Mindful of the dangers of luxury and too much ease, the Earl was strict with his children and sparing in his affection, though he did love them dearly. In fact, he believed that everything relating to the emotions was suspect and should be suppressed. Attachments were a sign of weakness, he believed, and grief best handled by internalising it. In *Philaretus*, Boyle explained his father's motives for fostering out his children – admittedly something that was widely practised among the aristocracy and had its roots in old Irish customs. It was done, he explained, so that his 'perfect aversion' to those who 'used to breed their children so nice and tenderly, that a hot sun, or a good shower of rain as much endangers them, as if they were made of butter or of sugar.' A short time after his birth, Boyle was given into the care of a country wet-nurse so that he could be exposed to 'a coarse but cleanly diet and to the usual passions of the air'.

The Earl's wife, Catherine Fenton, appeared to have no say in these matters. Having married the thirty-eight-year-old Earl possibly at the age of fifteen, she bore him fifteen children and seemed to have deferred to him in all domestic matters. Boyle later wrote an essay entitled 'The Duty of a Mother to Nurse Her Own Child', which clearly showed that he had given the matter some consideration. His mother had succumbed to tuberculosis and died when Robert was three years old. Given that his parents were absent in England for a good part of 1628 and 1629, and lived in Dublin following their return, Robert probably never again saw his mother after he was first handed over to the wet-nurse. In effect, Robert Boyle had no recollection of his mother and, speaking in the third person, he considered 'it amongst the chief misfortune of his life that he did never know her that give [life to] him.'

Arranging child brides and grooms was another area that occupied the Earl's attention. He was careful, however, to match the ages of his children and their partners and to establish companionate relationships in the households where they were to spend the rest of their lives, according to Canny.

It was only as adults that the Boyle children were allowed to join their father's company and enjoy it in a relaxed or familiar way. Canny notes that, despite the protracted absences, the Earl recognised every one of his children as individuals and was emotionally attached to each one of them. On the birth of each child and grandchild, he would enter in his diary the star under which each was born and map their progress. Despite his strictness, the Earl's daughter Mary remembers him as the 'best and kindest father in the world'.

There was a certain Peter Pan quality to Boyle. He never reached emotional maturity and was forever attached to his interests, like a child with a favourite toy. He comes across as self-sufficient, with few close friends and never having taken a wife – as would have been expected of him. Having had so many sisters, Boyle clearly felt at ease in the company of women and indeed relished it. In a letter to his brother Lord Broghill, the twenty-six-year-old Boyle writes that he had managed to acquire a reasonable knowledge of Hebrew scriptures within a year, in spite of the amount of time he spent 'in conversation with young ladies'. John Evelyn writes too that his friend was quite 'facetious in conversation with the young ladies'.

In the event, Boyle was to remain a bachelor all his life. Had the Earl lived, he would probably have concluded the marriage negotiations he had begun with the family of Lady Ann Howard, but his untimely death put paid to that arrangement. Perhaps at one point Boyle felt it his duty to marry, though, according to Pilkington, he felt that he would never be able to fulfil the duty of a husband adequately. Wooing women did not come easy to Boyle, and involved him putting on 'appearances', as his sister Katherine put it, which suggests a certain artificiality. This was the case in his courtship of one lady, whom John Evelyn called 'the beautiful and ingenious daughter of Cary, Earl of Monmouth'. Details are sketchy, but their courtship appeared to have been difficult, with the result that Boyle felt the pain of rejection when she married someone else. At the time, his sister Katherine consoled him with the words:

> You are now very near the hour wherein your mistress is, by giving herself to another, to set you at liberty from all the appearances you have put on of being a lover; which, though they cost you some pains and use of art, were easier because they were but appearances.

It is possible that Boyle idealised women and found none who could meet his exalted standards of womanhood. According to Pilkington, Boyle kept the emotion of love at arm's length. Furthermore, his siblings' marriages – often bad ones – did little to stop Boyle thinking about the travesty of married love. By his own admission, he felt that he had no capacity for love. In reply to a letter from his niece Lady Barrymore, who erroneously believed he had married, he wrote: 'But though this untamed heart be thus insensible to the thing itself called love, it is yet very accessible to things very near of kin to that passion; . . . esteem, friendship, respect, and even admiration.' Boyle took the letter in the spirit in which it was intended and was not offended. In all likelihood, Boyle had major problems in intimate social relationships. You could say that marriage was an impossible emotional hurdle for him.

The notorious celibacy of the Father of Chemistry is well documented and possibly had a religious basis too. A trip to a famous Florentine brothel in the company of his tutor Marcombes to witness the seedier side of life was ultimately repellent for him. Boyle did not partake in the activities on offer, and an aversion to sex followed. As far as can be ascertained, there is no evidence that Boyle was homosexual. In *Philaretus*, he relates an incident where he was attacked by homosexual friars on a visit to Rome in 1641. Clearly not welcoming their advances, he made good his escape, but his disgust was evident: he referred to them as 'sodomites'. In his decision to put God before marriage, Boyle effectively turned himself into a secular monk. It was noted by Bishop Burnet that Boyle was still a virgin in middle age. Indeed, Boyle does come across as asexual or androgynous.

Boyle, like Hamilton, was very much at ease in the company of older, matronly figures, who lavished care and affection on him. In particular he relished the companionship of his sister, Katherine, Countess Ranelagh – who was fifteen years his senior – and a particularly close friendship developed. Soon after his father died, Katherine essentially took over the parental role and mothered, advised and supported Boyle in all manner of ways. As well as providing a home for him, she also engaged him on an intellectual level. She was endowed with considerable intelligence, great wit and a prodigious memory herself. In addition, she had substantial influence among certain members of the Commonwealth parliament. Salons were held in her house in London for the benefit of the Invisible College and later the Royal Society. Boyle and Katherine shared a home together for more than twenty years, and he died, aged sixty-four, a week after her death. Many of his theological writings were dedicated to her, as 'Sophronia'. Pilkington writes about her:

> Throughout half a century she was his continual support, his confiden-tial adviser, and a person who fulfilled for him the role of the mother he had never known, and to a very great extent that of the wife he was never to have. Indeed, if Robert Boyle never came very near to marriage, it may well have been because no other woman could easily equal Katherine in his esteem or supplant the deep and lasting affection which he had for her.

Another sister, Mary, Countess of Warwick, shared many of Boyle's interests, and in character they were similar too. Not surprisingly, given the pious nature of the family, she was renowned for her remarkable spir-itual diary and book of spiritual meditations, which were highly popular in their day. Like Boyle, Mary had an independent and determined streak: she insisted on marrying the man she loved, despite being ostracised by her father and family for her actions.

*

Much is known today about Boyle's contributions to chemistry but little about his passionate and extensive writings on religion – and, somewhat incongruously, given the character of the man, on the nature of love. Indeed, Boyle lived during one of the greatest periods of religious and political upheaval in England. Aside from the political issues they involved, the English Civil Wars of the mid-seventeenth century pitted conformists, representing the established church, against non-conformist Puritans.

In the years before he was actively engaged in science, Boyle wrote numerous reflections on God and love. The final decades of his life also saw him produce more works on philosophy and theology, based on ideas that had been germinating in his mind over a period of many years: *Things Above Reason* (1681), *Christian Virtuoso* (1690), *Excellency of Theology, Compar'd with Natural Philosophy* (1674) and the important *Free Enquiry into the Vulgarly Receiv'd Notion of Nature* (1686). The period in which Boyle lived was certainly one in which religion permeated every facet of society – from politics to academia. He was reared an Anglican, as was his father, who had a fervent distaste of Roman Catholicism which he managed to instil in his favourite son. Despite being surrounded by religious turmoil, Boyle remained faithful to Anglicanism, even though he was sympathetic to the Puritans in some respects. Indeed, Boyle was so unwavering in his faith that Pilkington describes him as 'a rock amid the shifting sands'.

By today's standards – though not by those of the seventeenth century – both father and son had a puritan cast of mind. Canny writes that the Earl was 'by disposition a pious man' who remained 'steadfast in these principles' – like his son. Records show that the Earl was devout by nature. His diary and correspondence regularly refer to his spiritual reading material, mostly the Bible. In practice, he was generous, giving dowries, endowing free schools and alms houses, supporting preachers on his estates and building churches, defensible castles and bridges. Ever the pragmatic opportunist, the Earl was opposed to centralised control in ecclesiastical affairs and in favour of local control, but would never acknowledge this publicly. According to Richard Canny in *The Upstart Earl*:

The self-image cultivated by Boyle was that of the virtuous man, free from ambition, whose wealth and possessions had come to him almost by default, and which he cherished only insofar as they could be employed to honour God, serve his king, strengthen the commonwealth and enhance the reputation of his family and posterity.

Boyle's personal piety as a scientist in the service of God is at the heart of his writings. Science historian Michael Hunter notes that Boyle's 'deep theism informs his outlook in natural philosophy, as in life in general; in addition, it may be argued that the obsessiveness which he showed in his pursuit of his goals grew directly out of the religious imperatives which dominated his life.' He keenly felt God's boundless love in the world and he expressed forthright views on the subject in his work *Seraphick Love*. Married love was possible, he believed, but the highest degree of love could only be reserved for God. In fact, he rather distrusted married love if it was not constant. No doubt the experiences of his siblings coloured his view in this regard – several of their marriages had been miserable failures. Moreover, spiritual values, he felt, were the only safeguard in times of strife. In an age of tyranny and social disintegration, the effect of *Seraphick Love* on his colleagues and the public at large was uplifting, and the book went through six editions in Boyle's lifetime.

Boyle's religious writings are also imbued with a spirit of tolerance that was sorely lacking in an age of religious dissent, bigotry and intolerance. As well as studying the Christian scriptures in depth, he examined the teachings of the Muslim and Jewish faiths, which he balanced against the dogmas of Roman Catholicism and Protestantism. Boyle genuinely tried to improve the lot of humanity: this inevitably included spreading the Gospel. The Bible, he believed, should be available for all races, and hence translating it into languages other than modern European ones became a pet project of his. As the years progressed, his missionary zeal came more to the fore, and in 1660 he was appointed governor of the Society for the Propagation of the Gospel in New England. He was responsible for financing the translation and publication of the Bible into Malay, Turkish, Welsh, Irish and the Native American language of the Massachusetts Indian tribes. The Irish version, which was intended for the Scottish Gaelic, reputedly was not popular because the Roman alphabet had been used instead of the Gaelic one.

Boyle's interest in religion and the supernatural also extended to superstition. Having been exposed to a few near-fatal accidents in his youth – he was flung from horses and rescued from torrential floods – he was convinced that destiny, or Providence, played a decisive hand in shaping his life. In *Philaretus,* he admits that 'he was the object of Heaven's care'. By all accounts, he was preoccupied with the belief that certain days of the week brought either good or bad luck: May Day, which he called a 'day fatality', was particularly foreboding. Persons with Asperger's syndrome can be quite superstitious and have difficulty separating fact from fiction. In fact, a deep ambiguity often exists for these seemingly 'rational' people: they can be extraordinarily scientific on the one hand, yet fascinated by alchemy and magic, and overcome by all sorts of irrational fears, on the other. Many writers refer to Boyle's ambivalent attitude to magic, whereby he was fascinated with stories of people who had made contact with supernatural beings. However, Boyle tried to avoid conducting any experiments involving magic.

*

It is little wonder, given the extent of Boyle's religious devotion, that he had a rigid sense of right and wrong, especially when it came to what he perceived to be his duty. This has all the characteristics of an Asperger or autistic superego – which in Boyle's case was indeed harsh. Boyle never wavered in his sense of duty to God, and he could be described as a 'lay bishop', even though he never took holy orders. By all accounts, he never swore or blasphemed, and he would pause each time before he mentioned the name of God. Indeed, he was utterly inflexible on this point: when he was elected president of the Royal Society, he turned down the position because he objected to the use of God's name in the formal oath of office. Today, he comes across as a prudish and straitlaced figure who probably exasperated colleagues and associates. Certainly as a boy he was odd in that there was no typical childhood naughtiness, only traces of a stubborn streak. The devotion to duty, moral rectitude and altruism was also found in his mother's side of the family – the Fentons – in particular Boyle's grandmother Lady Alice Fenton and her father Robert Weston, a Lord Justice and Chancellor of Ireland from 1567 to 1573.

In all his dealings, Boyle was 'utterly, transparently honest', according to Pilkington. This absolute honesty is certainly characteristic of Asperger's syndrome. Needless to say, having such a strict conscience meant that he was often plagued by shame and guilt. He was so virtuous and disciplined that he reputedly never told a lie. In *Philaretus,* Boyle elaborates on the virtue of truth and how the vice of lying went against his nature:

> This studiousness observed in Philaretus endeared him very much unto his Father; who used (highly) to commend him both for it and his Veracity: of which (latter) he would often give him this Testimony; that he never found him in a Lye in all his Life time. And indeed Lying was a Vice both so contrary to his nature and so inconsistent with his Principles that, as there was scarce anything he more greedily desired then to know the Truth, so was there scarce anything he more perfectly detested than not to speak it.

In his aversion to war, his moral rectitude also comes to the fore. Despite his father's pleading for him to join the Prince of Orange in Holland if Ireland was overrun by rebels, Boyle could never conceive of becoming a soldier. Enlisting in the army of Charles I was equally distasteful to him, not only for the 'low life' it included in its ranks but also for the destruction and death wrought by war. Indeed, an aversion to armies and conscription is often found in those with Asperger's syndrome. In the face of calamity, whether family misfortune, death or illness, Boyle faced the world with a remarkable stoicism. Indeed, this stoic quality was rooted in Protestant moral balance, self-control and piety.

In 1662, Boyle's conscience was certainly troubled with Charles II's decision to make the esteemed scientist the beneficiary of income from various former monastic lands in Ireland. This decision, according to John Young, left Boyle worrying for the rest of his life about its moral legitimacy. To assuage his conscience somewhat, he devoted the entire revenue to the support of Protestant Irish clergy and missionary work in North America.

In terms of his lifestyle, the modest Boyle had no time for pomp or ceremony and chose to live simply. Indeed, his self-care bordered on neglect at times. One friend described the simplicity of his life: 'In his diet (as in his habit) he was extremely temperate and plain; nor could I ever discern in him the least passion, transport or censoriousness, whatever discourse or the times suggested . . . [he was] easy, serious, discreet and profitable'. Ever mindful of the afterlife, Boyle requested that there be no unnecessary pomp at his funeral. All his life he objected to great ceremony or any excess, believing it to be a monumental waste of money that could be better spent on the relief of poverty. There was always something decidedly distasteful to him about excessive private interests and what he saw as the loose morality of the day.

At Boyle's funeral in 1691, Gilbert Burnet, Bishop of Salisbury, delivered the eulogy and described a man 'of a most spotless and extemporary life in all respects. He was highly charitable and was a mortified and self-denied man, that delighted in nothing so much as in doing good. He neglected his person, despised the world, and lived abstracted from all pleasures, designs or interest.' In his youth, Boyle had something of a temper, but under the tutelage of Marcombes – who had a much greater temper – he was forced to exercise a little self-discipline. Indeed, all his life Boyle strove to control his temper when faced with all manner of grievances. There is little to suggest that he was highly controlling or manipulative. In fact, he was broad-minded and liberal, moving science away from its previous secrecy and isolation. Furthermore, Maddison writes how Boyle was always perfectly frank in imparting what he had learned, or discovered, to the public. However, other critics condemned him for being 'too open and credulous and giving too much heat to the relations of his informers in philosophical matters'. This openness, while admirable, might also be read as a certain naivety on Boyle's part – a trait seen too in those with Asperger's syndrome.

In comparison with other Asperger geniuses, Boyle took criticism of his work reasonably well. *Spring of the Air* in particular was attacked by such leading natural philosophers as Thomas Hobbes, Francis Linus and Anthony Deusing. In response, Boyle refuted their arguments calmly and methodically. Unquestionably, he was hostile to any view that did not recognise God's power in the universe or any premature system-building, like Aristotle's.

*

The range of Boyle's occupations is impressive – chemist, alchemist, naturalist, linguist, religious devotee and writer – and points to a restless, searching mind. Moreover, his need to sustain a coherent self-identity and his insecurity suggest that he experienced a degree of identity diffusion, widely seen in Asperger's syndrome. As a writer, he experimented with a variety of genres, from essays, treatises, reflections and romances, and on a wide range of topics, but generally on moral and religious themes. His

145

literary writings were not obscure, either. *The Martyrdom of Theodora and of Didymus* became the basis for Handel's opera *Theodora,* while *Reflection upon the Eating of Oysters* was the alleged inspiration for Swift's *Gulliver's Travels.* In *A Pious Meditation upon a Broom Stick,* the satirist Swift also ridiculed Boyle's earnest and pious *Occasional Reflections upon Several Subjects.*

Clearly, Boyle's early life had some bearing on his self-identity and emotional immaturity. The fact that there was considerable parental absence and that he had little or no bonding with his mother gave him a quasi-orphan status, and the sense of insecurity and abandonment that Boyle experienced during his teenage years was compounded by a crisis of faith and the loss of his much-loved father. Boyle speaks of himself during those teenage years, in the persona of Philaretus, in an extremely distant way, as though that person was different altogether from himself. All the insecurities of adolescence clearly collided, and coincided with a period of deep religious crisis for him. Once Boyle had fully embraced Christianity, however, his faith seems to have brought greater security and comfort to him and, more crucially, to have provided a direction in life from which he never wavered.

Indeed, the Earl's mission to 'make himself' in Ireland is the classic search for a self-identity, with a desire for public recognition and an obsession with lineage, given his humble origins. When Boyle came to write a reflective autobiography – in itself an innovative and novel enterprise for the time – he had no preoccupation with lineage, which was unusual, given the custom of the period. He routinely declined positions of power, though many offers came from distinguished quarters. Not for him president of the Royal Society, provost of Eton College, a peerage, a college fellowship or a bishopric. Other than the title of 'Honourable' which he was born with, the only other title he took was Doctor of Physics at Oxford in 1665. His interest in alchemy and the secrecy with which it was conducted in medieval times lent credence to rumours that Boyle and Newton were freemasons. However, there is no evidence to support this view of Boyle. Being apolitical, the issue of national identity or nationality does not seem to have figured strongly with him either. He had no emotional ties to Ireland and did not consider himself to be Irish, and especially had no desire to speak Irish, despite his obvious linguistic skills. In fact, its dearth of scientific circles and the difficulty in procuring chemical instruments made Boyle refer to Ireland as 'a barbarous country'.

*

From the many accounts of Boyle's life and his correspondence, he did not enjoy good health and was far from robust. There is much evidence to suggest that he had considerable sensory impairments too. He was frequently described as sickly or feeble, and by the end of his days he was quite emaciated. He had an endless litany of complaints, from agues (fevers, chills or rigors) to kidney stones and palsy. There is no knowing what toxic substances Boyle might have used in his experiments, which may have given rise to ill-health too. The frequent attacks of palsy were, according to one letter cited by Maddison, 'contracted, I fear, not a little by his often attendance on chemical operations'. Furthermore, Boyle self-medicated on a regular basis and was renowned as a prescriber. Given the increasing recurrence of 'distempers' (infectious diseases, possibly scarlet fever), he grew almost paranoid of infection, particularly viral ones such as smallpox and chickenpox. As a consequence, he would not allow anyone who had been in recent contact with these illnesses near him. From his time at Eton until his old age, Boyle had considerable gastrointestinal complaints and sensitivity or allergies to various kinds of food. This is not uncommon: leaky gut syndrome has been associated with autism in recent years. To minimise his gastrointestinal disturbances, Boyle rigidly adhered to a diet of plain food and refrained from any indulgence. Indeed, he was fastidious about his food and would prefer to fast rather than eat something he disliked. This may also indicate that he had hypersensitivities where taste and texture was concerned. His diary reveals that, in adolescence, he abstained from sweets and confectionery and was not partial to fruit. Clearly, he could be a hypochondriac and showed multiple somatic complaints, which also occurs in people with Asperger's syndrome.

In 1654, Boyle suffered a debilitating illness after a fall from a horse in Ireland; while still not fully recovered from the fall, he was forced to make a long journey in inclement weather. Afterwards, he suffered from recurrent attacks of 'anasarka' or 'dropsy', old-fashioned terms for oedema or swelling associated with a variety of causes. In addition, he was badly bruised, and his eyesight was permanently impaired. (He was already short-sighted and prone to eye infections.) Judging by his eye symptoms, it is possible that he had a detached retina and cataracts in the last years of his life. His night-time vision was poor, he had floaters – dark or grey spots within his field of vision – and 'something' seemed to 'fall slowly down'. Clearly, to judge from the various accounts, he suffered from photophobia or experienced some hypersensitivity to light. In his writings, he mentions how gazing at firelight, even candlelight, was painful for his eyes. So debilitating was his sight that Boyle became dependent on assistants to read and write for him, much like Joyce and de Valera. Around this time, he also had scurvy, or the 'scorbutic disaffections', as they were then called. Earlier, in 1670, he suffered a stroke, but encouraged others to help in his rehabilitation – getting them to perform passive exercises or physiotherapy on his arms and hands. He seemed to make enough of a recovery to continue his experiments and writings, but the weakness and semi-paralysis continued: the surgeon James Yonge noted in a visit in 1687 that he found Boyle 'a thin man, weak in his hands and feet, almost to a paresis.'

It is difficult to say whether Boyle had any hypersensitivities where his sense of hearing was concerned, but he did have a deep appreciation of music, as an expression of pure spirit. Indeed, Maddison claims that Boyle was good at music and singing, even though Boyle himself claimed that he had a 'bad' singing voice. It is not known whether he played a musical instrument, but the lute certainly appealed to him. Although there is no suggestion that he was hypersensitive to sound, his work featured the theory and transmission of music and sound from a scientific perspective.

Boyle's mental health has also come in for some scrutiny. In adolescence, he suffered from depression, especially at Eton. As an overly sensitive young man, and given all the upheavals in his young life and constant ill-health, this comes as no surprise. The depression clearly was severe enough that he considered suicide several times, but the guilt of committing such a sin prevented him from carrying through any such action. Indeed, those with Asperger's syndrome tend to get depressed or despondent easily and can have suicidal thoughts, especially in their youth.

Some biographers, like Pilkington, believe that Boyle had a persistent fear of death – something that is understandable, given the high mortality rates of the time and the early deaths of his mother and some siblings. He clearly had a paranoia or aversion to extremes of temperature – particularly cold, inclement weather – and kept a range of cloaks to wear, according to the temperature of the day. Religiously, he checked the temperature each day using a thermometer. Naturally, this lent an even greater air of eccentricity to him. In her maternal way, his sister Katherine scouted for suitable lodgings for her brother in 1654 before his move to Oxford and reported back that she had found 'the warmest room', to put his mind at ease.

There is little evidence as to whether Boyle had motor clumsiness or not. Fine motor control was evident from how well he mastered handwriting at a young age. At Eton, he loathed sports, and his tutor John Harrison had to practically force him to play games. While in Geneva, he learned how to fence and play tennis, and he enjoyed them both, which might suggest some proficiency in them. He also learned how to dance, but he detested this activity – which might suggest a lack of co-ordination and rhythm. Numerous accidents with horses in his youth might indicate that he was not skilled in horsemanship, or alternatively problems with balance and proprioception. It is clear that he had an deep affinity for animals: his companion for many years was his favourite dog, a spaniel.

*

Unlike Hamilton, Boyle did not place an inordinate significance on the imagination. As a scientist, he was principally interested in fact and demonstrating it by experiment. The imagination, he believed, was solely concerned with forming images in the brain after it had passed through the cognitive system. Nonetheless, Boyle had been a dreamy youngster, preoccupied with legendary romances of heroes and heroines, but apart from a few boyhood verses in French or Latin and some 'amorous, merry and devout ones' in English, he was not a man to let the muses flow. Any poetry he wrote as a youth he subsequently burned. Nonetheless, the hallmark of the Asperger genius was evident in Boyle in his innate and endless search for universal truth and simplicity. His friend the diarist John Evelyn observed that he was:

> A great and happy analyser, addicted to no particular sect, but as became a generous and free philosopher, preferring truth above all; in a word, a person of that singular candour and worth, that would draw a just character of him one must run through all the virtues, as well as through all the sciences.

With his innate capacity for analysis, Boyle's genius lay in creating the foundations of science – foundations which have stood the test of time.

149

WILLIAM ROWAN HAMILTON

On earth there is nothing great but man; in man there is nothing great but mind.

WILLIAM ROWAN HAMILTON, *Lectures on Metaphysics*

William Rowan Hamilton was the greatest Irish mathematical genius of all time and has been dubbed 'the Irish Einstein'. In 1865, having been voted the greatest living scientist by the newly established National Academy of Sciences in the United States, he was elected their first Foreign Associate. In his lifetime, he made major scientific contributions to geometry, optics and mechanics and changed fundamental views of algebra, which in turn spawned new fields of study, such as hypercomplex numbers, vector analysis and linear vector space. With his general theory of dynamics, he was able to describe any optical or dynamical system by means of a single or characteristic function; this function became the cornerstone of modern physics and entered the scientific lexicon as 'the Hamiltonian'. A man clearly before his time, his theories had their greatest impact in the twentieth century. He inspired Einstein in the field of relativity; Erwin Schrödinger in the field of quantum mechanics and Murray Gell-Mann, who discovered the smallest subatomic particle, the 'quark' (a term that Gell-Mann, a devotee of Joyce, took from a line in *Finnegans Wake*).

Hamilton is perhaps best remembered today for his formula of quaternions, discovered in 1843, which became a cornerstone of algebraic equations. Quaternions are now widely used in computer graphics, simulations, computer games, iPods, global positioning systems and space travel. Indeed, when the Mars Exploration Rover landed on the planet in 2004, the computer graphics beamed back to the Jet Propulsion Laboratory in Pasadena were based on quarternions. Hollywood too has benefited from Hamilton's creative genius: quarternions make it possible for the likes of Lara Croft to leap onto cliff ledges and Keanu Reeves to destroy the computer-simulated Earth in *The Matrix*.

Beyond doubt, Hamilton is a superb example of the Asperger genius. What set him apart from his contemporaries was an extraordinary intelligence, an acute poetic imagination and hyperperception. Into the bargain, he was a wildly eccentric man.

*

In appearance, Hamilton is described as being of medium height and broad-chested. His eyes, like those of many geniuses, were blue and his hair brown. There was a certain symmetry to his face that gave him a handsome look. Again, like many geniuses, his face at times could be transfused with a radiance or charm that was arresting for anyone who entered the room he was in.

Born on 4 August 1805 to Archibald Hamilton, a solicitor, and Sarah Hutton, William Rowan Hamilton spent the first few years of his life in Dominick Street, Dublin. Within a year of his birth, his mother was able to report that he 'walks quite stoutly now'. Due to precarious family fortunes, the two-year-old toddler was sent to live with his uncle James, an Anglican curate at Trim, County Meath, who was also schoolmaster of the Church of Ireland Diocesan School. Correspondence between various family members reveals that Hamilton was a hyperactive child: he seemed never to stop playing and jumping about. He especially liked noise and would try to beat time on a drum and would rock his head when marching.

Clearly, Hamilton experienced no language delay. His uncle James was an innovative educationalist, if not a prescient speech and language therapist by today's standards, who devised a spelling system which made the acquisition of language easier. First, he combed dictionaries and spelling books for monosyllabic words in which the letter 'a' occurs. After Hamilton had mastered this, he moved on to 'b', and so on through the alphabet. When all monosyllabic words had been covered, he moved on to words of two syllables, then three, and so on. This method of learning, which was largely logical and systematic, clearly suited Hamilton, as indeed it would for many with autistic spectrum disorders.

It soon became apparent that Hamilton was a child prodigy with an astonishing command of languages: he reputedly knew thirteen. With the aid of his uncle James, who had distinguished himself in Classics at Trinity College Dublin, Hamilton was reading the Bible in English by the age of three. He had also mastered Hebrew as a toddler, followed by Latin and Greek. Needless to say, he acquired modern European languages, such as French and Italian, effortlessly. Legend has it that his linguistic ability was so astonishing that, by the age of ten, he could speak several Oriental languages, including Persian, Arabic, Sanskrit, Chaldee, Syriac, Hindostanee, Malay, Mahratta and Bengali. In *William Rowan Hamilton: Portrait of a Prodigy,* however, Seán O'Donnell disputes Hamilton's proficiency in these languages and argues that his father had made exaggerated claims. Hamilton probably had an elementary knowledge of these languages but did not speak them with any degree of fluency. Indeed, in later years Hamilton had difficulty conversing in French with a visiting Italian astronomer. By his own admission, he found 'facility and pleasure in acquiring foreign languages so far as to read them; but not in learning to speak or write them.' Whether Hamilton ever learnt Irish or not is unknown.

Hamilton's voice had great variations in pitch, which commonly occurs with Asperger's syndrome. His friend and biographer Robert Perceval Graves, in *Life of Sir William Rowan Hamilton,* describes his voice as alternating between rich, sonorous and rhythmical when speaking in public and high-pitched when he was happy and cheerful. Indeed, his sister Eliza referred to it as his 'ventriloquist-like voice'.

As is frequently seen in those with Asperger's syndrome, Hamilton's learning often came across as pedantic – with people judging him to be an obnoxious show-off. This was also reflected in his manner of speech, which could be stilted and artificial at times. For example, he would complain about getting up early – reputedly at 5 AM – and grumble in heavily formal poetic speech, which was entirely inappropriate for the situation.

When writing to his mother, his aunt Sydney would recount her nephew's exact words: 'Though Diana had long withdrawn her pale light, yet that Aurora had scarce unbarred her gates, and therefore he begged to be allowed to lie still.' In addition, Hamilton's letters to his father were 'unnaturally formal and stilted', according to Thomas L. Hankins, writing in *Sir William Rowan Hamilton*.

Hamilton also had a tendency to deliver monologues. In his uncle's home, Hamilton did not reserve his 'prattle' for family or acquaintances but launched forth on anyone within his radar, such as Reilly the cabman and Fotterell the blacksmith. Not surprisingly, Hamilton showed considerable skills as an orator later. In his professional life, he was renowned as a scientific orator, particularly in the regular round of meetings of the British Association for the Advancement of Science. Clearly, like many with Asperger's syndrome, overblown rhetoric found its way into his speeches, which on occasions struck an adulatory tone. A letter from his friend the poet William Wordsworth, who had seen a copy of one of his speeches, came with the hope that his next speech would contain 'less flattery among the men of Science than appeared in that of the last year in Oxford'.

From his youth, Hamilton was an intense and early reader: he read the works of Dryden, Wilkie Collins, Milton and Homer with relative ease. His imagination ablaze with heroes, he would act out scenes from classical literature, such as the Trojan War. Further more, his phenomenal memory meant that he had a good grasp of geography by the age of four.

*

The first stirrings of mathematical genius came before Hamilton was six years old. His aunt Sydney reported that 'you would find it difficult to puzzle him in addition and multiplication; but even in that he must go some strange way unless he is fought with'. Like many geniuses, he reputedly did not favour traditional methods of computing and instead formulated his own. His skill in computation was recognised early on by his uncle James, who brought the twelve-year-old Hamilton to Dublin to meet Zerah Colburn, the famous American 'calculating boy', who was a year older than Hamilton and who, like Hamilton, showed an extraordinary talent for languages. When aged seven, Zerah had reputedly taken six seconds to calculate the number of hours in thirty-eight years, two months and seven days. The two boys engaged in trials of arithmetical skill: although Colburn naturally came off the better each time, Hamilton acquitted himself well. According to the mathematician Andrew MacFarlane in a lecture on Hamilton he gave in 1901, published in *Lectures on Ten British Mathematicians of the Nineteenth Century,* these meetings gave Hamilton a definite taste for arithmetical computation, and for many years afterwards he loved to perform lengthy operations in his mind, extracting the square and cube root of a particular number, and solving problems that related to the properties of numbers. No calculation was too big or too small, too mundane or too bizarre for him: the volume of the Egyptian tomb at Edfu or the velocity of Christ's ascension into the heavens!

Before the age of thirteen, Hamilton had little formal education in mathematics. Like many geniuses, much of his learning was autodidactic. Around this time, he began reading the eighteen-century French mathematician Clairaut's *Algebra* and composed for himself 'A Compendious Treatise of Algebra', which set down his new knowledge. At the age of sixteen, he studied differential calculus with the aid of a French textbook and began to read one of the leading mathematicians of the day, Laplace, who was known for his mechanical, deterministic view of the world. Not only could the young Hamilton comprehend Laplace's work, *Mécanique céleste,* but he could also identify flaws in the reasoning of the celebrated mathematician.

Rather bizarrely, Hamilton began attending Trinity College examinations – which were conducted in public in those days – four years before he actually entered the university, so that he would be as well prepared for them as possible. By this time, Hamilton could read mathematical treatises the way one reads a novel. His enquiring mind meant that he did not tend to follow the well-worn path either. In his preparation for the entrance examinations to Trinity College, he did not always read the books that were prescribed for the course of study but instead read widely outside the subject, predominantly the mathematical works of the French École Polytechnique. At the time, the French were the leading lights in pure and applied mathematics, and Trinity College was in the process of revising its mathematical curriculum, moving away from the theories of Newton and other British mathematicians towards the work of Continental thinkers.

At the age of eighteen, Hamilton entered Trinity College, which gave equal weight to the study of Classics and mathematics. His time at university was truly outstanding and unrivalled. In his first year there, he won a rare honour, *optime* (the very highest distinction), in an examination on Homer. In his second year, he was awarded two Gold Medals, one for a distinction in Classics, the other in mathematics. Eventually, his belief that he could add something new to the field made mathematics an obvious choice over the classics. Furthermore, his sheer enthusiasm and burning ambition to become a great mathematician propelled him ever onwards. In his third year, he added a distinction in mathematical physics to his credits, and the following year, 1827, he presented a paper on 'Theory of Systems of Rays' to the Royal Irish Academy. In a ground-breaking contribution to science, he applied algebra to the geometry of light (optics), and his findings were subsequently published in *Transactions,* the proceedings of the Society. This quickly brought him to the attention of Dr John Brinkley, the Royal Astronomer, on whom the young genius made a favourable impression. Indeed, so impressed was the eminent astronomer with Hamilton that when he resigned his post to become Bishop of Cloyne, Hamilton was duly appointed to his position, despite stiff competition from several College Fellows. Hamilton was then not yet twenty-two years of age.

At the age of twenty-seven, in 1832, Hamilton followed up this work with a theory which predicted the phenomenon of conical refraction. This was a highly original discovery in geometrical optics which claimed that, under certain conditions, a single ray of light that fell on a biaxial crystal would be broken up into a cone of rays and, similarly, that a single emergent ray would appear as a cone of rays. Within two months of his prediction, his colleague Professor Humphrey Lloyd dramatically verified it at Trinity College.

The business of abstracting and generalising was always far more important for Hamilton than practical results. He explained this in a letter to his friend, the poet and philosopher Samuel Taylor Coleridge:

My aim has been, not to discover new phenomenon, nor to improve the construction of optical instruments, but with the help of the Differential or Fluxional Calculus to remould the geometry of Light by establishing one uniform method for the solution of all problems in that science, deduced from the contemplation of one central or characteris-

tic relation . . . my chief desire and direct aim being to introduce harmony and unity into the contemplations and reasonings of Optics, considered as a portion of pure Science. It has not even been necessary, for the
formulation of my general method, that I should adopt any particular
opinion respecting the nature of light.

Hamilton then began to apply his new approach to the dynamics of
moving bodies. He held fast to the belief that light was transmitted in
undulations or waves, but believed that this was a mechanical problem to
be solved. This led to one of his greatest achievements – the general theory of dynamics, developed in 1834. Here he was able to describe any
optical or dynamical system by means of a single or characteristic function; this became known as the Hamilton Principle or 'Hamiltonian' and
became the cornerstone of modern physics. In effect, it was the most
general method known for describing the motion of a system of particles.
By establishing an analogy between optics and dynamics, Hamilton created an entirely new abstract theory of mechanics and cleared the way for
others to devise new experiments. His method of dynamics was to influence Einstein's work on relativity and the development of quantum
mechanics in Erwin Schrödinger's work nearly a century later. Hamilton
essentially rewrote Newton's Laws of Motion in a powerful, general way
by expressing the energy of mechanical systems as special variables.

Another of Hamilton's contributions to mathematics was his idea that
algebra is the science of pure time. Indeed, he also believed that geometry was the science of pure space. Under the influence of such philosophers as Immanuel Kant, he believed that an understanding of pure
(abstract) space and time was only possible through *a priori* knowledge –
i.e. that which is intuitive. Hitherto, no mathematician had been able to
adequately explain imaginary numbers – the square roots of negative
numbers, which do not exist. In fact, algebra failed to explain what hap-
pened when you subtracted a larger quantity from a smaller quantity and
got a negative number or an imaginary number. With his metaphysical
outlook, Hamilton was thus able to change the view of algebra as dealing
only with natural numbers or the science of quantity (+1, +2, +3, etc.).
To overcome this problem, he invented algebraic couples, which are complex numbers given as ordered pairs of real numbers. The result of this
was that negative and imaginary numbers became valid. The important
thing for Hamilton was that the symbols of algebra had to represent

something real – not in the sense of a material object in the physical world, but as a mental construct.

This led in 1843 to Hamilton discovering a new mathematical language, quaternions. This was a method of describing rotations in four dimensions. Quaternions are quite hard to grasp as a concept because of their highly abstract nature. A quaternion consists of four parts, one of which is real (time), and the other three are imaginary (space). In effect, the quaternion is a set of vectors which are mathematical objects that have magnitude and direction. Hamilton described it as follows:

> Time is said to have only one dimension, and space to have three dimensions. . . . The mathematical quaternion partakes of both these elements; in technical language it may be said to be 'time plus space', or 'space plus time': and in this sense it has, or at least involves a reference to, four dimensions.

Because Hamilton was not primarily concerned with solving practical problems in science, ideas could gestate for years before a solution presented itself. The ideas surrounding quaternions engaged his mind for fifteen years. The discovery in 1843 came in a flash of inspiration, which Hamilton explained to one of his sons.

> On the 16th day of October, which happened to be a Monday, and Council day of the Royal Irish Academy, I was walking in to attend and preside, and your mother was walking with me along the Royal Canal, to which she had perhaps driven; and although she talked with me now and then, yet an undercurrent of thought was going on in my mind, which gave at last a result, whereof it is not too much to say that I felt at once the importance. An electric circuit seemed to close; and a spark flashed forth, the herald (as I foresaw immediately) of many long years to come of definitely directed thought and work, by myself if spared, and at all events on the part of others, if I should even be allowed to live long enough distinctly to communicate the discovery.

The breakthrough for Hamilton was also that the quaternion formula had integrity: mathematically, it was possible for quaternions to be added, subtracted, multiplied and divided. The real value of quaternions was not that they were a method of calculation but that they were a way of representing physical entities in space: they were perfect for devising virtual-reality scenarios. In essence, Hamilton saw geometry as the language of the abstract world – how space could be expressed. Though he received much credit for the discovery at the time, quaternions became more fully applicable in the twentieth century with the advent of radio, television and radar. Indeed, in 1943, on the centenary of the discovery of quarternions, Éamon de Valera as Taoiseach had a commemorative stamp issued to show the high esteem in which he held Hamilton.

In the latter part of his career, in 1846, a method of describing planetary orbits was also introduced by Hamilton, which was a valuable contribution to astronomy. The intense, narrow focus of his interests meant that he progressed rapidly in his career: from brilliant student to professor of astronomy at Trinity College, Astronomer Royal, distinguished member of the British Association for the Advancement of Science and president of the Royal Irish Academy, and a knighthood in 1835. A perennial criticism of both contemporaries and biographers was that had he been more willing to give room to physical experiment, his work might have been more fruitful. History has recorded otherwise, however.

*

Hamilton had an overriding love of pure mathematics: for the abstract and the ideal. This coloured and tempered the way he looked at the world and his approach to mathematics, and it goes to the heart of the Asperger genius. Their visions are classically linked to a higher order of knowledge characterised by truth, beauty, simplicity, harmony and unity. Moreover, there is an integrity and timelessness to their ideas or discoveries. For Hamilton to write about anything, it had to be real in his imagination first, regardless of whether it existed in nature or not. In effect, the way he did mathematics was by visualising it or seeing it as pictures.

During the 1830s, Hamilton made a thorough study of natural philosophy, as the science of nature was then called. In his views on natural philosophy, he was influenced by many thinkers, in particular Kant, Wordsworth and Coleridge. These men were borne out of a tradition of German Idealism that had spawned the Romantic movement, which was in its heyday during Hamilton's life. To Hamilton's mind, the language of mathematics and of poetry shared common values: both were creative and universal, and both had their own mysteries and moments of intense revelation. Hamilton's interest in Romanticism, however, was confined to the imagination and the metaphysical concepts of pure space and time. As an original thinker, he arrived at his own ideas independently. But they were reinforced when he became acquainted with Coleridge and read Kant's *Critique of Pure Reason,* in particular the following passage:

> Time and Space are, therefore, two sources of knowledge, from which bodies of various *a priori* synthetical knowledge can be derived. Pure mathematics is a brilliant example of such knowledge, especially as regards space and its relations. Time and Space, taken together, are the pure forms of all sensible intuition, and so are what makes *a priori* synthetic propositions possible.

In Hamilton's day, there were two conflicting views on how science should proceed. Should it be *a priori,* using deduction, where one reasons from the principle to the facts? This method is highly subjective, involving meditation on inner ideas of power, space and time; Hamilton's formula for quaternions was deduced in this way. Conversely, should it be *a posteriori,* using induction, where one reasons from the facts to the principle? This method was objective, immersed in the physical world, discovered by observation and the generalisation of facts. An example here is Newton's Laws of Motion. As we know today, both methods are necessary for the advancement of science, but the situation was not so clearcut in Hamilton's days.

Science that flowed from the imagination was the only kind of science that Wordsworth entertained, but Hamilton, though agreeing with his friend, found this view too narrow and limited. The imagination, he believed, should be broadened to include the intellect, so that mathematicians could express their vision or ideas in mathematical form. For his part, Coleridge believed that poetry flowed from the imagination while science was controlled by the intellect. This was strongly opposed by Hamilton, who passionately believed that the intellect stemmed from the imagination. Hankins sums up Hamilton's view of the imagination:

> Hamilton insisted that imagination should be expanded to include the *intellect,* a faculty integrally tied to the imagination and one that allowed man to rationalise his vision of harmony into the forms of mathematics. He insisted that truth, the goal of the mathematician, and beauty, the goal of the poet, represented two different views of the same structure. Truth, for Hamilton, was the self-consistency or consistency of an object with its place in the universe. Beauty was the fitness of an object

to excite tender emotion. The two were quite different, but had an intimate connection in nature.

In essence, Hamilton had a gift for pure mathematics and *a priori* knowledge was more real to him. His mind was consumed with abstractions. On the other hand, Boyle for example was very much an *a posteriori* scientist, where observable fact took precedence. Both were reacting to what was more real or immediate to them.

*

Hamilton's achievements came at a price: he was a workaholic. Referring to himself, he often quoted Ptolemy's description of the astronomer Hipparchus: 'He was a lover of labour and a lover of truth.' The love affair with labour and truth yielded 135 papers and two books. Moreover, lodged in the archives of Trinity College are at least six thousand letters concerning Hamilton, and 252 notebooks – or, as Seán O'Donnell has suggested, at least ten million words. Hamilton's fanatical devotion to work meant that he continually neglected himself. He once told Wordsworth that he had become 'most studious and hermit like'. Similarly, in a letter to his friend the Countess of Dunraven, he wrote that he was 'sitting up and getting up later than ever, and grown so much of a hermit that unless I find a pair of garden shears in some of my few visits to the garden, my beard, which already defies razors, will rival the chins of old philosophers'. To his friend Aubrey de Vere, he called his work 'a mathematical trance'.

Hamilton's attention to detail was phenomenally intense. He would endlessly write and rewrite papers, such as 'Theory of Systems of Rays', until he was content with them. Many of his drafts were undated and many others were committed to flames when they were not to his satisfaction. This clearly made it difficult for science historians to piece together the evolution of this thought. His system of note-taking and journal-writing can be dated from his time at university; he followed a pattern of almost religious devotion in this area. Hankins refers to the curious way in which he wrote in his journals, which has all the hallmarks of a repetitive, ritualised style – not unusual in the Asperger genius. It involved beginning at both ends of a notebook. First, he would write from the front, filling only the right-hand pages. Next, he would turn over the book and write from the back, again filling the right-hand pages. Hankins notes:

> He wrote incessantly, usually in notebooks of all sizes and shapes, but also on pieces of loose paper, particularly if he was drafting an article or lecture. He wrote on walks, in carriages, during meetings of the Royal Irish Academy, on his fingernails if no paper was handy, and, according to his son, even on his egg at breakfast. Occasionally he attempted to achieve some order in this mass of papers, but never with success. The papers flowed over the tables, onto the floor, and under the beds. On one occasion, when he was giving a large formal dinner, he had to clear the library. It took two days of solid effort, and even then the task was accomplished only by resorting to bags and baskets to contain all the papers.

Working in an ambience of chaos and disorder is rather typical of the Asperger genius. That said, there was a certain method in his madness: Hamilton could always tell if his papers had been in any way disturbed. Indeed, those with Asperger's syndrome have an enormous capacity to notice difference. Overall, Hamilton comes across as the stereotypical eccentric professor. Similarly, MacFarlane paints a bizarre picture of the total absorption of the genius at work:

> After Hamilton's death the dining room was found covered with huge piles of manuscript, with convenient walks between the piles; when these literary remains were wheeled out and examined, china plates with the relics of food upon them were found between the sheets of manuscript, plates sufficient in number to furnish a kitchen. He used to carry on, says his eldest son, long trains of algebraical and arithmetical calculations in his mind, during which he was unconscious of the earthly necessity of eating; 'we used to bring in a "snack" and leave it in his study, but a brief nod of recognition of the intrusion of the chop or cutlet was often the only result, and his thoughts went on soaring upwards.'

Hamilton's massive attention to detail meant that he would sometimes get bogged down in less important aspects of his work. In essence he lacked proportion – a quality shared by many Asperger geniuses. He failed to stand back from his work and see the big picture, pointing to a lack of central coherence on his part.

During his most productive years, the 1830s, Hamilton seemed to have infinite energy. His eight-year tenure as president of the Royal Irish Academy was marked with voluminous correspondence, which is typically seen in those with Asperger's syndrome. Moreover, with his prodigious memory he had a detailed knowledge of the Academy's affairs – more so than any other previous president, according to Hankins. Frequently, at a moment's notice, he could resolve any issue thanks to his superior knowledge of the regulations and precedents of the Academy.

*

Ingrained routines and rituals forged in youth continued throughout Hamilton's life. One of these was walking and rambling. As a youth living in Trim, Hamilton was an inveterate rambler and liked nothing more than to wander around the many medieval ruins and monuments in the town or along the banks of the Boyne. Walking was a habit easily combined with friendship, either with Wordsworth in the Lake District or with companions along the Royal Canal in Dublin. It was also a source of inspiration: he would often frantically scratch an equation on a leaf of ivy with a sharp stone or, as in the case of his discovery of quaternions, on the stones of Brougham Bridge in Cabra in Dublin. And when friends were not available, a book was a good substitute. In fact, in the manner of many geniuses, books were his constant companions and he took 'a sizeable library with him wherever he went', according to Hankins. That author notes that Hamilton was in the habit of taking long walks, always with a book in his pocket or 'sometimes even with a sack of books. At night the books accompanied him to his bedroom, where he slept among them and would wake and read at any hour.' This preoccupation with books, with reading, and with carrying a library around with them is typical of people with Asperger's syndrome. Needless to say, Hamilton's eccentricities prompted myriad tales. On one occasion, when visiting England, he stored a number of prized books in a pillowcase. While travelling on an open-top coach in Birmingham, the pillowcase fell open, with disastrous consequences. Hankins describes the scene: 'He caught Laplace's *Calculus of Probabilities* just as it was disappearing over the side of the coach, but Kant's *Critique* had already slipped away'.

*

Little is known about Hamilton's sense of humour, though it is clear that there was a playful side to his character and he had a great zest for life. We read about him in adulthood playing hoops in the observatory garden with his friend and biographer Robert Graves, and shooting over the weirs on the river at Adare Manor and jumping into the water fully clothed. He seems, like so many with Asperger's syndrome, to have revelled in inventive language too. According to Hankins, Hamilton was particularly fond of a book on mathematical mnemonics by Thomas Kirkman, a colleague of his at Trinity College. Through this playful verse, he delighted in remembering the rules of various functions in trigonometry. Moreover, he visited an old college classmate in October 1832 and they spent the time together in riotous rhyming and 'comic storytelling' – which lifted his mood enormously. The 'riotous rhyming' would seem to suggest that he enjoyed the kind of humour favoured by those with Asperger's syndrome: punning, wordplay and neologisms – especially simple humour. Hankins mentions a particular incident where Hamilton engaged in punning. Two colleagues of Hamilton's at Trinity, James MacCullagh and Humphrey Lloyd, who were on opposing sides of the argument in relation to the undulatory theory of light, nearly come to blows over the theory. Hamilton stepped into the breach with a joke to calm his colleagues: he 'hoped it would not be supposed that the wave men were wavering, or that the undulatory theory was at all undulatory in their minds'. Solving puzzles and conundrums with his colleague and friend Augustus de Morgan also gave him great pleasure.

Hamilton also loved games and developed a board game on the strength of an icosian calculus he had devised in 1856. On the board there was a graph of an icosahedron (a polyhedron with twenty faces). One player begins a path or circuit by inserting five pins or markers in any five consecutive edges and the other player is challenged to complete the circuit. The rules are such that every vertex is visited only once, no edge is visited twice, and the ending point is the same as the starting point. Much like the Rubik's cube in the early 1980s, the icosian game was more a puzzle than a game. Some claimed that it was too easy to solve, however, and it never became a commercial success.

*

In spite of Hamilton coming across as charming, courteous and personable, he had major difficulties interacting with others. When growing up in Trim, County Meath, there is little mention of him playing with other children other than his siblings and cousins. Indeed, he preferred the company of adults than his peers and could capably converse with them. Clearly he did not see the point of engaging in the normal play activities of childhood, despite the encouragement he received in this area from his uncle and aunt. Indeed, his aunt Sydney remarked that 'he could no more speak or play as children in general do, than he could fly. Everything he must have reason for.'.

A good deal of misbehaviour and mischief was also seen in the young Hamilton. Once he ripped loose some railings near the gate of Trim Castle and threw them into the adjoining courtyard. In his defence, he pleaded that his actions were 'to show in a metaphorical sense [the] horribleness' of having the railings in a state of disrepair. What passed for 'roguery' in the nineteenth century might possibly be read as challenging behaviour today! According to his aunt Sydney, 'he is a most sensible little creature, but at the same time he has a great deal of roguery about him. [Uncle] James does not let him much out for fear of his being spoiled by praise for he says he thinks that is the reason so few clever children grow up clever.' Clearly, James was the disciplinarian who kept the young prodigy in check.

Hamilton perceived his childhood in Trim as happy, despite his quasi-orphan status. The enormous desire for solitude so evident in many of those with Asperger's syndrome did not run deep in him. He clearly relished the peace and tranquillity of living in the area around Dunsink Observatory but preferred to have the house peopled nonetheless. In company of those of any age or social class, he could prattle on to the point of pomposity in long monologues – a feature of Asperger's syndrome. In later years, his addiction to work would take precedence over socialising. Particularly when working on his magnum opus, *Lectures in Quaternions,* and later *Elements of Quaternions,* he became reclusive, devoting more and more time to expounding his work. In so doing, he shunned the world and practical affairs, where body and soul were just about held together.

Nonetheless, during his time at Trinity College he was not short of companions. Again, as so often happens with people with remarkable minds, he became highly sought after on the social circuit. At the age of eighteen, he was introduced to the celebrated Edgeworths of Edgeworthstown, County Longford, in particular the novelist Maria Edgeworth, who was then perhaps the most famous female literary figure in the British Isles. She describes Hamilton as 'a real prodigy of talents' who was 'gentle and simple' in manner – something that is in keeping with the temperament of many geniuses. By all accounts, Maria, then aged fifty-six, had a talent for putting people at their ease and drawing them out of their shells: Hamilton's friendship with her blossomed and she became his confidante and adviser. It was the typical mother–son relationship found in those with Asperger's syndrome. Another older, motherly type of woman, Lady Guy Campbell, daughter of Lord Edward Fitzgerald, also later filled the role of confidante for Hamilton.

Through the Edgeworths, Hamilton found company that interested him, including that of T. Romney Robinson, the astronomer at Armagh, and Francis Beaufort, a hydrographer at the Admiralty in London and a member of the Royal Society. Through Maria, he was also able to meet and develop close friendships with Wordsworth and Coleridge, both of whom were to became mentors to the young Hamilton. Again, as is typical of those with Asperger's syndrome, these friendships were sustained by a meeting of minds, with both parties being able to happily discuss poetry, philosophy and science. Indeed, according to Hankins, Hamilton always reminded Wordsworth of Coleridge, so alike in character and temperament were the two men. In later life, Hamilton would continue to develop close friendships with like-minded people, usually carried on through massive correspondence, such as with the English mathematician Augustus de Morgan.

The large brood of Edgeworths meant that there was a great deal of socialising and numerous eligible young ladies in attendance at their estate. Clearly Hamilton was attracted to women and appears to have had a considerable sex drive. Indeed, in his fifties he seems to have enjoyed flirting openly, going so far as to kiss various females in the Meridian Room at Dunsink, according to O'Donnell.

Though Hamilton had no shortage of friends, interacting with them was another matter altogether. This was particularly so in his relations with women. Socially naive and eccentric, he appears to have been rather shy in promoting himself as a suitor, something not uncommon in those with Asperger's syndrome. Indeed, he had an inability to express his feelings in a socially acceptable way. In temperament, he essentially had a romantic disposition. His highly sensitive, if not hypersensitive, nature meant that he felt disappointments keenly, particularly those which involved the opposite sex. During his early twenties, he fell in and out of love with such unfailing regularity that he was frequently driven to distraction and contemplated suicide. The waters of the Royal Canal on more than one occasion seemed a suitable balm to his suffering.

Inept at reading social cues, Hamilton frequently misunderstood intentions and signals. A number of encounters with young ladies saw him becoming rather fickle and unable to make up his mind as to who he should court – Fanny Edgeworth or Louisa Disney. Yet invariably, any disappointments in love prompted a retreat into work on his part. In his relationship with Catherine Disney, who became the love of his life, he showed himself to be rather highly strung. The Disney family lived in the nearby village of Summerhill on the estate of Lord Langford in County Meath. Thomas Disney was a wealthy estate agent whose five sons were educated at Trinity and became close friends of Hamilton. The day Hamilton met Catherine Disney, 17 August 1824, was a red-letter day for him, much like the day Nora Barnacle and James Joyce walked out on 16 June 1904. With his keen interest in numerology, Hamilton never forgot the date. In the manner of all great love affairs, he fell in love with Catherine on first sight. Right from the start, as a guest in her parent's home, Hamilton's behaviour was socially inappropriate – and typically Asperger-like. Hankins mentions that he committed all sorts of 'social blunders' on the first visit: he ignored Mrs Disney, whom he should have led into dinner, and took Catherine's arm instead, and monopolised her for the whole evening. Either too shy or constrained by society to express his feelings for her directly, Hamilton did not make his intentions known to Catherine, who, as it turned out, was in love with him. In the absence of any offer of marriage from Hamilton, when another suitor, the older and eminently respectable clergyman Reverend Barlow, proposed, the offer was accepted by her family. Hamilton's reaction, according to Hankins, was extreme: he 'experienced, in all but its last fatal force, the suicidal impulse'. Such powerful emotions were hard to contain, yet his work and ambition saved him from going ahead with any drastic action.

Overall, in Hamilton's courtships of women there is an 'aura of artificiality'. He filled pages with poetry about the accomplished Catherine, impressed with her beauty and noble heart and mind. Hankins is correct when he says that Hamilton expressed his love in a theoretical way and that 'love existed for him in some unearthly realm apart from this world'. In fact, Hankins is describing an Asperger relationship. In many respects, Hamilton's relationship with Catherine Disney Barlow is akin to that between Yeats and Maud Gonne: it always remained tremendously idealistic and perfect, but tragic because it could never be consummated. The emotional immaturity at the heart of these supersensitive and romantic men, Emmet and Yeats included, is seen time and again in those with Asperger's syndrome.

The infatuation with Catherine continued to preoccupy Hamilton throughout most of his life, even after his own marriage. In rather dramatic fashion, she re-entered his life nearly twenty-five years later, in 1848. By this time, her sons were studying at Trinity College and being tutored by Hamilton. Her marriage had not been a success and, clearly in some distress, she wrote to Hamilton over the course of several weeks, with the tone of the letters becoming ever more intimate. Given the social conventions of the day, this was a scandalous communication. When her husband found out about it and wrote to him, the upstanding Hamilton sought to put an end to the correspondence. The outcome was that Catherine took an overdose of laudanum in an attempt to end her life, but failed, and survived. Her illness tortured Hamilton, who still idolised her, and went so far as to visit her old family home of Summerhill, where he 'kissed, in the twilight, alone, the spot whereupon I first saw rest the feet of that Beautiful Vision!' Shortly before her death, however, they were reconciled. Afterwards, he immediately set about collecting memorabilia of her: her books, journals, poems, pencil case, locks of hair, and portraits. His obsession with Catherine continued, and he would pester others to talk about her or else gaze for hours at her portrait. In fact, he began to gaze at her image through a mirror when he discovered that her likeness was better when viewed in that way.

A second relationship in his youth, this time with Ellen de Vere, was marked by ardent feeling and unexpressed emotion. Ellen, who lived at Curragh Chase near Adare, was a regular visitor to the Dunravens of Adare. Her brother Aubrey had become a good friend of Hamilton's and they shared many interests. Despite the difference in age, the rather childlike Hamilton often enjoyed the company of younger minds, as commonly occurs in those with Asperger's syndrome. Ellen too became the subject of Hamilton's tender verses, waxing lyrical about her fragility, sensitivity and spirituality – qualities that invariably impress the romantic idealist. In courting Ellen, Hamilton again was too tentative and misconstrued her position. On the verge of proposing to her, he lost heart when she declared that she 'could not live happily anywhere but at Curragh'. Hamilton read this literally to mean that she would never leave the family home, and gave up much too easily. Certainly concrete thinking and the tendency to take things at face value is not uncommon in those with Asperger's syndrome.

By all accounts, Hamilton's choice of wife, Helen Bayley, does not appear to have been a good one. Given their poor social skills, naivety, idealistic natures and lack of common sense, those with Asperger's syndrome do not always pick life partners well. Hamilton was no exception. Judging by the protective nature of several of Hamilton's friends and colleagues, the general opinion of Helen was rather poor, if not vitriolic at times. MacFarlane, clearly no advocate of Lady Hamilton, had very definite views about the type of wife that would best suit Hamilton's needs:

> The kind of wife which Hamilton needed was one who could govern him and efficiently supervise all domestic matters; but the wife he chose was, from weakness of body and mind, incapable of doing it. As a consequence, Hamilton worked for the rest of his life under domestic difficulties of no ordinary kind.

Perhaps most unfortunately for Hamilton, Helen did not share his interests in mathematics and astronomy. Indeed, the view was widely held that Hamilton had married Helen on the rebound from his two failed romances and that she was inferior to both Catherine and Ellen in many respects: beauty, intellect, status, fortune and health. Like so many with Asperger's syndrome who cannot express their feelings face to face, Hamilton resorted to writing to make his message plain – at times rather too honestly, if not inappropriately. Once Helen had accepted his marriage proposal, Hamilton relayed to her his past romantic anguishes with Catherine Disney and Ellen de Vere.

Hamilton seemed to have little or no capacity to take care of himself, and his wife, due to illness, seemed unable to provide any help in this area either. The exact nature of her lifelong illness was something of a mystery, but there is some evidence that she was highly strung and insecure, and suffered from many psychosomatic complaints. Furthermore, the birth of each of her three children was followed by a period of postnatal depression. The burden of managing the Dunsink household frequently became too much for her, and she would retreat to her family in Nenagh, County Tipperary, for respite, or else her mother would arrive up from the country and restore order. Displaying few maternal instincts, Helen was an absentee mother to all intents and purposes – and worse, for Hamilton, an absentee wife. Naturally, this resulted in him having to fend for himself – he was no paragon of domesticity – and the isolation affected him greatly. Even when his wife was around, things were no better: Hankins notes that 'he had no regular meals, sometimes missed meals altogether, and dispersed the chill of the night with glasses of porter, when he should have had a warm fire and hot coffee'.

Like Pearse, Hamilton could appreciate women in their own right too. Certainly he had a liberal attitude towards women, which many could describe as 'feminist'. Having had no brothers, Hamilton's main male influence was his uncle James, whereas, given the abundance of sisters, aunts and cousins, the female influence on him was considerable. These women were maternal figures for him and were highly intelligent too. His earliest education had been in the hands of his aunts, Elizabeth and Sydney, who were knowledgeable in both Hebrew and Latin. His sisters, like himself, had been farmed out to relatives at a young age. They had abundant intelligence and talents and were fiercely independent: Grace, the eldest, was prized for her management of the household at Dunsink Observatory; Eliza, closest in age and temperament to Hamilton, shared something of his genius and literary talents; Sydney, the bold, adventurous type, emigrated to Nicaragua and later to New Zealand, where she lived out her days; Archianna, the youngest, was hardly known but, from O'Donnell's account, she was considered 'simple-minded' and 'retarded' – one wonders if she had autism. None of the sisters married and all lived with Hamilton at Dunsink Observatory before his marriage.

Undoubtedly, Hamilton idolised Eliza and saw her as his 'poet sister', a kindred spirit who nurtured him spiritually and intellectually. His uncle James had recognised signs of genius in her as well but was unable to provide her with the same education afforded to Hamilton because she lived in Gracehill, County Antrim, with her mother's people, the Willeys. Surprisingly, given the times, Hamilton was less prejudiced in his views about the intellectual merits of women. He was not convinced that domestic excellence was the chief virtue of women:

> I am not quite sure that in anything valuable the minds of men are real-
> ly superior to those of the other sex. In taste, in imagination, in feeling,
> in affection, in piety, in the enduring pain, and the charming away of dis-
> tress, women have, in general, almost an allowed superiority; and . . .
> there are some recorded instances in behalf of the fairer sex which may
> perhaps excite a suspicion that if there had not been more, the cause has
> been the want of opportunity rather than the want of ability.

In his analysis, Hamilton omits any reference to the ability to system-
atise, which is a trait more commonly found in men.

In regard to his three children, Hamilton appears to have been a remote figure, although he was an affectionate father. By his own admission, he was 'fond of children but not disposed to have them constantly with me'. Moreover, his concern for his children's welfare saw him frequently bail them out in straitened circumstances. As so often happens with the children of geniuses, the pressures to meet the standards of the parent are inordinately high, and an open invitation to failure. Indeed, the eccentricities of the father were replicated in the children. The biographer Robert Graves wrote that Hamilton's eldest son William Edwin, by profession a civil engineer, had 'no moral principle, has lived a most irregular life, and is now near Toronto, living from hand to mouth teaching and lecturing'. William constantly sought money from his father. His second son, Archibald Henry, a rebellious clergyman who inherited the intellect and morality of his father, fared no better: that 'eccentricity in him seems fast ripening into insanity. He commuted and compounded, as a curate, and has given everything away – mostly to the poor, and is now almost entirely dependent on his brother-in-law, Archbishop O'Regan'. Hamilton's only daughter, Helen Eliza, was a 'shy and rather eccentric girl', according to Graves. In many ways, she took after her father, being bright, morally upright and romantic in outlook: in adulthood she took to writing novels, but she died in childbirth. Hankins too makes reference to how Archibald became an increasingly eccentric figure and was 'not of this world'. It is possible that his children inherited many Asperger traits as well.

*

Hamilton had an extraordinarily naive and impractical side. Prior to his marriage, his sisters lived with him at Dunsink Observatory, where they managed the house and kept things in order on the domestic front. Astonishingly, he presumed that, on his marriage to Helen Bayley, they would continue to live with him and his new wife, and was genuinely baffled when they moved out.

As the Royal Astronomer, Hamilton took little interest in the day-to-day running of Dunsink Observatory. His initial enthusiasm waned and, over the years, measurement recordings were increasingly done by his assistants, sometimes his sisters Eliza and Sydney, who shared his interest in science. According to both MacFarlane and Hankins, Hamilton never attained any skill as an observer. Never a practical man, he was far from adept at using telescopes. The great meridian circle at Dunsink was the most accurate instrument of its kind in the world, yet Hamilton never practised long enough to gain sufficient skill to operate it successfully. At heart, Hamilton found the work extremely tedious, and exposure to the night's elements brought on colds and fatigue for him. In reference to Hamilton's organisational abilities, Hankins draws an amusing contrast between Hamilton's counterpart in Greenwich, George Biddell Airey, who became director in 1835:

> The Royal Greenwich Observatory under [Airy's] direction reached the ultimate of efficiency and precision, while the observatory at Dunsink under Hamilton's direction was characterised by moderate chaos and benign neglect. Airy kept careful files of all correspondence, memoranda and research documents, while Hamilton tended to shove them under the bed. Airy kept his accounts personally by double-entry bookkeeping; working on them was one of his greatest joys. Hamilton never seemed to be quite sure where money came from and where it went. . . . Hamilton often sent his poems to his regular correspondents, including Airy, but he thought Airy's reaction would probably be 'make three copies and file it'.

As is typical of Asperger geniuses, Hamilton's teaching skills were somewhat lacking, and he showed little social intelligence, common sense or empathy for less-skilled students. In this regard, Einstein was a notoriously bad teacher too. According to Hankins, Hamilton's sisters would have been more receptive to undertaking the work at the Dunsink Observatory had he been a better instructor. In addition, though he had a talent for oratory, getting his message across was a sometimes haphazard affair. Frequently, he could not modify the lecture to suit the audience: he either gave explanations that were so basic that they embarrassed his audiences or else launched into material that was so incomprehensible that they were well and truly confused.

Students fared no better with his writings. His 'Theory of Systems of Rays' was notoriously difficult to read. Commentators complain that there are no diagrams or examples to aid the reader through the dense jungle of his writings and that crucial information is buried under less interesting aspects of his theory. His *Lectures on Quaternions* are also lamentably compact and have been criticised for their 'diffuseness of style', according to MacFarlane. He certainly sometimes 'forgot the expositor in the orator'. The *Lectures* is therefore no manual of instruction for the benefit of students and teachers. The advice of his friends to keep things brief and to the point was disregarded, but soon after publication, the imperfections of the *Lectures* became all too apparent to Hamilton and he set about providing a – badly needed – manual. However, this was soon beset with digressions. By his reckoning, Hamilton believed that it would fill four hundred pages and take two years to prepare. In the event, it amounted to nearly eight hundred closely printed pages and took seven years. He worked with the desperation of the dying, often up to twelve hours at a time. Indeed, bronchitis and gout finished him off in 1865, aged sixty, before he could complete the work.

Like many Asperger's geniuses, Hamilton had problems with money and was constantly overdrawn at the bank. In this light, Hankins's assertion that Hamilton was never quite sure where the money came from and where it went to is not surprising. Indeed, checks and balances in the management of his funds were lacking.

*

Issues around self-identity, common to those with Asperger's syndrome, were found in Hamilton too. The identity diffusion was evident in the multiplicity of roles and occupations he had in his lifetime. As well as being a mathematician, he was at various times also a child prodigy, a linguist, a poet, a philosopher, an astronomer, and president of the Royal

Irish Academy. Curiously, like others discussed in this book, Hamilton was to all intents and purposes an orphan at the age of three, despite the fact that his parents were very much alive – although his aunts and uncles seem to have made good substitutes. This also raises questions about any possible emotional detachment in the parents. Economic necessity was cited as the reason why his parents chose to deliver Hamilton into the care of relatives. That said, boarding school and fostering were frequent occurrences in his social class at the time. Prior to both parents dying in 1819, when he was fifteen, he had little contact with them. A few letters and a visit to his father three months before his death seemed to sum up the entire contact. The first letter Hamilton received from his father, at the age of thirteen, was long, verbose and pompous yet full of fatherly advice, according to Hankins. In fact, it seemed to fit a lawyer–client relationship more than that between a father and son.

Fame was important to Hamilton because it confirmed and reinforced his identity as a brilliant mathematician. Clearly, like Joyce, he had abiding self-conviction in his genius and was deeply ambitious. Public recognition, when it came, was always welcomed by him, especially the bestowing of a knighthood, probably his highest accolade, followed by his election as first Foreign Associate of the US National Academy of Sciences. With a talent for self-advancement, Hamilton could ingratiate himself with key individuals who could further his career. A huge regard for posterity ensured that he kept his voluminous correspondence and virtually every scrap of paper on which he had ever written. Publicly, his tenure as president of the Royal Irish Academy was also quite successful. Certainly he does not appear to have been grossly scheming or calculating, and kept silent counsel when things became difficult. In general, he tried to defuse situations through compromise or sheer decency, with a keen eye on the rituals of protocol – much like de Valera.

The question of Hamilton's national identity was ambiguous too. He always considered himself to be a patriotic Irishman, despite being committed to the Act of Union and having an almost reverential regard for royalty. Like Daisy Bates, he saw the Empire as an inviolable structure and was attracted to ideal and absolutist states. Apparently, on Queen Victoria's ascent to the throne in 1853, he wrote a sonnet for the occasion, like an unofficial poet laureate, and sent it to her. Twelve years later, when Victoria paid her first visit to Ireland as queen, he composed another. Admittedly, Hamilton had good cause to feel well disposed towards the monarchy, as he had been added to the civil list of pensioners in 1843 by the Tory government and was granted £200 a year for life. Courageously, Hamilton continued to exercise his right to vote, despite the turmoil of the times and an open ballot. But with his sharp sense of morality, he was above bribery and could resist political pressure. Though he confessed to being a reformer in spirit, he could never support the Repeal of the Union and joined an Irish Protestant Conservative Society in 1834.

Hamilton the actor was yet another persona of his. Like others discussed in this book, including Pearse and Yeats, Hamilton had a flair for the dramatic. Aided and abetted by his adoring sisters, he would enact scenes from the classics, such as the Battle of Troy. On the occasion when, as teenagers, they briefly stayed with their father in Booterstown, Hamilton organised them into a government, entitled 'The Honourable Society of Four'. Hamilton was a peer, Eliza and Sydney were commoners, Grace was the Lady Lieutenant, and their father was King Archibald. Hamilton drew up the statutes; one of the first acts of the Society of Four was to petition their uncle James to allow Hamilton to stay longer with his father than the two months that had been agreed! The petition failed, but not for the want of trying. Hamilton, so immersed in the business of government, had neglected the more practical duty of taking care of his father, who was in poor health.

Like W. B. Yeats, Emmet, Pearse, de Valera and Joyce, Hamilton had an affinity for poetry – but he could be classed as an amateur in this regard. During his time at Trinity College, he composed some original poems, including 'On College Ambition', and in the spirit of a true poet laureate tended to mark important occasions with a poem: the discovery of the planet Neptune in 1846 saw Hamilton compose a poem for John Couch Adams, who had correctly predicted the existence of the planet and calculated its position a year earlier. Romantically, Hamilton saw poetry as something he needed to do to take care of his soul. As a poet, however, he lacked technique, though he possessed imagination in abundance. His poems therefore tended to be overly romantic, banal and conventional.

*

Hamilton appears to have been one of the least controlling figures discussed in this book. Admittedly, he tended to be bossy towards his sisters if they failed to write to him. Also, he was inclined to influence the direction of studies of his sisters as well, particularly Eliza:

> I have heard from various quarters, [that] your natural indolence . . . grows upon you — and you may be sure that if you allow it to do so — if you allow the habit to take possession of you, of not bending your whole energy of thought and mental power to whatever pursuit or study you are engaged in, those energies, however great, will as it were grow rusty and decay.

He forcefully expressed his wish that he wanted either Sydney or Eliza to become an astronomer, but this did not sit well with their wishes and plans. This may be read, however, as an expression of brotherly responsibility on his part, especially after his father died, when Hamilton was fifteen.

In the matter of his work, the issue of establishing scientific priority exercised him greatly as the years progressed. The desire to have his name credited with whatever discovery he had made came into sharp focus when his colleague at Trinity, James MacCullagh, claimed that he had first discovered conical refractions three years earlier. Though MacCullagh issued a retraction, the episode made Hamilton ever more cautious. Nonetheless, over the years other claims to priority were made by MacCullagh on the system of polar molecules and even quaternions. As a result, there was a growing tendency on Hamilton's part to monopolise all published work on quaternions. An autistic superego was evident too in his conservative behaviour, especially as he settled into adulthood.

There is some evidence that Hamilton was plagued with guilt, especially when his colleague MacCullagh committed suicide for no apparent reason in 1847. The Famine years also brought a level of guilt on his part at his inactivity, while friends such as Aubrey and Stephen de Vere threw themselves wholeheartedly into famine relief. Hamilton was far too engrossed in his own world, living in the 'here and now', to fully apprehend what was going on around him. In this respect, it is not surprising that he was largely apolitical. His continuing love for Catherine Disney also filled him with self-censure. Typically, Hamilton assuaged his guilt by redoubling his work efforts. His lapse into heavy drinking, particularly when he became somewhat agitated and violent and had to be restrained, brought him great anxiety as well. Clearly, he recognised that such behaviour was sinful. Increasingly, the upheavals in the Protestant church during the 1830s affected him, and he thus began a strict observance of all religious fasts and feast days specified in the Book of Common Prayer.

*

There is scant information on any sensory impairment or hyperacuity that Hamilton might have had. Nonetheless, we can glean that he was hypersensitive where temperature was concerned. According to Hankins, he did not like contact with water. As a child, he fought against his Saturday bath in a pedantic manner, proclaiming that, as he had begun to study Hebrew, he was observing both the Christian and Jewish Sabbath! He disliked being exposed to the elements, especially to the bitter coldness of Dunsink Observatory.

Rather surprisingly, given that many mathematicians are also gifted musicians, it appears that Hamilton had no aptitude for or appreciation of music, according to his friends. That said, there is little information regarding whether he liked or disliked music. Given that he frequented the houses of such patrons as Lord Adare and the Edgeworths, he was exposed to much dancing and recitals, which he clearly enjoyed, judging by a letter to his sister Grace:

> We closed the ball by a Coronation Dance, which began with a gentle and solemn music; with motion corresponding; but soon grew fast and furious, till the first couple had held a handkerchief for the ladies to dance under and for the gentlemen to leap over.

Disruptions to circadian rhythm are certainly evident in those with Asperger's syndrome, and Hamilton appears to have had sleep disturbances and was not known for being an early riser. We have already seen how he would complain about getting up early as a young boy. As an adult engrossed in mathematics, working into the night seems to have suited him better. He notes that, when working on 'Theory of Systems of Rays', he was 'sitting up and getting up later than ever'. Indeed, Hamilton was notoriously unpunctual and always arrived late for church, meetings, lectures and so on. You could say that preoccupation in his work at one level was the cause of this, but also the tendency to live in the moment, so apparent in those with Asperger's syndrome.

There is a suggestion that Hamilton had some degree of motor clumsiness. As a boy, his handwriting was poor and by the age of seven he still had a childish scrawl. His fine motor skills were so poor that his attempts to form capital letters were extremely forceful, and in the process often destroyed his aunt's pens and writing materials. In addition, he had little skill in horsemanship and frequently took falls, which may indicate poor co-ordination and some recklessness. In terms of sports and physical pursuits, he enjoyed swimming, which requires gross motor skills rather than fine ones. The practical work of science and dexterous skill at Dunsink Observatory, operating telescopes and such like, he left to his assistants.

During his lifetime, Hamilton enjoyed reasonably good health, aside from periodic bouts of depression. There is no doubt that the hypersensitive mathematician suffered from melancholy and anxiety. His early twenties were years of intense anguish in the pursuit of love; he told his friend Aubrey de Vere that he passed 'nearly eight years in a state of mental suffering' but that being able to work saved him from despair. By all accounts, Hamilton found work the perfect antidote to the many trials and tribulations he experienced. His home life was far from happy, and during the early 1840s, when his wife's illness forced her and the children away from Dunsink, he became despondent, if not depressed. The loneliness also coincided with his first difficulties with alcohol.

His unrequited love for Catherine Disney Barlow haunted him throughout his life, and he could never quite relinquish the powerful feelings he had for her. As those close to him died – such as his sister Eliza, his uncles James and the Reverend John Willey and his aunts – he felt their losses keenly. In a letter sent to his brother Robert, John Graves – a colleague at Trinity College – talked about the signs of strain evident in Hamilton's behaviour: there was a 'certain nervous irritability in his temperament' which seemed to accompany an overactive mind and workload. Indeed, the burden of creativity and lack of self-identity can result in depression on the part of the Asperger genius. Sadly, Hamilton took refuge in alcohol, yet another obsessive addiction, as recorded by Andrew MacFarlane:

> The explanation lay in the want of order which reigned in his home. He
> had no regular times for his meals; frequently had no regular meals at all,

but resorted to the sideboard when hunger compelled him. What more natural in such condition than that he should refresh himself with a quaff of that beverage for which Dublin is famous—porter labelled X^3?

In the twenty years prior to his death, his drinking increased. Indeed, this problem only became public knowledge when he became violent at a meeting of the Geological Society in 1846. The excesses of work, grief and loss, and domestic neglect came at a personal cost to his health. In later years, his eyesight declined and he wore glasses. Furthermore, he appears to have developed double vision and was somewhat colour blind: according to O'Donnell, whereby he could not distinguish blue from green. Epileptic seizures also occurred as did frequent bouts of bronchitis and gout, which precipitated his death in 1865.

*

Hamilton was a deeply religious man and by nature certainly had the sense of spirituality or religiosity often found in the Asperger genius. Indeed, personal piety was very much in evidence in the Hamilton family. On his mother's side, an aunt had married a minister in the Moravian Brethren, a group that was strongly Calvinistic, and it is thought that his sister Eliza's strong vein of piety came from this source. Hamilton was similarly pietistic, and for him the pursuit of the creative acts of mathematics and poetry were imbued with a religious tone and purpose.

The quality of his beliefs was put to the test in adulthood, and an instinctive leaning towards High Church practice was revealed. From the 1830s, a period of church dissent and reform raged throughout Britain, initiated by the Whig government, and inevitably the religious upheaval that beset the Anglican Church spilled over into Ireland. At first, Hamilton sympathised with the reforming zeal of the Oxford Movement, which concerned itself with reviving the Anglican Church, especially its doctrines of the apostolic succession, the priesthood and the sacraments, but the emphasis on authority and high liturgical practices remained. Hamilton became disenchanted with the reform movement, however. Many of its defenders, like John Henry Newman, converted to Roman Catholicism, as did his friends Aubrey de Vere and Lord Adare – this brought personal isolation to Hamilton for a time. His sisters Sydney and possibly Eliza became Calvinists. The move to Roman Catholicism, with the supreme authority of the pope and the 'idolatrous' veneration of Mary, was a bridge too far for Hamilton, however.

In essence, Hamilton was a hybrid of the Evangelical church and the Anglican church – an 'Evangelical Anglican', as he called himself in later life. He responded to the Evangelical church's emphasis on ministry and mission, and its simple services and personal piety, but the lack of a systematic theology in Evangelicalism was a stumbling block for the idealistic Hamilton, who took theology very seriously. Indeed, it could be said that de Valera and Pearse shared something of this disposition too. In a letter to Robert Graves, Hamilton declared: 'I had certainly leanings to high-churchism . . . But I have never allowed my views and feelings of religion to harden into any system; nor have I ever joined any party in the Church.' This essentially sums up the position of many Asperger geniuses in regard to religion: with their independent minds and spirits, they carve out their own place in established religions.

Hamilton's interest in religion extended to the supernatural and pseudoscience. Like many geniuses, he was fascinated by numerology, hypnotism, ghosts and phrenology – the study of the structure of the skull to determine a person's character and mental capacity. With typical mathematical logic, Hamilton calculated the exact date of the Council of Nicaea in 325 AD. Likewise, he was fascinated by the ten days that elapsed between Christ's Ascension into heaven and the arrival of Pentecost.

Hamilton's scientific achievements were so far-reaching that they continue to fascinate the world. His truly exceptional mind, eccentricity and creative nature all point to him being an Asperger genius. The words of the science historian L. Pearce Williams in *Foundations of Scientific Method: The Nineteenth Century* are quoted by Hankins to describe many of the men who were attracted to the ideas of Kant and the natural philosophy of the Romantic movement. Hankins claims that the description fits Hamilton as well, and indeed fits all of the Asperger geniuses discussed in this book:

> They were all highly sensitive men, seeking both beauty and truth in their philosophy. Most wrote poetry and expressed their emotions in verse. All had a deep sense of form and thought architectonically. The whole was always more important and more than the sum of the parts. All recognised the importance of and all felt the near ecstasy of creativity springing from the active mind. Spirit was as real to them as body. All underwent youthful crises and discovered Kant as the answer to their personal *Angst*.

6

DAISY BATES

One must love solitude for its own sake to taste in its fullness the perfect happiness that these beautiful open spaces give.

DAISY BATES, *The Passing of the Aborigines*

She may have lived most of her life in Australia but, like Joyce and Beckett, Daisy Bates could never quite relinquish her country of origin. Ireland, particularly its fertile landscapes and the innate spiritualism of its people, was never far from her thoughts. Her acquaintance with Irish customs from the first twenty years of her life, spent in Roscrea and Dublin, would in time colour her work as one of the first ethnographers of the Aborigines. Certainly the best-seller that made her name in 1938 in England, *The Passing of the Aborigines,* is littered with references to the Celts and the Irish – everything from turf fires to pigs and Kilkenny cats, and from cures, keening, fairy tales and speech rhythms to folk music and hurling.

Daisy Bates's contribution to the study and welfare of the Aborigines was truly unique, showing a true genius for ethnography. By 1920, at the age of sixty, she was firmly established as an authority on the Aborigines in the states of Western and South Australia. She had been the first female member of an Australian scientific expedition led by Cambridge University and was a member of both British and Australian anthropological societies, the first female Protector of the Aborigines (albeit an unpaid position), and the first female Justice of the Peace in two states. Despite these illustrious achievements, she was – and remains – a controversial figure in Australian history, not least for her beliefs that the Aborigines were doomed to extinction and were guilty of cannibalism. Today, the great body of her work remains in the archives of the National Library of Australia, largely unpublished.

In common with many of the characters discussed in this book, she tended to arouse strong emotions, ranging from admiration to acrimony. Yet of all these characters, Daisy Bates is perhaps the most eccentric, the most complex and the most neglected. Moreover, she was an Asperger genius who blended fact and fiction adroitly, and it was this aspect of her character that left her in poor standing with the scientific community. Even so, for Australian schoolchildren she is still a colourful figure who graces the pages of their history books.

Daisy's legacy has been a mixed bag: she has been indelibly branded both a saint and a liar, and also as romantic a figure as Laurence of Arabia or Florence Nightingale. She weaved a good deal of fiction into her accounts of her private life, especially regarding her social background. Like the 'Talented Mr Ripley' in Patricia Highsmith's novel and the film about the psychopathic Tom Ripley, she could pass herself off in the higher echelons of society as a well-bred lady of means and status.

Today, she continues to fascinate and intrigue. Since her death in 1951, her life has been the subject of numerous books, plays and films, and an opera by the Australian composer Margaret Sutherland. Hollywood legend Katherine Hepburn, who was enamoured with Daisy at one stage, commissioned two academics to research her life, intending to play the starring role in a film of the ethnographer's life. Needless to say, when such unsavoury details as Daisy's penchant for lies and bigamy emerged, the screen icon lost interest in the project.

*

The charisma and equanimity particular to Asperger geniuses was certainly to be found in Daisy Bates. There are many references to her magnetic personality in Elizabeth Salter's biography *Daisy Bates: The Great White Queen of the Never Never*. This magnetism was expressed by an intensity and vivacity that left men helplessly staring at her as she came into a room.

Pretty and feminine, her eyes were described as vividly blue and beautiful, her hair chestnut or reddish, her nose small and gently aquiline, her face frequently defiant, and her chin firmly protruding. Like many people with autism, her skin retained a softness and smoothness – wrinkle-free well into her seventies – making her face look rather girlish. Physically, she was rather delicately built, measuring five feet, three or four inches in height, with a size-three boot size. Her gait was unusual in that she walked absolutely poker-straight and briskly, and was rarely without a black umbrella that doubled as a walking cane. Equally, when sitting, her body was stiff-backed and erect. She had a natural elegance and was renowned for her dress sense, though, remarkably, she tended to wear Edwardian attire right up until her death in 1951. Her delicate hands were never without her ubiquitous white gloves, worn as much from habit as to act as a shield against contagion. Above all, Daisy Bates's daintiness belied her steely inner strength and determination.

*

The story of Daisy's origins contained in Salter's biography and others is largely fictional: there was no chaotic-but-happy childhood among the Anglo-Irish gentry and aristocracy. Research in recent years, much of it unpublished local history, has shed new light on the matter, in particular *Daisy Bates* by Emmet Arrigan and Elisabeth Monkhouse, published in 1999 in Irish.

Born on 21 October 1859 in Roscrea, County Tipperary, Daisy May (or Margaret, as she was baptized) was the third child of James and Bridget O'Dwyer (née Hunt). A twin brother, Francis, was also born but he died of tuberculosis when very young. There were two older sisters, Mary Anne and Catherine, and by 1864 three younger siblings, James, Anne and Michael, had joined the family. All the children were baptized in the Church of Saint Cronan, belonging to the established Church of Ireland. Though Daisy claimed that her father was Anglican, the O'Dwyers were in fact staunch Catholics well known in the town as cattle dealers and blacksmiths. Certainly at one time they were prosperous, with land in Scotland and Wales used for grazing cattle before they were shipped, in addition to land in two townlands outside Roscrea, Ballychrine and Ráth Liath (Ashbury), where they kept horses. In post-Famine times, when there was widespread poverty in Roscrea, it is not known how the

O'Dwyers fared. Daisy's father, who was far from well-off, seems to have eked out a living as a blacksmith in his forge at the back of the house where they lived on Main Street. There is also the suggestion from Daisy that her father, and indeed the O'Dwyers, were hard drinkers.

Like Hamilton, Boyle and de Valera, Daisy's early childhood was marked by parental loss. Her mother's death from tuberculosis occurred when Daisy was five years old and saw her matriarchal Grandmother Hunt, who lived in Ballychrine, take over her care and that of her two older sisters and her brother James (Jim). Within six months of his wife's death, James O'Dwyer had remarried a young Dillon girl from the neighbouring townland of Derrymore, and a short time later the couple left Ireland in search of a new life in Australia. It is likely that James intended to send for his family once he had made good, but this never materialised: he never arrived in Australia and possibly died from tuberculosis en route.

Of Anglican stock, the Hunts in their day had been well-to-do and could boast seventy-seven acres of land in Ballychrine. In the old farmhouse, by a great turf fire, Grandmother Hunt captured the young Daisy's imagination with tales of banshees, leprechauns, fairy forts, amadáns, death coaches and, not least, St Patrick driving the snakes out of Ireland. Indeed, the power of fairies and baby elves still inspired poetry in Daisy seventy years later. As Daisy put it: 'I have never grown out of my longing for you and my playmates of long ago.' In Daisy's gentrified account of her upbringing, her illiterate 'nanny' Allie was the person to whom she attributed her immersion in Irish superstition and folklore. This woman was in fact her cousin Allie (Alison) Dwyer, who kept house for Grandmother Hunt.

Everywhere the effects of the Great Famine were still to be seen. The countryside around Ballychrine, and indeed much further afield, was filled with poverty-stricken faces: families dispossessed and destitute as a result of death, famine and emigration. However, they could be 'merry in their misery' too. Sounds of the fiddle, singing, dancing and clapping carried in the night from wakes or shebeens around Ballychrine, and all were stored in Daisy's memory. It is clear that, from an early age, she was blessed with a sharp curiosity and was highly perceptive and observant of the ways of Irish peasantry. She committed all she felt, saw, heard, smelt, tasted and touched to memory. A strong Christian, Grandmother Hunt brought

Daisy to Sunday services at Ballychrine and was endowed with a spirit of charity, regularly visiting the poor and tending to the sick in their homes – a spirit that was undeniably passed on to Daisy.

Like Yeats, Hamilton and Beckett, Daisy spent much of her early childhood ranging and rambling over the nearby countryside with her brother Jim, exploring ring-forts, Carraig Hill and the lower reaches of Knockshegowna, usually in search of 'goblins and ghosties', as she called them. By her own admission, she appears to have been quite the tomboy, and fearless, and broke her leg on one occasion. She was quite hyperactive and seldom walked if she could run. Described as a difficult, spirited girl, she was restless and possibly had concentration problems at the local Sacred Heart school, where she was educated by Catholic nuns. In later life, she admitted to being a 'scatterbrain' – and in general was a problem child.

Upon the death of her grandmother, when Daisy was eight or nine, the family was broken up. Mary Anne (called Marian by Daisy) was now grown up; Catherine (called Kathleen) and Jim were dispatched to relatives in Dublin, while Daisy appears to have stayed in Ballychrine and was perhaps cared for by her grandmother's sister Biddy Cantwell or her aunt Elizabeth Hunt for a time. Before long, she was sent to Wales to live with a Mrs Goode, who was a close friend of the rector in Ballychrine or in Roscrea – or so Daisy claims. There Mrs Goode taught her how to be a lady. Daisy next claims that she returned to Dublin to live with relatives and continue her schooling. In Daisy's version of events, her education proper began when she was fostered or 'adopted' by the aristocratic Outram family, reputedly old English friends of her grandmother. However, Julia Blackburn in *Daisy Bates in the Desert* claims that the Outram family had no Irish connections and had never taken a young girl called Daisy May O'Dwyer into their care.

Despite abundant intelligence, teachers frequently reported that she 'would not learn', according to Salter. Inattention and boredom may well have prevented her from excelling at school. Ernestine Hill in *Kabbarli: A Personal Memoir of Daisy Bates* says that Daisy had a solid education, was fluent in a number of languages and was familiar with mythology, literature and theology. Some of this was probably achieved through her own didactic efforts. An avid reader, she acquired a taste for English classic writers such as Dickens, Scott and Thackeray. They also had a substantial knowledge of philosophy and was acquainted with the works of Nietzsche and Schopenhauer. Displaying an enquiring mind, she also showed a passionate interest in all things science, but her reading in this area, though extensive, was not encouraged as a teenager. In later life, Daisy bemoaned the fact that she had failed to come to grips with maths; had she done so, she believed she would have had a grip on the 'real world'.

It is likely that, by the age of eighteen, Daisy was employed as a family governess, possibly in Dublin. In 1884, she decided to emigrate to Australia, ostensibly in search of sunnier climes to cure a 'spot' on her lungs, afraid that tuberculosis would claim her life, as it had her mother. However, it is also believed from local Roscrea sources that she obtained a free passage to Australia through the nuns, who were setting up a mission to convert the Australian Aborigines to Christianity.

Once in Australia, the facts of Daisy's life are somewhat clearer. In the care of Bishop George H. Stanton, in Townsville, North Queensland, she lost no time in building up a network of influential friends and found work as a governess. Within weeks, she was married by a Catholic priest to Edwin Henry Morant (dubbed 'Breaker' Morant due to his prowess with horses), but the marriage ended within a month. A move to New South Wales almost immediately provided more governess work and wedding opportunities for her. In February 1885, she was married to Jack Bates and gave birth to a son, Arnold, a year later.

By 1894, an increasingly restless and unfulfilled Daisy had abandoned her husband and son, leaving the latter in the shared care of a boarding school and his grandmother Bates. Supposedly on doctor's orders, she returned to England, where she was to spend five years honing her talents as a journalist on the *Review of Reviews* and the spiritualist magazine *Borderline,* which were run by W. T. Stead. In London her interest in writing about matters Aborigine was awakened by a letter in *The Times,* which contained strong allegations of cruelty towards Aborigines by white settlers in north-western Australia.

With newfound purpose, Daisy returned to Australia claiming that she was a journalist hired by *The Times* to write about the Aborigines. This had the desired effect and opened doors for her. From 1899 until her death in 1951, she devoted her life to the Aborigines, forging a life not only as an ethnographer and writer but as their protector and friend. Imbued with an Aboriginal spirit, her research trail was truly nomadic and took her all over Western and South Australia. In between hospitalisations or writing stints in Adelaide and Perth, her work took her to Beagle Bay Mission in Broome, and six years were spent on the Maaba Reserve and around the south coast, some months on the infectious-disease colonies of Bernier and Dorré Islands and the prison colony of Rottnest Island, two years at Eucla on the edge of the inhospitable Nullabor Plain, sixteen years in the desert at Ooldea, four years on the banks of the Murray River at Pyap, four years in Wynbring, and finally two years around Streaky Bay in South Australia. In the last year or so of her life, she was cared for in a nursing home in Adelaide, where she died on 18 April 1951.

*

Qualities that are now almost a prerequisite of genius were unquestionably found in Daisy: intelligence, natural curiosity and novelty-seeking, determination, phenomenal memory, sharp observation and scrupulous attention to detail, hard work and prodigious energy, all-encompassing narrow interests, and a huge capacity for absorption. Beyond doubt, Daisy was exceptionally intelligent and probably had a very high IQ. While she often exhibited poor social intelligence, she possessed native intelligence or 'tribal knowledge', which some recognised as her own brand of 'common sense'. Like many with Asperger's syndrome, de Valera and Joyce included, she had a certain amount of innate cunning or wiliness. 'Cunning as a native' was how she was described by a woman called Mrs Thompson, in whose farmhouse in Streaky Bay Daisy lived for over a year, according to Blackburn. 'There was nothing wrong with her,' Mrs Thompson explained. 'She had her own common sense.'

Showing little interest in domestic or social chit-chat, Daisy preferred to engage in lively discussions about the literary and political issues of the day. In addition, a thirst for knowledge led her to read and discuss anthropological literature in her early years in Australia. Natural curiosity and novelty-seeking were evident in her pioneering spirit. For her, Australia, the bush and in particular the Aborigines were full of marvels and were infinitely fascinating:

> To live among them, to see them amidst their own bush surroundings
> and to note their everyday comings and goings, is to experience an ever

delightful feeling that you are watching the doings and listening to the conversation of early mankind. . . .

So close had I been in contact with them, that is was now impossible for me to relinquish the work. I realised that they were passing from us. I must make their passing easier. Moreover, all that I knew was little in comparison with all there was yet to learn. I made the decision to dedicate the rest of my life to this fascinating study.

I admit that it was scarcely a sacrifice. Apart from the joy of the work for its own sake, apart from the enlightenments, the surprises, the clues, and the fresh beginnings that were the stimuli of every day, the paths of never-ending high-roads and byways in a scientific study that was practically virgin country, 'the freshness, the farness' meant much more to me now than the life of cities.

Though lacking a formal training in anthropology and academic credentials, she managed to learn a great deal about the subject when she was left to her own devices. Autodidactic, she studied 'every note of the bibliography at my disposal' regarding the aboriginal tribes of Western Australia, South Australia and other states. Whatever deficiencies in learning she had were compensated for by instinct, experience, scrupulous attention to detail and, of course, burning passion. At all times she sought clarity, particularly in relation to the Aboriginal research done hitherto, much of which was contradictory. She therefore decided to 'seek the truth at the fountain-head'. Such was the compelling and obsessive nature of her interests that she described it as a 'virus of research' in her.

This curiosity and interest never faltered and was augmented by her tremendous ability for observation. With scientific detachment, she made records of whatever she observed in the bush. Popular with the Australian public, she gave many lectures. As reported in Salter's biography, one audience member reported her as 'possessing the infinite capacity for detail which, according to a well-known philosopher, is the stuff of which genius is composed'. In general, people with Asperger's syndrome have an intense focus on details and are much more interested in the external than in the internal world; this is very much the case with Daisy. Because she had a lot of time on her hands in the desert, a good deal of it was spent observing the natural world – from the microcosm to the universe. She kept records of dates, places, temperatures, the quality of soil, and even its mineral content; certainly the keeping of this kind of documentation is typical of people with Asperger's syndrome.

Not surprisingly, such people are attracted to science, or 'natural philosophy' as it was known in her time. In this respect, it could be said that Daisy was the consummate scientist, the naturalist par excellence – much like Robert Boyle. She combined many specialities during her time in the desert and the bush. An ethnographer, anthropologist, ornithologist, geologist and astronomer, in the desert she knew the name of every bird, animal, flower and star. Ever the naturalist, she would send off specimens of mountain lizard or sand burrowers preserved in spirits to the National History Museum in London. Like Robert Boyle, she had an interest in natural remedies too. Combining knowledge picked up from various sources – from the Aborigines to the Irish – she made and administered her own remedies, from cough syrups to eye balms, using concoctions of tea leaves or daisies – often to good effect. Like St Francis of Assisi, she could be found tending to sick birds, animals or reptiles: she once healed the split mouth of a lizard:

> My old-fashioned remedies were particularly successful, making me rejoice that I was of Ireland, where bone-setters and wise women could cure all and sundry. My grandmother's cough mixture, the simple recipe of six ingredients that she dispensed to coughing children for fifty miles around – honey, brandy, lemon, olive oil, powdered candy and vinegar (a tablespoon of each) was most popular.

Much like a missionary, she tended to the welfare of the Aborigines, albeit without any zeal to convert them. Setting herself up as a healer, she nursed them back to health when they had fallen foul of the 'white man's illnesses', massaging their bodies and giving them nourishment, remedies and cough mixtures.

*

Given her propensity for facts and details, it comes as no surprise that in her possession were many notebooks and diaries, something that people with Asperger's syndrome often carry around with them – like her fellow Aboriginal enthusiast Bruce Chatwin. Typically, her diaries are not a chronology of each day's doings and goings but poetic turns of phrase describing sunsets, birds, wildlife and so on. Her notebooks frequently contained endless lists – again typical of those with Asperger's syndrome.

She made lists of all manner of shells, shrubs and bushes that surrounded her: 'saltbush, bluebush, samphire, billy button, spear grass, silver grass, blue grass, cotton bush'. Allied to this was a collecting instinct too: over the years, she collected many shells, flints and little fossils, often which possessed talismanic properties for the Aborigines. Lists of vocabularies or lists of details of Aborigines who had passed through Ooldea were all compiled by her diligent hand, like a public register. Sometimes there are strange concoctions of grocer lists or snatches of internal monologues – not unlike something that Joyce might have put in one of his novels.

No permanent home – nardoo
toothpaste, salt, baking soda, chalk borax, Ina, Junbur
Whirlwinds
Telephones
Breakdown
Winds and winds
The dead days of the
afternoon.

When her supplies of paper were exhausted, she would write notes on the backs of envelopes or whatever else came to hand. She would often stitch sheets of paper together to use as diaries – anything from flour paper to brown wrapping paper. In Ooldea, one trunk was reserved for notes and diaries and another for her manuscripts and vocabularies:

My voluminous notes had been scribbled anyhow and anywhere, on white paper and brown, diaries and notebooks and fragments, intelligible and unintelligible to any save me, packed into any receptacle that would hold them in my eight by ten tent, where they became inextricably mixed and were in constant peril of destruction.

Putting any order on her notes was beyond her because her mind could never focus on the big picture. Like Hamilton, she was not a systemiser and her notes were destined for chaos as a result. The celebrated British anthropologist A. R. Radcliffe-Brown at first agreed to edit her work for publication but reneged when presented with her 'long and wandering work'. Clearly, Daisy did not have the wherewithal to have her work published, preferring instead to record the information before the

Aborigines became extinct. At first, she showed a degree of naivety about getting her work authorised by Radcliffe-Brown: in fact, he later plagiarised it. Towards the end of her life, when the National Library of Australia agreed to house her work, she achieved some measure of order, but by that time her research had drawn to a close.

Writing about the Aborigines for publication was another aspect of her all-encompassing passion. In many cases, it was done as much to gain recognition as a means of augmenting her meagre or non-existent income. As a writer and journalist, she contributed to many newspapers, journals and magazines, including the *Department of Agriculture Journal,* the *Australasian,* the *Western Mail* and *The Advertiser.* Her style of article varied from traveller tales to personal histories of the Aborigines. One criticism of her traveller's tales was that they had little narrative sense, which again one would expect to find in someone with Asperger's syndrome. She was a perfectionist when it came to her journalism. In fact, Salter remarks that, to the end of her life, writing was a 'hardship' to her: 'The drafts of article that she left behind show that she polished and repolished. Well aware of her tendency to exaggerate, she took trouble to research her subject and prided herself on her written word.'

The prodigious energy at the heart of the Asperger genius was certainly found in Daisy, who radiated energy even in her declining years. Once, over a seven-month period, she covered 5,400 miles, visited seventy towns and acquired thirty-four new dialects, according to Salter. Her work was all-consuming and marked by tremendous self-discipline:

> I would camp out sometimes for days, sharing my food, nursing the babies, gathering vegetable food with the women, and making friends with the old men. Thus I extended and verified my knowledge by gradual degrees until I gained a unique insight into the whole northern aboriginal social system, and its life-story from babyhood to age. Every moment of my spare time was given to this self-imposed and fascinating study. Not a word nor a gesture passed me by without opening up an avenue of inquiry, tactfully and methodically pursued.

A certain urgency always pervaded her work. Having witnessed the extinction of many of their tribes, she inevitably speculated their race was doomed, judging by her account at Maaba Reserve:

I would be on duty from night till morning, collecting scraps of language, old legends, old customs, trying to conjure a nation of the past from these few and homeless derelicts, always in haste, as they died about me one by one, in fear lest I should be too late.

Her persistence and resilience were truly staggering. Even when there was an engine drivers' strike, resulting in her receiving no supplies for months, she did not leave Ooldea, like all the families of the fettlers – the men who worked on the railways. Instead, undeterred, she stocked up and spent weeks alone in the desert. Her working conditions were extreme by any standards, especially in the matter of getting copy to the newspapers. The harsh desert climate did little for her hands – or her typewriters. Her hands would get burnt and blistered from the heat and dryness and from carrying water, and she was forced to use seven finger stalls when typing. In fact, she put great energy into everything she did: even in England when learning to type, she practised so hard that her fingers bled.

*

In terms of her contribution to science, Daisy was one of the first people to do proper field research, the mainstay of ethnography, which involves the study of a small group of people in their own environment. The numerous years she spent alone in the bush or on the edge of Aboriginal camps paid huge dividends in terms of research and was ground-breaking. Moreover, because ethnographers are not looking for the 'big picture' but focus instead on a detailed account of the circumstances of the people being studied, Daisy could both describe and interpret based on the significance of whatever she observed. Someone like Daisy, who had difficulty looking at the big picture, was eminently suited to this kind of research. She was one of the first to write down the stories of the Aborigines and their own words, and to record how they thought, their kinship systems, totem groups, taboos, rituals and rites of passage, marriages, and singing and dancing ceremonies called *corroborees*. She also made maps and compiled dictionaries of dialects, along with recording innumerable legends and myths.

Part of Daisy's genius was an instinctive appreciation for the storytelling culture of the Aborigines. Coming from Ireland, which also boasted an oral culture, she knew the value of superstition and magic. In this respect, the manner in which she chose to gain the trust of the Aborigines was instinctively cunning. Pretending that her native name was 'Kallower', she claimed that she was a magic woman reincarnated from one of the wives of the dreamtime patriarch, Leeberr. This cleverly paved the way for the Aborigines to accept her as a kindred spirit: 'I knew their simple social organisation, and could speak to them as one of themselves, a blood-relation, and listen patiently to the old songs and stories.' Such was her acceptance by the Aborigines that she was allowed to witness many initiation rites, something expressly forbidden to women. Her capacity to 'think black', as she put it, and to glean so much information from them was made possible by her ability to live in the timelessness, or 'here and now', of the Aborigine mind:

> The first lesson that I learned was never to intrude my own intelligence upon [the Aborigine], and to have patience, the patience that waits for hours and years for the links in the long chain to be pieced together. A casual soul, he knows no urgency. Yesterday and to-day and to-morrow are all the same to him. Naturalness in white company comes from long familiarity. Only when you are part of the landscape that he knows and loves will he accord you the compliment of living his normal life and taking no notice of you . . . his unconscious confidences are by far the most valuable. Most of my data is the gradual compiling of many, many years.

To put Daisy in context as an ethnographer is also to draw attention to the huge scientific controversies in which she was involved. Many of these disputes arose, at best, from her failure to see the big picture or, at worst, from a desire to gain recognition and an income. There is much truth in Salter's suggestion that Daisy's adoption of the black community was at first an intellectual rather than an emotional one. Like Elspeth Huxley in Kenya, Daisy made arguments in defence of the white settlers initially. Being pro-settler, she defended the kindness and decency of the English, but the more she immersed herself in Aboriginal ways, the less enamoured she became with the white man. And losing her objectivity marked the end of her scientific detachment.

The controversial issues that dogged her life's work were her assertion that the Aborigines were a doomed race, her rejection of half-caste children, her promotion of a segregated state headed by a High

Commissioner for Native Affairs and, most contentiously, unsubstantiated claims of baby cannibalism among the Aborigines. At heart, the Asperger inability to see the big picture prompted her to reject any notions of integration or assimilation.

As a scientists, Daisy was well aware of the massive population decline among the Aborigines. Before 1788, the Aborigine and Torres Strait Islander population was estimated at 750,000 people, with approximately seven hundred languages being spoken throughout Australia. Over the years, she would interview the surviving members of various tribes, increasingly believing that the oldest and most fascinating race of people in the world was passing away before her eyes. She probably underestimated the survival instincts of the Aborigines and the onward march of evolution. Instead, the new generation of Aborigines displeased her: she saw them as being contaminated by the white man and having no respect for the songs, rituals and ways of life of their ancestors. They often took to begging, stealing, drinking and prostitution. In fact, everything about the white settlers seemed to hasten the demise of the Aborigines:

On their own country [the Aborigines] were trespassers. There was no more happy wandering in the interchange of hospitality. Sources of food supply slowly but surely disappeared, and they were sent away to unfamiliar places, compelled to change completely their mode of life, to clothe themselves in the attire of the strangers, to eat foods unfitted for them, to live within walls.

Their age-old laws were set aside for laws they could not understand. The younger generations, always wilful, now openly flouted the old, and defied them, and haunted the white man's homes, protected by his policeman. A little while, and they resorted to thieving – where theft had been unknown – and sycophancy, and sold their young wives to the depraved and foreign element. Half-castes came among them, a being neither black nor white, whom they detested. They died in their numbers of the white man's diseases, measles, whooping-cough, influenza, and the results of their own wrong-doing. . . .

Can we wonder that they faded so swiftly? Can we blame them for the sudden reactions that found vent in violence in certain instances few and far between, punished sometimes with terrible reprisals on the part of the white man?

Contrary to Daisy's belief, the Aborigines did not disappear. Today the indigenous population is about 410,000, or about 2 percent of the entire Australian population. In effect, the Aborigines offered little resistance to change and allowed nature to take its course – something that Daisy instinctively understood. She believed that the Aborigines had much in common with the Celts and Orientals in respect of keening for their dead and storytelling traditions, but more so in their tendency for fatalism.

Indeed, Daisy's own instinctive preservation of sameness made her embrace this notion of fatalism and resist attempts at integration with the white settlers. She genuinely believed that few Aborigines assimilated easily and survived. Ever the purist and idealist, she did not want the West to contaminate the Aborigines. 'I did my best to arrest the contamination of civilisation', she declared. She believed that mixing with white people had turned them into 'derelicts' – her word for the down-and-outs of the Aboriginal groups.

*

Daisy Bates exhibited a considerable degree of social impairment. Her need for isolation grew greater with the passing years, or rather she found solace more and more in solitude. She was clearly very much at home alone in the bush but rarely felt lonely:

> I knew every bush, every pool, every granite boulder, by its age-old prehistoric name, with its legends and dreamtime secrets, and its gradual inevitable change. There was no loneliness. One lived with the trees, the rocks, the hills and the valleys, the verdure and the strange living things within and about them. My meals and meditations in the silence and sunlight, the small joys and tiny events of my solitary walks, have been more to me than the voices of the multitude, and the ever-open book of Nature has taught me more of wisdom than is compassed in the libraries of men.

The nomadic Aborigines suited her because they offered a variable mixture of company and solitude. She moved to the bush as much to get away from the social setting of white people as to be close to the Aborigines. In so doing, she created an autistic world for herself in which she controlled everything to her own satisfaction. Moreover, the Aborigines posed no threat to her, and she thus welcomed their company. The more time she spent with them, the more detached she became from her own social group. Admittedly, her controversial views often alienated her from people. In the end, she described herself as 'a stranger to the ways and thoughts of my own people'. With the coming of the east–west railway in 1917, linking Brisbane to Sydney, she felt threatened by the presence of white men and kept a revolver under her pillow at night and under her skirt by day. A visit to the cities of Adelaide, Melbourne and Sydney in 1933 after years in the desert made her feel like a stranger and an anachronism in her old-fashioned clothes. When she returned to Adelaide after living in Ooldea, she would saunter across busy streets, blissfully unaware of traffic lights and heavy traffic, like a female Crocodile Dundee.

That said, during her sixteen years at Ooldea, Daisy maintained a tenuous link with her old life and still enjoyed very occasional visits by her old friends. But like Beckett and Boyle, such visits were always carefully prearranged. At appointed times, she would meet friends for an hour or so, when the train called at the station. Contrary to popular opinion, she hated publicity and would hide or avoid people if she could – although she would sally forth for official engagements like meeting royalty or government officials. Indeed, like Boyle and Hamilton she was an unashamed royalist. Unsolicited visits from white people were another matter, however. Such was her popularity and notoriety after the publication of *The Passing of the Aborigines* that, when she set up camp on the banks of the Murray River at Pyap, hordes of tourists would arrive to chat and take photos of her. Such was her annoyance at these intrusion that – in a move reminiscent of Robert Boyle – she was forced to put up notices asking them to keep out and stay away.

In her interactions with people, there was a certain lack of empathy and social know-how. In this respect, she has been variously described as arrogant, rude, bigoted, egocentric and intolerant. Her difficulties in seeing things from the perspective of the Australian government and its civil servants meant that she was very poor at negotiating. To compound matters, a lack of deference and tact often characterised her dealings with people, whether they were her employers in London or government authorities in Australia. Quite simply, she rubbed people up the wrong way – often in an imperious manner. Moreover, she would exaggerate whatever crisis situation existed in order to get her own way – something which usually failed to strengthen her case. She also disliked having to collaborate with colleagues, and her impulse to shock did little to enamour her to civil servants, many of whom regarded her as 'an irresponsible eccentric'.

There are many accounts of Daisy's eccentric and inappropriate behaviour. Blackburn mentions how once, on her arrival in Adelaide, she confronted the doorman of the Adephi Hotel and asked if she could take a bath – much to his perplexity. Furthermore, depending on the company, Daisy could alternate between charm itself and downright rudeness, and she was often prickly and cold. In her latter days at Ooldea, she refused to talk openly to the German missionary Annie Lock, whom she believed had muscled in on her work with the Aborigines. She communicate with Lock, who lived close by, only through correspondence. At Wynbring, she rarely exchanged a word with the white settlers other than a stiff greeting, according to Blackburn. In the white community, she was very much an outsider – as people with Asperger's syndrome often are. She clearly did not fit in with their society, and they looked upon her with suspicion. Different from them in every way – in terms of dress, beliefs and customs – she soon became a figure of fun, laughed at and called a witch or crazy woman.

The nature of her personal relationships followed a similar pattern. In childhood, she tended to seek out the company of older people in preference to her peers – something which is typically seen in those with Asperger's syndrome. In fact, Daisy cared 'not one shake of a lame mouse's tail', as she put it, for the opinions of her own age-group. In essence, she had poor social relationships with her peers and failed to maintain long-term intimate relationships. As regards female friendships, these were few and often ended because of friction. These women tended to be in supportive roles, much like James Joyce's women. Among them were the journalist Ernestine Hill, the altruistic Georgina King, and Hester Cayley, who were essentially midwives to the birth of her books or serialisations.

Men, on the other hand, were her mentors. Clearly, she was fond of men and found discourse in their company more to her liking. People with Asperger's syndrome, who possess an 'extreme male' brain, are certainly more at home with a male type of discourse. If her earliest memories are to be believed, she worshipped her father, 'the loveliest father in

Christendom'. Among her male mentors were influential editors, clergy and political figures: W. T. Stead, Bishop Stanton, Bishop Gibney, William Hurst, Father Nicholas, Premier Sir John Forrest, Sir William Campion and Arthur Mee. Although she enjoyed conversing with men, she frequently corresponded with them. Echoing several of the figures discussed in this book – including de Valera, Joyce and Boyle – Daisy was a prolific letter-writer and correspondent. Writing letters brought a degree of safety from intrusion and freedom of expression for her, and her lack of social know-how and the stress of intimate interpersonal contact were thus avoided. Many of her friendships were conducted in this way for many years.

With men she could be flirtatious and especially charming. In particular, her correspondence with William Hurst, editor of the *Australasian,* was full of banter and coquettish charm. In fact, she could charm the birds off the bush or, as one admirer said, 'the swans off a pond'. Living in the here and now, the type of men that Daisy was attracted to each time were those who, like herself, were restless. The power, wildness and romance of the Australian outback fed her imagination, and horsemen and drovers epitomised the heroic, pioneering spirit of the age. Her romantic, impulsive nature made her fall in love quickly but out of it even more quickly – even if this meant serial bigamy. Clearly marriage was a resounding disappointment each time and failed to live up to her idealistic expectations. There are records of three bigamous marriages: to Edwin Henry Morant, Ernest C. Baglehole and Jack Bates. There are also possibly two unacknowledged engagements: to Philip Gipps in New South Wales and Carrick O'Bryen Hoare in England. A scandal possibly of a sexual nature is rumoured to have occurred in Dublin before Daisy first left for Australia. The suggestion that she had an affair with the young man of the house, which clearly ended badly because he committed suicide, has been made by Blackburn. One thing that seems certain is that, once living among the Aborigines, Daisy's life was one of asceticism. Her self-imposed celibacy would not allow any man to enter her tent, in observance of the Aborigine custom.

By all accounts, Daisy met her match in the larger-than-life Morant, who was intelligent, well read, charming and impulsive, as well as being a romantic poet with a capacity for reinvention, and a pathological liar. Like Daisy, his origins were shrouded in mystery: he was rumoured to be the illegitimate son of an English admiral. Their marriage lasted for about a month. After stealing a pig and a saddle, Morant spent a week in prison, and he also failed to pay for the wedding. The couple separated – at Daisy's instigation – and reputedly never met again. Later, he achieved greater notoriety, meeting his end in South Africa in 1902 when he was executed by the British during the Boer War.

True to form, Daisy soon fell in love with Jack Bates, who had a similar prowess with animals, in 1884 in New South Wales. According to Daisy's version of events, the equally impulsive and independent Bates proposed marriage when they were out riding one day, and he arranged for them to stop off at a church, where a preacher was in attendance. Impulsive as ever, Daisy agreed to marry him there and then, dusty and drenched with sweat as she was.

It is possible that their marriage failed because Bates was a loner and restless like herself, preferring the company of drovers and cattle to domesticity. Much of his life was spent on the trail moving cattle from one part of Australia to another, and this did not change after he married. His quiet and taciturn manner was in sharp contrast to her exuberant vivacity. In addition, he failed to live up to Daisy's expectations and provide the home she wanted, and his sense of purposelessness filled her with contempt. Furthermore, she disliked his smell, his manner, and even his face when he was asleep! Despite having a son together, they avoided each other's company for several years, before finally parting in 1912. According to Blackburn, she only spoke about him with affection when she decided that he was dead; from 1912 onwards, she would refer to her 'late husband' as though she were widowed, despite the fact that he was still very much alive.

Her obvious lack of maternal instincts left Daisy open to a great deal of criticism. Although she liked children and generally got on well with them, the same could not be said for her own child, Arnold Bates. People with Asperger's syndrome often remain rather child-like and can feel at home with children rather than with their peers, and this was certainly the case with Daisy. Her love for children was based, according to Salter, more on her feeling of affinity with them than on any maternal protectiveness. Her first reaction to being told she was pregnant by her doctor was an emphatic: 'I don't want a baby'. In practice, she never really changed her opinion and certainly did not distinguish herself when it came to her mothering skills. After the baby was born, she refused her husband's conjugal rights and did not settle down to raise her child, preferring to live in anonymous hotels or by herself. In the first eight years of Arnold's life, responsibility for him was often abdicated to the nursemaid or his grandmother. He was finally sent to a boarding school when Daisy returned to England alone in 1894 for five years.

To the end of her days, Daisy was adept at erasing people from her life, whether one of her husbands or her son. They simply ceased to exist for her. By all accounts, she was very cold towards Arnold and in later years, for reasons unknown, took to referring to him as 'William'. It is little wonder then that her son was described by his cousin Charles Carney as a 'withdrawn, self-contained boy, lacking . . . spontaneous warmth'. His interests were, perhaps not surprisingly, in engineering and music. According to Blackburn, she seemed to be embarrassed by him, because he was awkward, uneasy and 'difficult in one way or another like his father'. Once Arnold reached adulthood, his mother's contact with him was brief and she probably never saw her two grandchildren. Rather tellingly, she admitted: 'I loved my cannibals more than I loved my family.'

*

There appears to be no evidence of any speech and language delay on Daisy's part. It is likely that she spoke early, and she was certainly never short of something to say. The fact that she had considerable problems with grammar as a child may indicate she had some difficulties with syntax or sentence formation, however. Indeed, grammar continued to pose problems for her at school, and teachers often resorted to disciplining her. In her reference to primary schooling, Daisy mentions that she attended the 'dame school in the dell', where she learned to read, write and count. This was probably the local Convent of the Sacred Heart in Roscrea, where she was taught Latin, French, German and mathematics. It is also believed that Daisy learnt Irish there and could speak it quite well. Certainly the nuns instilled in her a love of languages. A postulant from the Irish College in Paris taught her French and no doubt opened up a new world for her, beyond poverty-stricken Roscrea. Daisy had an astonishing linguistic ability. In her lifetime, she mastered 188 aboriginal dialects, and Ernestine Hill in *Kabbarli* claims that she was fluent in

French, Latin, German and Greek. Much of her linguistic ability can be attributed to her logical mind and exceptional memory; indeed, the phenomenal memory found in Asperger geniuses was certainly present in Daisy. It was referred to as 'total recall' by Salter and 'photographic' by Hill.

A profound love of language was evident: as well as her writing and linguistic skills, she took great delight in the spoken words of the Aborigines. She revelled in the 'rippling murmurs' or rolling r's of their language, which reminded her of Irish speech patterns. Indeed, the musicality of language delighted her, as it did Joyce and Beckett. Ernestine Hill noted that she had a musical ear for phonetics. She also had a flair for neologisms common to many with Asperger's syndrome: words like 'honeythunderositiness', 'gigglywinks' and 'limpositiness' – often showing the influence of Dickens, her favourite author – peppered her speech. Acrostics too were a favourite of hers from adolescence, especially one from a suitor that used the letters of her name and which she memorized, according to Salter:

*D*ost, oh dost thou remember the night we first met,
*A*h dear the remembrance to me,
I to my death will ne'er forget,
*S*weet lady that dance with thee,
*Y*es that dance so pleasant by thee!

Being well read, she could talk with great wit and charm on diverse subjects. Whenever stimulated, she would talk in monologues, as Salter notes: 'Her talk bubbled with a child's inconsequence but her range of subjects extended from politics to the theatre, from books to the latest court cases, punctuated by an earthy store of Aboriginal anecdotes.' It comes as no surprise that she was a good public speaker and was regularly invited to give lectures. According to Salter, she possessed the two essentials of a born lecturer: a carrying voice, which was deep-toned and pleasant to listen to, and a bubbling wit that prevented her audience from becoming bored.

Most accounts of Daisy refer to her remarkably soft voice, which was gentle and low; others described her voice as sweet. There is no evidence of a high-pitched or flat tone. Hill recalls that, in her long association with

Daisy, her voice was never monotonous. However, in common with many on the autistic spectrum, Daisy's voice could vary and undergo change. There was certainly a capacity on her part to alter her natural Irish brogue. Hill writes that she had an Irish intonation but not a shadow of brogue. Her years in England certainly modulated her accent somewhat. On her return to Australia in 1899, her voice had become more noticeably English, with clipped tones. Nonetheless, the Irish lilt was still evident forty years later.

*

An impish and childlike sense of humour, common to many with Asperger's syndrome, persisted throughout Daisy's life. In her mid-thirties, onboard the ship *Macquarie* sailing for England from Australia in 1894, Daisy and another female passenger played juvenile games, sliding along the polished wooden deck on metal trays for the entertainment of crew and passengers. Her Irish grin was legendary and her laugh described as 'ripe, wicked [and] unexpected'. Even into her late eighties, her sense of fun had not deserted her, and she delighted in being pushed on a garden swing. She was quite at home in the company of children and loved playing with them, particularly singing rhymes such as 'Here we go round the mulberry bush', which she would translate into whatever Aboriginal dialect she was using at the time. Cat's cradle, hide-and-seek, marbles, and 'I spy' were other games in her repertoire. Not surprisingly, given her talent for reinvention, she was good at impersonations and enjoyed taking part in dramas with the Aborigine women on special days, such as Empire Day. Like de Valera, Pearse and Boyle, she enjoyed the humour found in cartoons. She tells of how, as a girl – if she is to be believed – she and her father would laugh at the cartoons in his favourite magazine, *Punch*.

Given her mischievous disposition, she was not slow to shock people. Whenever she was back in polite society, such as in the women's clubs in Adelaide and Perth, she would deliberately shock elderly ladies with risqué tales of the Aborigines. During the Beagle Bay Mission, when she was forced to share a wagon in the bush overnight with Bishop Gibney and Father Nicholas, she teasingly asked the bishop whether he had ever put his shoes and socks on in bed with a lady before. The bishop humoured her on that occasion but at other times would tick her off when she overstepped the mark. Indeed, Daisy revelled in the ridiculous and the absurd. On one occasion, when she rescued a blind Aborigine called Dowie from a clump of bushes and carried him on her back, the irony was not lost on her: he was blind, demented and naked, while she was a member of Perth's most exclusive women's club!

*

An obsessive desire for sameness and repetition was undoubtedly deep-seated in Daisy's case. Those with Asperger's syndrome like highly organised systems, and Daisy certainly reflected this in her regular act of writing, her pattern of interaction with the Aborigines, her personal daily routine and, rather dramatically, in her style of dress. In this respect, she earned a reputation as an extremely eccentric lady.

The act of writing was itself a ritual for her. Regardless of sore eyes or fatigue, she would write every day, even if it was just a couple of words hastily committed to paper. This was important to her because she felt that it was her duty to mark or register the passing of each day. Recording the information she gathered from the Aborigines was naturally of greater importance to her. Once she had witnessed some tribal event, initiation or rite, she would record her 'data' straightaway so that she never got a word wrong, even if this meant getting to sleep at three o'clock in the morning.

Her life in the bush took on a familiar pattern too. She would move from camp to camp, complete her vocabularies, record fragments of legends, take note of customs, nurse the sick and comfort the bereaved. Many of her routines were ingrained over decades of living in the bush or desert. She had rituals for everything – waking up, eating, taking exercise – and hardly ever wavered from them. Rising early, she would watch the sunrise and slowly take in the day, breakfast on tea and toast, shower using a basin and a perforated kerosene tin, do her exercises such as skipping, and dress in a methodical fashion. This probably took some time, given the intricacies of Edwardian petticoats! By her own admission, she was meticulous in her dress and preserved a 'scrupulous neatness and all the little trappings and accoutrements of my own very particular mode of dress, sometimes under difficulties'. Associated with her daily routines was her repetitive style of dress. Her style of fashion did not change with the times, and year after year she wore the same clothes, similar to the

Asperger-like Wittgenstein after the First World War. Salter notes how her underskirts dated back to her school days. It is no exaggeration to say that identical sets of clothes bought in bulk in 1909 lasted her a lifetime. Admittedly, this was as much due to preservation of sameness as to thrift and dire straits:

> [Each morning] I made my toilet to a chorus of impatient twittering. It was a fastidious toilet, for throughout my life I have adhered to the simple but exact dictates of fashion as I left it, when Victoria was queen – a neat white blouse, stiff collar and ribbon tie, a dark skirt and coat, stout and serviceable, trim shoes and neat black stockings, a sailor hat and a fly-veil, and, for my excursions to the camps, a dust-coat and a sunshade. Not until I was in meticulous order would I emerge from my tent, dressed for the day. My first greeting was for the bird.

Many of her routines had almost sacred overtones. A black umbrella used as a sunshade was sacrosanct to her. At a garden party in 1901 for the visiting royals in Australia, she had dropped the umbrella. The then Prince of York, the future George V, picked it up and handed it to her. After that, it was always her 'royal umbrella', and no public appearance was complete without it.

*

Beyond doubt, one of the most fascinating aspects of Daisy Bates's character is the Asperger identity diffusion she manifested so dramatically. Of all those discussed in this book, she had the greatest need for reinvention. It could be said that she had no coherent sense of self, rooted in reality, but was on an endless search for a self-identity. In a rare moment of revelation, she said of herself: 'I am two people, one I like and the other I do not know.' In a further show of the multiple selves that constituted her, she declared: 'A thing of patches am I – here an exultation of duty, there a love of fun and frolic and again of melancholy.'

Having a coherent sense of self is dependent on having a personal chronology, but the ability to place personal events in time or sequence is often lacking in those with Asperger's syndrome. As a result, they have poor personal memory or selective memory. At heart, Daisy did not have a chronological sense of time but lived in the here and now. Time was not felt or measured in terms of past or future, but only in relation to the present. In one of her notebooks, she writes:

The sun falling quickly.
Suppose one had neither past nor future, that
one only lived in the immediate twenty-four
hours. Loneliness does not block one's thoughts
and one wishes it would.

As a result, the past was always revised from the perspective of the present, and a blending of fact and fiction thus occurred. There was a high tolerance for ambiguity on her part, which made reinvention a constant possibility. Any ambiguities over reinventing herself were overcome by her supreme conviction and self-belief. Like Joyce, Daisy had a sense of her own importance and was able to reinvent herself largely because she believed absolutely in the roles she played. When things did not go to her liking, she was not ashamed to ask, imperiously: 'Do you know who I am?'

To begin with, she deliberately obscured the circumstances of her birth and social background. There was uncertainty over her date of birth (variously given as 1859, 1861 and 1863), as she gave different dates on her wedding certificate and in other documents. Even the names of her relatives varied: baptized Margaret, she was called Daisy May; her mother's name was Bridget but Daisy claimed it was Marguerette, which was actually her aunt's name. In Australia, she always claimed she was a product of Anglo-Irish gentry and had moved in aristocratic circles in Ireland and Great Britain. Beyond doubt, origins were important to her in that they conferred respectability and status. Like Joyce and de Valera, she traced her origins to nobler times, claiming that she was descended from the O'Dwyers, an illustrious line of Catholic chiefs and barons who had had lands in Kilnamanagh in Tipperary for ten centuries but were dispossessed during the Cromwellian Wars.

If she did change her origins, this was clearly done for self-advancement. All her life, she carefully controlled all information about her early life, destroying evidence, telling lies, conveniently forgetting things and being deliberately vague and elusive. She claimed that a freak flood on one of the ship's decks destroyed her entire collection of family and childhood photographs during her passage to England in 1894. A bonfire, started by herself, of her diaries, letters and papers in 1940 at Pyap in

South Australia, on the banks of the Murray river put an end to any hope of clarity in regard to her origins.

Clearly, to the outside world Daisy came across as having a selective memory. In a radio interview in the late 1930s, she was elusive about her early life: 'Oh, I couldn't tell you anything about years because the one thing I can't remember is years.' At the height of her popularity, when asked about her early life, Daisy was ready with the answers, as Blackburn relates:

> Daisy tells them everything that has come to mind, the story changing and changing again according to her mood. She tells of the beauty of her mother, the kindness of her father whom she loved so passionately, the good breeding and generosity of her grandmother. She remembers her brothers and sisters, the silver, the portraits, the lace dresses, dancing and riding on horseback. She will never forget the particular pleasure of shaking hands with Queen Victoria one bright sunny day [at Balmoral]. She couldn't have been more than six years old.

A restless spirit and need for recognition are just two manifestations of identity diffusion in the Asperger genius. The taste for high adventure was extreme in Daisy's case: sailing ships, cattle droving, going on expeditions, and so on. She once travelled three thousand miles in a saddle from Broome to Ethel Creek on a droving mission. She certainly felt most at home with the nomadic lifestyle of the Aborigines, as she realised in 1912: 'By this time I was a confirmed wanderer, a nomad even as the aborigines.' The sense of purpose she achieved among the Aborigines was so powerful that she endured the desert for sixteen years, relying on all her wits and resources to survive, and sometimes in poor health. Indeed, these must have been exciting times for her too, as she was resourceful and a good hunter.

In effect, Daisy was a consummate actress moving from one stage play to another: her occupations included that of governess, journalist, librarian, ethnographer, tribal matriarch and Keeper of Totems among the Aborigines. Her abilities meant that she could build up a circle of influential friends who welcomed her as a member of their clubs and societies. Blackburn writes that 'she did manage to jump from one stepping stone to another, inventing herself as she went along.' In the process, she was labelled a fantasist and an exaggerator, if not a pathological liar.

The most astonishing aspect of her life is her serial bigamy, where her capacity to embrace the moment negated all previous ties.

Recognition is necessary for those with Asperger's syndrome because it confers an identity, however brief or transitory. Numerous titles were proudly held by her: Fellow of the Anthropological Society of Australia, Honorary Correspondent of the Royal Institute of Great Britain and Ireland, Member of the Royal Geographical Society of Melbourne. Popular with public and press, in 1921 she was dubbed the 'Great White Queen of the Never Never'. Her celebrity status meant that she rarely failed to accept invitations to lecture, open fêtes or give out school prizes.

No doubt the role that she prized most was that of tribal matriarch. She learned from the Aborigines that there was no greater love than a mother's love, which was a love of never-ending service. It became her responsibility to care for the Aborigines with loving kindness, and this explains why she would refuse to leave 'her people' in the desert in the face of drought, famine or engine-drivers' strikes. From her writings, it is clear that she was a benevolent yet ever-watchful figure of authority who could command considerable power. 'There was none who dared to question Kabbarli', Daisy announced. It is clear too that she enjoyed the deference of the Aborigines. Ever patient, they would wait until they had summoned up the courage to approach her, as Kibbarli. Furthermore, they would walk from miles around to visit her:

> To the grey-headed, and the grey-bearded, men and women and children alike, I became *kabbarli,* the Grandmother. I had begun in Broome as *kallower,* a grandmother, but a spurious and a very young one, purely legendary. Since then I had been *jookan,* sister, among the Bibbulmun; *ngang-ga,* mother, among the scattered groups of Northampton and the Murchison, but it was at Dorré Island that I became *kabbarli,* Grandmother, to the sick and the dying there, and *kabbarli* I was to remain in all my wanderings, for the name is a generic one, and extends far among the western-central and central tribes.

There is a sense that Daisy cast herself in the role of saint and martyr, as a self-appointed Florence Nightingale of the natives who would endure all kinds of hardships and privations for them. Moreover, from her time on Dorré and Bernier Islands – an infectious-disease colony for Aborigines – she played the part of Lady Bountiful for the rest of her days, dispensing not only food and medicines, but also little treats and gifts: 'I did what I could among them with little errands of mercy; distributing rations and blankets from my own government stores when boats were delayed; bringing sweets and dainties for young and old, extra blankets in the rain, and where I could a word of love and understanding.' She maintained that little presents always promoted goodwill.

The Lady Bountiful aspect of her personality possibly had delusions of grandeur about it, but the distribution of alms was reminiscent of her very charitable Grandmother Hunt, and indeed Queen Victoria. She earned the reputation from government officials of being 'bad with money', and they soon tired of her demands for more supplies. While she was not personally extravagant, her generosity towards the Aborigines was boundless, and her small presents tended to make costs soar.

Being a tribal elder also contained an element of sexual ambiguity for her. The Aborigines, she claimed, had told her that in the Old Time she had been a man, a tribal elder, but that now 'I was neither man nor woman.' Clearly this gender fusion and confusion appealed to her, as indeed it appealed to Joyce, with his notions of the manly woman and the womanly man. Besides, her sexual identity became ever more asexual or celibate as time went on. By all appearances, from 1913 onwards Daisy was celibate and adhered religiously to the Aborigine custom of allowing no man other than her husband to enter her tent. 'I never forgot or ceased to obey that fundamental law', she said – not for the Bishop of Willochra or for royalty.

One of the highest honours bestowed on her by the Aborigines was that of Keeper of the Totems. No native woman had ever received this honour, whereby she was entrusted with the care of the sacred totem boards. In fact, her increasing immersion in the life of the Aborigines saw her adopting many 'spiritual' roles, as her 'patients' often responded to psychological rather than medical cures. Having acquired a magic stick, she at times came close to acting as a sort of witchdoctor. 'My healing and my Kabbarli wisdom,' she claims, 'were a source of all my power.' When caring for the Aborigines imprisoned on Rottnest Island, she objected to the practice of locking up members of different totem groups in the same cell and went to great lengths to soothe their minds.

Alas, practical recognition was slow in coming: she never published an academic book, much to her disappointment; she was passed over for paid commissions and appointments; and she was denied the paid post of Chief Protector of the Aborigines. On several occasions, she was passed over for government positions because of her age or her sex. Her visits to Adelaide, Melbourne or Sydney for meetings with governors or premiers, or for scientific congresses, excited her greatly, not least because she then felt part of the scientific community. Meeting distinguished anthropologists at one such congress in 1938 was a 'happy and exhilarating' time for her. Despite not receiving proper official or academic recognition, on a public and popular level she fared much better. By far one of her most rewarding acknowledgements came when she received the Order of Commander of the British Empire (CBE) in 1934. Though she was Irish, Daisy at heart never had any leanings towards nationalism and, like Boyle, Hamilton, and even Joyce to some extent, was content to bask in the glory of the Empire, as she saw it. 'This recognition from our beloved Sovereign,' Daisy rejoiced, 'coming as it did when my little camp was almost empty of provender and my heart of hope, has been the full reward of my life's service.'

It was only in the last decade of her life that Daisy fitted fantasy to fact, according to Salter. It could be argued that, by this stage, she had nothing left to prove.

*

In her lifetime, Daisy was called many things, from foolish and quixotic to rebellious and racist. More often than not, her actions were inexplicable or eccentric and inevitably gave rise to such judgements. Many of her actions were the product of an exceptionally harsh or autistic superego. Indeed, her moral vision was extremely sharply defined. All her life, Daisy's values and sense of respect, duty and pride were set in high relief. Exposed to Victorian dress in her formative years, she felt naked if her neck was revealed and would deplore the arrival of new fashion trends, which involved more and more flesh being exposed. Like Joyce, Daisy was no bohemian, for all her bigamous marriages and seductiveness. Paradoxically, she had a certain strain of puritanism and asceticism, not unlike that of Boyle, de Valera and Pearse. Those who crossed her path in life considered her to be either a true saint or a sanctimonious do-gooder.

Respect was a cornerstone value for Daisy: she felt that it should be accorded to the Aborigines, and also to her. In demanding respect, she could be imperious. Much like Joyce, she objected to being called by her Christian name, regardless of race or status, preferring instead the matronly 'Mrs Bates'. In order to maintain her matriarchal prestige among the Aborigines, it was vital that she bestowed on them gifts in exchange for the information they so gladly volunteered to her. By her own admission, she never attempted to alter the Aborigines' natural habits and environment. She never treated them like servants and respected their laws and customs. When Aborigines travelled for miles around to visit her, the visit followed a certain pattern, modelled on respect. First, she would welcome the visitor and give them tea and bread to put them at their ease, and would then clothe them before explaining the white man's ways and laws. Her pride was enormously important to her – pride in both position and appearance. Pride made her put on a cheery and chirpy mask – the 'mustn't grumble' disposition of true and loyal subjects of the Empire. So proud was she that she would never stoop to ask for charity and was incapable of playing the part of a civil servant.

In the maintenance of standards, she never brooked compromise. Things were either right or wrong, and there was no middle ground. Even in London, when working for Stead on the spiritualist magazine *Borderline*, she resigned her job rather than compromise her beliefs on Christian spiritualism. Furthermore, collaborations with various anthropologists were cast aside over the years with dismissive scorn. She was as unforgiving as she was uncompromising. When the Ooldea station master, A. G. Bolam, publicly accused her of killing any initiative the Aborigines ever had and of making them dependent on government aid, she cut him dead. Whenever she encountered him, she would walk right past him as though he were invisible and never spoke to him again.

Daisy's sharp superego also extended to certain purist views. There is no doubt that her beliefs were often idealistic, especially regarding half-caste children – something of which she disapproved strongly. During her time at Ooldea, she did everything in her power to restrict the practice severely:

No more half-caste children were born in Ooldea from 1920 until the temporary cessation of my work there in 1934, nor were any half-caste ever begotten in any of my camps. I had my own way of dealing with the problem. I walked delicately, by quiet persuasion preventing the black girls from haunting the white men's huts, and by equally quiet persuasion, from a different angle, deterring the white men from association with them, an appeal to the women of their own race and colour to play the game that never faded.

Aborigines, she believed, should be kept away from the dangers that interaction with the white man posed – begging, prostitution and stealing. Her notion of 'protector', however, was more akin to that of warden or moral policeman. In her maternal way, she wanted to warn and protect 'her' people from these dangers, but this tended to abnegate the rights of the Aborigines and turn the camp into a nanny state. Similarly, she wanted to create a separate, segregated state where all Aborigines could live to ensure the survival of their race. In this respect her idealistic, purist mind in the role of 'saviour' of her people brings to mind de Valera and his stewardship of the fledgling Irish state. Notions of race segregation inevitably raise the disturbing issue of race eugenics. Clearly Daisy left herself open to the charge of racism, however well intentioned she may have been.

Bestowed with an innate sense of justice and decency, Daisy's letters time and again make reference to her 'playing the game' – and to her disappointment when others failed to do so. Occasionally, when she thought the Aborigine system too harsh or cruel, as for example when a woman was punished by having her wrist or ankle bones broken, she intervened. A sense of fair play always governed her dealings with people, and she believed that the punishment should fit the crime. Sending people 'to Coventry', she argued, was the best punishment for an assortment of misdemeanours, and its results were effective.

*

If ever conflict was at the heart of genius, this was the case with Daisy. A reputation for being a rebel, a controversialist or indeed perverse dogged her. Typical of many of those with Asperger's syndrome, she seldom took advice, rejected received wisdom and was hypercritical. Many who knew her recalled how difficult she could be. In her newspaper articles, it was said that she frequently wrote in a dismissive way. Being controlling and dominating was one thing in the outback, where she was the ruling matriarch, but it proved extremely difficult in the 'white' centres of power. In her dealings with civil servants, she was positively hostile. This climaxed in 1920, which saw an end to her being given any further paid work by the government. As far as the civil servants were concerned, she was 'a self-willed eccentric who refused to acknowledge their authority' – she often went over the heads of officials and straight to top, usually the governor or premier. The depth of her moral outrages was considerable. Letters full of unashamed venom would land on officials' desk when she lost government appointments or commissions. Right was always on her side, as she saw it, and she protested fiercely.

In possession of an independent mind and tremendous willpower, Daisy naturally could be controlling in her behaviour, if not manipulative and vengeful. She openly admitted that she 'broke all the rules', as people with Asperger's syndrome often do. This tendency for control was evident from her early days in Australia: she was described as being obstinate, and her friend Hester Cayley recalled that she was 'a wayward girl, as stubborn as Paddy's mule'. In this respect, she also showed features of oppositional defiant disorder often seen in those with Asperger's syndrome.

Daisy might have advanced further in her academic career if she had been prepared to accept the authority of Radcliffe-Brown, who led the first Cambridge anthropological expedition in Australia. Their relationship was far from harmonious, however, and Radcliffe-Brown was as individualistic and dominating as she was. There was no question of Daisy yielding to his authority, however.

The vengeful side of Daisy was similar to that of Joyce or Boyle. Indeed, she would harbour grudges for many years before exacting revenge, usually quite spectacularly. At a scientific congress in 1914, where Radcliffe-Brown presented some anthropological material, the chairman duly asked Daisy, who was in the audience, to comment. Relating the story later to an interviewer, she recalled her words precisely: 'I said that Mr Brown had given my notes so nicely there was no occasion to add to them.' Because her work had been plagiarised by Radcliffe-Brown, she became paranoid about future collaborations. In fact, she refused to collaborate at all for the remainder of her life, even though this resulted in her work being largely unpublished.

*

Throughout her life, Daisy had several sensory impairments and sensitivities. Like de Valera and Joyce, she had considerable eye problems, and her
eyes appear to have been quite photosensitive. It is not known whether
she was short-sighted or not, but certainly by 1919 she had developed
severe eye strain and was using eyeglasses and a magnifying glass to read.
She also developed the chronic inflammatory eye disease known as sandy
blight. This condition was occasionally so severe that she developed near-
total blindness, but she generally declined surgery. The pain and disability, if not danger, it brought were a considerable trial to her, but she per-
severed in her work – much like de Valera and Joyce too.

Clearly, Daisy also had acute visual perception. The green landscapes
of Ireland were indelibly imprinted on her mind since childhood. The
diverse and visually appealing landscapes of Australia were a constant
source of stimulation for her too. The colours of the desert were especially vivid to her, and she loved to watch desert sunsets and the
afterglows that illuminated the sky. During the drought in Ooldea, a green
cabbage stalk propped up against an acacia tree outside her tent was both
restful for her eyes and a constant reminder of Ireland.

Like many Asperger geniuses, Daisy experienced sleep problems or
difficulties maintaining circadian rhythms. Her requirement for sleep was
very low indeed: she would wake after only six hours of sleep at night.
When witnessing initiation rites, storytelling or other night-time activities,
her hours of sleep were reduced even more. Even when the sun was at its
hottest, she was never able to sleep during the daytime. Although she lived
most of her life in the open air or in the deserts of Australia, her clothes
– long Edwardian dresses, gloves, hat and fly veil – meant that her skin
was never exposed to the sun and was also possibly deficient in melanin,
which has been linked to sleep problems in those with autism.

It is difficult to say whether Daisy was hypersensitive to sound, but it
seems certain that her hearing was acute. After living in the desert, her
hearing was sharper: she could hear a camel approaching from several
miles' distance by his muffled thud. While it is not known if she played a
musical instrument or not, she had an appreciation for music and liked to
sing, especially hymns from her childhood. The perfect unisons and har-
monies of Aboriginal singing were striking to her and reminded her of
Irish singing. Music as a form of expression was certainly important to
her – whether of songs or keening – especially for the surges of emotion
that it brought:

If you are a Celt you can sense what the singer is unable to express, and feel the varied emotions passing through him. Subjects that have lent themselves to epics in other lands can only be rendered by the aborigine in a crude sentence. His totem songs – a few words at most – are sung with wild abandon, the emotions they stir within him becoming stronger with every repetition, until finally, from excess of feeling, the singer will often fall unconscious, to be roughly massaged into life again.

She compared the Aborigines' crooning lullabies, with their soft melodies rising and falling, to an aboriginal Gregorian chant. She also enjoyed birdsong and the singing of whales, and was particularly attuned to the sound of the waves, especially in the years she spent at Eucla on the south coast of Australia: 'I love the whisper of the wind in the *mulga* [trees] [and] watch the movement of the stars'.

Daisy evidently relished movement, the more rapid the better. Through childhood and early adulthood, she liked fast activities and ones where good balance and proprioception were required, such as running, tennis, hockey, dancing and horseriding. In this respect too, she appeared to have good muscle tone and no motor clumsiness, although she once admitted to being 'all hands'. Sea voyages did not induce seasickness, and during her schooling her handwriting was neat and precise.

It appears that Daisy was hypersensitive to touch in some respects. According to Blackburn, as a child she confessed that she 'hated being photographed if the photographers were men, I disliked their touch on my shoulders and arms. As a small child I was untouchable by any person except my nurse.' The hypersensitivity was most acute when it came to the texture of her clothes: it is not surprising that she gained a reputation for being fussy and finicky. Silk next to her skin was the only material she would allow; anything else 'burnt her like acid'. The sensation of various winds, from sandstorms to zephyrs, on her skin was often poetically described by her; the ones she most liked were the gentlest breezes caressing her face. The texture of certain rocks appealed to her also. In her pocket she liked to carry a meteor stone, a shiny black bead of molten glass commonly found near the Ooldea Soak. The touch of flintstones, especially when they absorbed the warmth of her skin, was particularly soothing too. Indeed, the ritual of carrying and collecting stones was also seen in Joyce and in Beckett's character Molloy.

There is no doubt that Daisy, like Joyce, had an acute sense of smell.

Her environment was a vast olfactory lab for her. Living in a hot climate no doubt augmented certain smells, which made her even more sensitive. In fact, she learned to recognise people and tribes by their smell and could describe smells in great detail. The more she immersed herself in the life of the desert and the Aborigines, the more she objected to the smells of white men. Her writings and letters are often full of references to objectionable smells: that of her husband Jack, the 'oniony' smell of Annie Lock, the 'cloying' smell of the people who brought her in an ambulance to Port Augusta in 1945, and 'three odoriferous Chinese'. She did not find all smells unpleasant, however, and would savour the sweet, fresh scent of herbage after rain.

In terms of taste, her childhood 'memories' reveal that she had a sweet tooth, with an insatiable appetite for the pastries in a particular Dublin cake shop. In her later years, when collaborating with Ernestine Hill on *My Natives and I,* her sweet tooth had not deserted her, and in the offices of *The Advertiser,* where they worked, fruit and coffee with 'lashings' of cream was the order of the day. By and large, Daisy had fastidious if not frugal tastes when it came to food and always had a small appetite. She mostly liked simple foods and drinks, such as cold water and tea, and had a penchant (which was rarely indulged) for a drop of brandy – something she inherited from her father. Basically, she lived on tea and toast – or the unleavened bread known as damper – jam, honey, porridge and vegetables such as carrots and tomatoes, and fresh fish whenever possible. Never slow to accept Aborigine hospitality, she dined on roasted lizard, snake and grubs or the native game of kangaroo, emu, wombat and wallaby, when it was offered. By her own admission, she was no cook, ate little meat and tended towards vegetarianism:

> My own fare, day after day, throughout the years, has always been so simple that to myself I am a miracle. I have consoled myself with the reflection that the simpler our needs, the nearer we are to the gods. A potato in the ashes, now and again a spoonful of rice that nine times out of ten was burned in my absence or absentmindedness, occasionally the treat of a boiled egg, and always my tea – my panacea for all ills – were the full extent of my culinary craft.

Being close to nature, the senses of the Aborigines, especially touch and smell, were far more sensitive than those of the white man.

Like so many Asperger geniuses, Daisy did not always enjoy good health and was hospitalised numerous times, mostly for pneumonia, malnutrition and eye infections. Even so, illness rarely got in the way of what she wanted to do. Many of the deaths in her family were likely to have occurred due to tuberculosis. Diabetes also tended to run in the family, though there is no mention of Daisy developing it. From her years in the desert, sandy blight did untold damage to her eyesight, resulting in recurring bouts of blindness, while old age brought other illnesses, including skin cancer. She also suffered from periodic depression and anxiety. 'Anxiety was a constant companion . . . fear of want was directly responsible', Salter notes. Sometimes her ability to withstand all sorts of privation was not enough. Habitually, she had no concrete prospect of financial assistance and was too obstinate to give in and ask for help. She mentions a 'bad breakdown in health' that occurred in 1918, which necessitated a stay in an Adelaide hospital. In her later years, she developed signs of a persecution complex and could be quite paranoid. Furthermore, she was quite narcissistic. Salter notes how her pride would become 'inflamed to the point of mania' – something which is not uncommon in people with Asperger's syndrome. Usually work was her antidepressant, and being close to the sea or aboard a ship certainly helped her too. According to Blackburn, she would write descriptions of the skies to calm her in times of stress.

*

The sense of religion or religiosity, often found in Asperger geniuses, certainly pervaded Daisy's outlook on life. Not surprisingly, her religiosity was tempered by her religious heritage, both Anglican and Catholic. Depending on circumstance, she could adroitly mimic the rituals of both traditions. Indeed, her sister Catherine, though baptized an Anglican, later became a Catholic nun. Daisy's experiences of spiritualism as a young woman working in London made her cynical, however. At that time, she felt that spiritual phenomena were in God's domain and that, when they genuinely occurred, they should be left undisturbed and certainly not subjected to experiment. She considered anything else blasphemy and strongly disapproved of mediums. Equally, she disapproved of London psychic clubs such as the Fabian Society, which was patronised by a host of Irish literati, including Yeats, Shaw and Wilde.

Yet her spiritual genes were certainly much in evidence, in spite of the fact that she admitted no creed and practised no particular faith in adulthood. But, like Joyce, for all her denials she never quite relinquished her faith. She retained a copy of the Bible that had been presented to her as a young girl, and whenever the opportunity arose she would walk to church on a Sunday. We hear that she held the Trappist Mission in Broome, which she visited in 1899, in high regard and took part in their religious services, even though she was avowedly not a Catholic: 'Although I am an Anglican, I attended all religious ceremonies, morning and evening, during my stay, and loved to listen to the natives . . . intoning the Latin chants and responses.' This unorthodoxy also occurred with Pearse, de Valera, Joyce, Boyle and Hamilton.

Daisy's immersion in the ways of the Aborigines deepened her sense of spiritualism, in a universal, timeless sense. This was replaced by a feeling of being at home with the magic and superstition of the Aborigines. Moreover, she saw herself in the role of seer and referred to 'my clairvoyance'. The vein of mysticism in the Celtic character, she believed, helped her to relate better to the Aborigines. Moreover, she realised how similar the Aborigine imagination was to hers, albeit far more powerful. Indeed, the intensely vivid imagination she exhibited in childhood never deserted her – something that is certainly a recurring feature of the Asperger genius. She imagined the hills around her home in Tipperary to be vast burial grounds, with people and potatoes lying side by side, and that before the Famine hills had not existed. As a child, she delighted in peasant stories and in adult life would retell Irish fairy tales and legends, remembered from childhood, over and over again. She began to write poetry as a child and continued to do so into her early adolescence and for most of her adult life. In essence, Daisy had a medieval mindset, like many an Asperger genius: the mixture of the sacred and the profane was intrinsically logical to her.

From her time in the desert and among the Aborigines, the eternal and unchanging world came to take on a greater significance for Daisy. She came to understand how the Aborigine cosmology or creation myths of the dreamtime pervaded the fabric of their lives. Clearly the notion of dreamtime or the 'time before time' became spiritually important to her. Living in the desert, where the days rolled into each other, was like living in eternity, or where time was suspended. The dreamtime was fundamentally mystical in nature.

In the manner of many Asperger geniuses action was Daisy's yard-stick, and her motto 'Example, example always.' Echoing Joyce, she believed in 'deeds and not words' and found most religions wanting because 'they lack that humanity which should be the very pith and centre of spiritual activity'. Her sacrifice was her lifetime dedication to the Aborigines in the face of enduring hardship and privation. Like Pearse and Emmet, hers was a sacrifice embraced with great courage, and willingly. Had she been less fearless in her work with the Aborigines, she would have achieved little. 'I lived their lives, not mine,' she wrote. 'I have given up all my social life to my work and I am as happy as Larry over the sacrifice.'

7

WILLIAM BUTLER YEATS

I have no instincts in personal life. I have reasoned them all away.

W. B. Yeats, letter to Robert Gregory, 1909

In the hierarchy of poets, William Butler Yeats is an arch-poet. His work is celebrated today for its lyricism, its simple beauty and symbolism, and its profound love of Irish myth and landscape. The poetic genius of this Nobel Prize winner is beyond dispute. Many lines of his poetry have entered the nation's vernacular – *'I will arise and go now, and go to Innisfree'*; others have been set to music – *'Down by the salley gardens my love and I did meet'*; and others have become part of daily speech – *'All changed, changed utterly'*.

Yeats is remembered not only for his towering legacy to literature, specifically poetry and drama, but also for his association with the birth of the nation. His political and cultural links with the emerging Irish Republic saw him carve out a public niche for himself – as steward of the state. From the many accounts of his remarkable life, a compelling picture emerges of the Asperger aspects of his character. A diagnosis of Asperger's syndrome certainly comes close to bridging the excesses and eccentricities of his personality and his creative genius.

218

*

William Butler Yeats was born on 13 June 1865 in Sandymount, Dublin, the eldest son of John Butler Yeats and his wife Susan Pollexfen, whose family had milling and shipping interests in Sligo. In time, he was joined by three siblings that would survive childhood, Susan (Lily), Elizabeth (Lolly) and Jack B. Yeats. Each of the siblings possesssed a keen intelligence and was gifted and talented in their own right. The Pollexfens and the Yeatses were the products of Irish Protestant stock, though the family fortune sharply declined when John Yeats forsook a career in law to purse a precarious one as a portrait painter.

In appearance and demeanour, W. B. Yeats exhibited many features of Asperger's syndrome. He was tall and thin (though somewhat portly in later years), and handsome, with a crop of jet-black hair that silvered over time. The poet Katherine Tynan thought that he was beautiful to look at, as indeed did many others. Sallow-skinned, his face was narrow, with high cheek bones, a fine straight nose, and a small, sensitive, firm mouth. Furthermore, with limited expression, his face was no register of changing emotions. In this respect, Terence Brown in *The Life of W. B. Yeats: A Critical Biography* writes that the poet seemed 'cold, aloof, curiously without evident affect'.

While there are no reports of him avoiding eye contact, Yeats's eyes were certainly distinctive and mesmeric. Among his peers, they were the focus of much attention: Tynan described them as 'eager, dark eyes'; Maurice Bowra as 'dark eyes that peered into infinity'; and others saw them as 'slanting', 'penetrating', 'flashing' or 'luminous and black'. They often gave him an ethereal or otherworldly look. The historian A. L. Rowse observed the older Yeats as having 'a puckered look of a small child; weak eyes, visionary and estranged from the world'. The poet's peculiar eyes also came to the attention of the Ulster writer St John Ervine:

> He has a queer way of focussing when he looks at you. I do not know what is the defective sight from which he suffers, but it makes his way of regarding you somewhat disturbing. He has a poetic appearance, entirely physical.

In terms of his gait, the writer George Moore referred to Yeats as being 'excessive in gait' and having 'long heavy feet'.

In common with many Asperger geniuses, he had a powerful presence, which was infused with unmistakable charm, and had a way of captivating people. When reciting poetry, he would talk slowly, in a low voice that could hold listeners spellbound. Moreover, he had poise, aloofness and a certain aristocratic bearing that lent him an air of proud arrogance. Clearly, he often had an extraordinary impact on people. In 1930, he impressed the formidable Virginia Woolf with the 'force of his personality and the power of his conversation at full flood', according to R. F. Foster in his celebrated biography *W. B. Yeats: A Life*. On a lecture circuit in the United States, Yeats had a particularly profound impact on his audience. One undergraduate of Bowdoin College in Maine recalled that Yeats was the most impressive man he had ever seen; others were made uneasy by Yeats's otherworldly presence. When editing *Blake's Prophetic Books* with Edwin Ellis, Yeats completely unnerved Ellis's German wife. Keith Alldritt in *W.B. Yeats: The Man and the Milieu* records how she grew alarmingly uncomfortable in the presence of the great poet:

> [She] became alarmed by the shabbily dressed mystical poet who would throw his arms about rhythmically in her drawing room, as though conducting an orchestra. . . . On one occasion she threw him out of the house for, said Yeats, she was entirely convinced that she had thrown a spell on her.

Classmates were not immune from the effect of the young Yeats either. Alldritt relates how one of these classmates recalled that Yeats was a 'queer chap' and that there was something 'quietly repellent' in his manner which affected even his relations with his teachers. Yeats was not unaware of the effect he had on others and acknowledged that sometimes people were put off by his posing and artificial manner.

The childlike quality seen in many Asperger geniuses was present in Yeats too. All his life he had an astonishing inability to take care of himself. According to his son Michael, writing in *Cast a Cold Eye: Memories of a Poet's Son and Politician,* Yeats was helpless when it came to dealing with the ordinary requirements of everyday living. Like a child, he was liable to do anything and needed constant minding. Once, he ate a whole packet of opiated cough lozenges, according to Foster, and slept for thirty hours.

*

It comes as a surprise to many that Yeats, who had such a natural talent for literature, had considerable difficulties with language. There is strong evidence that he experienced a delay in developing speech and language. Alldritt notes that he was 'slow in mastering his alphabet and learning to read'. In later years, Yeats confessed that he 'was difficult to teach'. Certainly by the age of nine, he still could not read. Needless to say, this did not go unnoticed at home: the entire family tried to teach him to read and became convinced that he would never master the skill. In some quarters, this gave rise to anger and frustration. Michael Yeats records how his grandfather, judging his father to be a difficult pupil, 'boxed his ears' and set about teaching him to read himself, but to little effect. Naturally, given the sensibilities of the period, the Pollexfens came to believe that Yeats was both mentally and physically defective.

Having finally learnt to read shortly after the age of nine, Yeats, like Einstein, had problems with spelling and pronunciation. Michael Yeats recalls how his father was unable to spell even simple words correctly ('gas' would be spelt 'gass', for instance) and that his punctuation was 'peculiar'. Moreover, his handwriting was often wild and illegible. The erratic spelling and punctuation persisted all his life and was largely phonetic-based ('tecnic' for 'technique', for example). Yeats was not unaware of these shortcomings, however. Foster writes that the poet would admit his 'blindness to grammar, spelling and the appearance of "my lines upon paper" ' all his life. It is possible that Yeats had dyslexia, which often occurs along with autistic spectrum disorders. Nonetheless, once he had learnt to read, Yeats appeared to have no difficulty in comprehending what he read. In fact, he was autodidactic, like many with Asperger's syndrome, and read avidly.

Like Einstein, but unlike other Asperger geniuses, Yeats was a poor linguist. He took up French and German at the High School on Harcourt

Street in Dublin, but fared badly in these subjects. Numerous times in his life he tried to learn French, but its pronunciation got the better of him on more than one occasion. According to Foster, Yeats was 'constitutionally incapable of learning French or any other language'. At school, he appeared to have had some aptitude for Latin and enjoyed good marks in it from time to time. It is quite likely that he had a good grounding in Latin grammar. In contrast, he was unable to learn Irish, despite his fervent regard for it. In fact, it pained him that he could not acquire his native language. There are no accounts of the methods employed in teaching him Irish.

Yeats's schooling suffered because of the somewhat haphazard nature of his early life – a result of his father's bohemian existence, which involved him travelling between Sligo, Dublin and London to paint. Sometimes the family moved with him; at other times they remained behind while John Yeats sought commissions. For the first ten years of his life, the young William lived largely in Sligo, but he received a more conventional education during his early adolescence at the Godolphin School in Hammersmith, London, and completed it at the High School in Dublin. In the best tradition of various geniuses, including Einstein and Newton, he was a poor student; one headmaster said that he was sure that Yeats would never amount to much. Alldritt remarks that Yeats remembered his time at school as 'one of failure, misery and humiliation'. Indeed, he earned a reputation for idleness there. Yeats himself recalled that 'I spent longer than most schoolboys preparing for the next day's work and yet learnt nothing, and would always have been at the bottom of my class but for one or two subjects that I hardly had to learn at all.'

Natural curiosity motivated him to learn – something that came easily to him when he found the topic interesting, such as with the science subjects, including chemistry, biology and zoology. Biology and zoology in particular were a source of fascination to him; these subjects are often favoured by people with Asperger's syndrome because of their complex classification systems. Yeats achieved his best school results in mathematics and Euclidean geometry. His academic education came to an end, however, when he failed to meet the entrance requirements for Trinity College Dublin in Classics and mathematics – much to his family's displeasure.

Over the years, Yeats's verbal skills improved vastly. In his late thirties, while on the American lecture circuit, he discovered a talent for oratory. His delivery was passionate, forceful, articulate and energetic. It is likely that he inherited some flair in this area from his father. John Yeats too was an accomplished debater and 'controversialist' who, according to Richard Ellmann in *Yeats: The Man and the Masks*, took delight in expressing extreme views in order to get a rousing response from his opponents. In common with many with Asperger's syndrome, Yeats had an idiosyncratic or stereotyped way of speaking and recited poetry in a ritualised, chanting manner. Ellmann claims that this was a 'curiously rhythmical manner of speaking' which was difficult to reproduce. The poet John Masefield too was struck by Yeats's poetic delivery, as noted in *W.B. Yeats: The Man and the Milieu*:

> I often heard Yeats's method. It is not easy to describe; it would not be easy to imitate; probably it influenced all who heard it either for or against. It put a great (many thought too great) yet always a subtle insistence upon the rhythm; it dwelt upon the vowels and the beat. In lyric, it tended ever towards what seemed like Indian singing; in other measures towards an almost fierce recitativo. When reading or reciting verse to a friend, he was frequently dissatisfied with the rendering of a line. He would then say, 'no, no' and would repeat the faulty line with a more delicate rhythm, helping it to perfection with the gestures of his (most strangely beautiful) hands.

Others have commented on the deliberate nature of Yeats's speech. The author and critic Anthony Cronin described him as 'studied in manner and speech, unremittingly poetic'. Yeats's tone varied from high- to low-pitched; this meant that it could sound unnatural or contrived. Not surprisingly, he earned a reputation for speaking in an 'affected voice', according to his son. For his part, Michael Yeats preferred to call it a 'Sligo accent' with a 'strong voice'.

Repetition features prominently in Yeats's use of language too. Preoccupied somewhat with developing his son's mind, John Yeats noticed how his boy liked an appealing or resonant phrase, which, once heard, he would repeat over and over again. By Yeats's own admission, in *Autobiographies*, the pleasure he derived from rhyme was profound even from an early age. In an encounter with H. W. Nevinson, the jour-nalist noticed that Yeats would say 'D'y' see?' at every sentence. Clearly, verbosity and instinctive monologues that are seen in Asperger syn-drome were evident in Yeats's case. The notoriety he gained for dom-inating conversations with his endless monologues is legendary. This was apparent to Nevinson when he met Yeats; the latter talked inces-santly, moving his hands about a good deal, so Nevinson reports.

Yeats's laugh was described as 'stentorian' by the painter Augustus John, and indeed such inappropriate loudness was seen in Joyce too. In general, the type of humour typical of the Asperger personality is of a simple and slapstick variety. Generally there is little appreciation for subtle or satirical humour, although this was not always the case with Yeats. By all accounts, Yeats's sense of humour was simple and juve-nile, like that of his brother Jack: it took the form of 'prankishness', according to Ellmann. Indeed, his great 'silliness' did not escape the attention of the poet W. H. Auden. Over the years, reports of Yeats's behaviour inevitably gave rise to this view. For example, his interest in the occult led to many eccentricities. On one occasion, he tried to hyp-notize hens in a farmyard at Clondalkin, near Dublin. His son Michael reveals that he had a sardonic sense of humour – much like Joyce, Beckett and others. A contemporary of W.B.'s at the High School, W. K. Magee, recalled that no one could say that Yeats was without humour, but that it was of a 'saturnine' variety. He certainly did not suffer fools gladly – and in the poet's estimation he was surrounded by many. Not surprisingly, Yeats also relished malicious gossip.

*

In his lifetime, Yeats's interests were always pursued narrowly and with utter compulsion. Though varied, his all-encompassing passion for poetry, drama, literary revival, the occult and politics were closely inter-woven. From childhood, he had an enquiring mind: his father recount-ed that he was 'a joy to anyone who would tell him things out of ancient philosophy or modern science'. One of his first obsessions was biology and zoology, particularly from 1881, when the Yeats fam-ily moved back to Ireland and lived in Howth, County Dublin.

Captivated by the work of the evolutionary biologists Darwin and Alfred Russel Wallace, he went on frequent entomological field trips and, according to Alldritt, collected butterflies, insects and moths, 'in which he took a serious scientific interest'. Indeed, the collecting instinct – again an Asperger characteristic, with its focus on counting – was evident in Yeats, who also had a love of computing.

A penetrating intellect was also a boon to Yeats's creativity: he always quickly grasped the matter at hand. His fellow poet Seán O'Faolain noted how Yeats had a 'quick receptive mind and skims the cream off with ease'. Despite his poor school record, Yeats was autodidactic and essentially educated himself, like many with Asperger's syndrome. He read voraciously, with novels always taking second place to poetry and philosophy. In his lifetime, he amassed a library of three thousand volumes, including many works of Celtic mythology. His influences were myriad – writers, poets, mystics and philosophers of all stripes, from authors of works of Celtic mythology to Chaucer, Blake, Dante and Keats, and from Paracelsus and Neoplatonists to Emanuel Swedenborg and Freud.

In adolescence, he took his first steps into verse-making, often giving schoolmates a flavour of what was to come – something that they rarely forgot. Even at that stage, Yeats had absolute conviction in his genius. From the time he began writing seriously and left school in his mid-teens, he did not seriously entertain any other career, although he spent two years at the Metropolitan School of Art in Dublin. A friend of his father and professor of English literature at Trinity College Dublin, Edward Dowden, was in no doubt about Yeats's talent:

> He has genuine imagination, richness of diction & above all a power of writing easy musical verse quite remarkable in these days of Tennyson, Rossetti & Swinburne & their followers. One has to go back to Coleridge & Keats to find the same kind of gift. In fact he has poetic genius.

Recognition of Yeats's genius came particularly fast and early. By the age of twenty, he had had poems published in the *Dublin University Review,* and his first volume of poetry, *The Wanderings of Oisín,* was unleashed on the world in 1888, when he was just twenty-three years old. From then until his death in 1939, his literary output was colossal (nearly four hundred poems and some twenty-six plays and twenty-five stories); he also produced a great deal of material relating to the revival of the Irish language and literature and the need for a national theatre. His intense industry produced at least 87 books; 250 articles, essays and reviews; at least 50 books edited, prefaced or contributed to by him; and in excess of 80 lectures, speeches or discussions, amongst other miscellaneous writings. Ellmann gives a flavour of the frantic period from 1889 to 1903, during which time Yeats had so many interests and activities, 'with so little obvious relation between them, that a strictly chronological account would give the impression of a man in frenzy, beating on every door in the hotel in an attempt to find his own room'. Even as he approached his seventieth birthday, Yeats's literary energy and creativity had not waned.

Earning his stripes as a genius, Yeats was always original and innovative, instinctively devising new techniques and styles. By that stage he knew his own mind, which, in *Autobiographies,* he described as 'sensuous, concrete and rhythmical'. In time, he moved away from his earlier Romantic, symbolist period to a more modern, realist style. The style he forged became remarkable for its simplicity, clarity and naturalness. It was highly readable in comparison to the poetic styles that preceded him; he used contemporary words and syntax and engaged the reader with rhetorical questions. At the same time, his poems were full of pictures and images – often exotic or native landscapes. Crucially, with varying rhythms and melody he created a musical vocabulary borne out of Irish tradition. He believed that his poems should be either spoken (as drama) or sung, always with an emphasis 'to make my language natural'. Ever attentive to detail, he was attuned to the lack of prosody or 'common music', as he called it, in the poetry of others.

Yeats's focus was very much on his personal life and the world around him. He drew his themes from real life – conflicts with the self and will, unattainable desires, especially love, and communing with the dead. Sexual and religious ecstasy also became dominating themes in his work and part of his poetic imagination. All his life he took an interest in the occult and philosophy, and he joined various societies that took part in seances. Theatre techniques such as those of Japanese Noh in *At the Hawk's Well* were incorporated into his work to create a minimalist style that in time would influence playwrights such as Brecht and Beckett.

Yeats's early interest in science showed an innate preference for tiny details or elements. It is not surprising that Virginia Woolf noted that 'every twig was real to him': for Yeats, tiny details could contain immortal truths. One could say that, by examining the particular, he was led to universal meaning. The image conjured up by a tiny detail, such as a twig, was a concrete image, as was the swaying of a great chestnut tree or the movement of a dancer, as in his poem 'Among School Children'. Thinking in concrete images or fragmented pictures, something which is typical of autism, was how Yeats's mind worked. This is borne out in references to his autobiographical *Reveries over Childhood and Youth* found in *Autobiographies*. Ellmann quotes from Æ, who considered that the memoir was far from an autobiography but a 'chronological arrangement of pictures'.

The recording of details was important to Yeats, and he kept voluminous notebooks and diaries, recording aphorisms, reflections and, especially, astral events. Although he had a good memory for facts and details, this did not extent to remembering people's names. Foster refers to his 'congenital inability to remember names' and relates a story of when the poet took Lady Gregory in 1907 to visit his two elderly aunts in Dublin but could not for the life of him recall their names!

To judge from biographical accounts, Yeats had an astonishing ability to immerse himself in his interests with intense concentration. This was evident in childhood, when he habitually lapsed into reverie – much to the chagrin of his parents, who thought him lazy and 'addicted to reverie'. The fanciful, wildly imaginative side of his character was much in evidence in Sligo, where he roamed the countryside, his mind full of heroism and mythology – ships, haunted houses, ghosts, monsters and fairy folk – which would form the basis of much of his early poetry. Indeed, daydreaming or reverie can be a sign of mental preoccupation and not necessarily of time-wasting. This practice was to continue throughout Yeats's life and was indeed a necessary part of his creative process.

An ability for sustained concentration was also evident in his many lecture tours. On a given evening, he could talk tirelessly for more than two hours to crowds of over a thousand people. Like Einstein, Yeats's self-absorption was legendary. Such was his ability to lose himself in thought that, at an Arts Club dinner in Dublin, when told he had not yet eaten, he believed it, and went in and had a second dinner. Reflecting on his father's extreme absent-mindedness, Michael Yeats writes that, at dinner parties, his father would become so absorbed in conversation that he failed to register just what he was eating. On one occasion, after eating parsnips – a vegetable not to his liking – he turned to his wife and told her that it 'wasn't a very nice pudding'. Over time, his family became attuned to signs of him in creative mode, according to his son, and the fact that he could not recognise faces, even very familiar ones:

> One afternoon my sister Anne got on a bus on her way home to find the poet already sitting in a front seat, obviously deep in the throes of composition. So she left him alone and took a seat near the back. In due course they both got off the bus at the family gate and, as they went in, he looked at her vaguely and asked, Who is it you are looking for?

One legendary account of Yeats's absentmindedness was cleverly captured in a cartoon in the journal *Dublin Opinion* in 1925. In a classic Asperger pose, Yeats had his head in the air while, unbeknownst to him, he passed his old friend Æ by on the street. Michael Yeats describes the incident:

> On one occasion in the 1920s our house in Merrion Square was briefly in the public eye. We lived at No. 82 and my father's great friend George Russell (Æ), the poet and mystic, lived at No. 84. They were both very absent-minded, and one afternoon they set off simultaneously to visit each other. Russell as usual walked with his hands behind his back and his head down, my father with his hands behind his back and his head in the air. By chance a well-known cartoonist of the day, Isa McNee, was just across the street at this moment, and the humorous journal *Dublin Opinion* appeared the following week with a cartoon by her illustrating this event.

The tendency to live in the eternal present or 'here and now' was particularly evident in Yeats. This also meant that constructing a personal narrative was almost impossible for him. In *Autobiographies,* for instance, there is a distinct lack of chronology. Any sequence of time and events takes second place to a haphazard collection of descriptive images, casual thoughts, opinions and anecdotes. The attempt to recount his days spent in Paris as a young man was particularly arduous:

> I see Paris in the Eighteen-nineties as a number of events separated from one another, and without cause or consequence, without lot or

part in the logical structure of my life; I can often as little find their dates as I can those of events in my early childhood.

Clearly time-dependent literary constructs such as characterisation and plot were deficient in Yeats, as they are in many with Asperger's syndrome. Of his immersion in children's stories such as Grimm's fairy tales or the stories of Hans Christian Anderson, he says: 'I have remembered nothing that I read, but only those things that I saw or heard.' Though he read novels, he often forget their plots, much as Joyce did. A preference for formulaic novels was evident in the fact that he enjoyed reading detective novels, such as those by Agatha Christie.

*

The degree of social impairment in Yeats was particularly acute. The remote figure with a desire for isolation wrestled with constant cravings for an audience. In his early years, there is evidence that he was introverted and cut himself off from his schoolmates. Outwardly he had no interest in their games or play, or in sharing their interests. Often lonely, he generally developed friendships with others who were much older than him; in childhood, his 'principal friend' was the stable boy Johnny Healy in Sligo. Certainly his difference and awkwardness set him apart from other children. As a solitary child with peculiar interests – collecting butterflies and moths and incessant daydreaming – he became a figure of fun. At the Godolphin School in London among boys of his own age, he was labelled the 'Mad Irishman' and bullied. Ellmann describes how 'they laughed at his awkwardness and bullied him because he was weak'. The sensitive Yeats was not immune to their taunts, however, but sensed his difference. Alldritt notes that Yeats was a loner and 'felt himself set apart'.

Certainly in early adolescence Yeats took 'intense pleasure in being alone' and engaged in solitary wanderings, according to Alldritt. It was in these years that Yeats began composing verse. At the oddest hours, he took to wandering around the Hill of Howth, where his family lived following their return to Ireland in 1881:

He would pass the hours and eat and sleep in total isolation, on the excuse of catching moths. Sometimes, to his father's dismay, he would go and sleep at night among the rhododendrons and rocks in the wilder part of the grounds of Howth Castle.

229

References to Yeats being aloof and remote pepper the many accounts of him. Certainly a mixture of shyness and aloofness is often seen in those with Asperger's syndrome. By his own admission, as a boy staying at his grandparents' house at Merville in Sligo, he would hide in a hay loft when visitors called. Others, including his wife, speak of him being shy and timid; indeed, this was an enduring family trait. To compensate for his shyness, Yeats often projected an image of brash self-confidence. Foster records Yeats's views on the subject: 'I seldom get credit for an absurd amount of timidity and shyness, which has a way, when I meet anybody for the first time, or practically for the first time, of hiding embarrassment under a brazen manner.'

Like many Asperger geniuses, Yeats was hypersensitive in the extreme. In childhood, this fact was obvious to his father: 'Willy is sensitive, intellectual and emotional – very easily rebuffed and continually afraid of being rebuffed – so that with him one has to use great sensitiveness.' Alldritt too notes how he was 'a highly strung, imaginative child'. Yeats himself provides another explanation for the fact that he was not willing to interact with people – fear: 'sometimes the barrier between myself and other people filled me with terror'. This too has echoes of Beckett's horror of dealing with strangers.

In Yeats's aloof manner there were indications of an inability to express affection – something inherited in the Pollexfen family line. It is often said that his mother's lack of maternal love contributed to her son's social inadequacies. Clearly Susan Pollexfen had difficulties communicating and reciprocating feelings. In general, the Pollexfens had difficulty expressing love and affection, according to John Yeats, but this did not mean they were devoid of all feeling:

> All the time [the Pollexfens] were longing for affection . . . and their longing was like a deep unsunned well. And never having learned the language of affection they did not know how to win it. . . . I more than once said to my wife that I never saw her show affection to me or to anyone, and yet it was there all the time.

The aloofness and remoteness he displayed were also read as a lack of humanity – a charge frequently levelled at those with Asperger's syndrome. Brown quotes an acquaintance of Yeats who thought that his worst personal fault was 'a lack of ordinary good nature'. The poet

Louis MacNeice too bemoaned the 'constitutional inhumanity' of the great poet. This was a sore subject as far as Yeats was concerned. When his friend the poet Katherine Tynan rebuked him for being bookish and inhuman, he took great umbrage:

> I am a much more human person than you think. I cannot help being 'inhuman' as you call it. . . . On the rare occasions when I go to see anyone I am not quite easy in my mind, for I keep thinking I ought to be at home trying to solve my problems – I feel as if I had run away from school. So you see my life is not altogether ink and paper.

Ellmann notes how Yeats attempted to build bridges to 'connect himself with humanity' – attempts which were not always successful. In fact, this is a typical aspiration of those with Asperger's syndrome. Cutting himself off from the events of life dramatically diminished his ability to capture the human spirit: 'If we poets are to move the people, we must integrate the human spirit in our imagination.' Tellingly, his wife believed that he 'had no interest in people as such, only in what they said or did'. In this respect, Alldritt is correct in claiming that Yeats was interested in literary anthropology: he visited peasant homes to collect folkloric material around Gort, County Galway – something that mirrors Daisy Bates's work with the Aborigines in Australia.

While isolation was a particular feature of his early life, Yeats overcame this to a certain extent, becoming somewhat gregarious in later life. His desire for social contact – for an audience, to be specific – found expression in the many clubs, societies, dinner parties, lecture tours and country-house gatherings he was part of over the years. 'I was only self-possessed with people I knew intimately,' he stated in *Reveries over Childhood and Youth*. Therefore, he sought like-minded company and continued to feel out of place in the company of strangers and among those who were not close associates of his. He also confessed that he 'shrinks from all business with a stranger and is unnatural with all who are not intimate friends'.

In 1909, when writing an unsent letter to Robert Gregory, he drew attention to his lack of social instincts: 'I have no instincts in personal life. I have reasoned them all away & reason acts very slowly & with difficulty & has to exhaust every side of the subject.' By his own admission, he became aware of his social shortcomings: 'I began to make blunders when I paid calls or visits, and a woman I had known and liked as a child told me I had changed for the worse.' The nature of Yeats's social interaction bears all the hallmarks of Asperger-type behaviour: he had no appreciation of social cues or turn-taking, and spoke and behaved inappropriately. Indeed, his capacity for rudeness was legendary. His conversations consisted of monologues rather than dialogues, and he had no capacity for small talk. Quite simply, he did all the talking. The writer Vita Sackville-West met him in 1935 and was not impressed:

> He is the sort of person who has no small talk at all, but who either remains silent or else plunges straight into the things that matter to him. So little small talk has he that he doesn't even say 'How do you do?' when shaking hands on arrival. He just sits down on the sofa, looks at his nails for two minutes' silence, and then tells one stories about [Gerard] Manley Hopkins or Lady Gregory or [Oliver St John] Gogarty; or else expounds his views on T. S. Eliot and *les jeunes* . . .

Interacting with Yeats was never easy for his peers. Brown quotes St John Ervine, who recalled conversations he had had with Yeats during the 1920s:

> It is not easy to talk to him in a familiar fashion, and I imagine he has difficulty in talking easily on common topics. I soon discovered that he is not comfortable with individuals: he needs an audience to which he can discourse in a pontifical manner. . . . I doubt very much whether he takes any intimate interest in any human being.

Dealing with issues that could be considered outside his remit often left Yeats foundering. He once accompanied his wife to St Columba's College in Dublin, where they were considering educating their son. Instead of enquiring about obvious matters like entry requirements, sports, or the facilities that were available, he asked the warden for a full explanation of the state of the college drains – believing that, by doing so he was behaving like a normal parent.

Yeats was often oblivious to those who struggled to understand him, as one schoolmate observed: 'He was a good talker. He would argue and discuss matters with the master. . . . he used to spout reams of poetry to us, which none of us could comprehend as his delivery was so fast . . . [and he was] rather fond of attitudinising.' Those with Asperger's syndrome are often labelled narcissistic and egotists, and Yeats's habit of constant talking about himself and his interests, uninterrupted, came to be seen as self-centredness by many. The wife of David Cecil, whom Yeats had met as an Oxford undergraduate, summed up the great poet as 'a thundering egoist'. Another feature of those with Asperger's syndrome that often sees them labelled as arrogant and ignorant is poor face recognition. Both Ellmann and Foster recall an incident where Yeats dined with a group of academics at Wellesley College in the United States in December 1932. The poet T. S. Eliot sat beside him, but Yeats failed to recognise him, despite the fact that he had met him numerous times before:

> Yeats, seated next to Eliot but oblivious to him, conversed with the guest on the other side until late in the meal. He then turned and said, 'My friend here and I have been discussing the defects of T. S. Eliot's poetry. What do you think of that poetry?' Eliot held up his place card to excuse himself from the jury.

This failure to recognise faces, no matter how familiar, can be accounted for by a weak visual memory.

Those with Asperger's syndrome make poor listeners and are often incapable of meaningful dialogue. A case in point is the meeting between Yeats and General Eoin O'Duffy, leader of the Irish fascist party, the Blueshirts. According to Ellmann, when they met, O'Duffy's wife noticed that 'they spoke on different lines and neither listened to the other'. Over time, however, Yeats became aware of this trait, noting: 'I do not listen enough.' Crucially, Yeats realised that, as a poet and dramatist, by not listening to people he was removed from their cares and concerns, and thus from reaching an understanding of the true fabric of their lives.

In his dealings with others, Yeats was also renowned for his lack of tact – something that Foster refers to as his 'moments of superb tactlessness'. Foster also refers to Yeats's 'habitual indiscretion' and relates how he often betrayed confidences. Once, in Dublin, he regaled others with the exploits of Dorothy Coates, one-time mistress of the Irish-American lawyer and collector John Quinn. Certainly the Asperger genius does not always see the harm in gossiping and breaking confidences.

In the conduct of his romantic affairs, Yeats was quite often socially inappropriate. A telling example concerns his hunt for a suitable bride.

Having failed to woo Maud Gonne's daughter Iseult, he quickly settled on marrying Georgie Hyde-Lees but did not purchase new clothes for their wedding, deciding instead to wear those he had bought to pursue the enchanting Iseult. This was a detail that Lady Gregory found particularly distasteful, according to Brown: 'The mistress of Coole was particularly scathing about Yeats intending to marry Hyde-Lees in the clothes he had purchased to woo Iseult.' On the occasion of his marriage to Georgie, he thought it unnecessary to inform his two sisters and family of his nuptials, despite the fact that he was on good terms with them all at the time.

In his dealings with his children, Yeats's social impairment was particularly obvious. Whereas Yeats saw his own father as being 'affectionate but intellectually dominating', Michael Yeats regarded his father as a 'remote figure'. It is worth noting that, when Yeats died in 1939, Michael says that he did not feel any profound sense of personal loss. His father had always been a 'formidable, towering figure' to him. In fact, it was like 'living with a national monument', he declared. Moreover, Michael claims that Yeats himself had no notion of what it was to be a 'normal' father, i.e. someone who is 'young and energetic, plays with the children, goes on picnics with them, takes an active part in family discipline'. His father did none of these things. Judging by Yeats's poetry, however, he was evidently pleased to have a family, but had no idea of how to talk to his children. Michael recalls that only once in their childhood did his father exercise any kind of family discipline. This took the form of a poem – albeit on the subject of goodness – being read aloud, which left them 'bemused' rather than suitably chastised!

The nature of Yeats's close friendships forms a similar pattern to those of other Asperger geniuses. In his youth, men tended to be mentors, such as his father John Yeats, the Trinity professor Edward Dowden and the Fenian John O'Leary. Throughout his life, Yeats demonstrated an ability to form and maintain a number of friendships. In essence, they were always with like-minded people who shared his interests and pursuits closely: poets, dramatists, actors, artists and occultists. The quality and durability of the friendships often proved problematic, however. Like many with Asperger's syndrome, particularly Joyce, Yeats quarrelled and fell out with friends, in particular male ones. In some cases, friendships were severed irreparably, while others were renewed periodically. Perhaps his most constant and lifelong male friends, despite some turbulent times, were J. M. Synge, Arthur Symons (also a close confidant) and George Russell.

The nature of Yeats's relationship with women is highly complex. The singular most important female relationship for the Asperger person is often with their mother. Curiously, Yeats's mother does not figure prominently or fondly in his accounts of childhood, aside from references to her love of storytelling. Several biographers have commented on her withdrawn nature and how undemonstrative she was in her affections. This raises the issue of whether she possessed some Asperger traits herself. By all accounts, she had an acute lack of desire to interact with her peers. Ellmann described Susan Pollexfen as being 'so silent, so instinctive, so deep-feeling' that she was the exact opposite of her husband, who had 'sought the opposite to his own affable, argumentative, opinionated mind'. Terence Brown describes her as an 'uncommunicative, apparently emotionless companion' to Yeats's father. Brown quotes Yeats's own words about his mother: 'She was not sympathetic. The feelings of people around her did not concern her. She was not aware of them. She was always in an island of her own.'

Certainly Yeats gravitated towards women who were maternal towards him, in particular Lady Augusta Gregory. Their association was legendary, and she became his lifelong friend, patron, collaborator and confidante. Their mutual interests in literary and cultural matters ultimately led to an Irish literary revival and the establishment of the national theatre, the Abbey Theatre. The women who shared his interests tended to be patrons, writers, poets, actresses, patriots, occultists and spiritualists. He often projected a loveable quality where women were concerned, and this sometimes pointed to an innate cunning intelligence on his part. In his impecunious early years in London, he figured out that by visiting female friends at 5 o'clock and taking tea and toast with them, he could save his pennies for the bus home.

By and large, his friendships with women were passionate and unconventional attachments. Foster notes that, even in the years prior to Yeats's death, his need for company, particularly female, 'raged unchecked'. The lines of friendship were often blurred by infatuations, short-lived romances and sexual encounters, with the exception of Lady Gregory. From his teenage years, given his potent imagination and sexual immaturity, he idealised, indeed idolised, women. It appears, however, that he had little involvement with them in early adulthood, admitting: 'with women, I was timid and abashed'. Having avoided intimacy at all costs, he reputedly was still a virgin at the age of thirty.

In his affair with the married Olivia Shakespear, whom he referred to as 'Diana Vernon', at the age of thirty Yeats did not know how to conduct the affair, for since childhood 'he had never touched a woman's lips', according to Ellmann:

> In 1895 and 1896, when a beautiful married woman fell in love with him, he spent the first year in idealised chastity, meeting her only in museums and railway carriages; and then, when they finally went to bed together, he kept expecting love to end until finally it did, and he returned to his former hopeless adoration of Maud Gonne and to his twilit state between chastity and un-chastity.

Although their liaison was idealised, the friendship with Olivia Shakespear continued for forty years, until her death. Yeats's most celebrated relationship was with the revolutionary Maud Gonne, whom he met in 1889 at the age of twenty-three. From the start, he was captivated by this independent, beautiful and ethereal woman, who fired his imagination and emotions like no other woman would in his life. Idealised as a kindred spirit, she became the focus of much of his poetry and was immortalised in his poem 'No Second Troy'. His 'courtship' of her, however, was quite naive, and its failure frequently sent his spirits plunging. Though his love for Maud Gonne was unrequited – she had been conducting a secret affair in France for many years and had a child – the liaison endured for fifty years and appears to have been briefly consummated nearly twenty years after they first met.

Despite several affairs and infatuations, not least with Maud Gonne's grown-up daughter Iseult, Yeats's desire to marry had become urgent by the age of fifty-two. His choice of bride, however, was influenced more by astrology than emotion, and he looked about for a 'friendly, serviceable' woman. His bride was a member of the circle of psychics he frequented in London, the twenty-four-year-old Bertha Georgie Hyde-Lees, whom he had known for a number of years. Any previous reservations he had about the marriage were confirmed on the wedding night. Shockingly honest, he told his young wife that 'he could summon up no desire for her'. Unfazed by his confession, the resourceful Georgie tried to save their marriage. A week later, she introduced 'automatic writing', claiming to be a bearer of occult messages, for his benefit. (Basically, she wrote down words, which she claimed not to understand, as though they had been communicated through her.) Heartened, the poet believed that she was his new source of inspiration, and the marriage survived. In time, her role as muse and mediator grew into that of 'helpmeet, secretary and domestic organiser', according to Foster. In fact, she became the typical Asperger wife, like Sinéad de Valera, in complete control of the household.

As he grew older and settled into married life, Yeats began to equate sexuality potency with poetic inspiration to an ever greater extent. In fact, he was so obsessed with sexual vitality that, when he began to experience impotency in the 1930s, he had a vasectomy. Thus the Steinach operation was performed to increase his production of testosterone and so preserve his potency. It is doubtful whether the operation was entirely successful, although it seemed to satisfy Yeats somewhat and led to two affairs in quick succession, first with the actress Margot Ruddock and then with the journalist Ethel Mannin. Other relationships, of a kind, developed with Dorothy Wellesley and, lastly, with Edith Shackleton Heald.

*

The instinctive desire for ritual, routine and repetition, so pervasive in those with Asperger's syndrome, marked all aspects of Yeats's life. 'I have a great longing for order and routine,' he once declared. In fact, he could think of one place where it could be happily indulged. In a letter to Lady Gregory, he mused: 'I always long for a life of routine. . . . I think a monastery, if only it could come to terms with your sex, would be the most exciting & delightful place imaginable.'

Beyond doubt, Yeats displayed stereotypies classically associated with autism. Stereotypies describe repetitive motor mannerisms, such as finger- or hand-flapping, that appear to have no obvious purpose or function. In Yeats's case, these ritualised movements were accompanied by a dissociated or trance-like state when he was composing poetry. In effect, this acted as a stimulus or aid to creativity. His hand-flapping must have seemed both extraordinary and alarming to those who observed it for the first time. Alldritt describes how he roamed the streets of Dublin 'sometimes flapping his arms about as he recited or composed poems aloud'.

Accompanying the great poet in long walks around Dublin, Katherine Tynan too noticed how Yeats would flail his arms around in a violent way that 'intrigued policemen'. The stereotypy in Yeats's case also involved a highly unusual speech element: a repetitive, chanting murmur. John Yeats's recollection of the times his son would compose poetry at home is found in *W. B. Yeats: The Man and the Milieu*:

> Oblivious to everyone else, [Yeats] would start to murmur, developing lines of poetry. Then he would speak them louder and louder. And louder. Then, still utterly preoccupied, he would chant and declaim. Finally, as John Yeats remembered, 'his sisters would call out to him, "Now, Willie, stop composing!"'

Composing and its accompanying stereotypies were likely to happen at any time, as Michael Yeats points out:

> All the family knew the signs, we were careful to do nothing that might interrupt the flow of thought. Without warning he would begin to make a low, tuneless humming sound, and his right hand would wave vaguely as if beating time. This could happen at the dinner table, while playing croquet, or sitting in a bus, and he would become totally oblivious to what was going on around him.

Yeats himself was not unaware of his eccentric behaviour. 'I have a way of acting what I write and speaking it aloud without knowing what I am doing,' he confessed in *Reveries over Childhood and Youth*.

From Æ (George Russell), we know Yeats's working routine: he disciplined himself to write for two or three hours a day, whatever the outcome. Repetition too was a key element of his work. Certain topics formed the cornerstone of his poetry and plays: truth, beauty, love and nationalism. According to Ellmann, Yeats kept asking the same questions over and over again until they became profound: 'What is truth? What is reality? What is man?' Consequently, his search became never-ending and repetitive. He particularly relished certain ideas that incorporated concepts of return and rebirth. For example, he believed that history followed a repetitive two-thousand-year cycle, with events taking place in a continuum rather than being unique and singular. Cyclical repetition in the form of lunar cycles also claimed his attention, in that human personalities could be assigned to different phases of the moon.

Another compulsive ritualistic habit seen in Yeats was his collecting instinct in childhood. For years, he collected insects, particularly moths and butterflies, because it was possible to obtain several hundred, if not thousands, of them. In adulthood this collecting habit shifted to volumes of literature instead.

Occult rituals were built into his routine too. From early adulthood until old age, he took part in seances and occult investigations, and clearly was addicted to the rituals associated with these practices. For many years, Monday evenings at Woburn Buildings in London were the seat of his dabblings in the occult. Like many Asperger geniuses, walking was a ritualised habit that was important to him. From childhood he was an inveterate walker, whether in the countryside or on city streets; he enjoyed moonlit walks in particular.

Yeats's style of dress came to be ritualised too. He generally dressed in the same manner every day and was fastidious and particular about his clothes all his life. Depending on his age, his style was distinctive; some would call it his 'uniform'. According to his son Michael, as a young man his father would dress in an unusual fashion with 'a long black cloak, dropping from his shoulders, a soft black sombrero on his head, a voluminous black silk tie flowing from his collar, long black trousers dragging untidily over his long, heavy feet'. The image perhaps scored in the public mind is of a sixty-year-old smiling public man in a three-piece suit, with necktie and beribboned pince-nez. Clearly, his appearance was linked to a certain amount of personal vanity. He was, like a contemporary rock star, striking a pose. Interestingly, his grandfather William Butler Yeats was also noted for his extreme vanity. In *Reveries over Childhood and Youth,* Yeats recalls that he was 'so dandified a horseman' that he split three riding breeches in a day, presumably because he insisted upon wearing them so tight.

*

Evidence for an autistic superego is certainly present in the case of Yeats. By adolescence, the combined legacy of the Yeatses' clergymen predecessors and the Pollexfen puritanism had inculcated a sharp sense of right and wrong in him. It led him to admit that 'I was as prudish as an old maid' and 'self-rightous'. His conscience was certainly a strong force throughout his life, as he admitted in *Autobiographies*: 'the voice [of conscience] has come to me at moments of crisis, but now it is a voice in my head that is sudden and startling. It does not tell me what to do, but often reproves me. It will say perhaps, "That is unjust" of some thought; and once when I complained that a prayer had not been heard it said, "You have been helped."'

It is clear too that, when his standards of perfection fell short of the mark – or whatever he visualised – the hypersensitive Yeats perceived it as a failure, and this inevitably gave rise to guilt. By his own admission, in *Reveries over Childhood and Youth,* he was always ashamed of his lack of physical courage and the way in which other boys were able to bully him. Ellmann remarks that Yeats went into 'sieges of self-criticism' from 1908 to 1910. In 1908, he began to keep a diary recording dissatisfaction with his life and his attempts at reformation. His widespread use of masks to hide behind led to an even greater sense of deception. Ellmann writes that:

> In 1933 [Yeats] admitted that, though he had overcome his shyness a lit-
> tle, "I am still struggling with it and cannot free myself from the belief
> that it comes from a lack of courage, that the problem is not artistic but
> moral". Although of late years he had spoken more directly he was still
> unsatisfied and felt that he had played his inner being false by dressing
> it in costume and metaphor instead of expressing it directly.

Yeats clearly had a strong sex drive, although, given his degree of dis-appointed and unrequited love, he was sexually frustrated, particularly in early adulthood. According to Foster, he was consumed with sexual guilt, which was implicit in his sexual frustrations and in his attempts to relieve these frustrations through masturbation.

The conflict so often at the heart of genius was certainly a driving force behind Yeats's creativity. Like his father with painting, Yeats's con-stant reworking of his poetry and plays meant that conflict and struggle dogged his path. In this respect, Ellmann says that few poets had found mastery of themselves and of their craft so difficult or had sought such mastery, through conflict and struggle, so unflinchingly as had Yeats. The absolute need for the acquisition and maintenance of control seen in the Asperger genius is inherently linked to a struggle for perfection and a belief in the absolute rightness of their work or vision. Moreover, manip-ulating others in order to sustain their creativity is also instinctive in those with Asperger's syndrome. In practice, for Yeats this gave rise to all sorts of problems associated with dealing with the world. Disharmony generally arose because of his controlling nature. He reputedly liked to repeat the words of his friend Charles Rickett, who believed that those who have something to give to the world are always 'troublesome'. Certainly troublesome, if not meddlesome and relishing controversy, is a fair assessment of Yeats the man. Foster notes how Yeats needed to belong to organisations and that, once attached to them, he had to shape them into the image he desired. The need to be involved in activity or to be a part of things certainly spurred him on: 'It was no business of mine and that was precisely why I could not keep out of it.'

Because Yeats saw things literally and in concrete terms, there was no middle ground, no consensus, and no seeing things from another person's perspective. Everything was either black or white, or, as his wife Georgie put it, 'everything had to be either geese or swans to him'.

When provoked, Yeats could be arrogant, bullying and aggressive. There are many instances of his violent temper and aggressive behaviour, especially towards family members. Indeed, these outbursts show all the hallmarks of autistic aggression. Certainly his bad temper was a prominent feature of his involvement with his sisters' printing ventures, Dun Emer and Cuala Press. During one quarrel over the editorial policy of Dun Emer, John Yeats described his son as behaving like a 'demi-god'. Alldritt remarks that Yeats was a combative man with a 'violent temper that sustained him in many nasty quarrels . . . a brawler and scrapper'. His sister Lolly declared in a letter to Lady Gregory that 'it is quite useless trying to talk reason to Willie, who can never see any side of anything but his own & who if at all opposed at once becomes overbearing and rude. . . . He does not understand practical life.'

In all phases of his life, Yeats's tenacious hold on power seemed to be in step with his genius. Not alone was he extremely controlling in relation to his family but also towards his friends: he once tried to control Katherine Tynan's life by planning her career. In many respects, Yeats was manipulative, especially where female relationships were concerned, and he rarely allowed others to exercise control over him either.

A reputation for being difficult and stirring up rancour preceded him at every turn: he became a force to be reckoned with in combat. He was involved in squabbles over artistic and managerial control of the Irish

National Theatre Company or control of the administrative councils of the Order of the Golden Dawn, an occult group with which he became involved in London. When things got out of hand, his constant threats of resignation hung over the National Theatre Company like the sword of Damocles. Actors and younger writers frequently left the Abbey Theatre in dispute, having made an enemy of him. Ellmann refers to Yeats's controlling nature, whereby he became 'a terrible man in combat, who could compel by sheer force of personality, or, as he would put it, by power of his mask, a jeering crowd into silence'. Certainly he fearlessly took on the audience during the riotous debate at the performance of J. M. Synge's play *The Playboy of the Western World,* at the Abbey Theatre.

The Irish government incurred his wrath in a well-known incident in 1933. Fianna Fáil, who were in government at the time, heeded influential Irish-American societies and individuals who condemned the Abbey Theatre's American tour of the previous year. The Irish government threatened to withhold funding for the Abbey until the plays were suitably sanitised – that is, displaying far less bad language and instances of drunkenness, murder and prostitution, and a generally poor image of the Irish. Yeats refused point-blank to change the programme. Alldritt quotes from him: 'We refuse such a demand; your Minister may have it in his power to bring our theatre to an end, but as long as it exists it will retain its freedom.' A meeting was then arranged between de Valera and Yeats, and the matter was brought to a peaceful conclusion, with Yeats receiving the necessary funding. There was a certain meeting of minds between Yeats and de Valera: Yeats was not slow to show his admiration for de Valera and he praised the statesman's simplicity and honesty.

A tendency for control and discipline was certainly found in the Yeats family line. There were very definite views on how children should be disciplined. Ellmann describes Yeats's paternal grandfather as an 'unusual clergyman'. Indeed, his form of discipline tended towards the unorthodox. On one occasion, he boxed the ears of his son John, Yeats's father, and afterwards 'shook hands with him and hoped he was not offended'. A firm belief in harsh discipline led him to send John to a school run by a Scotsman whose 'floggings were famous', as Ellmann remarks. The controlling element in John's personality was also apparent; certainly, where his precocious son was concerned, he took an active and formidable role in his education. A degree of aggression was also found in Yeats's maternal grandfather William Pollexfen. He kept his own counsel but his authority was unquestioned. His temper was such that he kept a hatchet beside his bed 'in readiness for burglars'. In his *Reveries,* Yeats remembers the 'silent grandfather, inspiring fear and deference'.

*

Beyond doubt, Yeats was a highly complex individual – something that was in no small measure due to his identity diffusion. The search for identity and its shifting and evolving nature became a lifelong pursuit of his in terms of both his work and life. From the outset, the conflict borne out of identity diffusion was a boon to his creativity, as indeed it is to many, if not all, Asperger geniuses. He once declared that 'a poet always writes of his personal life. It is the quarrel with oneself.' His identity diffusion was also affected by his tendency to live in the 'here and now'.

According to Alldritt, Yeats as a young man spoke 'only of the terrible inner turmoil, the churning sense of inadequacy within. As he approached his twentieth birthday his sense of self was unformed, still volatile and a mass of contradictions'. As a result, Yeats manifested identity diffusion to an extraordinary extent. There was never a moment when he was not reinventing or adjusting himself through the use of masks, myths and myriad occupations. Like many Asperger geniuses, he distinguished himself in many fields in his lifetime: as a poet, dramatist, writer, painter, theatre director, occultist, astrologer and senator in the newly established Irish State during the 1920s. Giving the multiple roles and identities that Yeats displayed – some serious, some outlandish – it is little wonder that some people were dubious of his bone fides and unsure whether he was a genius or a charlatan. Following the publication of his *Ideas of Good and Evil* in 1903, an article in the English journal *Leader* cast aspirations on exactly who or what Yeats was – and with not a little spite:

> What after all is Mr Yeats? He is one of the most complex personalities we have. There is a touch of the real poet in him, and a spice of the amateur (but not insincere) politician. Added to these, he is a sort of quaintly-comic man, who confuses matters for us by letting on to let on that he takes himself seriously. Added to this again, he is as handy a man as any under the sun at successfully 'planting' his literary wares: 'no flies on him' there! As to the spook business and the seeing of visions, probably nobody but Mr Yeats himself could tell how far he is in earnest. Indeed,

he has been so long posing in that peculiar spiritual line now, that probably not even he himself could tell if he really sees anything – and in any case it doesn't matter.

Given his own highly developed aesthetic, along with that of his father and brother Jack B. Yeats, it is no surprise that painting featured in the panoply of Yeats's interests. John Masefield in *Some Memories of W. B. Yeats* remembers that Yeats always spoke of painting as a painter speaks. For a time, he considered becoming a painter: he attended classes at the Dublin Metropolitan School of Art, where he painted 'adequate' watercolours, according to Foster.

Unlike many with Asperger's syndrome, Yeats was not apolitical, like Joyce and Beckett. On the contrary, Irish identity and nationalism were vital to him. He was proud of his Irish Protestant heritage, which was deeply rooted in Ireland, and in Sligo in particular. In 1885, as a young man, he embraced Fenianism and took the oath of the secret Irish Republican Brotherhood. He later supported Home Rule under Redmond's Irish Parliamentary Party. Clearly, his deep sense of nationalism and close identification with many of the leaders of the 1916 Rising and the later War of Independence was evident in his poetry and drama. Following Independence, he supported the Treaty. As a senator in the newly established Irish Senate, he distinguished himself with his progressive ideas on education and equality, and helped to draft a new Copyright Act and develop a new Irish coinage. As a politician, however, he was never outstanding, as he had little knowledge of or interest in economics or the practicalities of politics.

Yeats's political views were often controversial, given the climate of the time. The rise of fascism during the 1930s and the establishment of more fundamentalist forms of governance seemed to him a sound cure for the ills of democracy. He was impressed by Mussolini's elitist government and supported the Irish fascist movement, the Blueshirts. Fundamentalist ideas are often appealing to the Asperger mind, and Yeats was no exception. He was certainly seduced by fascist thinking and later, with regret, referred to the period as his 'flirtation with authoritarianism'. In effect, Yeats's hostility to democracy was the product of political naivety. During this period, Yeats also advocated eugenics and individualism. Admittedly, his reason for joining the Eugenics Society in 1937 was not racial prejudice but his fears in old age about educational and cultural decline in Ireland, now that the impact of the Anglo-Irish gentry was waning.

Many biographers, most notably Ellmann, have remarked on Yeats's tendency to construct myths, earning him the reputation as 'the Poet of Shadows'. Alldritt too considered Yeats to be a master craftsman, with one of his most skilful constructs being his own image. Yeats's anxiety over identity particularly led to an interest in the occult and astrology, like Robert Boyle. Here the notion of the transmutation of the soul struck a deep chord with him. Transmutation made it possible for the self to be remade over and over again. In this regard, Ellmann notes how Yeats believed that the human mind had power to control the universe, to make and unmake reality. As a result, Yeats put great store in his alter ego, Leo Africanus, encountered in séances. Literary alter egos were also constructed to express the different facets of his personality – Michael Robartes, Owen Ahearne and Red Hanrahan – according to Foster. So much so that, according to Ellman, Yeats believed that his true identity lay in his poetry:

> Sometimes he was content to think his real self was in his verse. 'My character is so little myself', he put in a manuscript book, that all my life it has thwarted me. It has affected my poems, my true self, no more than the character of a dancer affects the movements of a dance.

In later life, Yeats's preoccupation with identity, masks and personality saw him complete a second version of his work *A Vision,* presenting a theory of the variation of human personality.

Depending on the occasion, Yeats presented multiple faces to whoever he met, and these faces were not always flattering. Michael Yeats observed that his father was 'a man of many masks, and could project totally different images, depending on the person he was meeting or the circumstances of the time'. Certainly the issue of identity was one that preoccupied Yeats on first meeting Maud Gonne. Ellmann writes that, when Yeats met her he immediately fell in love, and the question was 'which of his two selves should he show her? He had to show her his inmost heart, so with her he was John Sherman, the wild yet timid dreamer'. His use of masks also points to an intellectual approach to people, typical of those with Asperger's syndrome, rather than an emotional one.

In later life, Yeats showed a certain dissatisfaction with masks and the multiple personas he presented. This can be read as an attempt by Yeats to make more meaningful contact with other people. After his marriage, his wife's support and encouragement had a stabilising influence on him. Had he remained a bachelor, he may well not have become the Nobel Laureate poet who is celebrated today. Moreover, Yeats did appear to change, as people with Asperger's syndrome sometimes can in later years. By his own admission, as he grew older he confessed that 'he was not the same timid clumsy boy who twenty-five years before had put on a pose so he could face the world'. He had overcome somewhat both his shyness and his deep dissatisfaction with his self-identity.

With Asperger's syndrome, the effect of identity diffusion is a restless individual, both in mind and spirit – and both temporally and spatially. 'I long for a life without dates and without any settled abode,' Yeats once declared. Largely inheriting a pattern from his father, Yeats rarely stayed in one place for long. All his life he divided his time between Ireland and England, in particular Sligo, Galway, London, Dublin and Oxford. Tours in the United States would later demand his attention, and he also went on working holidays in Italy and France.

Like Joyce, the effect of a divided self saw Yeats became preoccupied with tradition and family memory in later years. Much to his sisters' surprise, he expressed the desire to inherit the family miniatures, which were at the time in the possession of his maiden aunts in Dublin, once they died. The obsession with origins and legacy, and recognition of his own place in the scheme of things, saw him compose his epitaph:

Cast a cold Eye
On Life, on Death,
Horseman, pass by.

Although ever conscious of his age, he did not welcome the coming of old age.

Yeats's later preoccupation with his legacy raises questions about his need for recognition. Many biographers and commentators claim that he was a dedicated careerist, adroitly promoting his own interests, preoccupied with money and indeed snobbish about seeking social standing. Yeats was certainly more than a little narcissistic and quite good at promoting his work, getting good reviews by using others for his benefit, particularly in the 1890s with the poets of the Rhymers Club in London. 'Always eager to promote himself' was how Aldritt described him.

All his life, he had a certain ambivalence when it came to money, as is typical of people with Asperger's syndrome. According to his son, he was careful about money. Alldritt records that, when Yeats won the Nobel Prize for Literature in 1923, one of the first questions he asked the bearer of the news, the journalist Bertie Smyllie, was: 'How much, Smyllie, how much is it?' Indeed, throughout his life Yeats was preoccupied with financial worries – he constantly supported his own family, sisters and father – and was greatly relieved when he was placed on the Civil List, which meant that he received a pension of £150 a year. His attitude to money is probably best explained by the experiences of his father: the poverty and hardship suffered by the Yeats family throughout their father's bohemian years had affected them greatly.

In effect, the contradictions at the heart of Yeats had to be reconciled in some fashion. Clearly, Ellmann understood the ambiguity in Yeats's work in terms of a divided mind:

> Given his sense of a divided mind, Yeats had to try to achieve in his verse what Coleridge called the 'balance or reconcilement of opposite or discordant qualities'. . . . His shortcomings in the 'nineties was that he conceived of his art . . . as a see-saw sometimes between scepticism and belief, sometimes between natural and supernatural love, sometimes between action and the dream, sometimes between the peasant and aristocratic traditions.

*

Throughout his life, Yeats did not enjoy good health. Like many Asperger geniuses, his immune system was far from robust. According to Foster, he grew up 'lanky, untidy, slightly myopic and painfully thin – possibly tubercular'. All his life, and particularly in his latter years, he battled against numerous illnesses and diseases, including infantile tuberculosis, dyspepsia, heart disease and angina, high blood pressure, tonsillitis, rheumatic fever, rheumatism, brucellosis, bronchitis, pneumonia, kidney disease, oedema, hernia and impotence. He was constantly bothered by fevers, influenza and colds; he was also short-sighted and suffered eye inflammations periodically. In 1894, he was diagnosed with a conical cornia, according to Foster, which was especially bad in his left eye. So debilitated had he become in his old age that his wife and friends would read to him, and he periodically needed an amanuensis.

By his own admission, some of his illnesses were psychosomatic; these included neuralgia, fatigue, rheumatic pains, anxiety, insomnia, 'nervous weaknesses', 'nervous collapses' and 'mental confusion'. But for all his physical infirmities and weakness, his mental energy and faculties were indefatigable. 'It is a curious experience to have an infirm body and an intellect more alive than it has ever been,' he once revealed.

There is some indication from Yeats that his mother's family were prone to depression, particularly the Pollexfen men, whom he described as 'strange melancholic uncles'. In addition, mental instability in the form of manic depression was present in his aunt Agnes Pollexfen Gorman, her daughter Elma and another aunt, Elizabeth Pollexfen Orr. One uncle, William Middleton Pollexfen, died in an insane asylum. Yeats's father suspected that his daughter Lolly had inherited some mental illness from the Pollexfens too.

Depressive-type illnesses are commonly seen in Asperger geniuses. It is uncertain whether Yeats suffered from depression or not. Ellmann notes how he talked about his 'dreadful despondent moods', leading one to believe that he may have suffered from recurrent depression. Given his hypersensitivity, he appears to have been highly strung on occasions. 'Composition strained my nerves and spoiled my sleep,' he admitted in *Autobiographies.*

There is some evidence to suggest that Yeats had motor clumsiness. Poor dexterity in handling or manipulating objects was evident in his poor handwriting and when he took part in sports. As a child, his awkwardness and physical weakness kept him from being a favourite of his mother's family, who were all excellent athletes. Yeats showed poor horsemanship: in *Autobiographies,* he reveals that his father was extremely disappointed that his son 'did not learn to ride well'. Yeats's gross motor skills were good, however. He was good at running, like Joyce, and won a cup in 1879 for a half-mile race at the Godolphin School in Hammersmith. And, again like Joyce, he excelled at diving and swimming, especially underwater, according to his son Michael.

Sensory impairments and hypersensitivies often found in those with Asperger's syndrome were prominent in Yeats's case too. The sights, sounds, textures, tastes and smells of nature could be overwhelming for him, and his audiovisual imagination was exceptionally acute. Despite poor eyesight, he was addicted to immersing himself in nature, where he could feast his senses on the changing seasons. Indeed, his great love of colour, painting and landscapes found expression in poetry. Like Joyce, Yeats had a particular preference for the colour blue – in his case, dark blue – which, he wrote in *Reveries,* 'always affects me'.

In terms of hearing, Yeats seems to have disliked loud noise and was tone deaf. In fact, he had no capacity for singing – his singing was usually high-pitched and out of tune – and his family went so far as actively to discourage him from singing when he was young! Nonetheless, he had a remarkable ear for language, which the BBC producer George Barnes, who on a number of occasions broadcast Yeats reciting poems, observed first-hand: 'He could not hum a tune as his notion of pitch was wildly inaccurate . . . [but] his ear for the sound of speech was so accurate that it outran comprehension'. Foster claims that Yeats had a gift to control the 'music of words' to an almost extrasensory pitch. Like his brother Jack, Yeats had a peculiar gait which was described as heavy. In *Reveries,* Yeats notes how his grandmother would try to stop him 'stumping' on his heels as a boy. The journalist H. W. Nevinson, when he met Yeats as a young man in 1899, noted that Yeats had a rather stooping posture. Clearly there was some degree of poor proprioception and poor balance. As a child, he frequently took falls from his pony and suffered from seasickness.

The instinctive affinity with animals, commonly seen in those with Asperger's syndrome, was present in Yeats, as it was in the entire Yeats family. As a child, Yeats became preoccupied with two dogs and followed them everywhere, and throughout his life animal cruelty appalled him.

*

It has long been recognised that Yeats was endowed with 'pure imagination'. This has made him not only the people's poet but also the poet's poet. It was something that was evident to those around him, notably fellow poets and writers. In this respect, Foster refers to a meeting in 1902 between the nearly forty-year-old Yeats and James Joyce, then in his early twenties. The 'mesmeric beauty' of the early Yeats poems, such as 'The Adoration of the Magi' and 'Who Goes with Fergus?', was scored in

Joyce's mind forever. In later life, Joyce admitted that he himself lacked 'pure imagination', which Yeats 'pre-eminently possessed'.

Yeats's imagination was predominantly visual. As a child, this gave rise to all sorts of fears and phobias, usually of monsters and ghosts. We have no knowledge whether he was unable to engage in 'pretend play' as a child – something that is classically seen in autism – but we know that a certain vagueness and remoteness on his part dominated that period. With greater exposure to the world, his aesthetic imagination grew more and more defined, and he was always impressed by poets and painters, including Dante, Keats and various Byzantine artists, who could think in pictures.

The effect of having 'pure' imagination, creating something out of nothing, meant that Yeats could capture something – a casual thought, mood, emotion or image – which was brilliant in its simplicity, beauty and truth, and make it concrete. This skill was there in abundance in such poems as 'Innisfree', 'The Fisherman' and 'The Fiddler of Dooney'. His imagination was also linked into the universal memory of tradition, as Foster notes.

Given the vibrancy and potency of his imagination, it is no surprise that Yeats took an interest in religion, metaphysics and the esoteric. For an enquiring mind such as his, these belief systems offered a truth and knowledge that was not readily accessible in everyday life. Crucially, the religious disposition or religiosity he displayed had definite familial roots, as indeed had his scepticism and superstition. Yeats's forefathers were indisputably men of the cloth. His great-grandfather John had been rector of Drumcliffe, Sligo, while his grandfather William Butler Yeats had been a deeply orthodox rector of the Church of Ireland in County Down. Yeats's maternal grandmother, Elizabeth Pollexfen, was intensely religious and also superstitious. In *Autobiographies,* Yeats writes that his childhood memories of Sligo are filled with 'the quiet religious grandmother interested in nature cures'. A strong mystical trait was also present in the Pollexfens, evident in his uncle George's interest in the occult. By contrast, his own father, John Butler Yeats, was a confirmed sceptic.

From biographies, we learn that Yeats had a curiosity about religion from an early age. Ellmann records that, as a young boy, Yeats would ask questions like: 'What religion do the ants have?' In addition, Yeats as a youth was full of thoughts about God and was 'intensely religious by nature'. As an adult, a defining moment in his life came when he joined the Order of the Golden Dawn. His attraction to the occult was far from faddish and indeed sustained him throughout his life. Yet, as he had never quite relinquished his childhood religion, his wife saw fit to arrange for an Anglican clergyman to pray over his dead body in 1939.

Given such a family legacy, Yeats developed, in Ellmann's estimation, an eccentric faith 'somewhere between his grandfather's orthodox belief and his father's unorthodox disbelief'. This curious hybrid of sceptic and believer is found in many Asperger geniuses, who find it difficult to surrender completely the twin powers of science and religion. Amid the logic and reason, there is an innate predisposition towards magic and mystery. This was seen in Yeats's work *A Vision,* where he attempts to structure life into categories and cycles. This book, which draws heavily from the occult and philosophy, is laden with symbolism. It is the work of a logical mind with a taste for abstraction and schematizing – commonly found in those with Asperger's syndrome – but, according to Ellmann, Yeats's system had 'a sort of anti-system' built into it. You could say that Yeats's focus was inherently mystical.

From a sceptic's point of view, a belief in the supernatural is always likely to raise questions of naivety and gullibility in the person who holds such a belief. Such traits are also associated with Asperger's syndrome, where individuals can be too trusting and are not equipped with the social skills required to detect deception. Certain commentators believe that, by absorbing himself in masks and esoteric creeds, Yeats distanced himself from reality, or rather from common sense. In particular, the critic John Carey in the *Sunday Times* (18 June 1999) noted that, as time went on, Yeats accumulated 'a bizarre panoply of creeds that could liberate him from the prison of common sense – Rosicrucianism, reincarnation, cyclical patterns of history based on the phases of the moon'. In fact, Yeats did not need to be liberated from common sense since he was singularly deficient in it all his life – as are many with Asperger's syndrome! Brenda Maddox, in *George's Ghosts: A New Life of W. B. Yeats,* states that Yeats was gullible, but only because 'he believed in faith'. This belief sprang from his genuinely held belief that he could access secret knowledge through the occult, especially when his wife introduced automatic writing in the early days of their marriage and assumed the role of medium. There was no reason for him to believe that his wife could be deceiving him. Even so, Yeats's poetry moved to a different plane with the advent of the use of automatic writing. As Maddox notes, automatic writing moved him from being a good poet to being a 'great one'.

Like many Asperger geniuses, Yeats's later work became more enigmatic. Its quasi-mystical dimension meant that it was not always open to easy interpretation. Terence Brown refers to this phenomenon as 'the absence of communicable meaning' – as was also found in Joyce's *Finnegans Wake* and Beckett's later works. Yeats's poem 'Sailing to Byzantium' was also criticised for its 'senselessness' by Carey. Increasingly, Yeats came to the conclusion that 'man can embody truth but he cannot know it'. Truth was beyond reason: hence the mystical endpoint of his work. Like Beckett, for Yeats faith and instinct outweighed rational or abstract argument. The belief, held by Yeats, that 'poetry and religion are the same thing' has echoes too in Beckett's belief that 'all poetry is prayer'. In the final analysis, for Yeats, the Asperger genius, faith and instinct rather than logic and reason formed the pole star from which he took his light.

8

JAMES JOYCE

To be narrow, peculiar, and irresponsible, and at the same time all-encompassing, relentless, and grand, is Joyce's style of greatness.

RICHARD ELLMANN, *James Joyce,* 1959

No book on Irish geniuses would be complete without reference to the country's greatest writer of the twentieth century, James Joyce. The genius of Joyce is undisputed and his works *Ulysses* and *Finnegans Wake* richly deserving of their description as 'masterpieces'. Beyond doubt, Joyce was a complex genius – or a man of 'blatant inconsistencies', as Edna O'Brien suggests in her book *James Joyce*. In the opinion of the French writer André Gide, his genius was an enigma to the end. Clearly Joyce was a mass of contradictions: he could be charming and cruel, aloof and affable, secretive and open, imperious and childlike, bohemian and prudish, strong and fragile, restrained and reckless. Ultimately, given his extraordinary intelligence, much of the enigma can be understood through the prism of Asperger's syndrome, especially in relation to traits he inherited from his father, an exceptional character in his own right.

Born into middle-class respectability on 2 February 1882 in Rathgar, Dublin, James Joyce was the first son of John Stanislaus Joyce and his wife May Murray and the eldest of the couple's ten children. By the time Joyce reached early adulthood, however, the family fortunes had declined to the point of grinding poverty due to his father's improvidence – something that was to be replicated in the son.

*

In appearance, Joyce was tall and slender and quite a good-looking man. Indeed, his wife Nora Barnacle always loved his 'looks'. Others, including his brother Stanislaus, were taken by his distinguished bearing, which could be stately and aristocratic at times. The unmistakeable charm and equanimity so commonly found in those with Asperger's syndrome was present too in Joyce. Many drew attention to his self-possession or poise. His friend the poet Padraic Colum in *The Joyce We Knew: Memoirs of Joyce* recalls that, no matter how shabbily dressed or hungry he was, Joyce always had 'fine composure'. His presence was profoundly affecting even to fellow geniuses such as Sergei Eisenstein and Samuel Beckett. Following a meeting with the taciturn Joyce in a dark room, Eisenstein came away thinking of it as 'a ghost experience'. Others were less flattering: many of his fellow students and his pupils thought him 'weird'.

Colum also remembers that Joyce had a narrow forehead with a small, well-shaped head and that his jaw was close to his chin. His mouth was sensitive, mobile and thin-lipped, and his pale blue eyes were distinctive. Richard Ellmann, in his celebrated biography *James Joyce*, wrote that his strong brown hair and stubborn jaw were the strongest part of his face but that otherwise it was quite delicate. By all accounts, Joyce could maintain eye contact but sometimes had a 'fixed stare', a 'piercing gaze', a 'medusoid stare', an 'icy look' or a 'gleam in his eye' – certainly a trait of Asperger's syndrome. His face frequently registered no emotion; it was described by his friend Eugene Sheehy in *The Joyce We Knew* as an 'impassive poker face'. Even so, his face retained a sort of boyish look well into maturity. At the age of fifty, he still had the softness, colour and glow that a child's face has, according to Colum.

There was always something juvenile about Joyce in adulthood, from his schoolboy laugh and prankish behaviour to his unbroken voice. A habitual retort of Nora's was that her husband was 'childish' – a comment not infrequently made by many spouses or partners of those with Asperger's syndrome. In fact, Nora scolded Joyce all his life like a recalcitrant child. This notion of arrested development struck Joyce too. In later life, he explained to the Swiss writer Jacques Mercanton why his young tenor voice had stayed unchanged: 'It's because I've not developed. If I had matured, I wouldn't be so committed to this *folie* of writing 'Work in Progress' [*Finnegans Wake*].'

*

For one who became a genius at expression, the young Joyce experienced no speech and language delay. The earliest family recollection of him is of an amusingly independent three-year-old, who uttered 'Here's me! Here's me!' as he eagerly made his way downstairs from the nursery to the dinning room, where his parents were entertaining guests one evening. Little is known about his early schooling other than that in the first six years of his life he was taught to read and write by an educated woman called Mrs Conway, otherwise known as Dante, who would feature in both *A Portrait of the Artist as a Young Man* and *Ulysses*. Learning posed no problems for Joyce and he showed exceptional intelligence in the Jesuit schools he attended: Clongowes Wood College in Kildare and Belvedere College in Dublin.

Like many Asperger geniuses, Joyce's possessed remarkable linguistics skills. It was a natural progression for him to study modern languages at the Royal University of Ireland (later University College Dublin), which he entered at the age of sixteen and a half; he was conferred with a BA honours degree in modern languages (English, French and Italian) in 1902. (Despite his proficiency, Joyce had not bothered to study and obtained only a pass mark.) In particular, he excelled at Latin, French and Italian, and achieved fluency in all of these languages very quickly. Remembering their time together, Sheehy says that Joyce spoke Italian like a native, even though at that time he had never left Dublin. In later years, he acquired Danish and German too, but it was a constant regret to him that he had never studied Greek. His love of languages also extended to Irish, which he took up for about a year, attending classes given by Pádraig Pearse. The scorn in which Pearse held the English language prompted Joyce to abandon the lessons, however, although he retained an interest in Irish all his life. Many with Asperger's syndrome find Irish a very difficult language to learn, unless they have a clear understanding of its grammar, and subsequently abandon it, and it is possible that this occurred with Joyce too.

Clearly Joyce was in love with language, like his father before him, who had an eloquent and caustic wit. At Belvedere, Joyce came under the influence of the English teacher George Dempsey, who nurtured his talent in English composition. Each week, Dempsey would get Joyce to read out his compositions as models of good writing. As a result, he won many prizes for English composition during his five years at Belvedere. Joyce had a good ear for language – especially its musicality, something which is commonly found in those with Asperger's syndrome – and his prose captures the inflections in the speech of everyday Dubliners. It did not take long for those around Joyce to notice that his talent for language was no mere linguistic skill but a profound obsession with words. Edna O'Brien calls him the ultimate wordsmith. He revelled in endless wordplay, puns, rhymes and limericks – as do many with Asperger's syndrome. Crucially, for Joyce the rhythm and musicality of language was far more important than its meaning or sense. This was later seen in *Ulysses* and *Finnegans Wake,* especially when he gave advice to translators of these works. Songs and rhymes of every description, and indeed musical stylistic devices such as assonance, alliteration and consonance, can be found throughout his work. The absence of punctuation in *Ulysses* further stresses the rhythm and tempo of the words, such as in Molly Bloom's famous soliloquy, rather than the sense.

Joyce's voice was subject to variations in tone, as commonly occurs in those with Asperger's syndrome, but it was never monotonous. His natural speaking voice was a pleasant tenor, according to Stanislaus, but whenever he was excited or inebriated, his tone tended to become high-pitched. In fact, Joyce was a gifted tenor who once shared a platform with Count John McCormack in Dublin. In spite of a sweet and mellifluous voice, he was considered a weak tenor because his voice had never broken, according to Ellmann.

The tempo and delivery of Joyce's speech varied widely too, but it nonetheless followed a distinct pattern. Generally, in conversation he spoke rapidly if he was dealing with a topic with which he was familiar, according to Stanislaus. On the other hand, when giving something his earnest consideration, he spoke slowly and chose his words carefully. Moreover, depending on the company, or his mood, he alternated between being entirely unresponsive and silent or overly talkative and pedantic in conversation – a feature that is not uncommon among those with Asperger's syndrome. His pedantic nature and verbosity meant that he usually dominated conversations. Indeed, friends and acquaintances were subjected to frequent Asperger monologues or 'set speeches'. Among his coterie in Trieste, Joyce's conversation often began with a 'flat dismissal of subjects that interested his friends', according to Ellmann. Colum reported that Joyce delivered many set speeches in his youth: he would launch into verse or recite long Latin passages. Furthermore, Wyndham Lewis remarked that Joyce kept a standard set of things to say to people and had 'carefully arranged modes of behaviour'. On the other hand, Joyce could be disconcertingly silent in company. His father's friend, Alfred Bergan, who accompanied Joyce on many of his exceptionally long walks around Dublin, found either Joyce 'affable' or 'utterly silent'. Showing a distinctively autistic way of relating, by his own admission Joyce wanted his imagination to grow when he was with people, 'otherwise it was silence', according to O'Brien.

Like many Asperger geniuses, Joyce could capture an audience with his skills in oratory – which were well honed during his Jesuit education. In 1900, John Joyce attended a meeting of the Literary & Historical Society at which his son read a paper and greatly impressed the audience. The proud father later declared that his son had held the place spellbound. Indeed, Peter Costello and John Wyse Jackson in *John Stanislaus Joyce: The Voluminous Life and Genius of James Joyce's Father,* note that John Joyce had advised his son to become a barrister: 'I often told Jim to go for the bar, for he had a great flow of language and he speaks better than he writes.'

*

From an early age, Joyce's interests were highly focused and circumscribed. Chief among these was his obsession with language, in particular style and expression. He had an insatiable thirst for learning and absorbed numerous literary styles. Like many Asperger geniuses, he was autodidactic. From the age of ten, a decline in the family fortunes meant that he was removed from private schooling for nearly two years and left to his own devices. Every hour of the day, he would harass his mother to set lessons for him and examine his work, whether he was at home or on picnic trips to Howth or Bull Island. According to Stanislaus, Joyce would bring notebooks of summaries of literature or history, or lists of French and Latin words for his mother to quiz him on. This autodidacticism continued into adolescence, when he would often read outside prescribed coursework. At university, his obsession with language and drama led him to visit the theatre whenever he could, and write reviews, poetry, plays and dissertations on English rather than concentrating on his studies. As a result, his BA results were disappointing for one who showed so much promise. At the age of eighteen, he wrote a celebrated article on Ibsen's new drama *When We Dead Awaken,* which was published in the *Fortnightly Review,* the leading literary English review at the time.

So voraciously and eclectically did Joyce read that Ellmann believed that he had 'read everything' by the time he was twenty. William G. Fallon in *The Joyce We Knew* remembers how his friend Joyce would comb book-stalls every Saturday looking for new books to read. He also borrowed from Capel Street Public Library some scandalous or risqué books, like *Tess of the d'Urbervilles,* which regularly raised eyebrows among po-faced librarians. Joyce became a familiar figure at the National Library, where he would read every day until it closed at 10 PM, and at the Bibliothèque Nationale when he was in Paris in 1902. When writing *Ulysses* and *Finnegans Wake,* he devoured all manner of books, pamphlets, manuals, street directories and rhyming dictionaries – indeed anything that might satisfy his obsession with lore and learning. Edna O'Brien reports that, when he died, there were almost a thousand volumes in his library. Joyce never stopped thinking about Dublin: the city would become an autistic obsession, along with other objects of his affection, such as his father, Nora Barnacle, and anyone else who had strongly impinged upon his consciousness.

In relation to his ability to sustain his creativity, Joyce showed many hallmarks of genius, and of Asperger's syndrome: a strong will and absolute persistence; phenomenal memory, discipline and hard work; intense concentration; daydreaming; insatiable curiosity and observation; and an intense focus on details. In particular, he had seemingly endless reserves of energy. He laboured over *Ulysses* for seven years and estimated that it entailed 20,000 hours of work; *Finnegans Wake* took seventeen years to complete.

Joyce's great powers of concentration were obvious from his teenage years. Stanislaus remembers how, when writing his English compositions each week, Joyce would write quickly without making a rough copy beforehand. Such was his concentration that he rarely made a mistake –

an interesting parallel with Robert Emmet, who also wrote error-free letters. Similarly, Joyce's first serious attempt at writing a play, *A Brilliant Career,* required hardly a correction in the entire manuscript.

Even when he was under pressure, Joyce could channel all his energies and concentrate on the matter in hand. Once, after reading a paper to the Literary and Historical Society on Ibsen, he listened to the vehement opposition to his paper and then answered his critics. This took forty minutes without notes, as Eugene Sheehy observed, and he masterfully won over the audience. The ability to marshal his thoughts and express them in a sustained, concentrated way is something he shared with great orators like Emmet and Pearse.

From his adolescent days, Joyce was something of a dreamer, and would transcribe his dreams into a copybook and analyse them. Although he did not daydream on the same scale as Yeats, Pearse and Boyle, he used dreaming as a link between the conscious and the unconscious – a technique he used to unique effect in *Ulysses.*

Joyce, like many with Asperger's syndrome, was also insatiably curious and had a great capacity to notice difference. According to Stanislaus, Joyce never seemed to be observant but was nonetheless capable of taking note of the smallest detail. Joyce himself said that he did not see things but that, rather, he absorbed them. William Fallon remembers:

> One of the most notable things about him at school was his flair for observation linked to an uncanny memory. Incidents, not even of passing interest – a house that seemed to be unrelated to its fellows alongside, boys playing at marbles at the kerbstone of a roadway, a clump of dwarf trees, a distant view of a chimney stack of a brewery suddenly swinging into sight at a particular bend in an avenue – were all imprinted on his mind with photographic accuracy.

This feature of extensive detail-processing is prominent in those with Asperger's syndrome and reflects a weak central coherence or high-level cognitive processing. In fact, the ability to process an incredible amount of detail can often be said to be the secret of genius. Joyce's mind was described by Stanislaus as 'minutely analytical'. Again, like many of those with Asperger's syndrome, Joyce was an inveterate list-maker. *Finnegans Wake,* for example, lists all the great rivers of the world, as well as great Irish cricketers! His capacity for making detailed lists was first apparent in

Clongowes, where his letters home were full of requests, which the rector of the college likened to 'grocer's lists', according to Ellmann. In Zürich, he confided to his friend Frank Budgen that he had a 'grocer's assistant's mind'. Ellmann writes that Joyce's memory was not photographic but retentive, and Stanislaus states that Joyce could 'quickly commit prose as well as verse to memory and keep whole visual scenes in his memory'. One method that he used to remember pictures of Dublin, according to Fallon, was to memorise a series of business names in shopping areas. Many biographers recount how Joyce's father said that, if Joyce were ever set down in the Sahara, he could draw a map of Dublin from memory alone.

The originality and innovation of the Asperger genius was to be found in Joyce too: he, more than any other writer of his time, broke the conventional mould of literature and its taboos. He became the great experimenter with style and expression who was to change the course of literature in the twentieth century. In many respects, Joyce can be compared to Robert Boyle, who altered the course of modern science in the seventeenth century. Literature, no longer the preserve of high-minded philosophy, like science turned its attention to the mundane and the lowly. Committed to ground-breaking realism, Joyce became an 'empirical' writer who, with great curiosity, observation and precision recorded the 'facts' of human nature in his work. Indeed, he records details in a very factual style. The uncompromising Joyce emerges from his writing too: realism for him also meant recording the less-than-sublime aspects of humanity such as sex and bodily functions, along with the sordid and the seedy.

The desire to attain truth, again a great motivator of the Asperger genius, was certainly evident in Joyce. His obsession with style and experimentation was another way of trying to capture reality or truth, and he wrote in many different genres. Grim realism marks his collection of short stories *Dubliners,* while *A Portrait of the Artist as a Young Man* has a linear, biographical structure; in *Ulysses,* myriad styles and techniques are used. In his formative years, Joyce had tried to imitate all the leading English stylists, including Carlyle, Newman, and de Quincey, and later, in *Ulysses,* he emulated them. Indeed, Edna O'Brien declared that the eighteen chapters of *Ulysses* were so varied that the book could be described as eighteen novels between the one cover.

For the reader, the lack of a coherent narrative in Joyce's work can be confusing and bizarre. It is not surprising that Joyce's writing has been erroneously described as 'psychotic' and *Finnegans Wake* as 'the product of a clever schizophrenic', by psychiatrist Nancy Andreason. In *The Joyce We Knew*, Arthur Power talks about Joyce's 'telegraphic style', which consisted of short, pungent sentences – which Joyce considered 'proper for the present day'. In effect, *Ulysses* is an autistic narrative, with a rapid-fire delivery or fragmented discourse, and obsessed with the minutiae of life, without focusing on the big picture. *Finnegans Wake* continues in this vein in an even more pronounced way.

Joyce had little capacity for plot as a literary device. As a result, his novels were strikingly plotless – and not novels in the traditional sense. Stanislaus recalls that Joyce often failed to remember the plot of a book he had read:

> [Joyce] devoured books, while I was a slow reader. It sometimes surprised me, however, to find both that my brother remembered little or nothing of most of the books he read so voraciously and that at need he could make good use of the one or two things he did remember from his reading. He read quickly, and if the book or the author did not appeal to him he forgot them quickly.

Instinctively Joyce reacted against plot, considering it a literary convention to prevent flagging interest on the part of the reader. Hence his inclination for 'plotless sketches', according to Stanislaus. For example, there is no plot in *Ulysses* other than the recording of every minute of one day in the life of its two central characters, the 'everyman' Leopold Bloom and the 'artist' Stephen Dedalus. Those with Asperger's syndrome often fail to appreciate plot, probably because of their weak central coherence. The concept of character development was also somewhat alien to Joyce. A criticism by William Archer of Joyce's early play *A Beautiful Career* was that the characters were 'not sufficiently individualised', but he commented that the purely imaginary characters had impressed him. Indeed, in Joyce's work fact and fiction are too closely intertwined for readers to empathise with his characters in a meaningful way. The more Joyce experimented with his writing, the less accessible his works became for the general reader: by the time he came to write *Finnegans Wake,* Stanislaus got the impression that his brother had lost interest in communication altogether, according to Ellmann. In Edna O'Brien's estimation, *Finnegans Wake* is a book in which 'people were not only people, they were as well rivers, bushes, mounds, boundless embodiments of Irish mythological figure, human longings, human impulses caught in an archetypal sweep.' Indeed, this book has all the hallmarks of an autistic narrative. It was essentially an experiment to prove that the history of people is the history of language and to re-create a language connected with human origins.

Although Joyce did not appreciate plot, he was aware that he still had to make his novels hang together. He opted for a structured or formulaic approach – something that is always popular among those with Asperger's syndrome. *Ulysses* had a tight framework and the chapters were as patterned as the Book of Kells, a manuscript that never failed to amaze him. A title, a scene, an hour, an art, an organ, a colour, a symbol and a technique are found in each of the book's eighteen chapters. The structure of *Finnegans Wake* was influenced by the ideas of the eighteenth-century Italian philosopher Giambattista Vico, whose work *Scienza nuova* put forward the idea that human history is cyclical and endlessly repeating itself.

*

Humour was an integral part of Joyce's character and work. Joyce himself had a lively sense of humour: Eugene Sheehy remembers that he was 'always good for a joke'. Both *Ulysses* and *Finnegans Wake* are intrinsically comic novels, in which the humour is closely intertwined with language. (Joyce was surprised that the reviews of both books seldom pointed out how funny they were, as he saw it.) Like many with autistic spectrum disorders, Joyce enjoyed simple humour such as practical jokes, mimicry, charades, parlour games and clowning. Like Pearse and de Valera, Joyce was a clever mimic, impersonating the mannerisms and pet sayings of various school teachers – to the great amusement of his fellow students – and his capacity for improvisation in parlour games was unrivalled. Joyce's ready laugh was distinctively schoolboyish – a loud whoop or 'Ha! Ha! Ha!' cackle, in which he would throw his head back, according to Fallon. On one occasion, when Joyce was among a group of boys outside the gates of the National Library, his laugh was so loud and inappropriate that a passer-by enquired whether he was ill and needed to be taken home.

By and large, Joyce used humour as both a shield and a weapon.

William Fallon recalls how he would suddenly change from laughter to solemnity. For all its simplicity, Joyce's humour was sophisticated too: satire and irony were mainstays of his sense of humour. For instance, he lampooned his Dublin publishers Maunsell & Co. in verse in 'Gas from a Burner', and many others attest to his sardonic wit. Indeed, his taste for comic insights, scathing wit and caustic put-downs was undoubtedly inherited from his father.

Joyce was acutely attuned to the nuances and subtleties of language – not just in English but in the many languages which he had mastered or of which he had a smattering. Among his university friends, such as J. F. Byrne and Oliver St John Gogarty, his linguistic humour was supreme: endless wordplays (especially with homonyms), multilingual puns, spoonerisms, dog Latin, jokes, riddles, paradoxes, malapropisms and neologisms. For example, Joyce coined the word 'Dubliners', as hitherto the term Dublinmen had been used, according to Costello and Jackson. You could say that Joyce was like a jester poet laureate, marking every event of note with a rhyme or limerick. The polyglot punning in *Finnegans Wake* is unrivalled. Clearly, he shared his inventiveness with language, as well as a whimsical and impish sense of humour, with Mozart.

With schoolboyish zeal, Joyce delighted in slips of the tongue, particularly risqué ones, such as when his brother requested the book 'Jude the Obscene' instead of *Jude the Obscure* from the public library. Another example concerned his attempts to dance with Mary, the sister of his long-time friend Eugene Sheehy, at one of the many lively Sheehy soirées held in Mountjoy Square. So awkwardly and limply did Joyce hold Mary Sheehy while they were dancing that she was forced to ask him to 'hold my thumb'. Joyce misheard and thought she had said 'hold my tongue' – upon which he exploded with laughter. Indeed, he loved scatological and obscene language so much that he dubbed his style 'arsthetic'.

*

Routine and ritual were mainstays of Joyce's life. These features, inherently linked to the Asperger desire for preservation of sameness, gave rise to many of his idiosyncrasies. To begin with, he was a ritual note-taker all his life. According to his wife Nora, his first action each morning was to reach for the pencil and paper that were beside the bed. He habitually carried around a copybook or notebook, or, like Hamilton, would jot notes down on scraps of paper or whatever was at hand. Ellmann says that he carried dozens of small slips of paper in his wallet, and loose in his pockets, to take notes on. When he had filled up these slips, on both the front and the back, he would continue to write on them diagonally (i.e. across his earlier writing). Anything from slang to anecdotes was duly copied down on these slips of paper.

So rigidly did Joyce adhere to his routines that Nora and his family were left with little choice but to fall in step with them. When writing, he often spent between ten and sixteen hours a day at work. Even a bad hangover would not deter him, although illness sometimes would, as when he was forced to rest his eyes during a flare-up of one of his many eye complaints, or following surgery. Curiously, he had a habit of wearing certain items of clothing when he was writing. The painter Arthur Power, whom Joyce knew in Paris, recalls that Joyce always wore a short white coat, like a dentist's, when working.

Joyce's obsession with Dublin was similarly rooted in his desire for preservation of sameness. Even though he left Dublin in 1904 at the age of twenty-two and returned there briefly on three occasions, after 1912 he never set foot in the city again. Nonetheless, the city continued to preoccupy him, and Dublin memorabilia surrounded him. In one flat in Paris, Padraic Colum noticed that Joyce had large potted phoenix palms, to remind him of the Phoenix Park, and a carpet interwoven with the course of the River Liffey. In *The Joyce We Knew*, the Irish diplomat Seán Lester recalls that Joyce tuned into Radio Éireann daily when he lived in Paris and kept it on all day. All his life, his appetite for information about Dublin was insatiable. Irish visitors to Trieste, Zürich and Paris were endlessly plied with questions about the city and its characters, and visits turned into endless rounds of reminiscences. Like many people with Asperger's syndrome, it distressed him to hear of any change – whether deaths, the changing of street names, or the demise of monuments, businesses or houses. Back home, his aunt Josephine was pressed for all manner of precious facts and for Dublin newspapers, magazines, train timetables, and so on. Her death was a great loss to Joyce; he then resorted to getting stenographers to visit his bedridden father in Dublin to record the old man's memories, idioms, speech rhythms and answers to set questions.

It could be said that Joyce imprisoned his sources of inspiration. He tended to deny any change to the situations of his father, wife or daughter. This may also account for why he never visited his father in Dublin and refused to acknowledge his daughter's mental illness at first. In his mind, he had a certain image of his father and his habits, and he had no wish to alter it. Many traits of his father – the inability to manage everyday life, including an endlessly repeated pattern of moving flats, borrowing money, spending wildly, being threatened with eviction, and coming close to starvation – became those of Joyce too. Ellmann writes about Joyce's aversion to change, in particular his desire not to return to Ireland.

> Whenever his relations with his native land were in danger of improving, he was to find a new incident to solidify his intransigence and to reaffirm the rightness of his voluntary absence. In later life he even showed some grand resentment at the possibility of Irish independence on the grounds that it would change the relationship he had so carefully established between himself and his country. 'Tell me,' he said to a friend, 'why you think I ought to wish to change the conditions that gave Ireland and me a shape and a destiny.' That Joyce could not have written his books on Ireland is likely enough, but he felt the need for maintaining his intimacy with his country by continually renewing the quarrel with her.

Certain events were religiously observed by Joyce. With his excellent memory, he remembered birthdays, various events and feast days, and would habitually send letters and greeting cards. He always celebrated his own birthday in style. Deadlines for his printed works were always set for his birthday; a copy of *Ulysses* was delivered on his fortieth birthday, and *Finnegans Wake* on his fifty-seventh – almost as birthday presents for himself. Having been steeped in religious ritual, a trace of it remained with him all his life. In Trieste, Zürich and Paris he would attend certain religious events without fail, such as ceremonies on Holy Thursday and Good Friday. That said, many of these religious routines were carried out from rote or for entertainment value rather than because they had any spiritual meaning or significance.

The notions of variation and sameness, particularly in space and time, preoccupied Joyce, as Ellmann suggests in his biography. This is particularly evident in *Finnegans Wake*. In relation to this work, Joyce said, as reported by Ellmann: 'there is no present and no past, that there are no dates, that time – and language which is time's expression – is a series of coincidences which are general all over humanity'. In essence, this reflects the inner sense of time that those with Asperger's syndrome manifest. Living in the 'here and now', the eternal present, is generally far more real to them than chronological, linear time. As a result, Joyce was largely apolitical. Although, like Beckett, he had a tendency to identify with the underdog, he was seldom moved by social injustice or political turmoil.

*

The way in which Joyce related to people was fraught with problems and ambiguity. Like many people with Asperger's syndrome, he was a difficult and exasperating person to love. Nonetheless, it is not true to say that he showed no desire to mix with his peers or was reclusive. Neither is it true that he was unable to relate to people. In fact, his desire to interact with others, particularly his family, was very strong indeed. Whatever fear of loneliness he possessed, he had an even greater need to be appreciated.

Like Beckett, Joyce was selective about the company he kept, had little social awareness and a good deal of social phobia, leading to all kinds of social impairments. Nonetheless, he possessed abundant native cunning or intelligence. He was a master borrower and wheedler of funds; he knew all the tricks of the trade, having acquired considerable cunning from his father. Indeed, Joyce would infamously turn up at the house of a friend or family member at mealtimes to cadge food.

From the many memoirs and biographies of Joyce, there is ample evidence that he was frequently aloof, detached, coldly indifferent, shy and unapproachable. Costello and Jackson describe this as his 'customary *froideur*'. Certainly, as Joyce grew older and more celebrated, he became more remote, inaccessible and formal in his dealings with others. Eugene Sheehy recalls that Joyce's mood alternated between 'cold, slightly haughty aloofness and sudden boisterous merriment'. Sheehy, however, felt that Joyce sometimes used this abrupt manner as a 'cloak for shyness'.

Joyce had little appreciation of social cues, despite his background in 'polite' middle-class society. As a result, his behaviour or manner could be inappropriate or artificial. He often lacked social graces and lurched between extremes of politeness, being either excessively grand or excessively rude. Arthur Power recalls that Joyce's social manner was not easy for those around him:

He surrounded himself normally with a kind of mental barbed wire – but his exquisite manners were reminiscent of the Dublin of the Grand Days. That remarkable Irish courtliness, he always had. It had the detachment and nobility to it of a grandee, and was as superior as a diamond is to glass to what passes for manners among the provincial gentry and nobility. It was the outward sign of inward refinement; and like all remarkable men he had no conceit; no boorish arrogance.

This old-fashioned courtliness was probably in large part inherited from his mother, who in turn had acquired it from two aunts who ran a school for young ladies in Dublin. The poet T. S. Eliot recalled too that Joyce could be overly polite or overly grand, depending on how he viewed his interlocutor. For the most part, however, people were on the receiving end of his impolite behaviour. He could be wilfully rude, coarse and cruel – largely because he hated falsity of any kind and reacted strongly to it. He certainly liked to shock – much to his brother's dismay:

> He has a distressing habit of saying quietly to those with whom he is familiar the most shocking things about himself and others, and, moreover, of selecting the most shocking times for saying them, not because they are shocking merely, but because they are true.

In Stanislaus's opinion, there was little courtesy in Joyce's nature:

> Impartial courtesy was one of the social graces that my brother lacked. With those few people who, he felt, were his friends, he was open and frank even to excess, but with acquaintances whom he knew but little or whom he thought he saw reason to distrust, there was a coldness and aloofness in his manner that frequently aroused hostility. Moreover, social intercourse is based on falsities of all kinds, which my brother could not stand. . . . His distant manner was not a pose prompted by arrogance: it was, as in many less sensitive people, a form of self-protection. . . . It came inevitably from an awareness . . . of the gulf between the thoughts and aspirations that tormented him and the apparent preoccupations of more normally constituted people.

Evidence of his discourtesies was legion. His ingratitude for financial, domestic or literary help exasperated Stanislaus, often to the point of violence. Joyce displayed little appreciation of the lengths to which people would go to help him, and he could be indifferent to their distress. Displaying the lack of empathy common to those with Asperger's syndrome, Joyce was pathologically tactless and frequently betrayed confidences: loyalty, discretion and confidentiality were important to him only in an abstract sense. Rather cruelly, he once betrayed Nora by repeating to Stanislaus some of her most precious secrets from girlhood.

Closely linked to his tactlessness was a naivety and imprudence – something associated with the Asperger trait of lack of common sense. Many observed this deficiency: Ezra Pound, for instance, admitted that he never had any respect for Joyce's common sense or for his intelligence, apart from his gifts as a writer. Joyce, who was not always alert to danger, had money robbed from him on a number of occasions, including serveral times during a brief stay in Rome in 1906–7. Not being a wise judge of character, Joyce had also been foolish enough to allow chapters of his work to circulate in Dublin. As a consequence, many so-called friends of his, such as Gogarty and Vincent Cosgrave, were intent on causing him trouble, for example by telling lies about Nora, either from jealousy or caprice. Joyce was also the subject of bullying both at Clongowes and Belvedere but, according to William Fallon, did not yield to his attackers.

For all his bad behaviour, Joyce could be tender, kind, gentle and caring. He could also be hypersensitive, as indeed many people with Asperger's syndrome are. A cross word or look from Nora would wound him deeply and incur a chilly response that might last for days. Once, on a trip to Dublin, he grew insanely jealous after hearing a story, which had been concocted by Cosgrave, about Nora's alleged infidelity with Cosgrave. True to his recurring sense of betrayal, Joyce overreacted and berated Nora at home in Trieste in a series of letters before she could defend herself. Joyce 'raged at the slightest rejection', according to O'Brien.

A perennial criticism of Joyce is that he was insensitive, arrogant and lacking in humanity. When accused by Arthur Power in Paris that he was 'a man without feelings', Joyce replied in a most haughty, scornful way: 'My god – I am a man without feelings.' The sensitive Joyce was not beyond tears from time to time – usually when he was overwrought with emotion or frustration. He wept bitterly over the death of his father, his charming younger brother George, Nora's alleged betrayal, the crippling failure of George Roberts to publish *Dubliners,* and his daughter's mental illness. Furthermore, he was stung too by his family's reaction to *Ulysses:* Nora had not bothered to read it, while his father failed to comment on it in any meaningful way.

The quality of Joyce's friendships and relationships was often complex, and he did not always find it easy to maintain friendships. Correspondence was his preferred method for conducting friendships. Like Boyle, Hamilton, Yeats, Pearse, and de Valera, Joyce was a prodigious letter-writer: in his lifetime, he wrote thousands of letters, and his correspondence today fills many volumes. By means of letters, he could, in typical Asperger style, express himself far more clearly and courageously than he was able to do face to face, especially to his father and to his patron, Harriet Weaver. When Joyce was briefly apart from Nora in 1909, he wrote letters to her in Trieste once if not twice a day.

Many of Joyce's dealings with other people were as part-object relationships: he saw them as objects to be manipulated. People were fodder for his imagination. His interaction with others therefore had a distinctly utilitarian purpose – as helpers and supporters of his talent and livelihood, and as sources of inspiration for his work. Friends and enemies became characters in his novels. Indeed, he showed a gross lack of empathy towards Stanislaus, his family and Harriet Weaver. In this respect, he could be said to have used people, and he was, as Edna O'Brien put it, 'deaf to the cries of his family'.

The Asperger genius has few intimate friends but hundreds of acquaintances, as it is possible for them to deal with many people on a superficial basis. Forming deep, respectful and empathic friendship was something else entirely: Joyce lacked a deep capacity for real friendship based on reciprocity and mutual respect. William Fallon believed that Joyce was 'a little too distant to be a close friend'. Instinctively, he gravitated towards people who shared his interests – learning, literature, drinking, singing and carousing. His relationships with men tended to be provocative, such as those with Vincent Cosgrave and Oliver St John Gogarty, and Joyce seems to have been incapable of sustaining close friendships over his lifetime. He frequently fell out with people, or friendships lost their warmth or vigour, as in the case of J. F. Byrne in Dublin, Frank Budgen in Zürich, and Arthur Power in Paris – although sometimes differences were patched up. Certainly growing up he was an intimate friend of Richard and Eugene Sheehy. Byrne and Joyce would parade together around Stephen's Green or Mountjoy Square and talk for hours. The English painter Frank Budgen had been particularly close to Joyce in Zürich, sharing ideas and a capacity for drink and frolics. Soon he became a confidant. In later life, the writer James Stephens developed a friendship with Joyce, who believed him to be his natural successor and hoped he would finish *Finnegans Wake* if blindness prevented Joyce from doing so. It seemed to Padraic Colum, however, that this relationship was an 'occupational relationship' rather than a genuine friendship. The two were like actors or strolling players, he felt. Indeed, Joyce's relationship with Beckett was one in which both men tended to lapse into long, comfortable silences in each other's company!

By far the most important male relationship that Joyce had was with his father. John Joyce favoured his precocious son James above his other nine children. The two were strangely alike; indeed, John Joyce exhibited Asperger traits. Furthermore, it is worth noting that both John Joyce and John Yeats possessed talent but lacked the driving spirit of the artist which their respective sons possessed in abundance. Beyond doubt, John Joyce was one of his son's greatest sources of inspiration. In particular, his language and wit were central to Joyce's oeuvre. John was a raconteur, old-style *seanchaí* and bon vivant, and his wit could be both eloquent and caustic, not to say foul-mouthed. The relationship between Joyce and his father was always strained and often childish. In spite of being devoted to his father, Joyce despised him for his shabby treatment of the family. This led to various estrangements, some of which were patched up, but in the last twenty years of his life John Joyce never once saw his son. Moreover, it could be argued that the central theme of *Ulysses* is failed fatherhood.

Joyce could essentially only appreciate people, especially his father, from a distance. Correspondence kept the bond alive, and John Joyce was the frequent subject of Joyce's voluminous letters. In this respect, Costello and Jackson are correct when they say that 'mystical kinship rather than the routine of daily life suited father and son better'. The high regard in which Joyce held his father can be judged by the fact that, in his pocket, he carried around a photograph of the portrait of his father painted by Patrick Tuohy. On his deathbed, John Joyce's last words were: 'Tell Jim that he was born at 6 o'clock in the morning', perhaps knowing that such a remark would please his son no end – which indeed it did.

The relationship between Joyce and his brother Stanislaus is also quite revealing. The early days of the relationship were marked by comradeship and intense admiration. The Joyces were almost always together – much like Pádraig and Willie Pearse – and Stanislaus, three years younger than

James, would follow Joyce everywhere, even to Trieste. Over the years, Joyce would faithfully send Stanislaus manuscripts for his valued opinions and advice – though this advice, when it came, was rarely heeded. Stanislaus had the thankless job of being his brother's keeper, disciple, underling, 'umbrella', 'whetstone', personal banker and surrogate father. Many years prior to the publication of *Dubliners,* Joyce had told Stanislaus that he would dedicate the book to him, but in the event he did not. Indeed, Stanislaus never received the recognition that his generosity towards and unfailing support for his brother deserved. Instead, there was only ingratitude and endless sponging. In the end, Stanislaus decided that he had had enough: between 1920 and his death in 1941, Joyce and Stanislaus met only three times.

Like Yeats, Joyce was not the most dutiful father: writing occupied all his time and excluded other activities. Unquestionably devoted to his children in spirit, he indulged them but never disciplined them. His son Giorgio was generally left to his own devices, and Lucia he treated as a source of inspiration, denying for many years that she had any kind of mental illnesses. In Paris, the publisher Sylvia Beach was able to watch the Joyce family at close quarters and, according to Brenda Maddox, felt that, although Joyce boasted about the 'supremacy of the family', his efforts to look after them were 'pathetic'. In fact, he had no idea how to take care of them and was oblivious to how bizarre his home life had become or to the torment that those who lived with him endured.

Like many with Asperger's syndrome, Joyce had a particular bond with his mother. Eugene Sheehy remembers that May Joyce was very proud and fond of her son and that he worshipped her. In fact, he was her favourite. For her part, May Joyce was gentle and had a good sense of humour, and was musically accomplished. Unfortunately, her docility towards her husband and to her priest confessors turned her into a helpless victim, rearing ten children in impossible circumstances – something for which Joyce despised her. His treatment of his mother when he briefly decamped to Paris in 1902 showed the most appalling lack of empathy, and he seemed incapable of seeing life from her perspective. He sent many begging letters to her for all kinds of provisions. Still cherishing her ungracious firstborn, she scrimped to send him whatever he needed. Consumed with his own mission as a great artist, he was indifferent to her burdens, as Edna O'Brien points out:

With a mindless insouciance he informs her that his friend (an enemy) Oliver St John Gogarty wrote to say that another friend remarked that there was 'something sublime in Joyce standing alone'. She wires money when she can wheedle it from her husband though it means depriving the other children of food or clothes. She had to sell a carpet to send the next instalment and he hopes that it is not the new carpet. She is scolded for having once wired the money on a Saturday as it could not be cashed on the Sunday.

Shortly afterwards, on his mother's death from liver cancer at the age of forty-four, Joyce showed no visible grief and rarely made a verbal reference to her again. However, he seems to have experienced some guilt in regard to his actions towards her: when he first met Nora Barnacle, he explained that his mother had died from his father's poor treatment of her and his own 'cynical frankness of conduct towards her'.

Joyce's relationships with women – with the exception of Nora and his mother – did not have the same intensity or provocativeness as his relationships with men. In general, the women in his life were in either motherly and supportive roles or in idealised ones. Women served a function: as prostitutes, patrons, publishers and aides. Harriet Weaver, Sylvia Beach, Maria Jolas and his aunt Josephine, among others, were motherly towards him: they became his friends and confidantes and were all-forgiving towards him – something that made them all the more attractive to him. His relationship with his wealthy patron Miss Weaver was quite artificial, for instance. She treated him like a demi-god; their relationship was largely conducted through correspondence, and they met very infrequently. He treated her abominably, shamelessly spending her money and plying her for more funds with ever-greater ingratitude. Indeed, O'Brien estimated that Weaver supported Joyce to the extent of about £1 million sterling in today's terms. Sylvia Beach, who arranged the publication of *Ulysses*, was similarly mistreated.

From childhood onwards, women who were sources of inspiration to Joyce were remote and idealised; these included his childhood neighbour Eileen Vance, cousin Katsy Murray, his friend's sister Mary Sheehy, fellow student Elizabeth Mary Cleary and Marthe Fleischmann, a liaison of his in Zurich. In many respects, Joyce's wife Nora was all things to him. Apart from his sisters, the female company that Joyce kept was either with respectable middle-class girls or with prostitutes. He was shy, awkward and reserved in the company of the former and not so much in the latter.

Charges of misogyny have been levelled against Joyce because he claimed that women were 'cold' and tended to see them as either whores or madonnas and of their largely supportive roles in his life. Nonetheless, his attitide towards women – as with almost everything else about him – was not clear-cut. In his writings, he often portrayed women as morally superior and claimed that Ibsen's work had persuaded him that women actually had a soul! Central preoccupations which reflect his vision of reality are the womanly man (Leopold Bloom) and the manly woman (Molly Bloom). As with de Valera and his affectionate letters, with Joyce there was some discrepancy between what was contained on the written page and what he practised in reality. It could be said that Joyce was too detached to appreciate women in their own right. He had very few strong female role models growing up; Nora, by contrast, was a strong woman who bossed Joyce around and could skilfully wheedle gifts and money from him. Indeed, some would argue that she henpecked Joyce, forcing him to peel vegetables or buy knitting patterns for her. Brenda Maddox writes in *Nora: A Biography of Nora Joyce*:

> [Joyce] seems to have longed to establish in himself all aspects of the bond of mother and child. He was attracted, particularly, by the image of himself as a weak child cherished by a strong woman, which seems closely connected with the images of himself as victim. . . . His favorite characters are those who in one way or another retreat before masculinity, yet are loved regardless by motherly women.

There is no evidence that Joyce had any significant love interest before Nora Barnacle, the love of his life. The autobiographical *Portrait of an Artist* suggests that Joyce had an emotional but idealised attachment to the fictional Emma Clery, based either on Mary Sheehy, sister of his friends Richard and Eugene Sheehy, or, more likely, Mary Elizabeth Cleary, a fellow student of his at university, according to Costello and Jackson. The day that Nora and Joyce walked out together, 16 June 1904, has become an iconic one: Bloomsday, the date on which the events portrayed in *Ulysses* took place. Joyce declared that no human being had ever stood so close to his soul as Nora did. With Nora, Joyce experienced real love, but their relationship was highly ambivalent. Nora was all things to Joyce:

native and earthy, instinctive and right, among other things. She was the person he exploited most for the purposes of his work. He wanted to know all Nora's secrets and later encouraged her to have affairs with other men so that he could write about her experiences, particularly for his play *Exiles*. Nora's refusal to accede to these demands – and his jealously – forced him back from the brink. It is not known whether Joyce was ever unfaithful to Nora, though he did have 'affairs' with three women: one in Trieste and two in Zürich. Varying degrees of sexual intimacy occurred and inappropriate letters were sent, but, as Ellmann suggests, it was probably nothing more than 'adultery in the mind'.

Yet for all its ups and downs, the relationship between Nora and Joyce was constant and enduring, notwithstanding that she threatened to leave him many times. She was a strong woman with what Arthur Power described as 'rock-firm common sense', yet she was dependent on Joyce too. According to Brenda Maddox, Nora 'loved and desired Joyce but despised him because he did not provide for his family'. Even so, he was the uxorious husband, lavished gifts on her, depended on her and could not bear to be apart. Once, when Nora had to undergo an operation, Joyce refused to be separated from her and had a bed set up for himself in her hospital room. In sum, it is doubtful whether Joyce would have achieved anything like as much as he did without her constant companionship and support. She was an 'Asperger wife', as Georgie Hyde Lees was for W. B. Yeats.

*

In *My Brother's Keeper,* Stanislaus writes that Joyce had extraordinary moral courage. You could say that his actions were always underpinned by an innate sense of virtue. The inevitable outcome of a Catholic upbringing for Joyce was that notions of good and evil, right and wrong, sin and redemption were indelibly imprinted on his mind. It was no idle boast that, as a writer, he wanted to become the conscience of his race. By nature he had a harsh or autistic superego. The burden of creativity often conflicted with his superego, and his great restraint yielded to great recklessness. Ellmann notes that, in this respect, all releases from 'excessive consciousness' attracted Joyce.

Joyce was 'brutally' committed to truth and honesty, and was extremely tactless. Eugene Sheehy claims that he was a very truthful man and outraged or upset people when speaking bluntly on the merits or demerits of someone's literary work. But Joyce always felt that right was on his side. On the charge of immorality, he once declared that he was more virtuous than 'all the lot' he had scorned in his poem 'Gas From a Burner' – publishers, printers and leading Irish literary figures. Once he had made his mind up, according to Sheehy, he would never condescend to argue a point. That said, if Joyce changed his mind about someone, e.g. James Clarence Mangan or Yeats, he would publicly admit so.

In particular, he disliked false sentiment: he hated going to funerals – which led many to conclude that he was heartless. He was particularly given to moral outrages against the Catholic Church. The hypocrisy shown towards his mother by the priests – advising her to put up with her husband's hard drinking, often violent, dissolute life – was particularly galling for him. With such a harsh superego, it was inevitable that Joyce would choose rectitude and integrity over blind servility to the Church. It was of considerable importance to him that his future relationship with Nora Barnacle was not founded on falsity either. Not long after they first met, he bared his soul and told her about his hatred of the Church and his visits to brothels. Even when she told him that she did not want to know about such things, he insisted she hear him out.

For all his obsession with obscenities in literature, it was another matter using them in public. Indeed, there was a side to Joyce that permitted everything on paper but not in his presence. He certainly had streak of propriety and prudishness in him – not unlike Boyle, Pearse and de Valera, among others. In a letter to Nora written in 1909, Joyce reiterated to her that he never used obscene phrases when speaking and disliked dirty jokes intensely. When living in Zürich, he would read excerpts from *Ulysses* – then in manuscript form – for his students but would censor certain paragraphs when young ladies were present. Later, in Paris, he would blush heavily if someone said a rude word, according to Maddox.

Even though Paris of the 1920s and 1930s was a fairly heady place, the Joyces were not as bohemian as one might expect. But they were not hypocrites either, as Maddox points out. They openly expressed their disapproval of promiscuity but welcomed stable relationships of whatever hue. Indeed, Joyce and Nora themselves had lived as man and wife for nearly thirty years until they were officially married in London in 1930 – so as to ensure inheritance rights for their children. All his life, Joyce strongly disapproved of both contraception and abortion. Ellmann suggests that Joyce had a special reverence towards birth and believed that conception should be considered natural and fated. The biographer also relates an incident in 1933 when, over several hours, Joyce and Paul Léon counselled Léon's niece into not having an abortion. Such incidents confirm Joyce's sharp moral compass and autistic superego.

For all Joyce's superego, he also had, by his own admission, an extravagantly licentious disposition. Stanislaus too declares that Joyce had 'a proud wilful vicious selfishness'. Undeniably, Joyce was a man of excess, particularly where money, drink and sex were concerned. On this point, Ellmann says that 'sexual continence was impossible for him. He felt he must chose between continual guilt and some heretical exoneration of the senses.' Undeniably, too, there was a certain degree of perversity in Joyce. He showed persistent paranoid traits and his indifference to the qualms and suffering of his mother and others bordered on an autistic psychopathy.

To begin with, he was extravagant to the point of recklessness and showed poor management of his everyday life. An improvident husband and father, he did not always repay financial favours and was slow in settling debts. He and his family dined out in style regularly, even though they could often ill afford it. Joyce would also tip extravagantly – much to Nora's fury. In Trieste, he would spend the last of his salary on expensive gifts for Nora, like hand-painted silk scarves, rather than food for supper. Although he was teetotal until the age of twenty-one, Joyce seems to have spent the remainder of his life making up for lost time, and a liking for carousing always accompanied his drinking. Edna O'Brien notes that 'as soon as he got his salary he drank it'. His capacity for alcohol was small, according to Ellmann, and he was prone to drunken collapses.

From early adolescence, Joyce had uncontrollable sexual impulses. Some biographers believe that he lost his virginity at the age of fourteen, while others put it at sixteen. Either way, by his late teens he was promiscuous and was patronising brothels, where he found 'his much-desired abasement', according to O'Brien. In these matters, there was no question of self-restraint, and his sexual excesses veered towards fetishism and sadomasochism. At first, his relationship with Nora was highly sexualised. Over time, she became aware of Joyce's odd sexual tastes, such as a fetish for woman's underclothes and furs. Clearly sadomasochism played a part in their sexual relations, as exemplified in 1909 in a series of 'dirty letters' between Joyce in Dublin and Nora in Trieste; the letters contain sado-masochistic fantasies, with a great focus on scatology. Nora entered into the correspondence and reciprocated the sexually explicit content. Essentially, the letters were aids to masturbation for Joyce, and possibly an attempt by Nora to prevent her husband from visiting brothels, according to Maddox. Though the letters initially filled Joyce with disgust and shame, he seemed to overcome these feelings enough to continue with them.

It is not known whether actual sadomasochism was a regular feature of the Joyces' sexual life or not; most likely it was not. Maddox believes that, by the 1930s, the Joyces' marriage was celibate: Nora mockingly referred to Joyce as a 'saint' in that respect. It is possible too that an inherent strain of asceticism found expression in his middle age. Another Joyce perversity was voyeurism, but again this seems to have been limited. For a time in Zürich in 1918 and 1919, he stalked a young woman he was briefly in love with. From across the street in which she lived, he would watch her at her window reading his letters.

The association of sex with sin was one that Joyce never relinquished. If his autobiographical novel *A Portrait of the Artist as a Young Man* is to be taken at face value, the guilt he associated with sex was overwhelming. Without doubt, residues of Catholic guilt remained with him, even after he had abandoned Catholicism. But there were other areas of guilt too: over his treatment of his mother and father, his daughter's mental illness, his extravagances, and his drinking. Nonetheless, the guilt was never strong enough for Joyce to mend his ways. Like Beckett and indeed many others with Asperger's syndrome, Joyce suffered all his life from anxiety and fear: some of his health complaints were due to 'nerves'. More than likely he assuaged his guilt, however temporarily, by working. It is possible that his work in effect kept him sane.

*

Control and domination were part and parcel of Joyce's character, and there is evidence that he displayed an autistic aggression. Instinctively argumentative, Joyce was hypercritical of both others and himself – something Stanislaus called his 'vigilant habit of self-criticism'. Ellmann too refers to Joyce's habit of disparaging himself, though he often did this in a way that was tinged with irony. Sparing in his praise, his hypercriticism was frequently directed towards others, whom he expected to meet his exactingly high standards. In particular, he held academics in contempt and declared – rightly, it would seem – that *Ulysses* and *Finnegans Wake* would keep them occupied for centuries. With an abundance of cynicism, he would reject received wisdom or deference to established poets and writers. In a much-celebrated, albeit exaggerated, account of his meeting with Yeats, he reputedly said to Yeats that the poet was too old for Joyce to help him, but both deny that this was said with any contempt. Indeed, Joyce took grave exception when others accused him of lacking feelings or humanity. On those occasions, a torrent of abuse was likely to follow.

Endless salvoes of criticism preceded and followed publication of his works, whether from publishers and printers or critics and the reading public. The critics and the public attacked his 'technical monstrosities, his anti-humanist indifference, his desecration of style and his obsession with bodily functions which bordered on the macabre', according to O'Brien. Joyce, hypercritical to a fault, often burnt his bridges and spoilt the previously good relations he had enjoyed with people who had otherwise helped and supported him, like Lady Gregory. He also had a notorious temper and instilled fear in people. Endless wrangling over and editing of the 'questionable material' in *Dubliners* held up publication of that book for nearly ten years and turned Joyce into a litigator. His belligerence and litigiousness extended not only to critics but also to publishers, copyright infringers, or anyone else, like amateur actor Henry Carr, who had, he felt, seriously wronged him.

Joyce's desire for control was inherently linked to his absolute vision where his work was concerned. He was a perfectionist, meticulously and constantly rewriting and revising proofs – and exasperating editors and printers, not to mention creating significant extra expenses for them by rewriting large parts of his books after the type had been set. Early chapters of *Ulysses* had been serialised in the *American Little Review* from 1918 onwards; when Sylvia Beech agreed to publish it as a complete book in 1921, Joyce set about adding corrections from memory, thereby expanding the book by a third. The matter of his official biography was also subject to significant revision and change. Like de Valera, Joyce took an active interest in 'editing' the work of his authorised biographer Herbert Gorman and was hugely controlling in this respect.

His great pride meant that Joyce never forgot or forgave anyone who had ever wronged, betrayed or crossed him – many people with Asperger's syndrome have little capacity for forgiveness. Indeed, Joyce's vengeful nature could be quite disturbing. In his case, revenge was carefully and meticulously exacted by ridiculing and distorting various transgressors in his various books. Padraic Colum says that Joyce was prone to the 'suspicion of persecution', while O'Brien writes that he was more than half in love with persecution. Indeed, the notion of betrayal was central to his make-up: he identified with figures such as Jesus Christ and Parnell. John Joyce had also blamed many of his problems on being a victim of circumstance and betrayal. His parting advice to his six-year-old son, when he deposited him at Clongowes for the first time, was: 'Never peach on a fellow'.

*

Asperger geniuses are often viewed as enigmas because their personalities are confusing, undefined or multiple. A colleague of Joyce's at the Berlitz School in Pola, Italy, Bruni Francini had the measure of Joyce from the very start. He thought him 'a composite of incompatibilities'. Unquestionably, Joyce showed considerable identity diffusion and had a fragmentary sense of self; however, the conflict this engendered was almost certainly a boon to his creativity.

The development of a coherent sense of self has roots in childhood experiences as well as in a person's genes. In his early life, Joyce had to deal with considerable trauma: habitual changes of residence; deaths of siblings, in particular his much-loved brother George; declining fortunes; the unhappy marriage of his parents; a violent and abusive father; and, perhaps most poignantly, a downtrodden and submissive mother who disappointed him. It seems likely that Joyce suffered psychologically from such trauma and that it engendered in him certain insecurities.

The development of identity is also linked to having a sense of self in terms of chronological time. The Asperger genius frequently operates in the timeless world of the here and now, and this causes deficits in personal memory. While Joyce had a phenomenal capacity to remember facts and details, this could not be said of his own chronology. Growing up, he learned more about himself from sneaking a look at Stanislaus's diaries than from inward reflection. Indeed, he never kept a diary. From Nora, we know that Joyce had no concept or sense of time: he never knew what time of day it was. He was forever responding to his own internal clock or intuitive time and would, for example, leave the house just as lunch was put on the table. Like Hamilton, he was notoriously late, whether for trains, meetings or classes.

Constructing a personal narrative was thus exceptionally difficult for Joyce. Though his novels *A Portrait of the Artist as a Young Man* and *Stephen Hero* are 'autobiographical', a good deal of fact and fiction are intertwined in them: Joyce is remade and revised in the figure of Stephen Daedalus. There is no question that Joyce would ever have been able to write a proper autobiography — no more than Yeats, de Valera or Hamilton was able to do so. Over many years, Joyce vacillated about helping his official biographer, and in the end he insisted on receiving the final proofs and previous corrections; he extensively edited the proof before he gave it his blessing. This clearly arose from a deficient sense of self and of course the inevitable desire to control the identity that was created.

Consumed with confidence and absolute conviction, his identity as a writer of great genius was the one that mattered most to him. His friend in Paris, Arthur Power, called this his superconfidence. In his role as a creative genius, he saw himself as a creator, artificer, priest, prophet, shepherd and demigod, especially when it came to creating a pure form of language in *Finnegans Wake* — what could be described as the stem cells of literature. One of his most distinctive features, according to Stanislaus, was his 'inflexible sincerity as an artist and his firm belief that artists are the true spiritual shepherds of the flock'.

Like many Asperger geniuses, Joyce was cast in the role of outsider, outcast or exile — figures who are, by their nature, detached from others. Like his hero Odysseus, the restless Joyce in time would become a nomadic traveller, albeit of urban landscapes, gracing the cities of Dublin, Pola, Trieste, Rome, Zürich, Paris and Geneva, among others. The figure of the wandering Jew or Moses was also one with which he identified strongly. Indeed, like Beckett, Joyce did not have a strong national identity: if anything, he considered himself to be European rather than Irish. To a large degree, Joyce the outsider plied his trade in solitude: there were few warm welcomes within literary establishments — at least not in his lifetime. He was not interested in being a professional writer; he was not part of any literary clubs or esoteric groups, and he disliked discussing literature in any formal setting. The only exception was perhaps in his formative years at university, where he engaged with various people, including Thomas Kettle, Francis Skeffington and Arthur Cleary, usually in the environs of the National Library on Kildare Street. Hence *Ulysses* is littered with outcasts. Edna O'Brien remarks that Joyce was 'determined to reinvent the city where he had been marginalised, laughed at and bared from literary circles'. Indeed, he identified with betrayed and persecuted figures such as Parnell, Hamlet, Dante, Lucifer, Byron and Jesus Christ.

Joyce pictured himself in several other roles, some of which were inherited from his father: that of actor, singer, businessman, *flâneur* or idle man-about-town. Indeed, Joyce held a considerable number of occupations in his life. In his early days, he dallied with the idea of pursing a medical career, as his father had done. Another early ambition of Joyce's was to become a singer: indeed, all his life Nora bemoaned the fact that he had not become a successful concert singer. At one point, Joyce considered becoming a travelling minstrel in England. He also earned quite a reputation for his dramatic abilities, and Eugene Sheehy believed that he would have made a great actor. He did indeed receive acclaim for his part in a play written by Sheehy's sister Margaret called *Cupid's Confidante,* in which he played the villain Geoffrey Fortescue. For one night only, in 1901, this play was staged in the Ancient Concert Rooms in Dublin. In a review in the *Freeman's Journal,* a leading newspaper of the day, the critic praised Joyce's 'extraordinary skill' and described him as a 'revelation'.

One of Joyce's lesser-known occupations was that of businessman. Stanislaus readily admits that Joyce was 'by no means lacking in business capacity'. This aptitude may in part have being inherited from his father and his wealthy Cork antecedents. According to Costello and Jackson, John Joyce had a good head for figures and also had experience as an accountant. For his part, Joyce's get-rich-quick schemes involved becoming an agent for Donegal tweeds in Trieste and importing fireworks. The first venture was successful; the other was not. Thanks to Joyce too, Dublin opened its first cinema, the Volta Cinema, on Mary Street in 1909.

In the main, Joyce supported himself through teaching and tutoring, often grudgingly. Like many Asperger geniuses, he was unorthodox: he used unorthodox methods when teaching, although some of these methods are now employed in the teaching of modern languages. Ellmann writes that Joyce was impatient with the early stages of learning – like de

Valera – and as a result the more able students tended to fare better. In Pola and Trieste, the lessons were rather unstructured: after a quick drill, Joyce would converse or sing Irish ballads and songs, or play language games with the students. The lessons were finally concluded when Joyce slid down the banister!

For those with identity diffusion, recognition of their work and the need to be appreciated often become pressing features of their lives. Though Joyce obviously achieved fame and was celebrated accordingly, he hankered after respectability and the need to establish his family credentials, whereby notions of origin, heritage and posterity concerned him greatly. Indeed, origins and identity were dominant themes in his work – possibly because they were shifting entities in his own persona. To prove that his origins had been that of a gentleman, he took great care to display his coat of arms and ancestral portraits in all the flats he occupied in Trieste, Zürich and Paris, and counting Daniel O'Connell, the Liberator, as one of his distant relatives gave him enormous pride.

The ancestral portraits were the only remnants of respectability that the impoverished John Joyce had preserved for his son. Paternity conferred status and continuity, and Joyce, by his own admission, would have felt incomplete if he had never fathered a child. So much so that, in 1923, he commissioned a painting of his father by Patrick Tuohy to complete a set of family portraits. Later, in 1938, he arranged for a photo to be taken of the four generations of Joyces: he, his son Giorgio and his grandson Stephen posed in front of the portrait of John Joyce. No shrinking violet where his own image was concerned, Joyce had a penchant for getting his photograph taken or his portrait painted. In fact, the Joyces patronised the best studio photographers in Trieste, Zürich and Paris. Many of these visits to photographers and painters can be seen as attempts by Joyce to reinforce his identity as a creative genius.

In his style of dress, Joyce was conscious of his identity, especially as an artist and gentleman. In fact, his dress and personal appearance vacillated between these images. The influence too of his father was not inconsequential: John Joyce was flamboyant in dress and, according to Sheehy, sported a military moustache and an eyeglass and cane, and wore spats.

Joyce seems to have had little sense of personal vanity, however. As a young man, Joyce's hair was frequently dishevelled and his clothes unkempt, reflecting the poor self-care that is often associated with the Asperger genius. At various times he was clean-shaven, sported a beard or goatee, or later wore a moustache. His style of dress was eccentric too: unique but repetitive. In his early twenties, fresh from Paris, he wore a wide-brimmed soft felt hat, a flowing butterfly bow and a long black over-coat. He would frequently dress in black, like many artists of his genera-tion. Others remember him cutting a dash as the 'artist', dressed in yacht-ing cap, grey flannels and white tennis shoes, and carrying an ashplant or rowan stick. Indeed, the use of walking canes is particularly common among those with Asperger's syndrome. In his years in Europe, Joyce's dress became more dapper, as he achieved increasing celebrity – a devel-opment for which Nora must take much credit. The image of Joyce as a gentleman was one they both cultivated. A family prized possession, rem-iniscent of better times, was a hunting waistcoat that had belonged to Joyce's great-grandfather and that was decorated with the heads of stags and hounds. Joyce would wear it on his birthday or for special family occasions.

*

Many readers of Ulysses are struck by the vividness of Joyce's descrip-tions of the sights, sounds and smells of Dublin. *Ulysses* is particularly redolent of the smells of turn-of-the-century Victorian Dublin. There is much evidence to suggest that Joyce showed hyperacuity or hyperaware-ness in some senses and impairments in others – common traits in those with Asperger's syndrome.

Like so many with Asperger's syndrome, Joyce suffered from myopia or short-sightedness and wore glasses from about the age of six. His pale blue eyes grew steadily weaker as he became older: they were under great strain, given the amount of close reading and writing Joyce did. By all appearances, Joyce's eyes were sensitive and possibly photophobic. Over the course of his life he suffered from a recurrent array of eye complaints – including iritis, conjunctivitis, cataracts and glaucoma – that resulted in more than ten operations and, eventually, blindness in one eye. In 1940, he explained to Seán Lester, then acting Secretary-General of the League of Nations, based in Geneva, that he had a small magnifying glass for reading, while for writing he attached a special glass to his spectacles. It is a testament to his indomitable will that he never admitted defeat and ploughed on regardless, much like Beethoven, who continued to compose despite his deafness.

There was certainly a hyperacuity where Joyce's sense of hearing was concerned; as commonly occurs, this became sharper as his eyesight grew weaker. He was hypersensitive to certain sounds, such as thunder, which also filled him with great fear. Joyce appears to have been sensitive to very high and very low sound frequencies and intensities: typically, thunder and silence. Once, a friend loaned him his apartment for some months. Although the flat seemed to offer the perfect ambience for a writer – absolute silence – Joyce could not bear it and had to leave. He did not dislike noise in general and confided to Arthur Power that he needed a certain amount of activity around him when he was writing. Clearly he could filter out sounds well when he was working. At times, his voice could be loud and raucous, and he may have been unaware of the volume it reached – something which is commonly found in those with autistic spectrum disorders.

The entire Joyce household had a great appreciation of music. They attended concerts and musical evenings when funds were available, or played the piano at home – at least until they were forced to pawn it. Joyce sang from an early age and could 'play' the piano by the age of four. However, he sang by ear only and never learnt how to write music or sight-read, according to Peter Costello in *James Joyce: The Years of Growth 1882–1915*. The importance of sound, mediated through language, in his work cannot be overstated. One of his most significant compositions is arguably the 'Circe' episode in *Ulysses,* which O'Brien describes as a dazzling feat in terms of sound and narrative. In terms of balance and proprioception, Joyce, like de Valera, suffered from severe seasickness when crossing the Irish Sea or the English Channel. Whenever he sat for his portrait to be painted, he could not keep still, and painters had to employ various devices to distract him.

Smell was an extremely important sense to Joyce: he told Arthur Power that a city could not produce literature until it had 'vintaged' and that it 'must have an odour'. In *Portrait of the Artist,* the smells of cabbage, 'horse piss', and rotted straw fill the pages, while *Ulysses* reeks of lemon soap, fried kidneys and the perfumed smells of prostitutes.

There is strong evidence that Joyce was hypersensitive to touch as well. Arthur Power remembers that his hands were noticeably fine and slight-fingered, while Padraic Colum remarks that his hands were soft and sensitive. The sense of touch is also well developed in those who play musical instruments, and Joyce was an accomplished pianist. As his eyesight failed, he came to rely on his sense of touch (and hearing) to a greater extent. Certain textures appealed to him more than others. As an adult, he relished throwing himself on a beach and letting his fingers run through the sand or fingering pebbles, as he had done in childhood. The feel or sensation of water was problematic for him, however. Although he enjoyed swimming, the same could not be said for washing and bathing. By his own admission, he was hydrophobic where personal hygiene was concerned. His pet aversion, he declared, was soap and water. Like Robert Boyle and Beckett, extremes of temperature did not agree with Joyce either. After swimming in the sea, he would shiver uncontrollably for a time afterwards. Equally, he would complain bitterly about the cold winters in Zürich and the stultifying heat of Parisian summers.

In gustatory matters, Joyce was fussy when it came to food, and he suffered many gastrointestinal upsets throughout his life. Poor diet and malnutrition in adolescence, possibly a sweet tooth and a lack of fruit and vegetables, caused significant dental decay. Like Beckett, complaints of a mouth full of dental caries – teeth rotting in his head, toothaches and abscesses – were constant. Some teeth were filled and extracted in Trieste and seventeen were later extracted in Paris. Moreover, being a smoker all his life is likely to have affected his sense of taste. We know that he drank black coffee and tea, disliked red wine and favoured white wine and absinthe. Given his habit of dining out frequently, it is possible that he had a fastidious and refined palate; he admitted to Marcel Proust that he had a liking for truffles. Although the motif of eating is a significant one in *Ulysses*, Joyce, unlike Bloom, could not stomach the inner organs of animals and fowl.

*

Poor health seemed to haunt Joyce throughout his life – though it never lessened his resolve to become a great writer. Indeed, Bruni Francini declared he was 'constitutionally fragile'. As well as near-blindness, he had a poor immune system; he was also something of a hypochondriac. From infancy, he was a delicate boy and far from robust. Much of his early days at Clongowes were spent in the school infirmary, often with gastrointestinal complaints. The suggestion that Joyce contracted syphilis possibly in adolescence or in later life has not been substantiated, although he frequented brothels and was morally opposed to the use of condoms. In Trieste, he was hospitalised with rheumatic fever while Nora gave birth to Lucia. The stress and scale of his work clearly took its toll on him. He had a succession of headaches, sciatica, colitis, 'nervous collapses' or fainting fits, tonsillitis, and arthritic back pain. In later years, stomach pains, passed off as 'nerves' by many, turned out to be duodenal ulcers. A perforated duodenal ulcer led to peritonitis, for which he required surgery; he subsequently developed postoperative complications and died. A postmorten showed evidence of peritonitis along with an obstructed bowel. Joyce often complained of insomnia, and his sleeping pattern was erratic: he generally kept late hours and was a habitual late riser, according to Stanislaus.

Bouts of depression, despondency and melancholy affected Joyce too, as commonly occurs in those with Asperger's syndrome. Judging by Bruni Fancini's comment that Joyce was 'hysterical' – and other similar remarks – it would appear that he was highly strung. His daughter developed schizophrenia but, from Maddox's *Nora,* we learn that there was a history of serious mental illness in Nora Barnacle's family, with two relatives of her family being hospitalised, almost certainly for schizophrenia. There was no evidence of schizophrenia in the Joyce family, however. This view is supported by Robert Kaplan in the article 'Madness and James Joyce', in which he also discounts the theory that Joyce had a schizoid personality.

There is strong evidence to suggest that Joyce had poor muscle tone and hyperflexibility, which is sometimes seen in autistic spectrum disorders. Although he was never a brilliant sportsman, he took a spectator's interest in cricket and rugby, which was played on the school grounds at Belvedere and Clongowes. Problems with fine motor co-ordination meant that Joyce was not adept at ball games, something which is common in those with Asperger's syndrome. William Fallon recalls that Joyce lacked the co-ordination for games, although he enjoyed the fun and companionship of other boys. He could not kick a ball properly and would kick it with his heel. Solitary sports that involved gross motor co-ordination suited him better, like running, swimming and walking events, which rely on speed and rhythm. Stanislaus remembers that his brother won many prizes for the hurdles and had great speed and endurance when running.

By all accounts, he was a great swimmer – partly a result of his determination and lithe build. He favoured the breast stroke and the 'trudge' stroke – a double over-arm motion – according to William Fallon. Despite his speed, he was not a graceful swimmer – Stanislaus described him as a 'splashy' swimmer – which is certainly in keeping with his poor motor co-ordination. As for gymnastics, Eugene Sheehy remembers that Joyce could do 'interminable' pump swings on the parallel bars, again relying on rhythm and momentum. Gymnastic routines that required fine motor co-ordination were not so easy for Joyce: Fallon recalls his 'antics' on the horizontal bars, where his lanky figure would become entangled in the bars.

Numerous contemporaries and biographers draw attention to the fact that Joyce was loose-limbed and floppy, and that his handshake was almost 'boneless'. This suggests poor muscle tone and considerable hyperflexibility. Being so flexible and loose-jointed, he was famous for his contortions: he was able to cross his legs twice over when sitting and, when inebriated, would perform his 'spider dance' or impersonate the mother of modern dance Isadora Duncan, with her infamous flowing limbs and high kicks. Undoubtedly, Joyce was an indefatigable walker, like his father, as indeed are many with Asperger's syndrome, and would walk everywhere rather than take a tram. His books, not least *Ulysses*, are a testament to his rambles all over Dublin. He once walked fourteen miles to Celbridge, County Kildare, and then back, on the same day.

*

Like many Asperger geniuses, there was a deeply spiritual dimension to Joyce. Naturally his Catholic upbringing and religious instruction by the Jesuits shaped this aspect of his personality immeasurably. At first, his piety and devoutness genuinely ran deep. This climaxed in adolescence, when he was prefect of the Sodality of Our Lady from the age of fourteen until he left Belvedere at sixteen. From then, he gradually rejected Catholicism, a shift motivated by his abhorrence of falsity. The spiritual life afforded by Catholicism, he felt, was false and exacerbated by clergy that sought to victimise its adherents, like his mother. Sex, guilt and redemption were profound stumbling blocks for him: repentance for him was prompted by religious terror rather than sincere feeling.

It was inevitable that someone of Joyce's nature would break with Catholicism. Fiercely independent in both mind and deed, he was a go-it-

287

alone figure whose spirit would never submit to authority – certainly a key feature of the Asperger genius. In addition, his father and grandfather before him were anticlerical to the marrow. Unlike Pearse and de Valera, who chose to remain unorthodox Catholics, with Joyce there were no half-measures: a complete break was required.

Yet Joyce could not entirely cut God off. Indeed, the bond – as in the Latin *religio*, 'to bind together' – could not be undone. In fact, Joyce was a hypersensitive man with an enormous capacity for feeling. There is much truth in Stanislaus's assertion that, if someone experiences a sense of the divine, that experience stays with them all their life. Some critics, like O'Brien, claim that Joyce had been so indoctrinated by his mother and by priests that he could never quite shake off the shackles of religion. In fact, his religiosity was innate. Indeed, William Fallon always felt that there was a side of Joyce's character that was spiritual, and that he had an emotional and intellectual attachment to the rituals of Catholic ceremonies. The majesty of the Church excited Joyce, according to Ellmann, and this feeling never left him. To the end of his days, he liked to attend church on special occasions. For Joyce, the Church rites were powerful dramas, in particular the Mass and Good Friday ceremonies, with powerful symbolism. He loved sacred music and counted Palestrina among his favourite composers. Because of his liking for singing and the Catholic liturgy and ritual, Catholicism represented the 'oldest mysteries of humanity' for him. During his years in Europe, he even liked to wear purple cravats during Lent.

After Joyce's break with Catholicism, there followed a period of soul-searching. Like Yeats and Pearse, Joyce gravitated towards mysticism, the occult and astrology, in particular theosophy. The Theosophical Society, which was frequented by many leading Irish literary figures, studied the world's religions, philosophies and sciences, with particular emphasis on the hidden mysteries of nature, including the psychic and spiritual powers latent in man. During this time, mystical figures like St John of the Cross and the mystic scientist Paracelsus – so revered by alchemists like Boyle – claimed Joyce's attention. In life, many regarded Joyce as a mystic figure – an ascetic monk of sorts. Certainly there was a simplicity and honesty at his very core. But Joyce cared little for the people who frequented the theosophy meetings and considered the enterprise a waste of time. He was equally divided between the call of reality and the call of the imagination. His dalliance with theosophy disappointed him because he felt that it was self-deluding. More crucially, as a writer it did not give him access to a higher reality. That said, mystical theology does feature in his work, in particular in *Ulysses* and *Finnegans Wake*.

Because religiosity and spiritualism are inherently linked to the imagination, it is not surprising that Joyce was attracted to the supernatural. Like Beckett, Robert Boyle and Daisy Bates, Joyce was exceptionally superstitious and had many supernatural fears. According to O'Brien, he was a man who believed in portents: 'names, numbers, matter to him and he was able to read hidden augury in a shooting star or the passage of a flight of seabirds.' Indeed, he was full of paranoid fears, including the fear of thunder already mentioned. Furthermore, he had a lifelong – and more understandable! – fear of blindness and wore a ring as talisman against losing his sight. For him, May was a lucky month, thirteen a lucky number and blue a highly significant colour. It was the colour of his eyes and of the Greek flag – he had a particular reverence for Ancient Greece – and had talismanic importance for him. It comes as little surprise that he wanted the blue and white colours of the Greek flag to grace the cover of *Ulysses*. To ward off bad luck, he wanted books published and delivered by his birthday, regardless of how much pressure this put printers under. He considered that nuns brought bad luck and would cross the street to avoid them. Rats induced fainting fits in him, and since being bitten by a dog as a child he had a lifelong fear of them. He saw flying in aircraft as very dangerous and feared that he would be shot dead if he returned to Ireland.

Beyond doubt, Joyce possessed a powerful imagination, and he recognised the primary importance of the imagination. From his childhood, his imagination was fired with heroes from antiquity and ideas from myriad thinkers and writers, including Greek philosophers such as Aristotle, as well as St Thomas Aquinas, Bruno, Dante, Vico and Shakespeare, and mystical poets like Blake, Byron and Shelley. It was the work of Tolstoy and Ibsen, however, that fundamentally shifted his imagination towards realism. In essence, his imagination could be characterised as medieval, drawing on extremes of asceticism and decadence. Recollecting their many discussions, Arthur Power said it was the medieval and the medievalists which attracted Joyce most. Moreover, Joyce held that medievalism was the true spirit of Europe. In medieval Ireland, the golden age of monasticism had left a magnificent legacy, and throughout his life Joyce kept a copy of the Book of Kells and drew inspiration from it, according to Power.

In many respects, Joyce had a powerful auditory imagination. Perhaps he experienced words as sounds or music. As a consequence, he had more in common with the genius of Mozart than with that of Yeats. In effect, Joyce cared more for the sound and rhythm of language than its sense. It could be argued that his work was the product of a hybrid imagination that straddled the disciplines of music and literature.

The claim has been made that Joyce was not an original writer. In his introduction to *My Brother's Keeper,* Ellmann says that Joyce's gift was for transforming material, not for originating it. Much the same point is made by Costello and Jackson, who claim that Joyce was either 'unwilling' or 'unable to invent very much'. For his part, Joyce believed that he had little or no inspiration or imagination but worked laboriously instead. With rare humility, Joyce singled out writers like W. B. Yeats, Emily Brontë and Rudyard Kipling as possessing pure imagination. Certainly, in his early career he was preoccupied with the fact that Yeats had more talent as a poet than he had, and 'he said so repeatedly' to Stanislaus. Joyce's most celebrated biographer, Richard Ellmann, believed that he was never a creator *ex nihilo*: 'he composed what he remembered, and he remembered most of what he had seen or had heard other people remember'. In essence, imagination was memory for Joyce.

Stanislaus fancied that his brother was like a scientist, holding a microscope over human nature, and his work no less important than that of the scientist. In many ways, Joyce as quasi-anthropologist is akin to Boyle and Daisy Bates, who were also preoccupied with the detail of the everyday world. But Joyce was no slavish follower of realism or the physical world. For him, the pursuit of science could be as barren and inhuman as the pursuit of religion, according to Stanislaus:

> In early youth, my brother had been in love, like all romantic poets, with vast conceptions, and had believed in the supreme importance of the world of ideas. His gods were Blake and Dante. But then the minute world of earth claimed him, and he seems to regard . . . his youth deluded by ideals that exacted all this service. . . . Yet he believed in them wholeheartedly – in God, in art, or rather the duty imposed on him by the possession of talent. The faculty of ardent belief in the absolute is

like the poet's gift. It does not come by fasting or praying or consuming midnight oil, but it hallmarks the man who possesses it. It hallmarked my brother even when he deliberately chose for his subject the commonplace person and the everyday incident, the things that are despised.

Through his life and writing, Joyce demonstrated that conflict is the source of creation. Conflict, whether of personal identity, or of space and time, feeds the minds of poets, mathematicians, scientists, composers, painters and politicians alike. Joyce's genius lay in recognising that the imagination was capable of bringing opposite poles of the mind together. Like Yeats, de Valera, Pearse and Beckett, he appreciated the power of symbolism. A striking symbol for him was the Norse ash tree from mythology – the Yggdrasil – which symbolised the higher and lower reaches of life. It could be said to stand for Joyce's own life, which brought together the sublime and the profane.

9

SAMUEL BECKETT

All my life, since we must call it so, there were three things, the inability to speak, the inability to be silent, and solitude – that's what I've had to make the best of.

SAMUEL BECKETT, *The Unnamable,* 1959

The highest public honour that can be conferred on a genius today is undoubtedly the Nobel Prize. In 1969, Samuel Beckett was awarded the Nobel Prize for Literature, the third Irish recipient of this prize, and a richly deserving winner of it. As a poet, novelist and playwright, the modernist Beckett presented a vision of the human condition in a unique, innovative way. His style was often stark, spare and bleak but not without humour. His characters deal with suffering and struggle with meaninglessness and nothingness but are saved from utter despair by a sense of hope. Indeed, evolution's rallying cry, from *Waiting for Godot,* has become immortalised: 'I can't go on. I'll go on.'

Gifted with exceptional intelligence and erudition, Beckett's works are rooted in his experiences of real life and are not merely cerebral. The mark of the master is still felt today: subsequent generations of writers, poets and playwrights, from Vaclav Havel to Harold Pinter, continue to be influenced by Beckett and his work.

With his genius came burdens too: illness and depression plagued him throughout his life. His desire to be away from people conflicted with his desire to seek their company. His aesthetic imagination was so finely tuned, and his senses and emotions so hypersensitive, that the characters and scenarios in his work have striking resonances of 'autistic' situations. A highly revealing picture of Beckett emerges in three excellent biographies, which together provide valuable insights into his character, work, and social and cultural background. The first appeared in 1978, Deirdre Bair's *Samuel Beckett: A Biography*; two more followed in 1996, *Damned to Fame: The Life of Samuel Beckett*, the authorised biography by James Knowlson, and *Samuel Beckett: The Last Modernist* by Anthony Cronin. Certainly, a picture of Beckett as the tortured Asperger genius emerges.

*

In appearance, Beckett inherited a number of physical traits from his mother, many of which are found in those with autism. Tall and thin with a hawk-like nose, he had pale blue eyes and a piercing stare, with the suggestion from a former lover Peggy Guggenheim that he avoided eye contact. In time his aquiline nose and face grew as craggy as that of de Valera's. Beckett's hair, a reddish gold was inherited from his mother – later a reddish brown – and was described variously as spiky, crew-cut but invariably dishevelled. In fact all his life it was rather like a schoolboy's hair cut. Like his mother, his bearing could be imperious and austere though he had natural poise and grace. Indeed his presence has been described as powerful by many, and with a striking gentleness of manner that on occasion could become awkward. His hands were thin and his fingers distinctively long and slender. His gait was idiosyncratic. Some remarked that it was 'curious' whereby he walked with lurching strides, with his feet splayed outwards – seen in autistic spectrum disorders. Cronin writes that he seemed to lift his feet from the ground as if its contact hurt him. Beckett's enigmatic nature puzzled many a friend and acquaintance. Yet the moody, reserved and aloof Beckett could and did cohabit with the witty companionable Beckett. Above all, the charm, so evident in those with autism, was present in Beckett. In *Damned to Fame,* a school friend, who later became General Sir Charles Jones, recalls his memory of Beckett:

Although withdrawn and sometimes moody, he was a most attractive character. His eyes, behind his spectacles, were piercing and he often sat quietly assessing in a thoughtful and even critical way what was going on around him. However, he had a keen sense of the ridiculous and a great sense of humour; from time to time his face would light up with a charming smile and change his appearance.

*

For someone so taken with portents and symbols as Beckett was in his early life, being born on 13 April 1906 was significant indeed: it was both a Friday the 13th and a Good Friday. To begin with, a life of certain privilege was in store for the young son of William Beckett, a quantity surveyor from a family of prosperous building contractors. Originally poplin and silk manufacturers descended from the French Huguenots, the Becketts were middle-class Protestants who lived in a well-appointed family home, 'Cooldrinagh', in Foxrock, County Dublin.

The young Beckett enjoyed all the trappings of a middle-class existence: private schooling, high teas and tennis parties. His earliest schooling took place at a nursery school run by the Elsner sisters in Foxrock. Then from the ages of eight to thirteen he attended Earlsfort House School in Dublin, whose tradition of strict discipline meant that he was no stranger to corporal punishment. The school's French headmaster, Alfred Le Peton, ensured that Beckett was exposed to the language he would later adopt as the perfect medium for expressing his ideas. According to Knowlson, it was at Earlsfort that Beckett decided that he liked English composition, and he received good marks for his compositions.

One of the most curious features of Beckett's childhood is his complete lack of fear. Consistent with autism, he showed little or no appreciation for danger and engaged in spectacular feats that would strike fear into the heart of any parent. As a boy, he would climb to the highest branch of the great fir tree in the family garden and throw himself off, allowing the lowest boughs to break his fall. He did this over and over again, despite repeated warnings – and beatings – from his austere mother. Another incident involved dropping a lighted match into a can of petrol beside the kitchen door in order to test the petrol's flammability! The experiment yielded nothing more for the ever-curious Beckett than singed eyebrows and a burnt face – and, of course, his mother's anger. In fact, all his life Beckett was rather accident-prone. Whether riding motorcycles or driving motorcars, he was a reckless driver: he often crashed vehicles and injured himself and others, and was prosecuted on one occasion. Even into his eighties, he would alarm friends due to his obliviousness to heavy traffic when crossing busy streets in Paris.

Following in the footsteps of his only sibling, Frank, Beckett's education continued at Portora Royal School in Enniskillen, alma mater also to Oscar Wilde. In the tradition of many Asperger geniuses, Beckett's schooldays were not marked by brilliant academic achievement. In fact, if anything his grades were fair to middling, and the work he turned in veered towards the sloppy and slapdash. He had no aptitude for science and was decidedly poor at physics and chemistry, though much better at mathematics. However, in an early indication of his talents to come, he won some prizes for French and English on a number of occasions, in particular the Seale Prize for English composition.

From Portora, Beckett progressed to Trinity College Dublin, where he studied modern languages. Much of his time there at first was spent compiling lists – as many with Asperger's syndrome do – to offset his crippling boredom. One such list, described by Bair, was decorated with doodles and listed how many times his English professor Trench had said 'at all' during the course of a lecture. Nonetheless, by the time he graduated in 1927 Beckett's linguistic brilliance was recognised. He got a first-class degree in modern languages (French and Italian) and was placed first in his class, for which he received the Gold Medal. For a period afterwards, he worked as a teacher in Campbell College, Belfast, but the experience – for pupils, staff and Beckett himself – was largely unfavourable. The year 1928 saw him become an English lecturer at the École Normale Supérieur in Paris as part of an exchange programme with Trinity. During this stay in Paris, he was introduced to James Joyce by his fellow Trinity man and friend Thomas MacGreevy. The meeting was to have a profound effect on Beckett, who before long was assisting Joyce with dictation and copying down parts for 'Work in Progress'. The association led to Beckett's first published article in 1929: an essay entitled 'Dante. . . . Bruno.Vico..Joyce' – with deliberately odd punctuation – as part of a collection of critical essays about *Finnegans Wake* called *Our Exagmination Round his Factification for Incamination of Work in Progress*. This was followed soon afterwards by the publication of Beckett's first short story, 'Assumption', and a year later the poem 'Whoroscope'.

Soon afterwards, Beckett returned to Trinity College as an assistant lecturer in French and completed his MA. Much to his mother's disapproval, however, the disillusioned and ever-restless Beckett left Dublin two years later and travelled around Europe – to London, Paris and Kassel, Germany, where his aunt Cissie Sinclair lived with her family. As the years progressed, Beckett gradually got various work published, all the while battling writer's block, chronic conflict with his mother, the untimely death of his father, anxiety and depression. An acclaimed essay on Proust was followed by a collection of stories set in Dublin, *More Pricks Than Kicks*; a cycle of poems, *Echo's Bones;* and his first novel, *Murphy,* a study of a man who sought spiritual release by tying himself naked to a rocking chair and rocking obsessively.

A near-fatal stabbing by a Parisian pimp saw the 'Irish poet' hospitalised in early 1938 amid a blaze of publicity which brought him to the attention of Suzanne Descheveaux-Dumesnil, who was to become Beceket's lifelong companion, and later his wife.

The postwar period in Paris saw Beckett at his most productive, with the publication of several novels, *Watt, Mercier* and *Camier,* and a trilogy in French, *Molloy, Malone Dies* and *The Unnameable,* and his play *Waiting for Godot.* The death of his mother in 1950 was a particularly traumatic event in his life and had a profound impact on his work. *Waiting for Godot* shot him to international fame when it was given its world premiere in 1953. Beckett, now firmly established as a ground-breaking playwright, thereafter engaged in an endless round of new writing – among other works, *Endgame, Krapp's Last Tape* and *Happy Days* – translating previous works into French or English, and assisting with or directing his own plays in Paris, London and Berlin. Always innovative and eager to use new media, in the late 1950s he began writing for radio, with *Embers,* and in the 1960s for television, with *Film.* Over the course of his lifetime he produced twenty dramas or short plays, eleven works of fiction, thirty-two short prose pieces, twenty plays for various media, and numerous poems and miscellaneous material. Like Yeats, he worked indefatigably, often in poor health, right up to his death. He had lived most of his life in Paris and died in a nursing home there on 22 December 1989, six months after the death of his wife Suzanne.

*

From an early age, Beckett's interests were strikingly obsessional. Whether they involved sport, literature, music or art, these interests were narrow, highly focused and often circumscribed. Though he often complained of his indolence and failure to write, when immersed in something Beckett seemed to have endless reserves of energy.

An intense, all-absorbing passion for sport and games, to the virtual exclusion of everything else, characterised his school life. The drive, energy, focus and concentration that would later be channelled into his work was initially expressed in sport. Clearly, his desire for action, such an instinctive feature of those with Asperger's syndrome, was deeply ingrained and found expression in rugby, cricket, tennis, golf, swimming, tennis, boxing and motorcycle rallying. His sporting prowess meant that he found himself repeatedly on teams for rugby and cricket. At Portora, his friend Brian Coffey noted how much shrewdness and 'low cunning' Beckett was endowed with, which made him an excellent bowler. He had a sportsman's eye for precision and could apply logic and reason to any game. He became an all-rounder at cricket and, while at Trinity, earned a mention in *Wisden,* the cricketer's almanac.

A motorcycle enthusiast since his early teens, he joined Dublin University Motorcycle Club and was often found tearing around the Wicklow Hills like a modern-day joyrider. With autistic fearlessness, he was a reckless driver and came a cropper many times. Swimming was something he enjoyed all his life. Taking early-morning swims in the freezing waters of Lough Erne at Portora or joining his father and brother at the Forty Foot in Sandycove were strong childhood memories of his. Board and card games occupied his mind too, and he was an avid chess and bridge player. Indeed, it was in bridge that he first showed signs of a phenomenal memory. Friends recalled that he had the kind of memory that kept track of every card and hand, and even remembered hands in games that were long past. In time, sport was supplanted by literature in his affections, though he retained a lifelong interest in games and sport. In his eighties, while in the nursing home in Paris, a television set that he kept under his bed was resurrected during rugby internationals, especially when Ireland was playing.

As he became more immersed in Trinity College, his focus switched to literature. By this time, his exceptional intelligence, love for pure knowledge, erudition, and talent for writing had come to the attention of Thomas Brown Rudmose-Brown, professor of Romance languages. Under Rudmose-Brown's tutelage, Beckett engrossed himself in the plays of Racine, the poetry of the French Symbolists, and the work of Petrarch, the sixteenth-century humanist poet Ronsard, and modern French writers such as Proust and Gide. Having taken Italian as his second subject, Beckett's was soon awakened to the delights of Dante, who was to become one of the most important influences in his life, presumably because he wrote in pictures – as he was too for Joyce. Indeed, Beckett's student's copy of Dante's *Divine Comedy* was on his bedside when he died. Later, other writers and philosophers, including Descartes, Schopenhauer and Bishop Berkeley, would influence his thought.

Because Beckett had an audiovisual imagination, music and painting became important components of his writing. He drew wholeheartedly from the world of music, painting, theatre, variety and film. Certainly Dublin at the time was an exciting place for theatregoers, with the works of Synge, Yeats and O'Casey being staged, along with those that were influenced by European experimentalism. Theatres such as the Abbey, the Gate, and Queen's, on present-day Pearse Street, were all patronised by Beckett. Dublin too had its fair share of variety, cabaret and burlesque shows, all of which Beckett immersed himself in with great gusto. Variety shows at the Theatre Royal fascinated him as much as the emerging film industry, especially the work of actors such as Charlie Chaplin, Laurel and Hardy, Harold Lloyd, Buster Keaton and the Marx Brothers. In this respect, his tastes, which were discrete and eclectic, were all mixed in the giant cauldron of his creativity. Many of the years he spent reading and experimenting – although outwardly directionless or unproductive – were in fact tempering him for the life of a writer.

Beckett's deep love of music began in boyhood, when he learned to play the piano and made himself commit the music of Gilbert and Sullivan, Chopin and Mozart to memory. Many years later, he still knew the music by heart. He would often attend concerts or musical gatherings, although he hated the social aspect of these events. During the rehearsal of his plays, Knowlson says that Beckett was more like a conductor than a director. Indeed, the voices of actors – especially the musical quality, tone and depth of the voices – impressed him far more than the individual's acting ability; his firm favourites were Jack MacGowran, Patrick Magee and Billie Whitelaw. Beckett would frequently visit museums and galleries in Dublin, London and Paris, and in 1936 he fully immersed himself in art during a six-month tour of German museums and galleries. Because Beckett's inner sense of time was the eternal present, there is a static quality to his plays and novels, in which frequently 'nothing happens'. This static quality was in part influenced by his innate sense of time, and also by the works by other writers such as Racine, but also by his love of painting. Indeed, many of his works in later life are like 'pictorial compositions', as Cronin suggests — suggesting the 'thinking in pictures' associated with autism.

With the focus on excessive detail that is characteristic of autism, Beckett became absorbed in whatever activity he was engaged in. The early war years saw Beckett translating and transcribing intelligence material for the French Resistance in Paris. The friend that recruited him into the Resistance, Alfred Péron, noticed that he 'had astonishing powers of concentration, a meticulous attention to detail, and the ability to organise, reduce, and sift very diffuse material so as to make it succinct and intelligible for the British SOE [Special Operations Executive]'. Like many geniuses, Beckett was obsessed with dates and facts. He kept copious notebooks and was always jotting down new phrases, witty sentences and words that took his fancy. Quotations from various books he was reading were copied down and often served up in his own works later. While in Germany from 1936 to 1937, he kept diaries, but these mainly record facts and details about the places he visited, the people he met and the paintings he saw.

Beyond doubt, Beckett had extraordinary powers of concentration and exhibited signs of hyperfascination. In *Damned to Fame,* Knowlson relates how the painter Avigdor Arikha recalled that Beckett could spend as much as an hour in front of a single painting, 'looking at it with intense concentration, savouring its forms and its colors, reading it, absorbing its minutest detail.' So well could Beckett remember the details of various paintings that Knowlson suggests that he had a photographic memory. Although he did make notes, Beckett absorbed great detail from merely looking at a painting, or listening to a piece of music, and could reproduce some fine detail in a later work. Indeed, such was his retentive memory that he could quote vast passages of poetry, knew Dante's *Divine*

Comedy word for word, and, like a human thesaurus, could list off more than twenty synonyms of a particular word. When he was in creative mode, his level of absorption was enormous and he was hugely productive. His most intensely creative period occurred from 1946 to 1950, after which the 'siege in the room', as he called it, came to an end. Within the space of four years, he had written three novels and the play that was to make his name. So wholly absorbed was he in writing *Waiting for Godot* that the 'handwriting is lucid, flowing, attesting to the ease with which he transcribed his ideas to paper', according to Bair. An air of preoccupation and gloomy introspection often hung over him, as he sat alone in cafés starring moodily in front of him. Or else at home, in the silent throes of creativity, he would sit at his table for two or three hours, unable to pen a single word.

A single-minded determination characterised many of his activities, whether he was working as a postwar ambulance driver at the Irish Red Cross hospital that had been set up in the bombed-out town of Saint-Lô in Normandy or when controlling theatrical productions. On Christmas Eve 1946, he drove to Le Havre to pick up the hospital matron off the ferry and then drove at speed for ten hours, practically non-stop, on war-damaged roads to Saint Lô, where, after only a few hours' sleep, he then drove on to Paris. Fellow workers remember that 'sheer obstinacy, an unwillingness to give up' was a constant trait in his character. At the height of his career, Beckett worked industriously – writing new material, translating previous works, proofing, personally answering a colossal amount of correspondence, directing, and attending endless meetings with actors, agents, directors, publishers and scholars – not to mention the times when he felt duty-bound to meet old friends and relatives.

An obsession with exactitude became the hallmark of Beckett's work. His genius lay in focusing on a single aspect of the human condition, namely suffering and meaninglessness, but in a highly original way that gave it a value not hitherto recognised. There was innovation in both what he said and how he said it – that is, in both style and content, which to him were the same thing. Rigidly minimalist but exact, he used bleak language to mirror bleak situations. And because all traces of his personal life were stripped away, his work took on a universality. The ideas of philosophers interested him but only took him so far. Many of Schopenhauer's ideas confirmed his own, such as the 'intellectual justification of unhappiness'. The eighteenth-century Irish philosopher Bishop Berkeley, with his belief that 'to be is to be perceived', also struck a chord with Beckett, as did the presocratic philosopher Parmenides and his concept of 'non-being'. Though interested in philosophers, Beckett was far from being an idealist and instead drew from his own senses and perceptions to represent what he saw as reality. He readily admitted that he was more interested in the shape of ideas than in the ideas themselves. 'I am not a philosopher . . . One can only speak about what is in front of one and that is simply a mess,' he said.

The mess in front of Beckett was indeed his own life. Like Joyce, Beckett drew from his own life experiences and in this respect was a realist. For many years, Beckett had struggled to become a successful writer, amid deep frustration, anxiety, despondency, poverty and illness. Underneath it all was a hypersensitivity, seen in those with autism: his capacity for feeling was limitless, and life was lived second by second. Conflict with his mother, his lack of identity, and the deep sense of loss and grief at the deaths of his father, mother and brother affected him profoundly. Similarly, he mourned the passing of dear friends and first loves such as Ethna McCarthy and Peggy Sinclair with great sadness. It is little wonder then that Beckett felt the major sin was 'the sin of being born'.

*

As his work matured, Beckett in effect created an autistic-like style or narrative. Often there is little or no narrative plot, characterisation or dialogue in his work. Issues of space, time and the self dominate his work – again, things which those with autism experience differently to the neurotypical or average person. The lack of a fully integrated brain in autism can result in isolation, exile and the seeming separation of mind or body – themes that Beckett returns to time and again. Indeed, his characters and situations resonate with autistic features, giving an enigmatic tinge to his work. To begin with, his characters frequently inhabit a limbo-like space – often womblike or tomblike – devoid of any human place or landscape, where they appear to be cut off from the rest of humanity, such as the character May in the play *Footfalls*. Always the sense of time is arrested or suspended, like in *Happy Days, Play* and *How It Is,* which ostensibly reflects the influence of the French philosopher Bergson.

In Beckett's work, time is rarely linear or chronological but static or cyclical, as in *Waiting for Godot* and *Murphy*. Here pessimism predominates, because of an inability to look at the big picture or beyond the present. Furthermore, the identity of characters is obscure: they are effectively lost souls, depersonalised by having letters attributed to their characters, such as in *Play, Rough for Theatre I and II*; identified as 'he' or 'she' in *Rough for Radio I*; disembodied voices or mouths in *Cascando* and *Not I*; different voices of the same person in *That Time*; or the nameless teller of tales in *How It Is*.

In numerous Beckett works, speech and language patterns come to reflect those seen in autism: monotone and flat voices, monologues, repetitions of phrases, wordplay, and disjointed and idiosyncratic language. By his own admission, Beckett wanted to achieve 'a sort of synthetically elaborate joke style' – which could be a description for autistic speech. Because of distortions in identity and time perception in those with Asperger's syndrome, the tendency to combine fact and fiction occurs, as in *Watt*. Similarly, repetitive rituals that either stimulate or comfort abound – repetitive pacing in *Footfalls*, repetitive rocking in *Rockaby, Film* and *Murphy*, obsessional walking in *Molloy*, non-functional or idiosyncratic gestures in *Molloy* and *Waiting for Godot*. When rigid routines or habits are broken, for example with Moran in *Molloy*, the characters cannot cope with change. A childlike obsession with objects, parts of objects or body parts is also present in much of Beckett's work too. There is a fixation with feet in *Waiting for Godot*, with stones in *Molloy* and with disembodied mouths, voices and heads in various other plays. There is also an anal fixation, evidenced by the scatology in *Murphy* and the Trilogy, and a focus on degrading functions of the human body in *Endgame*.

With ever-increasing minimalism, Beckett focused on literal meaning in an attempt to make his words more concrete. Annoyed when actors and directors wanted him to explain a character or scene, he would retort 'I meant what I said', insisting that they accept the surface meaning only. Similarly, another mantra of his was: 'No symbols where none intended'.

People with Asperger's syndrome often have excellent visuo-spatial skills in addition to logic and reasoning skills. Beckett was certainly not deficient in these areas: many of his stage directions for various plays contain geometric designs for the exact positioning and execution of the performance, such as in *Act Without Words I, Film, Come and Go, Ghost Trio,*

. . . but the clouds . . ., and *What Where.* With mathematical precision, he gives instructions for the positioning, timing and duration of lighting, sound effects, and so on.

*

There is no evidence that Beckett had any speech and language delay as a child. However, he had a very minor speech impediment that never quite resolved itself. Some friends and acquaintances observed a slight lisp, and Cronin notes that he had difficulty pronouncing 'r' sounds. In conversation, Beckett generally spoke in a soft, low voice, choosing his words with care, but there is no suggestion that he spoke in a noticeably flat monotone or that his voice was high-pitched – as is commonly the case in those with autism. 'A grainy, almost silent voice, a curious Irish lilt and lisp, with a repressed lean bark' was how the American screenwriter Clancy Sigal described it.

Depending on the situation, friends and acquaintances often observed that he was tongue-tied and loath to speak. He avoided public speaking at all costs – the most notorious example being his refusal to go to Stockholm to receive his Nobel Prize, when he sent his French publisher Jérôme Lindon in his stead. As a lecturer in French at Trinity, students remember him as self-conscious, and standing up to speak was excruciatingly painful for him. That said, he had developed some debating skills at Portora and was prominent in the debating society there: he once took part in a debate supporting women's emancipation and showed a talent for eloquence and passion. To speak or not to speak was a conflict at the heart of Beckett's work, and suggestive of Asperger's syndrome. In *The Last Modernist,* Cronin writes that the 'simultaneous and contradictory necessity and impossibility of giving utterance' would become a theme running through his work.

The Asperger love of language was evident in Beckett from an early age. His nanny, Bridget Bray, affectionately known as Bibby, immersed him in folklore, rhymes and catches, homespun wisdom and commonplace sayings. Knowlson records that Beckett learnt to read quickly and would wander off alone and become absorbed in a book. All his life, new words excited his interest, as did word games, crossword puzzles, rude limericks and tongue-twisters. From his earliest writings, he showed a precocious command of language and languages, according to Knowlson.

When directing his stage play *Footfalls* in Berlin in 1976, he gave directions to the German actress playing the part of the strange girl May. 'Words are as food for this poor girl,' Beckett said. 'They are her best friends.' The same could be said for Beckett himself.

Beckett was extremely conscious of the music of language; in his plays, punctuation was used as a musical as well as a grammatical device. Like Joyce, the sounds of words and their inherent rhythm and musicality were important to him. Both were in essence trying to turn literature into a kind of music, since they regarded music as pure spirit. As a boy, Beckett committed to memory the lyrics of comic operas. His neighbour and friend Mary Manning remembers that he was 'almost word-perfect over the whole range of Gilbert and Sullivan operas'. The double- and triple-rhyming and punning widely used in Gilbert's lyrics no doubt held a particular charm for Beckett. He was inventive too with language and liked to coin his own words and phrases. Indeed, his late novel *Worstward Ho* is a tribute to this aspect of language: he creates neologisms mostly around 'worse' and 'worst' and uses nouns as verbs and vice versa.

Not surprisingly, given that he had a logical mind, a good memory and a musical ear, Beckett was an exceptional linguist. Having learnt French and Latin at an early age, he went on to master French and Italian at university. An autodidact, he later taught himself German, Spanish and Portuguese. His decision to write in French rather than in his mother tongue came about because he felt that English was too rich a language – with all its homonyms and synonyms, which lent themselves to wordplay, punning and rhetoric – thus making it difficult to express things simply, 'without style', which is wanted he wanted to achieve. He felt the inadequacy of English far more than his mentor did: 'Joyce believed in words. All you had to do was rearrange them and they would express what you wanted', Beckett commented.

In fact, Beckett was searching for the perfect language medium to articulate his vision of humanity. 'And more and more my own language appears to me like a veil that must be torn apart in order to get at the things (or the Nothingness) behind it,' he once declared. In truth, he wanted to get rid of grammar and style altogether and achieve a sort of joke style – a style that mirrors the speech patterns of autistic children. Many autistic children have difficulty with syntax and sentence construction and tend to play with words instead, speaking in rambling monologues. Indeed, many of the monologues in Beckett's plays, such as in *Play* and *Not I,* consist of a torrent of words delivered at breakneck speed in a monotone. They are in effect autistic narratives.

*

Much of Beckett's humour was associated with language and situation, especially where it involved toying with logic and reason. Like Joyce, de Valera and Pearse, Beckett had a sardonic wit. His sense of humour, according to Cronin, was like Joyce's and was of an 'uncompromising, often cruel Irish kind, which has aspects of gallows humour in it, rather than the gentler, more whimsical English variety'.

Certainly Beckett in his formative years gravitated towards comedy and humour in whatever shape or form it came. As a young boy, the cartoons in back copies of *Punch* absorbed him. Another particular favourite was the detective Sexton Blake – a Sherlock Holmes lookalike – who featured in the *Union Jack* comic and which spawned a lifelong love of whodunnits in Beckett. In later years, French, English and American detective novels and thrillers from Ellery Queen to Agatha Christie were part of his staple reading diet. With their sardonic wit, simple and predictable plots, anti-heroes, puzzles, rules of fair play, mannerisms and excitement, it is not surprising that they were attractive for someone with Asperger's syndrome. Indeed, many consider *Molloy* to be a detective story of sorts.

An early introduction to Beckett's favourite type of humour also occurred at Portora, where he and his friend Geoffrey Thompson became acquainted with the work of the humorist Stephen Leacock. In *Damned to Fame,* Knowlson writes that 'Leacock's playful wit, somewhat unsubtle games with the reader, amusing parodies, wordplay, and interest in unusual words would certainly have appealed to two bright adolescents.' Later, this kind of humour found its way into Beckett's novels *Murphy* and *Watt.* Earthy, schoolboy humour was never far from Beckett's mind either. His particular brand of lavatorial humour, or fixation with scatology – something he shared with Joyce and indeed Swift and Mozart – was certainly obvious in adolescence, when, in a memorable ode, he waxed lyrical on the symmetry of turds. In fact, he remained somewhat immature all his life and never lost his childish, impish sense of fun – as indeed is the case with many of those with Asperger's syndrome. This sense of humour was as inventive and spontaneous at the age of seventy as it was when he was younger, according to Knowlson. The biographer also relates a memorable encounter between Beckett and Duncan Scott, a lighting operator at the Royal Court Theatre in London:

> I came across [Beckett] looking confused on the staircase leading from the upper circle to the Theatre Upstairs. 'Where are you trying to get to?' He explained that he was looking for the main auditorium. At the Royal Court this is situated below street level. When he was reminded of this fact, [he commented]: 'Oh dear. I seem to have lost my sense of altitude!'

In fact, Beckett had a true sense of the ridiculous, and at Portora was masterful at teasing his teachers. Indeed, his novels and plays are rife with his sense of the ridiculous and the absurd. In *Molloy,* the mathematical permutations of Molloy trying to work out how each one of sixteen sucking stones is not sucked more than once in any one round of his four pockets is hysterically funny.

As has been noted, in early adulthood Beckett patronised Irish variety shows in Dublin which featured a diverse range of acts, from comedians to acrobats and performing dogs and seals, and the advent of the silent screen brought slapstick and knockabout humour to his attention. Beckett himself had a capacity for imitation and improvisation which was rarely seen because of his dislike of entertaining at home or giving personal performances. When lecturing at Trinity, he attended one party where he had to imitate a famous person. Bair writes that he did an impeccable imitation of Benito Mussolini, complete with rapid-fire mangled Italian – much to the horror of the guests.

Indeed, there is a great deal of hilarious comic writing in Beckett's work, and a vein of caustic humour runs through much of it. Beckett had an uncanny ability to poke fun at the worst aspects of human existence. You could say that this was his antidote to the awfulness of life. For example, humour in his celebrated play *Waiting for Godot* offsets the work's suffering and gloom. Moreover, it also points to humour as being something essential to survival.

*

One of the many ambiguities that Beckett endured in his life was his conflicting need for solitude and company. This ambiguity is certainly

dominant in the Asperger genius. In *The Last Modernist,* Cronin puts it succinctly: 'He was inconsistent, liking company sometimes when he was in
it, but not on principle, and rarely admitting to liking it in prospect, or
even retrospect'. In practice, this tension led to all manner of social
impairments. From early childhood, the solitary aspect of his character
was evident. By his own admission, he was lonely as a boy and liked to
ramble on his own around the Foxrock neighbourhood and nearby countryside towards Leopardstown racecourse, Carrickmines and the
Ballyogan Road. There he would often read in silence or talk aloud to
himself in different voices to imaginary characters. Though he was popular at Portora and made some friends, Beckett was mainly moody, taciturn and uncommunicative during his time there. Clearly in adolescence
he had problems with authority at Portora and was frequently indifferent
towards his teachers. They took this attitude for insolence and arrogance,
and he was often severely disciplined. Like Joyce, he never showed emotion when receiving a beating at the hands of his masters and remained
self-contained and in control of himself.

As he grew older, other solitary pursuits developed. He frequently cut
an isolated figure playing chess or golf by himself or, during his later days
at Trinity, engaged in solitary pub crawls. Certainly at Trinity in his leisure
hours he would 'avoid humanity', as he put it. Later, in Paris, as his fame
spread, the need for a retreat quickly became a necessity. The outcome
was the purchase of a cottage at Ussy-sur-Marne outside Paris where he
could work and relax and, more importantly, was released from any social
commitments he had in the city. Silence and solitude undoubtedly sustained him when he was in the throes of creative work.

For Beckett, the realm of the imagination was infinitely preferable to
that of plain reality. Needless to say, the times when Beckett engaged with
others were usually fraught with difficulty, unless they involved family, relatives or close friends. To begin with, he was, as some have remarked,
pathologically shy. Coupled with his shyness was an air of remoteness or
self-containedness and gloom that was hardly inviting to others either!
Recalling his sense of remoteness, one fellow student at Trinity, R. B. D.
French, recalled that Beckett 'seemed to be a man that everyone knew of
but no one knew well'. He unquestionably had an inability to relate to
people and the outside world. As a child, he tended not to mix with his
peers but with adults, as is often the case in those with Asperger's

syndrome. At Earlsfort House School, it was noticed that he was far more comfortable in conversation with his masters and their wives than with his classmates.

The occasions when Beckett, as a young middle-class Dublin Protestant, socialised with his peers tended to be children's parties, Sunday teas and tennis parties. During these events, he made no show of enjoyment for his mother's sake and was invariably silent, sullen and unwilling to take part in whatever entertainment was organised. Increasingly, he came to loathe these parties, which were usually rigidly controlled by his mother. All his life, large social gatherings made him uneasy, though in early adulthood he often put himself through great torture by attending parties. Detached and introverted, he usually stood in the corner, head hung low and seldom speaking, and endured the evening until the bitter end. By his own admission, he had a phobia of public situations: strangers in groups frightened him and he had a horror of small talk. However, he appears to have become somewhat more relaxed in the company of strangers by the 1960s. Beckett was capable of making friends, but they were always carefully selected, as Knowlson writes:

> At school and Trinity College, he had been really friendly with a very few individuals. This suited his shy, retiring nature and allowed him to choose carefully those with whom he wanted to spend his time. As a young man he was intolerant of those who irritated him and suffered fools badly. When bored or annoyed, he would lapse into deep uncomfortable silences that people interpreted (often correctly) as rudeness and lack of civility. Yet, because he had been brought up to believe in courtesy and good manners, he became upset when he knew he had been impatient, rude, or discourteous.

Clearly, the numerous incidents where Beckett showed inappropriate behaviour were not simply due to ignorance or poor manners. During his schooldays at Portora, he showed little or no deference towards his teachers and could be openly cruel. For one who would later recoil against cruelty, this showed a deep ambiguity and depth of social impairment on his part. The maths and science master, Mr Tetley, was particularly disliked by Beckett. In class, he would draw pictures of Mr Tetley bending over with his head between his legs staring upwards against well-endowed buttocks, and then would openly flaunt these pictures for the master to see.

Naturally, Mr Tetley confiscated them each time but was unable to hide his dismay and disappointment. Beckett's behaviour was entirely inappropriate and soon his classmates were shocked and shamed by his antics. Inappropriate behaviour also often resulted from his lack of empathy and naivety. In *More Pricks than Kicks,* he viciously satirised friends and included love letters from his cousin Peggy Sinclair, who had died from tuberculosis. So upset was his aunt Cissie by his actions that she broke off relations with him for a time. Cronin notes that there appears to be a good deal of physical cruelty in Beckett's own work, and indeed perversity can be a feature of Asperger's syndrome.

Another inappropriate incident concerned Beckett's instant infatuation with Betty Stockton, an attractive American who visited Ireland in 1936 with a friend of the Beckett family. Though she was already engaged, Betty had no inkling of Beckett's feelings and certainly did not reciprocate them. If anything, Beckett was rather vague with his intentions and remained aloof in her company. On their third meeting, Beckett called to her hotel and presented her with a love poem that made obscure references to 'abort', 'nine months' and 'if you do not love me I shall not be loved'. Not surprisingly, his behaviour embarrassed and disturbed her. Inappropriate behaviour was not always confined to his dealings with women. When fleeing Paris as the Germans were about to occupy the city in 1940, Beckett and Suzanne hid in the home of the Sarrauté family. Because both he and Suzanne were late risers, he would tramp through the kitchen carrying his chamber pot as the entire household sat down to lunch, oblivious to their disgust and revulsion.

Being a poor communicator, like many an Asperger genius, the practicalities of teaching were lost on Beckett. Putting himself in the place of his student and pitching his material to suit their language level or the curriculum was never a consideration with him. It therefore comes as no surprise that there were considerable complaints about his teaching. At Campbell College in Belfast, where he taught briefly, he was antagonistic towards less able students, and the parents complained to the headmaster, a Mr Gibbon. When told by Mr Gibbon that the pupils were 'the cream of Ulster', Beckett replied: 'And rich and thick.' At Trinity, he detested lecturing, and his teaching techniques were unorthodox – a common complaint with geniuses. In Paris, his first lesson with a French student who was learning English, George Pelorson, consisted of them trying to read through *The Tempest* together!

The question of empathy is a curious one with regard to Beckett. Certainly in his earlier life he showed a distinct lack of empathy and his behaviour frequently gave rise to conflict. With the passage of time, however, and especially with the experience of war, a certain humbling seems to have taken place on Beckett's part. He was thrown into the company of people he would probably never have encountered in regular circumstances and ended up sharing their plights. It is likely too that this reponse coincided with Beckett's innate sympathy for the underdog – who certainly took centre stage in his works. Certainly, when friends experienced loss or bereavement, he immediately offered his help.

It is not uncommon for children with Asperger's syndrome to be subjected to bullying and victimisation. At school in Portora, Beckett was bullied and baited, according to Knowlson, although he put up a good fight. The victimisation did not end with his schooldays, however. In 1938, as has been noted, he was subjected to a vicious attack by a pimp on a Paris street late at night. In 1937, Beckett appeared as a witness for the prosecution in a libel trial against Oliver St John Gogarty who, in his memoir *As I Was Going down Sackville Street,* had libelled Beckett's aunt's in-laws, the Sinclairs. Although the case was ultimately successful, Beckett came off rather badly. The skilful manipulations of the defence lawyer Fitzgerald saw Beckett depicted as a blasphemous and decadent intellectual living in Paris, a city then regarded as a den of iniquity. Indeed, Beckett possessed a certain naiveté and innocence of which people took advantage. Because of his spontaneously generous nature, he was considered a soft touch for money, especially when he had become successful. Indeed, Brendan Behan, among many others, plagued Beckett for money or favours.

Like many with Asperger's syndrome whose instincts are finely tuned, Beckett had a natural affinity for animals and hated cruelty towards them. Indeed, the death of a family pet dog during his time in Trinity plunged him into such depths of grief that he contemplated suicide.

*

The manner in which Beckett conducted his close relationships and friendships was strikingly complex and enigmatic. It seems that Beckett could relate much better to men than to women, with certain exceptions. Men were far more likely to share his interests, whether in matters relating to his work, music, art, sport or Trinity College. Naturally, he was comfortable too with family and close relatives, as is often the case in those with Asperger's syndrome. He had a deep love for both his father and his brother Frank, even though they appeared not to understand him. With Beckett's mother becoming increasingly difficult to live with, Bill Beckett withdrew from home life and became more solitary. Beckett saw his father as 'essentially lonely and almost beyond communication'. On their deathbeds, he nursed his father and brother in turn with tender loving care, and their deaths plunged him into depression. Indeed, his loyalties to his family ran deep and he was always obliging towards his sister-in-law, nephew, niece and other relations.

Once you had gained Beckett's trust or admiration and he was at ease in your company, he was a different person. With friends and close friends, his shyness and silences were not awkward but companionable. Moreover, he could be charming, erudite and quick-witted, and entertaining company. The complexity of his friendships was noted by Cronin:

> His friends tended to fall into two categories: those with whom he felt sufficiently at ease to maintain a mutual and comprehending silence, and those who were talkative enough to fill the silence and distract him — even, in some cases, with gossip and chatter. He was a good listener, seeming to give all his attention to what one was saying and inclining his head a little as he listened.

Male friends were carefully selected and tended to be compartmentalised: Irish friends or relatives were kept separate from European, English or American ones, and rarely introduced to each other. Also, rendezvous generally tended to be one-to-ones in cafés. Only on rare occasions were friends invited to his sanctum in Ussy, and if an invitation was extended Beckett made sure that the visitor was seen off again on the train in the evening of the same day. Clearly, he could not face the intimacy and terror involved in having to entertain guests overnight.

Principled loyalty seems to have been a mainstay in Beckett's life, and he remained thoroughly loyal to his friends. Indeed many ties that he forged in his early life lasted a lifetime, in particular with his Portora schoolfriend Geoffrey Thompson, Trinity men Alfred Péron and Thomas MacGreevy, and Con Leventhal, a friend who married Beckett's early love Ethna McCarthy. Because they shared common interests, his friends tended to be publishers, actors, directors, artists and writers. The friendship with MacGreevy was especially important: he became Beckett's confidant and indeed the only person to whom he was completely truthful. The friendship lasted for more than forty years and a huge correspondence built up between them: at least three hundred letters from the mid-1930s until MacGreevy's death in 1967 exist today. In James Joyce, Jack B. Yeats, Bram van Velde, Giacometti and Avigdor Arikha, Beckett found kindred spirits, where companionable walking in silence was often a pleasure, and a distraction from the lonely struggle of creative work. Indeed, if anything Joyce and Jack Yeats were mentors for the young Beckett.

A deep ambivalence existed at the heart of Beckett's relationships with women. The root of his difficulty with women lay in the fact that their roles were rigidly compartmentalised in his life. He could relate to them at separate levels which were each important to him – maternal, spiritual, intellectual and sexual – but not in any integrated way. This lack of psychological integration is seen in autism, manifesting itself in a juvenile view of women and, by extension, a lack of emotional maturity with regard to them. Moreover, his frequent inability to reciprocate feelings meant that an often unbridgeable gulf existed between Beckett and whatever woman was the focus of his attention at the time. As a result, women tended to be objects of contemplation. Indeed, he also showed a passivity with regard to women and liked to be at their mercy.

Did Beckett ever experience genuine love and demonstrate affection? There is the suggestion from Bair that, as a child, he did not show affection – something which is commonly seen in children with autism. She writes that his mother was 'determined to conquer his stubborn refusal to be reached, his unwillingness to show all the ordinary emotions, from fear to affection'. For all his early love poems and the rejections he experienced in his youth, Beckett later seems not to have believed in love and appeared to be convinced that he was incapable of loving.

The most important female relationship and also the one that yielded the greatest conflict for Beckett was that with his mother May. There was a certain coldness in her make-up and an evident lack of empathy. One key incident from childhood that Beckett never forgot was when he and his mother were walking home from the shops hand in hand along Cornelscourt Hill Road one day. Looking up at the blue sky, Beckett asked her if the sky was as far off as it seemed to be. Her curt reply wounded him deeply: 'It is precisely as far away as it appears to be.' Family friends such as May Manning recall that 'Sam suffered from emotional malnutrition.' In fact, the only type of love that the austere May seemed to dispense was that which her son described as 'savage loving' – an excessively undemonstrative and controlling kind of love.

It would seem likely that May Beckett had some degree of high-functioning autism, possibly Asperger's, which was complicated by depression. In her own childhood, she was high-spirited, novelty-seeking, undisciplined and described as a 'problem child'. In later years, she cut an odd figure. Photographs reveal a woman who was 'strikingly mannish' with a huge head, according to Manning. A penchant for flowered hats was her only concession to frivolity, and they added greatly to her eccentricity.

May Beckett's level of social impairment was such that it contributed greatly to the disharmony between herself and her family, especially Beckett. Withdrawn and moody, she disliked social gatherings unless they were confined to family relatives or a few close friends. Only among those who shared her interests in gardening and animals would she come alive. With children, particularly her nephews and nieces, she could be wonderful company. She had an endless stock of impersonations, jokes and funny stories, which revealed in her a sense of the ridiculous that she certainly passed on to her son. In fact, she oscillated between being great fun and being frenzied. A disruptive force in the household and a habitual insomniac, she also suffered from migraines and depression. Bair describes these 'mercurial swings of temperament' as being distressing for her sons.

Although she was capable of great kindness and generosity in times of need, May's deep piety and puritanical moral code made her a formidable figure. She made no secret of her displeasure at what she perceived to be her son's failings: he had no respectable job, an aimless life, and brought shame on the family, with court appearances for drunken driving and the Sinclair libel case, and was still financially dependent on her at the age of thirty. Even in adulthood, she treated Beckett as a child, reducing his allowance if his behaviour was particularly unruly or violent.

Not surprisingly, Beckett gravitated towards maternal figures – mostly female cousins – as he grew older, and in particular his rather bohemian aunt Cissie, who seemed to supply any deficits when it came to maternal love. For Beckett, the experience of 'love' in his youth tended to be in a highly abstract, idealised form, where he wanted to enter into some kind of spiritual union with his beloved. In this sense, women were no more than love objects for his contemplation. At Trinity, he formed a deep spiritual attachment to Ethna McCarthy, a highly intelligent fellow student who featured as 'The Alba' in his early fiction and poetry. Like a medieval troubadour, Beckett wanted women to 'excite his soul but not his body': there was no question of sex, and so he kept his distance.

Perhaps the most illuminating of Beckett's relationship was the one with his first cousin Peggy Sinclair. As with Ethna, he idolised and romanticised Peggy from afar – she in Germany, he in Dublin or Paris – and was obsessed with her face more than her physical presence. Indeed, as their affair progressed, he was at his happiest when she made no demands on him. Beckett began to see sex as a natural way to 'transcend the conditions of ordinary existence' – to negate the awfulness of being. Alas, in his eventual sexual encounters with Peggy she did not live up to his ideals. By his own admission, he detested her body: her fat ankles, her Botticelli thighs and her knock-knees.

Increasingly, Beckett had difficulty translating feelings of love into sexual desire or associating the act of sex with other forms of emotional involvement. Prostitutes and masturbation were infinitely preferable for him. Like Joyce, Beckett in his student days patronised brothels in Dublin and he continued to do so in Paris all his life. Not surprisingly, Beckett gained a reputation as a misogynist and his sexual desires increasingly found expression in perversities such as infantilism, voyeurism, masochism, buttocks-fixation and womb-fixation.

Because he feared entanglements, he prized casual affairs in which there was little emotional investment. This emotional immaturity appears to have lessened somewhat in later life, however. The type of women that Beckett was attracted to were generally intelligent women, usually working in the creative arts, and were strong-minded, talkative, charming and independent. It is said, however, that he was uneasy around unattached women and wary of those who were clearly very much in control of their lives. Brief affairs – with the wealthy American art-gallery owner Peggy Guggenheim – became the norm for Beckett, but he would lose interest once the woman involved became too demanding of his time, energy, space and privacy. Lucia Joyce, Joyce's daughter, has often been mentioned in connection with Beckett, and while it is clear that he was captivated by her to some degree, he prized his relationship with her father above that with her. With characteristic passivity, he naively did little to discourage Lucia's attentions until her deteriorating mental health, eventually diagnosed as schizophrenia, prompted him to reject her categorically.

The two women who were to have a lasting attachment to Beckett were the music teacher Suzanne Descheveaux-Dumesnil, who became his wife, and Barbara Bray, an English script editor for drama at BBC Radio. The former relationship lasted fifty years, the latter, thirty years, until Beckett's death. During those years, Beckett still conducted brief affairs, as discreetly as possible. When Suzanne entered Beckett's life in 1938 after he had survived a knife attack, she became a stabilising force at first, in the mould of Nora Barnacle with Joyce and Georgie Hyde Lees with Yeats. It is likely too that in the early years of their relationship she fulfilled many roles: sexual, maternal, supportive and intellectual. By his own admission, he was 'fond' of her but 'dispassionately' so. It was largely through her efforts and her belief in his genius that his work was first published. Beckett, despondent and lacking in the social know-how required for dealing with publishers, would wait idly in cafés while she hawked around his manuscripts and knocked on doors.

Like Beckett, Suzanne was intensively private. Indeed, she was even more reclusive than him: she disliked social gatherings and thus avoided his friends. With no home life to speak of, neither she nor Beckett were interested in having children, and it is likely that sex was not a feature of their life; she described it to a friend as 'a *ménage à celibataire*'. Beckett's decision to marry Suzanne after they had been living together for thirty years has been seen by many as enigmatic and bizarre. The marriage took place secretly in 1961, essentially so that she could inherit his literary estate. But the marriage was, as Bair suggests, a mockery; there was little warmth between the two and they had little in common. In effect, Beckett and Suzanne led separate but parallel lives, almost mirroring the non-interactive parallel play of children with autism.

Some years before his marriage, Beckett had formed a close liaison with Barbara Bray, a young widow whom he had first met in the 1950s when she was working for the BBC. Extremely intelligent, attractive, talkative, independent, and a gifted French translator, she had many things in common with Beckett – not least her sense of humour. Her deep attachment to him, probably built on admiration and respect for his genius, evolved into what Cronin describes as a 'very intimate and personal' relationship. This relationship no doubt prompted her to leave her job in London and move to Paris in 1961 with her two children. It appears that Beckett agonised over marrying Suzanne but that duty and guilt won out in the end. In the months after her death in 1989, Beckett admitted: 'I owe everything to Suzanne.' Despite its unorthodox nature, his relationship with Barbara endured for three decades and appeared to be a stabilising force in Beckett's life.

*

Beckett was frequently described as a creature of habit who lived a carefully regulated life. Certainly rituals and rigid routines formed an important part of his life. Many of the rituals were carried out to facilitate his writing, to exert control over his life – in particular against the intrusion of others – and to maintain the status quo. Indeed, his desire for preservation of sameness can be seen as an attempt to maintain a certain mental equilibrium. The arrival of fame and wealth did little to change Beckett's essential habits once he had allowed for the solitude and space he required for writing, in the form of his new apartment on the boulevard Saint Jacques and a cottage in Ussy-sur-Marne outside Paris. When it came to money matters, however, he still returned to the bank he had used near his old flat on the rue des Favourites in the neighbouring arrondissement.

Beckett was generally a late riser, as many with autism are, but could function well into the night. When he finally consented to having a telephone installed in his flat, he would respond to calls only between the hours of 11 and 12 o'clock in the morning, and a red light would flash, in preference to a ringing tone. Callers were given careful instructions by his friends or publishers on how to use this system. As regards time management, he was extremely punctual when attending meetings or appointments, or when giving lectures, unlike Joyce. As a rule, if people contacted him with a view to meeting him, he would send instructions about the time and venue. On arrival, he would indicate how long the meeting would last – usually an hour – and then depart once the allotted time had elapsed. Sometimes this rule was relaxed if he found a kindred spirit, and then a long drinking session was likely to ensue. He had a rule about not drinking before 5 o'clock in the afternoon, which he observed as much as possible.

316

Walking and pacing were firm habits of Beckett's. From his earliest childhood, he developed a passion for walking, no doubt engendered in part by his father, with whom he would walk for hours around Foxrock and its neighbouring districts as well as in the nearby Dublin and Wicklow hills. In Paris he would take long solitary works – occasionally in the company of Joyce or Giacometti – or when visiting a new place or after a long day involved with the production of a play in London or Berlin. During intense periods of writing *Murphy* in Dublin, he walked up to ten miles a day. Often a whole day was given over to obsessional walking. Pacing was another ritual, done frequently at his writing retreat at Ussy. Usually in times of anxiety, especially when suffering from writer's block or on first learning that he had won the Nobel Prize, he would pace back and forth across his room. This tendency for repetitive pacing was inherited from his mother, who had the carpets removed from the floorboards in the family home so that she could hear the sound of her footfalls – a trait that found its way into his play *Footfalls*. These repetitive autistic actions, done as much for stimulation as to relieve frustration, were a necessary part of his life.

Recurring themes, phrases and motifs were another aspect of Beckett's liking for repetition and preservation of sameness. Throughout his life, certain phrases would be repeated in his correspondence, such as 'must it be it must be it must be' – a phrase borrowed from Beethoven, questioning the acceptance of death.

*

Beneath his calm exterior, Beckett experienced a powerful and often paralysing sense of guilt. His conscience was nothing short of puritanical, and this arose directly arose from the harsh superego forged in his youth – which is commonly seen in those with Asperger's syndrome. The product of a rather puritan upbringing, Beckett's moral code was more finely developed than most, and he admitted as much when he told the psychoanalyst Dr Wilfred Bion that Puritanism comprised the simple, straightforward and dominant part of his personality. From his days at Portora, certain qualities and values were deeply ingrained in him: loyalty, honour, integrity, politeness and respect for others. At home, these traits were reinforced by his mother, who had a rigid moral code herself and whose superego was possibly even more severe than that of her son. Frequently, these values were to the fore, most noticeably when Beckett had achieved a certain degree of literary success. Having been well drilled in good manners, he could conduct himself with great, if not excessive, politeness when in company, as Peggy Guggenheim observed. There was also an old-world courtliness to him akin to that seen in Joyce – and far more pronounced in Beckett's case. Unlike Joyce, Beckett could be extremely considerate and accommodating, and contrite if he had caused ill feeling, embarrassment or hurt. Like many with autism, Beckett was unable to tell lies and was scrupulously honest. His English publisher John Calder said that Beckett's 'only real social lack is that commonest of social accomplishments – hypocrisy. Beckett is unable to tell the smallest white lie or engage in the smallest dishonesty.'

Stoical by nature, any calamities that came his way were accepted without too much fuss, such as the time he was stabbed in Paris. In his work too he was conscientious, whether he was producing his own work, helping the Resistance, or driving an ambulance and being quartermaster for the Irish Red Cross at Saint-Lô in the aftermath of the war. He had an innate sense of justice but was not overtly political and frequently refused to be drawn into pledging or signing petitions for causes in public. That said, his innate abhorrence of war saw him refuse to join the Officer Training Corps at Portora, according to Knowlson. Essentially, his sense of justice had its roots in fair play for all, and, from his time at the multi-denominational Earlsfort House School, he certainly accepted all Jews, Catholics and Protestants. He identified strongly with the underdog, and many of the figures in his plays and novels are such characters. Victims of totalitarian regimes, whether fascist or communist, were often the beneficiaries of his kindness and generosity. During the Nazi occupation of France, he gave bread rations to Lucie Léon after her husband Paul had been deported to a concentration camp.

The central place occupied by guilt in Beckett's life inevitably arose from his clash of conscience and duty, and his own creative urges. This was particularly the case as he ploughed a lonely furrow in becoming a writer. He would set impossibly high standards, resulting in much grief, frustration and guilt. Beckett had strong family loyalties and so felt guilty about the various occasions when he failed to please his family. The fact that his mother disapproved of his work, neither commenting on them nor displaying them at home, caused him great pain and anxiety. While his parents lived, he was also financially dependent on them – a situation that sat comfortably with neither son nor mother. He often took refuge in alcohol and reckless pursuits, and experienced panic attacks.

Sometimes the call of duty was as strong as the voice of solitude for Beckett. He would agonise over whatever choice he was making and, not surprisingly, earned a reputation for being indecisive. Peggy Guggenheim relates how, outside her house door, Beckett would go through 'the most terrible agonies' trying to decide whether to come in or not. The conflict between the desire to oblige people by sharing their company and staying away from them in his own space was a constant challenge and source of frustration to him.

During his relationship with Suzanne and their later marriage, he experienced enormous guilt over his affairs with other women. The effect of his superego is perhaps the best explanation as to why Beckett decided to marry Suzanne, despite having embarked on a significant affair with Barbara Bray some years before. Clearly understanding Beckett very well, Barbara later responded: 'One of Sam's main characteristics was loyalty and gratitude and I would never ask anybody whose main characteristics were loyalty and gratitude to be disloyal and ungrateful. On the contrary.'

Beckett's loyalty to Joyce was almost reverential, and he took a special interest in the welfare of his daughter Lucia. No doubt feeling guilty for having rejected her advances and precipitating her illness, he would visit her when she was hospitalised in Ivry and later corresponded with her when she was in England, helping her out whenever he could.

As the years progressed, Beckett's superego appears to have become more harsh and his scruples more pronounced. Highly critical of himself, five years before his death he was still tormented by his 'cruelty to people'. He suffered a great amount of mental anguish, according to Bair, because he loved his father more than his mother. This brought him guilt and shame, because his mother was a seeming paragon of virtue, while his father was clearly not. He even felt guilty for existing at all, and indeed many observers have remarked on the somewhat masochistic nature of his suffering. Welcoming or wallowing in humiliation and abasement did seem to be part of his nature. When his friend George Pelorson was at Trinity, he had a sense that Beckett was in some way relishing the extreme discomfort caused by an enormous cyst he had on his neck.

Sometimes Beckett put himself through the torture of meeting new people or strangers or took a perverse pleasure in misery and suffering – in what he called the nothingness of being. It is possible that by doing this he felt he was atoning for any wrongdoings he had accumulated and that this acted as a form of expiation or compensation for him. Indeed, doing good was often a tonic for Beckett.

*

The controlling behaviour so frequently found in those autism and indeed in geniuses was evident in Beckett too. There seemed to be no area of his life where control was not an issue. When control was lost, he inevitably experienced anger and hypercriticism, if not anxiety and depression. According to Knowlson, Beckett had a violent temper and once went berserk when he was bullied by a gang in Portora, lashing out at them using his best boxing skills. In later years, however, Beckett had excessive self-control where his temper was concerned and always hid his anger in public, according to Bair.

So formidable was Beckett's presence, Bair says, that no one would dare to criticise him about his work, his behaviour – which often involved drunken binges – or his clothes, which were frequently dirty and unkempt in his early years in Paris. 'For he met all comments, no matter how slight, with a cold stare and blank visage. He brooked no criticism of anything he did, and usually dropped the intrusive offender forever', Bair notes. Certainly, when he was crossed he could be unforgiving and he harboured grudges – not least towards the many publishers who had rejected his works in the early days of his career.

Like many Asperger geniuses, Beckett was critical of received wisdom and was sometimes anti-academic. He worked alone and never solicited advice or opinions while he was in the process of writing. Scornful of critics and criticism, particularly in his youth, he was not slow to mock them either. In his poem 'Whoroscope', he pokes fun at academia and at the poet T. S. Eliot and his epic poem 'The Waste Land'. Similarly, in 1934 he launched a broadside at Irish poets: those that excluded self-perception from their works were labelled antiquarians. For his part, Beckett hated having to explain his writings because he believed that all the interpretations of the text was contained therein: i.e. the text spoke for itself.

The extent to which Beckett exerted control over the production of his work is legendary. He never hesitated to say 'no' when an interpretation differed from the one he had envisaged. When directing his own plays, there was usually a rigid rehearsal schedule, and he was frequently demanding, expecting more and more from the actors. He had an excessive perfectionism that never wavered. In his mind, he had a picture of how his plays should be performed and he went to great lengths to actualise it and found it very hard to compromise. Once, in Paris, he held up the opening performance of *Play* for a week because of incorrect lighting equipment.

If his texts were altered or edited in any way, he often flew into a rage, as for example when an extract of *The Unnameable* was printed in a French review, *La Nouvelle Revue Française,* minus one passage. Equally, he expressly refused the gender of a role to be changed and was horrified when an all-female cast wanted to perform *Waiting for Godot* in America. Translating his work into English or French was also problematic, and he ran into difficulties with translators in the early days: for example, with *Molloy* he finally decided to do all his translation work himself.

In the matter of his social relationships, Beckett exerted huge self-control over the way in which he interacted with people so that his equilibrium or capacity to write was not impaired. The excessive discipline and control he exerted over himself indicates an obsessive personality. Revealing himself to others, especially strangers, was never countenanced. On the other hand, he sometimes had no option but to do as, as when he sought the help of psychoanalyst Dr Wilfred Bion for acute anxiety and depression in 1933. Bair writes:

> Probably the most important aspect of Samuel Beckett's self is and always has been best described as 'control'. Until this time he had always been the one in any of his relationships to decide how close he would allow others to come to him. He was the one to arrange meetings or engagements, and these were always in public places from which he could easily and gracefully escape. He rarely invited friends to his family home, or later to his rooms and apartments, because then he would have been forced to entertain them, perhaps long after he was tired of their presence or bored with them. And consistently, in conversations and interviews with persons who claim to have been his lifelong friends, the realisation comes that it has always been Beckett who set the pace and direction of the friendship. For a person such as Beckett who has raised his personal privacy almost to a religious fetish, it must have been

extremely difficult to begin a professional relationship in which total and absolute openness about every aspect of his life was the only ground rule upon which the relationship could be established.

Fame and recognition brought considerable ambiguity for Beckett, who essentially wanted success on his terms. Although his literary reputation was certainly important to him, he did not want it to encroach on his private life and went to great lengths to maintain control of it. In this respect, he had a passion for secrecy. All the publicity for his works was left in the hands of his publishers, or Suzanne in many instances, and media interviews were routinely turned down.

*

'Identity is so fragile', Beckett once admitted. In fact, he showed clear signs of identity diffusion and indeed doubted the very existence of man. Non-being was more valid to him than being, and he liked to quote Democritus: 'Nothing is more real than nothing.'

A watershed moment for Beckett occurred when his analyst Bion brought him to a lecture on dreams given by Jung in 1935. Jung related the case of a patient, a ten-year old girl, who was experiencing bizarre mythological dreams. In Jung's estimation, this girl was merely existing and not living. 'She had never really been born,' he said. This episode immediately struck a deep chord with Beckett: it seemed to explain his sense of isolation from the world and why he could not fit in and relate to others. More crucially, it shed light on his ambiguous attachment to his mother. To Beckett, his failure to be born 'psychologically' meant that the child was still not separated from the mother and its mind was confined to the mother's womb, whereby he equated the womb with the tomb. Indeed, in *The Last Modernist* Cronin writes about Beckett's feelings of being 'assassinated' before his birth. Beckett often drew on psychological theories, only to reject or satirise them in his later works. He never jettisoned this concept, however, which is present in many of his works, notably *All That Fall* and *Footfalls*. Indeed, in *Malone* Beckett writes: 'Nothing is less like me than this patient, reasonable child, struggling alone for years to shed a little light upon himself, avid of the last gleam, a stranger to the joys of darkness.'

The failure to develop a sense of identity is at the core of autism and is part of a wide range of arrested developments. It is evident in early childhood, when children refer to themselves in the third person, and may partly explain the huge attachment to their mothers that is commonly seen in such people. The failure to develop a sense of identity results in a lifelong search for an identity, which can involve a switching back and forth between various identities – what Beckett would call the 'unattainable self' and the 'non-attainable non-self'.

Right from the start, Beckett's personality was an enigma. His fellow students at Portora could not understand how he could be so moody and withdrawn and then so charming and quick-witted, and an unmerciful teaser. A frustrating search for identity meant that Beckett entertained many roles, some of which he embarked upon for a time, like teaching and writing critical reviews, while others were fanciful. In 1935, he wrote to the celebrated Russian director Sergei Eisenstein asking him if he could study to be a cameraman under his tutelage in Moscow – he received no reply. On another occasion, he seriously considered becoming a commercial pilot, even though he had never flown in an aircraft. Some jobs were done from necessity, like farm work in the village of Roussillon near Avignon, to which he and Suzanne had fled after having been betrayed to the Gestapo in 1942. Similarly, he drove an ambulance for the Irish Red Cross in Saint-Lô so that he could remain in France after the war.

Recognition for his work was always an ambiguous affair: he welcomed it because it confirmed his identity as a writer but it also terrified him because of the tide of publicity that followed in its wake. Two honours in particular gratified him: that of Honorary Doctor of Literature from Trinity College in 1959 and later the Nobel Prize for Literature in 1969. On the other hand, when the Croix de Guerre and Médaille de la Résistance were awarded to Beckett by the French government for his bravery during the Nazi occupation, he dismissed his efforts as 'boy scout stuff'.

Because of the great deal of upheaval and suffering in his life, Beckett, like many other geniuses, tended to identify with the martyred figure of Christ. Indeed, he made great play of the fact that he was born on Good Friday. Especially in his early adulthood, the absence of a self-identity caused him to gravitate towards figures that he admired and respected, in particular Joyce and Jack B. Yeats, who became mentors to him and had a similar artistic temperament. So great was his admiration for Joyce in his early days in Paris that he tended to imitate his mannerisms, in particular wearing the same shoe size as the master – several sizes too small! This practice ruined his feet, and he needed an operation to correct a hammer toe some years later.

Intensively private, secretive and controlling about his personal life, Beckett religiously turned down any approaches for an authorised biography. Perhaps, because he could not make sense of his own identity and the conflict it engendered, he did not want an outsider to try to do so either. Around the time of his mother's death in 1950, he burnt nearly twenty years' worth of old letters, confining them to the past once and for all. The question of biography is always problematic for someone with identity diffusion, given that distinguishing truth from fiction is a near-impossibility for them and that dealing with guilt can be traumatic.

In 1971, he wryly greeted Deirdre Bair, his first biographer, with the words: 'So you're the one who is going to reveal me for the charlatan that I am.' Despite telling Bair that he would neither hinder nor help her in the writing of the biography, this was a magnanimous step for Beckett, who, approaching seventy and in ill health, felt a duty to the literary world and was perhaps more at ease with his success than he had been before. An earlier attempt by the American scholar Laurence Harvey to carry out the research for a critical study was effectively censored by Beckett: the pain of exposure, with his private life being laid bare, was no doubt too much for him. Following publication of Bair's biography, which Beckett reputedly did not read, he subsequently authorised a biography to be written by Knowlson.

The issue of sexual identity also arises in the context of Beckett's identity diffusion. Because of his immature emotional responses and ambivalent attitude towards women, he could not form stable, loving relationships with them – with the possible exception of Barbara Bray in later life. By all appearances, Beckett's sexual orientation was heterosexual, with deep sexual appetites, and in his lifetime featured promiscuity, masturbation, celibacy and possibility impotence. That said, in *Damned to Fame* his former lover Peggy Guggenheim is quoted as saying that she believed him to be homosexual, for reasons not cited. Cronin suggests that there was a homoerotic quality to his relationship with MacGreevy – who was homosexual – and many other of his male friends.

*

Excessive sensitivity or hyperaesthesia is often associated with genius. Beckett had extraordinary sensory perception: his senses were so finely attuned that they powered his visual and auditory imagination. It is no coincidence that Proust, with his celebration of the senses in *Remembrance of Things Past,* was the subject of Beckett's first critical study in 1931. The sights and sounds of Dublin and its environs from his childhood, along with those of Greystones and Dún Laoghaire, were indelibly imprinted in his mind, and images of the Forty Foot, the Bailey lighthouse, and the Irish countryside, with its mountains and harbours, were all reproduced in his work. Yet while his writing benefited from such hypersensitivity, it often made life very difficult. Barbara Bray had occasion to witness Beckett's hypersensitivity at close quarters. In *The Last Modernist,* Cronin writes:

> A very fineness of perception, amounting, in her view, to hyperaesthesia, or specially heightened consciousness, made him suffer more than most people did in company or circumstances which were antipathetic to him. He was she thought like the man Rousseau speaks of, who finds himself out in the tempest without his skin. At the same time his ultra-sensitivity was balanced by humour and insight.

Although Beckett had poor visual acuity and needed glasses for short-sightedness, he nonetheless had a strong visuo-spatial aesthetic. A deep love of painting and art was evident in him, and he had a great appreciation of architecture. Variations in light and shade were very noticeable to Beckett and not surprisingly the Dutch Masters were his favourite painters. In life, he hated to be deprived of light and felt miserable when this occurred. Jack B. Yeats was one of a number of modern painters that he regarded highly; in fact, the only paintings in Beckett's possession were two by Yeats.

Beckett too had an exceptionally acute sense of hearing. Hypersensitive to sound, he once exploded with anger at his cousin's house in Dublin because of the ticking of the clock. As a boy he was always attentive to sounds of varying qualities and pitch – dogs barking, church bells, distant lawnmowers, a rake over pebbles, the click of a croquet mallet and ball. Gifted with a musical ear but not a singing voice, he had a deep appreciation for music and attended many concerts. As a young boy, he learned to play the piano and had a tremendous ability at sight-reading. On rare occasions, he would play for others and, according to Cronin, showed 'great musicality, style, and phrasing'. The tin whistle was also in his repertoire. His favourite composers included Mozart, Beethoven, Chopin, Haydn, Schubert and Schumann, and modernists like Satie and Bartók. Allusions to composers and music featured in Beckett's work, and music was used in a number of his plays, with repetitions and variations in key, rhythm, tempo and pitch.

With his attentive ear and love of music, it is no surprise that Beckett loved birdsong. Like Daisy Bates, he was a master at recognising bird species and imitating their calls. His interest in bird-watching was first awakened during the many occasions he and his father walked together in the Dublin and Wicklow hills. At his cottage at Ussy, Beckett would take up binoculars and watch the comings and goings of birds with rapt attention. In the last months of his life, he fed biscuits to the pigeons each day in the courtyard of his Paris nursing home. Many of them would feed from his hands, like St Francis of Assisi.

Hypersensitivity to smell is certainly a trait of Asperger's syndrome, and Beckett manifested an acute sense of smell. Indeed, like Proust, his sense of smell was so highly refined that it was linked to powerful memories, especially those of childhood. As an old man, he could vividly recall smells such as that of his mother's lemon verbena, which grew in Cooldrinagh. It is possible that Beckett's skin was hypersensitive, as he was prone to rashes and boils, and he hated wearing collars. Although he was not necessarily tactile with people, touching and collecting inanimate objects such as certain bones and stones became an obsessional interest of his, as it did for his character Molloy in the eponymous novel. Beckett also appears to have been hypersensitive to cold weather and would make sure to wrap up in layers whenever it was inclement.

In terms of culinary tastes, Beckett was quite ascetic. He ate very little and was even more frugal as the years progressed. He was always thin; Bair notes that, if he missed one meal, he did not go out of his way to eat before the next one. Although his tastes were simple, he was quite fastidious and as a child adamantly refused to eat margarine, possibly because it had an unnatural taste. Fish, in particular sole and mackerel, was a favourite of his. Under Suzanne's influence, he lived mainly on vegetarian meals such as salads, grated carrots, cheese, rice and eggs, and he ate meat only if he was presented with it as a guest at dinner. When alone in Ussy, he would often eat a monotonous diet of scrambled eggs or rice, and stewed prunes, over and over again.

*

It is unclear whether Beckett had motor clumsiness or not. At school, his skill in ball games and his neat handwriting would seem to indicate that he had fine motor skills. That said, he was an unorthodox cricketer and could be an awkward player at times. His piano teacher from childhood noted that he played the piano in a rather heavy-handed, mechanical fashion – you could say, in a somewhat autistic style. In terms of his driving ability, his recklessness and frequent accidents might indicate that he could not co-ordinate gears and pedals smoothly. His gross motor skills seem to have been good: he was a good swimmer, for instance.

Variously described as 'curious', 'stooped' and 'lumbering', Beckett's gait was affected by Asperger's syndrome, whereby his feet splayed outwards and his lower limbs appeared to be stiff. This made him the subject of much teasing at school. Similarly, in his eponymous novels he gives Watt and Molloy awkward, unbalanced gaits. In terms of balance, there is the suggestion in *Damned to Fame* that Beckett had a fear of heights when he climbed the 318-foot-high tower of the Andreaskirche in Brunswick, Germany. He made the ascent in fear and trembling; he was quite nauseated at the top and hardly dared to look at the spectacular view, possibly indicating some vertigo too. Given his dislike for dancing, it seems safe to assume that Beckett could not keep a rhythm. In addition, sometimes he unconsciously imitated movements, which sometimes occurs in those with Asperger's syndrome. During conversation, this involved a tendency to mirror the posture, gestures and mannerisms of the other person – usually a person with whom there is a strong rapport or harmony. This symmetry of body language was most noticeable when he was in conversation with Joyce. This mirroring of gestures was described by Joyce's biographer Richard Ellmann, when Beckett visited Joyce to work on *Finnegans Wake*: 'Joyce sat in his habitual posture, legs crossed, toe of the upper leg under the instep of the lower; Beckett, also tall and slender, fell into the same gesture.' Knowlson writes that Beckett used to ape Joyce's way of dressing and adopted some of his habits or mannerisms, including wearing shoes that were too narrow for him, as has been mentioned, and also drinking white wine and holding his cigarette in a certain way.

*

From a medical perspective, the level of illness and disease that Beckett encountered in his life was considerable. Ever since he put pen to paper, there has been an extraordinary interest in his mental health. Clearly, he had a depressive personality and showed signs of acute anxiety and depression, with a tendency to exaggerate his ailments and an element of hypochondriasis. The depressive personality was probably inherited from his mother, who showed signs of depression too. According to his biographers, Beckett took lithium for his depression from time to time, which suggests that a diagnosis of depression was made at some point.

From childhood, Beckett had all sorts of fears and anxieties, and he suffered from nightmares, no doubt augmented by a vivid imagination. After leaving Portora at the age of seventeen, he had a depressive mood swing and withdrew more and more into himself. The years when he struggled to gain recognition as a writer were turbulent, with ongoing conflict with his mother and a self-perceived lack of identity that led to greater anxiety and depression. As a young man, suicide preoccupied his thoughts, especially in Paris. Although he scared friends with his earnest talk on the merits and demerits of various ways of committing suicide, his talk of suicide was more philosophical than real. 'Life,' he said, 'was not worth the trouble of leaving it.'

Some friends described him as full of nervous energy, and he frequently suffered from insomnia. Like many with Asperger's syndrome, Beckett's sleeping pattern seems to have been somewhat erratic all his life. Certainly as a child he could not sleep at night. He was generally a late riser, especially in early adulthood, often waking in the afternoons. In his youth, he began to smoke and drink a great deal and neglected himself, either absorbed in his work or depressed. Cronin writes that Beckett dressed in sweaters and trousers which showed 'plentiful traces of food, drink and other matter'. His trench coat was usually in need of cleaning and his shoes were 'permanently dirty and in need of repair'.

Upon the sudden death of his much-loved father in 1933 from a heart attack, it is clear that a crisis point was reached. Beckett began to experience panic attacks that were far more severe than the ones he had had before. He would wake up in the middle of the night with the fear that he was having a heart attack, along with feelings of imminent suffocation. The panic attacks were accompanied by all sorts of psychosomatic problems and neuroses: acute stomach upsets, fevers, colds, palpitations, dizziness, boils, cysts, facial rashes, nightmares and urinary retention. So disabling were his symptoms that he sought medical help, first from his friend Dr Geoffrey Thompson and later in London from the Jungian psychoanalyst Dr Wilfred Bion. As a result, he spent two years in therapy, as Bair notes:

> For years I was unhappy. Consciously and deliberately ever since I left school and went into TCD, so that I isolated myself more and more, undertook less and less and lent myself to a crescendo of disparagement of others and myself. But in all that, there was nothing that struck me as odd. The misery and solitude and apathy and the sneers were the elements of an index of superiority; guaranteed the feeling of arrogant 'otherness' which seemed as right and natural and as little morbid as the ways in which it was not so much expressed as implied and reserved and kept available for a possible utterance in the future. It was not until the way of living, or rather negation of living, developed such terrifying physical symptoms that it could no longer be pursued, that I became aware of anything morbid in myself. In short, if the heart had not put the fear of death into me I would still be boozing and dreaming, lounging around feeling that I was too good for anything else.

Having observed the ill effect that Beckett's mother had on her son, Bion tried to persuade him to reduce all contact with her. This advice fell on deaf ears, however, because of the ambiguous nature of their relationship, rooted in guilt and duty. The therapy came to an end when Beckett grew sceptical about its efficacy and concerned about the value for money – his mother's money – that it represented. Two years of analysis, however, helped Beckett to become more sociable, more humble and more tolerant with others. While in analysis, many of his symptoms reduced, but they later returned. Even so, the panic attacks were never as severe again. It is possible that Beckett got the technique of free association of ideas from his experiences in psychoanalysis, and this may have liberated some of his true potential. Work, and perhaps music to some extent, was ultimately the antidote to his depression.

Not all of Beckett's illnesses were purely psychosomatic or resulting from neuroses, however. That said, it was often impossible to distinguish between his physical and psychological ailments, as Cronin suggests. His poor health was not helped by his erratic diet and poor nutrition, his heavy drinking and smoking, and his failure to get prompt medical attention.

The range of illnesses that Beckett experienced in his lifetime runs like a medical dictionary. Judging by the extent of his chronic infections and inflammatory conditions, he seems to have had an exceptionally weak immune system, and, naturally, when he was anxious or depressed his resistance to infection was reduced even more. All his life he was prone to general coughs, colds and influenza, and contracted them with increasing regularity. From adolescence onwards, he developed a litany of recurrent bacterial skin infections: boils, abscesses and cysts on his neck, fingers, palms and groin; anal cysts were not uncommon either. Often the suppurating abscesses in various parts of his body had to be surgically drained. A mouth full of rotten teeth led to a succession of jaw abscesses that failed to heal after surgery, necessitating the grafting of a new palate. On the occasions when he was admitted to hospital, blood tests usually revealed that he was anaemic, and he was given iron and vitamin injections. Indeed, the state of his blood was often described by doctors as 'in a mess'.

Pneumonias, pleurisy and lung abscesses were to dog him after the knife attack in Paris, and a lung tumour was treated successfully with radiation. In later years, he developed Dupuytren's contracture, bursitis, periarthritis, lumbago, arthritis, severe emphysema, an enlarged prostate and an atypical Parkinson's disease; his mother in her later years also developed Parkinson's disease. Like Joyce and de Valera, Beckett developed glaucoma in both eyes and cataracts, for which he underwent surgery.

*

On the question of religion, Beckett admitted to having no religious feeling. Nonetheless, he possessed a certain religiosity or spiritualism that is frequently seen in those with Asperger's syndrome. As Protestants, Beckett's parents worshipped in the Low Church tradition, with its emphasis on Sunday worship, Bible study, private prayer and a puritanical moral code. However, the experience of being taken to church each

Sunday usually left the young Beckett frowning or with a 'glummer expression then the rest of the congregation', according to Cronin. Years later, Beckett would comment that he was brought up 'like a Quaker'. As an adult, Beckett was inclined towards agnosticism and always showed a deep scepticism about religious matters; like Joyce, he could be anticlerical. A staunch believer in individual freedom, he deplored how much control was exerted by the Catholic Church during the late 1920s and early 1930s on issues of contraception and censorship.

Even so, one of the few books that he kept in his possession all his life was the Bible. This was more than a mere reference book to him: indeed, his knowledge of scripture was almost word-perfect, according to Knowlson. Whether Beckett wanted to recognise it or not, there was a certain religious tone to his work. Like Joyce, religious motifs and references figure highly in his work, though he would later dismiss them as nothing more than literary devices. His statement that 'all poetry is prayer', however, suggests that he believed that there was a spiritual dimension to his work. Through the influence of Joyce and MacGreevy, he had some knowledge of Catholic theology and, as Cronin points out, often his religious vocabulary is more Catholic than Protestant, employing terms such as 'Assumption' and 'Annunciation'. From MacGreevy, he borrowed and read Thomas à Beckett's *The Imitation of Christ* and was impressed with its aspects of quietism or passivity, where the self is effaced and detached from the world, leaving the soul free to unite with the essence of God or Godhead. Elsewhere in Beckett's work, a tendency for mystical unions with his beloved or transcendence from ordinary life is also found, particularly in his earlier writings: the short story 'Assumption' and the novel *Dream of Fair to Middling Women*. Much of Beckett's mystical experiences was influenced by medieval ideologies such as Neoplatonism. Certainly he had a desire to transcend ordinary experience and was obsessed by the aim of creating what he called 'a literature of the unword', involving the negation of speech. However, it must be said that Beckett ultimately never took philosophy as his lodestar but instead relied on his inner compass to rationalise what he felt and perceived.

Beckett was preoccupied by the quasi-mystical significance of numbers. Indeed, numerology fascinated Beckett as much as it did Joyce, though he appeared to be far less superstitious than Joyce. All the same,

331

numerical patterns and recurrences were met with a suspicious eye on Beckett's part.

Much of Beckett's agnosticism stemmed from his condemnation of a God who allowed suffering in the world. In his play *All that Fall,* he attacks a God who does not exist, for being cruel and unjust. The desire to go on living in the face of endless suffering is a constant theme running through Beckett's work. The instinct for survival is a theme of *Waiting for Godot,* however, and *Murphy* features a religiosity of sorts and is rooted in Beckett's vision of eternity. It was his belief that, when things are beyond our control, we must look at life from the aspect of the eternal – *sub specie aeternatatis.* He took this view from philosophers such as Spinoza, Descartes and Geulinex but, unlike them, he did not place God at the centre of eternity. For Beckett, the belief in the existence of the eternal was the only justification to go on living. It could be said that, by holding firm to a belief in eternity, Beckett possessed religiosity or survival genes. The genius of Beckett ultimately lay in affirming evolution.

FURTHER READING

CHAPTER 1: ROBERT EMMET (1778–1803)

d'Haussonville, Comtesse Louise. *Robert Emmet*. Belfast: 1858.
Elliott, Marianne. *Robert Emmet: The Making of a Legend*. London: Profile Books, 2003.
Emmet, Thomas Addis. *Memoir of Thomas Addis and Robert Emmet* (2 vols). New York: 1915. Kildare: Warfield Press, 2003.
Geoghegan, Patrick M. *Robert Emmet: A Life*. Dublin: Gill and Macmillan, 2002.
McMahon, Seán. *Robert Emmet*. Cork: Mercier Press, 2001.
Madden, Richard R. *The United Irishmen, Their Lives and Times*. Dublin & London: 1858-60.
Ó Brádaigh, Seán. *Bold Robert Emmet 1778–1803*. Dublin: Cló Saoirse, 2003.

CHAPTER 2: PADRAIC PEARSE (1879–1916)

Edwards, Ruth Dudley. *Patrick Pearse: The Triumph of Failure*. London: Gollancz, 1977.
Lee, J.J. 'In Search of Patrick Pearse', in Máirín Ní Dhonnchadha & Theo Dorgan (eds), *Revising the Rising*. Derry: Field Day, 1991.
Lyons, F.S.L. *Culture and Anarchy in Ireland 1890–1939*. Oxford: Oxford University Press, 1979.
Moran, Seán Farrell. *Padraig Pearse and the Politics of Redemption*. Washington DC, Catholic University of America Press, 1994.
Ó Buachalla, Séamus. *The Letters of P. H. Pearse*. Gerrards Cross, Bucks: Smythe, 1980.
———. *A Significant Irish Educationalist*. Dublin: Mercier, 1980.
Pearse, Mary Brigid. The Home Life of Pádraig Pearse. Dublin: Mercier, 1979.
Pearse, P. H. *Political Writings and Speeches*. Dublin: Talbot Press, 1966.
Ryan, Desmond. *The Man Called Pearse*. Dublin: Maunsel, 1919.
Sisson, Elaine. *Pearse's Patriots: St Enda's and the Cult of Boyhood*. Cork: Cork University Press, 2004.

CHAPTER 3: ÉAMON DE VALERA (1882–1975)

Bowman, John. *De Valera and the Ulster Question 1917–1973*. Oxford: Oxford University Press, 1984.
Bromage, Mary C. *De Valera and the March of a Nation*. London: Hutchinson 1956.
Coogan, Tim Pat. *Michael Collins: A Biography*. London: Hutchinson, 1990.
———. *De Valera: Long Fellow, Long Shadow*. London: Arrow, 1993.
de Valera, Terry. *A Memoir*. Dublin: Currach Press, 2004.

Dwyer, T. Ryle. *Eamon de Valera*. Dublin: Gill and Macmillan, 1980.

———. *Big Fellow, Long Fellow: A Joint Biography of Collins and de Valera*. Dublin: Gill and Macmillan, 1998.

Faragher, Seán P. *Dev and his Alma Mater*. Dublin: Paraclete Press, 1984.

Longford, Earl of, and Thomas P. O'Neill. *Eamon de Valera*. Dublin: Gill and Macmillan, 1970.

MacManus, M. J. *Eamon de Valera: A Biography*. Dublin: Talbot Press, 1944.

O'Brien, Mark. *De Valera, Fianna Fáil and the Irish Press*. Dublin: Irish Academic Press, 2001.

Ryan, Desmond. *Unique Dictator: A Study of Eamon de Valera*. London: Barker, 1936.

CHAPTER 4: ROBERT BOYLE (1627–1691)

Canny, Nicholas. *The Upstart Earl*. Cambridge: Cambridge University Press, 1982.

Hunter, Michael (ed). *Robert Boyle by Himself and his Friends*. London: Pickering & Chatto, 1994.

Hunter, Michael, Antonio Clericuzio & Lawrence M. Principe (eds). *The Correspondence of Robert Boyle* (6 vols). London: Pickering & Chatto, 2001.

Maddison, R. E. W. *The Life of the Honourable Robert Boyle*. London: Taylor &Francis, 1969.

Pilkington, Robert. *Robert Boyle: Father of Chemistry*. London: John Murray, 1959.

Young, John. 'Robert Boyle, First Earl of Cork.' The Literary Encyclopaedia, 2004. http://www.litencyc.com/php/speople.php?rec=true&UID=522

CHAPTER 5: WILLIAM ROWAN HAMILTON (1805–1865)

Graves, Robert Perceval. *Life of Sir William Rowan Hamilton* (3 vols). Dublin: Hodges, Figgis and Co., 1889.

Guthrie Tait, Peter. 'Sir William Rowan Hamilton', *North British Review* 1866; 45: 37–74.

Hankins, T. L. *Sir William Rowan Hamilton*. Baltimore, MA: Johns Hopkins University Press, 1980.

MacFarlane, Andrew. *Lectures on Ten British Mathematicians of the Nineteenth Century*. New York: Wiley, 1916.

O'Donnell, Seán. *William Rowan Hamilton: Portrait of a Prodigy*. Dublin, Boole Press, 1983.

Wilkins, David R. *Sir William Rowan Hamilton (1805–1865)*. http://www.maths.tcd.ie/pub/HistMath/People/Hamilton/

CHAPTER 6: DAISY BATES (1859–1951)

Arrigan, Emmet and Elizabeth Monkhouse. *Daisy Bates*. Dublin: An Gúm, 1989. [In Irish]

Bates, Daisy. *The Passing of the Aborigines: A Lifetime Spent Among the Natives of Australia*. London: Murray, 1938.

Blackburn, Julia. *Daisy Bates in the Desert*. London: Secker and Warburg, 1994.

Broderick, Marian. *Wild Irish Women: Extraordinary Lives from History*. Dublin: The O'Brien Press, 2001.

Hill, Ernestine. *Kabbarli: A Personal Memoir of Daisy Bates*. Sydney, Australia: Angus and Robertson, 1973.

Kelly, A. A. *Wandering Women: Two Centuries of Travel Out of Ireland*. Dublin: Wolfhound, 1995.

Salter, Elizabeth. *The Great White Queen of the Never Never*. Sydney, Australia: Angus and Robertson, 1971.

Chapter 7: William Butler Yeats (1865–1939)

Alldritt, Keith. *W. B. Yeats: The Man and the Milieu.* London: John Murray, 1997.

Brown, Terence. *The Life of W. B. Yeats: A Critical Biography.* Dublin: Gill and Macmillan, 1999.

Ellmann, Richard. *Yeats: The Man and the Masks.* London: Penguin, 1979.

Foster, Roy. *W. B. Yeats: A Life* (2 vols). Oxford: Oxford University Press, 1997, 2004.

Hone, Joseph H. (ed). *John Butler Yeats: Letters to his Son W .B. Yeats and Others, 1869–1922.* London: Faber & Faber, 1999.

Maddox, Brenda. *George's Ghosts: A New Life of W. B. Yeats.* London: Picador, 1999.

Pyle, Hilary. *Jack B. Yeats: A Biography* (2nd edn). London: André Deutsch, 1989.

Yeats, Michael B. *Cast a Cold Eye: Memories of a Poet's Son and Politician.* Dublin: Blackwater Press, 1999.

Yeats, W. B. *Autobiographies.* London: Macmillan, 1955.

Chapter 8: James Joyce (1881–1941)

Anderson, Chester G. *James Joyce.* London: Thames & Hudson, 1967.

Andreason, Nancy. 'James Joyce: A Portrait of the Artist as a Schizoid', *Journal of the American Medical Association* 1973; 224: 67–71.

Arnold, Bruce. *The Scandal of Ulysses.* London: Sinclair-Stevenson, 1991.

Costello, Peter. *James Joyce: The Years of Growth 1882–1915.* London: Kyle Cathie Ltd, 1992.

Ellmann, Richard. *James Joyce* (2nd edn). Oxford: Oxford University Press, 1982.

Jackson, John Wyse and Peter Costello. *John Stanislaus Joyce: The Voluminous Life and Genius of James Joyce's Father.* New York: St Martin's Press, 1997.

Kaplan, Robert. 'Madness and James Joyce', *Australasian Psychiatry* 2002; 10(2): 172-176.

Maddox, Brenda. *Nora: A Biography of Nora Joyce.* London: Minerva, 1988.

O'Brien, Edna. *James Joyce.* London: Weidenfeld & Nicholson, 1999.

O'Connor, Ulick (ed). *The Joyce We Knew: Memoirs of James Joyce.* Dingle, County Kerry: Brandon Books, 2004.

Stanislaus, Joyce. *My Brother's Keeper: James Joyce's Early Years.* New York: Da Capo, 2003.

Chapter 9: Samuel Beckett (1906–1989)

Bair, Deirdre. *Samuel Beckett: A Biography.* London: Jonathan Cape, 1978.

Cronin, Anthony. *Samuel Beckett: The Last Modernist.* London: HarperCollins, 1996.

Knowlson, James. *Damned to Fame: The Life of Samuel Beckett.* London: Bloomsbury, 1996.

PUBLISHERS' ACKNOWLEDGEMENTS

Acknowledgement is given to the various individuals and organisations who granted permission for the images used on the cover of this book to be reproduced: Daisy Bates, © State Library of South Australia; Samuel Beckett, © Jane Bown, from a photograph in the collection of the National Portrait Gallery, London; Robert Boyle (after Johann Kerseboom, circa 1689–90), © National Portrait Gallery, London; James Joyce, © Gisèle Freund, from a photograph in the collection of the National Portrait Gallery, London; and W. B. Yeats, © the Estate of W. B. Yeats. The publishers have made every effort to trace holders of copyright material but would be happy to make good any omissions in this regard and to make acknowledgement in future printings of this book.